Doing Gender in Media, Art and Culture

Doing Gender in Media, Art and Culture is an introductory text for students specializing in gender studies. The truly interdisciplinary and intergenerational approach bridges the gap between humanities and the social sciences, and it showcases the academic and social context in which gender studies has evolved. Complex contemporary phenomena such as globalization, neo-liberalism and 'fundamentalism' are addressed, which stir up new questions relevant to the study of culture. This vibrant and wide-ranging collection of essays is essential reading for anyone in need of an accessible but sophisticated guide to the very latest issues and concepts within gender studies.

Rosemarie Buikema is Professor in Art, Culture, and Diversity at the Department of Media and Culture Studies, Utrecht University (NL) and Scientific Director of the Graduate Gender Programme in Utrecht. She has published widely in the field of comparative literature, visual studies, transnational justice, gender studies, and post-colonial critique. Her next book will be entitled *The Sacred Home* (University of Wales Press, 2010). See also www.genderstudies.nl.

Iris van der Tuin is Lecturer in Gender Studies at the Department of Media and Culture Studies, Utrecht University (NL). She teaches undergraduate and graduate courses focusing on feminist classics, feminist theory, and philosophy of science, and publishes on the same topics. See also www.genderstudies.nl.

Doing Gender in Media, Art and Culture

Edited by

Rosemarie Buikema
Iris van der Tuin

Routledge
Taylor & Francis Group

LONDON AND NEW YORK

First published 2007
by Coutinho Publishers in Dutch,
by Routledge 2009 in English
2 Park Square, Milton Park, Abingdon, Oxon, OX14 4RN

Simultaneously published in the USA and Canada
by Routledge
270 Madison Avenue, New York, NY 10016

Routledge is an imprint of the Taylor & Francis Group, an informa business

© 2009 Rosemarie Buikema and Iris van der Tuin
for selection and editorial material

Typeset in Times New Roman by
Florence Production Ltd, Stoodleigh, Devon
Printed and bound in Great Britain by
CPI Antony Rowe, Chippenham, Wiltshire

British Library Cataloguing in Publication Data
A catalogue record for this book is available from the British Library

Library of Congress Cataloging in Publication Data
Buikema, Rosemarie.
  [Gender in media kunst en cultuur. English]
  Doing gender in media, art and culture/[Rosemarie Buikema,
  Iris van der Tuin].
      p. cm.
    Includes bibliographical references and index.
  1. Feminism. 2. Mass media. 3. Art. 4. Culture. I. Tuin, Iris van der.
  II. Title.
HQ1101.B85 2009
305.4201 – dc22   2008053671

ISBN10: 0–415–49382–X (hbk)
ISBN10: 0–415–49383–8 (pbk)
ISBN10: 0–203–87680–6 (ebk)

ISBN13: 978–0–415–49382–6 (hbk)
ISBN13: 978–0–415–49383–3 (pbk)
ISBN13: 978–0–203–87680–0 (ebk)

Contents

Illustrations

The following were reproduced with kind permission. Every effort has been made to trace copyright holders and obtain permission. Any omissions brought to our attention will be remedied in future editions.

Contributors

Cecilia Åsberg is Distinguished Researcher of Linköping University, Sweden, and Assistant Professor at the Department of Gender Studies at the same university, where she is also setting up an interdisciplinary research platform, The Posthumanities Hub. She teaches and publishes in the fields of feminist technoscience studies, but also on the visual media cultures of history and popular science.

Maaike Bleeker is Professor in Theatre Studies at the Department of Media and Culture Studies, Utrecht University (NL). She publishes on contemporary theatre, dance, and visual arts and is especially interested in issues of perception, the senses, the physical, and the political. Her book *Visuality in the Theatre: The Locus of Looking* (2008) appeared with Palgrave Macmillan.

Marianne van den Boomen is Lecturer in New Media and Digital Culture at the Department of Media and Culture Studies, Utrecht University (NL). She publishes on Internet communities and participatory culture, with a focus on the role of metaphors.

Sarah Bracke is Assistant Professor in Sociology of Religion and Culture at the K.U. Leuven, Belgium. She carries out ethnographic research on (female) religious subjectivities within Christian and Islamic traditions in a European context, and writes on modernity, religion, and the (post)secular.

Rosi Braidotti is currently a Distinguished Professor in the Humanities, founding Director of the Centre for the Humanities at Utrecht University (NL) (www.hum.uu.nl/cfh), and Honorary Professor at Birkbeck College, London. She was the founding Director of the Women's Studies programme at Utrecht (1988–2005). Her publications include: *Patterns of Dissonance* (Polity Press, 1991); *Nomadic Subjects* (Columbia University, 1994); *Metamorphoses* (Polity Press, 2002); and *Transpositions* (Polity Press, 2006).

Rosemarie Buikema is Professor in Art, Culture, and Diversity at the Department of Media and Culture Studies, Utrecht University (NL) and Scientific Director of the Graduate Gender Programme in Utrecht. She has published widely in the fields of comparative literature, visual studies, transnational justice, gender studies, and post-colonial critique. Her next book will be entitled *The Sacred Home* (University of Wales Press, 2010). See also www.genderstudies.nl.

renée c. hoogland is Associate Professor of English, Wayne State University, Detroit, USA. She publishes on gender and sexuality, culture, and critical theory.

Anne-Marie Korte is Senior Lecturer in Systematic Theology of Christianity, Tilburg University (NL) and Professor in Women's Studies in Theology, Utrecht University (NL). She publishes on religious representations and theological interpretations of the body. Her current research is oriented on gender and blasphemy.

Ann-Sophie Lehmann is Lecturer at the Department of Media and Culture Studies, Utrecht University (NL). She publishes on the representation of the human body and the history and theory of picture making in old and new media cultures.

Geertje Mak is Lecturer in Gender History at the Institute for Gender Studies, Radboud University Nijmegen (NL). Her publications include studies on sex and gender in the nineteenth century and migration. She is currently working on a book on hermaphrodites, body, and the self in the nineteenth century.

Maaike Meijer is Professor-Director of the Centre for Gender and Diversity, University of Maastricht (NL). She publishes on songs, poetry, popular culture, Dutch literature, and lesbian existence. She is currently working on a biography of the Dutch poet Vasalis.

Sandra Ponzanesi is Lecturer in Gender Studies and Postcolonial Critique at the Department of Media and Culture Studies, Utrecht University (NL). She publishes on transnational feminism, postcolonial theory, migrant literatures, media studies, and postcolonial cinema. Her publications include *Paradoxes of Postcolonial Culture* (SUNY Press, 2004) and *Migrant Cartographies* (Lexington Books, 2005).

María Puig de la Bellacasa is currently a Research Associate at the Group for constructivist studies at the Philosophy Department of the Free University of Brussels, Belgium. She has published on feminist knowledge politics and works at the crossroads of feminist theory, contemporary continental philosophy, and science and technology studies. Her latest publications include a special issue of *Subjectivity* (September 2009).

Anneke Smelik is Professor in Visual Culture at the Department of Cultural Studies, Radboud University Nijmegen (NL). She publishes on cultural memory, human and machine, authenticity in fashion, and visual literacy. Her latest (co-edited) books are: *Bits of Life: Feminism at the Intersections of Media, Bioscience, and Technology* (University of Washington Press, 2008) and *Technologies of Memory in the Arts* (Palgrave Macmillan, 2009).

Iris van der Tuin is Lecturer in Gender Studies at the Department of Media and Culture Studies, Utrecht University (NL). She teaches undergraduate and graduate courses focusing on feminist classics, feminist theory, and philosophy of science, and publishes on the same topics. See also www.genderstudies.nl.

Berteke Waaldijk is a historian and holds a Chair in Language and Culture Studies at Utrecht University (NL). From 1988 to 2004, she was involved in the development of the curriculum of women's studies at Utrecht University. Her publications include: with Maria Grever, *Transforming the Public Sphere: The Dutch National Exhibition of Women's Labor in 1898* (Duke University Press, 2004) and, with Sabine Hering, *Guardians of the Poor – Custodians of the Public: Welfare History in Eastern Europe 1900–1960* (Opladen, 2006).

Gloria Wekker is Professor in Gender and Ethnicity at the Department of Media and Culture Studies, University of Utrecht (NL) and Director of GEM, the expertise centre for gender, ethnicity, and multiculturality in higher education. Her most recent publication is *The Politics of Passion: Women's Sexual Culture in the Afro-Surinamese Diaspora* (Columbia University Press, 2006).

Marta Zarzycka teaches Gender Studies and Art History at the Department of Media and Culture Studies, University of Utrecht (NL). Her research is focused on the cutting edge of gender and art, with particular focus on photography and its transport across the genres and media.

Acknowledgements

Doing Gender in Media, Art and Culture is the product of twenty years of close cooperation of several generations of lecturers and students in gender studies at Utrecht University, the Netherlands. Here we would like to thank those lecturers and guest lecturers who have coordinated and taught in the course 'Introduction to gender studies'. In particular, Berteke Waaldijk, Anneke Smelik, Maaike Meijer, Gloria Wekker, and Rosi Braidotti have laid the foundations for a course which is nowadays a core course of the Department of Media and Culture Studies of the Faculty of the Humanities, and which attracts over two hundred students on a yearly basis. We want to thank all those generations of students who have participated in the course in a critical and engaged manner. They have taught us how to best teach feminist historiography and have sharpened our views. In the academic years 2006–2007 and 2007–2008, we discussed drafts of *Doing Gender in Media, Art and Culture* with our undergraduate students. Their input was invaluable to us. The Ph.D students of the UU Graduate Gender Programme discussed the outline of the book in the programme's *Ph.D Reading/Writing Seminar* with us in 2006–2007. Their critical-creative remarks were highly valuable as well. Mariecke van den Berg, Daria Ukhova, and Stephanie Walker acted as our student assistants when we were finishing the manuscript. They have been our external hard drive, as well as our hands and feet. Aleid Fokkema's Lighthouse Texts has translated most of the chapters from Dutch into English. Thank you all.

Rosemarie Buikema and Iris van der Tuin

Introduction

Rosemarie Buikema and
Iris van der Tuin

The present book, *Doing Gender in Media, Art and Culture*, is designed as a textbook for humanities students specializing in gender studies. Gender studies is a relatively new branch on the science tree, if one realizes that it was only about thirty years ago that the first scholars were assigned to set up a line of teaching and research in *women's* studies, as it was first called. Since then, a multitude of course curricula have been developed for women's studies and gender studies, while new departments were formed and established, new staff appointed, and the first Ph.D theses in gender studies were completed.

And so this is the second textbook put together by the Department of Gender Studies at Utrecht University (NL) – the first, *Women's Studies and Culture: A Feminist Introduction to the Humanities,* was published in 1993 (Buikema and Smelik, 1993; 1995). Mapping the first outcomes of research in women's studies, that book described how women's studies had evolved into an autonomous academic discipline. At the time, an important component of that development was centred on the equality-difference-deconstruction debate. In summary, this debate was focused on a number of core questions:

- Is it the objective of women's studies to add women in art and culture onto a male dominated canon, or is the legitimacy of women's studies based on the aim to change that canon and the patriarchal structure of the historiography of culture?
- Is women's studies looking for some sort of 'female' essence, or does it rather depart from the notion that there is no such thing because of the differences between women and the disparity in geopolitical circumstances?
- Do questions of 'race'/ethnicity, sexuality, class, and age pertain to women's studies?

As a result of these critical reflections on the research domain for women's studies, the term women's studies was gradually replaced by gender studies to accommodate the fact that women's studies is not just concerned with women, but also with the mutual differences between women and even the differences within a single woman. The latter notion allows for habitual shifts of context: in a given situation, being woman carries predominant weight but in another, one's identity is foremost determined by one's being a student, and in the next perhaps age, class, or ethnicity plays an important part. Different social categories together often influence the way identity works. No one is therefore determined by the same factors in all circumstances. Identity is a fluid and shifting concept.

*

'Gender' is the overarching concept for research which is oriented on the inventory and analysis of power relations between men and women and also *within* men or women. Gender is the social-cultural counterpart to sexual difference. Gender studies is guided by the social-constructivist insight brought home by Simone de Beauvoir (1990 [1949]) that we are not born as women (or as men) but that we are made woman in a society characterized by patriarchal gender relations. Research in gender studies is concerned with critically reviewing the rigid patterns of patriarchal relations and is not bogged down by a biological, deterministic concept of men and women.

Descriptive research focused on tracking power relations at an individual, institutional, national, and geopolitical level is one aspect of gender studies, but specifying recommendations to implement change is also a concern. Gender studies is interested, for example, in the statistics and surveys that reveal in which cases women and men are either or not equal to one another, but it also studies feminist utopias and other possible world imaginings. These investigations are subsumed in the term 'gender', because it is a theoretical and multi-layered concept which demands for researchers to be competent or at ease in more than one academic discipline. As per Sandra Harding's definition (1986), the term 'gender' shows in what sense individual, social and institutional structures and symbols are male or female or have masculine or feminine connotations. In the majority of cultures it is still the case that masculinity – whether referring to concrete persons of the male sex or to symbols with masculine connotations – is valued higher than femininity. Because of the many dimensions involved in gender, researchers in gender studies require the knowledge and insights from diverse academic disciplines in order to fathom the complexity of core problematics in gender studies. Interdisciplinarity is therefore an essential constitutive requirement for gender studies.

*

Doing Gender in Media, Art and Culture is the successor to *Women's Studies and Culture*. A great deal has changed in the past fifteen years. It is significant that gender studies has taken root and that the study of culture is taking part in an altered context. Complex contemporary phenomena such as globalization, neo-liberalism, and 'fundamentalism' stir up new questions relevant to the study of culture. The old answers to old questions are subjected to scrutiny. Traditional centres of gravity within the humanities are shifting ground as a result of social-cultural and geopolitical developments and of changes within the academy. Due to such changes in the humanities, the role of gender studies in that context has altered too. *Doing Gender in Media, Art and Culture* supplies the academic and social context for the ways in which gender studies has evolved and offers, moreover, insight into certain developments within specific humanity disciplines.

This new textbook for gender studies signals that gender studies has become a fully-fledged academic discipline. As a demonstration, this book *reconsiders* the history of feminist theory and *canonizes* feminist thought again. The book as a whole reflects on commitment and innovation within the academy. We do not think that innovation and change within the academy result from breaking with received academic traditions, but believe they reflect the perpetual mobility of traditions in the knowledge factory. This book describes the transformations spawned by gender studies in the study of culture as a process of reconsidering, subverting, and rearranging what was and what is.

Constituting a new phase in the discipline, this textbook is also a form of documentation. The different ways of writing the history of women and of gender studies as a discipline are classified, documented, and addressed. As the latter term indicates, the idea of dialogue or debate involved in our historiographical method departs from the notion of a present 'in conversation' with previous versions of the past. The trails of the past serve to delineate the paths for the future. Or as Sara Ahmed said: 'Perhaps when we think about the question of feminist futures, we need to attend to the legacies of feminist pasts, in order to think through the very question of what it would mean to have a world where feminism, as a politics of transformation, is no longer necessary' (Ahmed, 2003: 236).

This process of reconstruction and constitution, of retelling and looking ahead, is illustrated by the figure of a heroine for each different chapter, a woman warrior as it were, presiding over each outlook. In each contribution, this figure serves as a prism of gender studies research in dealing with stories by and about heroines which have been circulating for some time in traditional disciplines involved in the study of culture. In other words, the story of each heroine has dwelt in different contexts, changing ever so slightly. The genealogy of those stories is traced and retold. These heroines, both the well-known and the lesser known, are put on the map again and the authors in this book subsequently initiate a debate with (or about) fellow scholars.

Although a review of debates, disciplines, and heroines, the base structure for each chapter is the same. Each chapter presents a heroine first and then details how her struggle has been interpreted at different locations and in different time periods. The chapters begin with a micro-narrative (the story of the heroine) and work towards a macro-narrative (a debate, as in Part I, or a description of the development of gender studies research within a particular discipline of the humanities, as in Part II). Each chapter thus documents and interprets transformations of a specific narrative about a heroine. In Part I, these exemplary case histories lead to a discussion of a number of central debates in gender studies. In Part II, those narratives serve to illustrate how various humanity disciplines have related to gender studies. Part III brings together the lines of thought which emerge from the previous two Parts and further explores the potential of research in gender studies in referring to one last woman warrior.

The narratives of women (heroines) do not necessarily yield a gender sensitive story. We mean to show that selecting a woman as an object for research offers the opportunity for feminist analysis, but such a selection does not self-evidently warrant feminist outcomes. The first step in gender studies research usually consists of making women present who have been forgotten or inadequately described, but even so this might lead to gender insensitive and/or sexist analyses of these heroines. As a sample of the potential of gender sensitive analysis, each chapter will again demonstrate that this is all about *what kind of questions* a heroine is being asked, and *what theories about gender* are being used.

Debates

PART

I

The arena of feminism: Simone de Beauvoir and the history of feminism

1

Iris van der Tuin

1.1 *Simone de Beauvoir at work.*

Simone de Beauvoir (1908–1986) is best known for her treatise *The Second Sex* (*Le deuxième sexe*). The book was published in 1949. It probes the view on women and discusses the way they are represented, how women see themselves, and what the future holds for young girls. De Beauvoir advances the theory that women are classified as second-class citizens in relation to men. She also maintains that men as well as women persist in affirming this unequal relationship, both in the choices they make and in their actions, as these appear to be the fruit of fixed patterns. Men are in control of the economy, of history, education, and representation. It looks as if women can improve their position by finding a suitable marriage partner, but as soon as they give up their jobs to have children, they are in fact finished. They can no longer fulfil themselves and are imprisoned in their homes from this day forward. Preoccupied with silly chores, housewives and mothers just cannot find the time for personal growth, nor for contributing to society in any significant way.

On the face of it, de Beauvoir appears to be saying that women are stuck in an inescapably hopeless situation. Yet her analysis offers room for change. She posits that *'on ne naît pas femme, on le devient,'* a phrase usually translated as 'one is not born a woman, one becomes one.' It is a social-constructivist statement meant to indicate that women are not determined by biology. Because one is *made* female, because femininity is a social construct, alternatives can be designed (de Beauvoir, 1988 [1949]: 734).

De Beauvoir's oeuvre is known throughout the world. *The Second Sex* is a true feminist classic, a bulky and widely translated book. A million copies were sold in France alone (Rodgers, 1998: 310). The English translation sold over a million copies in the USA (Glazer, 2004), and the number of translated copies sold in a minor language such as Dutch approaches 100,000 (Vintges, 1992: 252, note 18). Part I of *The Second Sex* is devoted to historical and symbolical examples of how second-class citizenship for women is actually realized. Part II concentrates on the social relationships between men and women and discusses the ways in which women give shape to their lives. Here, de Beauvoir addresses the subjects of marriage and (lesbian) sexuality. She shows that women are in a way complicit to acquiring their second-class position and limited possibilities; it appears women are generally reconciled to their situation from the kinds of choices they make.

As is argued in *The Second Sex*, this situation should come to an end. Economic independence and women's right to vote (only since 1944 in France) are a step forward in an endeavour to design a new kind of femininity and a more balanced relationship between men and women. Apart from that, however, women will have to liberate themselves in moral, social, and psychological terms as well. In aspiring economic independence, women should acquire an active attitude – which is, de Beauvoir maintains, entirely against their nature (de Beauvoir, 1988 [1949]: 689–91).

De Beauvoir was radically ahead of her time with her statements on the position of women. However, for a long time she considered 'feminism' to be a dirty word. *The Second Sex* readers are urged to be wary of men judging women, of women's enthusiasm about 'real women', and of men glorifying the abominable position of women. But then she adds the following: 'We should consider the arguments of the feminists with no less suspicion, however, for very often their controversial aim deprives them of all real value' (de Beauvoir, 1988 [1949]: 26). Hence, the project of *The Second Sex* consists of freshly investigating the so-called 'woman question'. She posits: 'If we are to gain understanding, we must get out of these ruts; we must discard the vague notions of superiority, inferiority, equality which have hitherto corrupted every discussion of the subject and start afresh' (de Beauvoir, 1988 [1949]: 27).

Yet, as is attested by *The Second Sex*'s mottos, she too relies on the work of earlier thinkers who are generally seen as feminists *avant la lettre*. One of these mottos is derived from the French enlightenment thinker François Poulain de la Barre (1647–1723), who wrote that 'anything written by men on women should be treated with suspicion, because they are both judge and interested party in the conflict'. Poulain de la Barre's work is firmly secured in the feminist canon, to the extent that only recently it was admitted to the philosophical canon at all (Stuurman, 2004). In fact, the same is true for the work of de Beauvoir. It was not until 1992 that Karen

Vintges made a case for interpreting de Beauvoir's oeuvre, and in particular *The Second Sex*, in philosophical terms. Until then, despite de Beauvoir's initial aversion of the term, her work had carried the label of feminism, which shows that apparently the 'feminist' and 'philosophical' categories are mutually exclusive (Braidotti, 1991). However, as is demonstrated by Berteke Waaldijk and Geertje Mak in this book, the process of canonizing is gendered, but still can be manipulated by (individual) women.

The German feminist Alice Schwarzer made a documentary film about de Beauvoir in 1974. Writing mainly for periodicals, Schwarzer was also the general editor of *Emma* and, as such, the equivalent of Gloria Steinem, who ran the major feminist magazine in the United States, *Ms*. In the documentary, de Beauvoir is portrayed as *the* feminist and the viewer can see that she appears to be entirely comfortable in this role. Schwarzer, who also wrote about de Beauvoir, interviews her and offers us a glimpse into her life. We see a living room littered with souvenirs and a desk piled with various papers. We witness de Beauvoir taking a stroll, reading the newspaper, and varnishing her nails. She is then introduced by a voice-over as the world-famous author of novels, autobiographies, travel accounts, and political and philosophical essays, including *The Second Sex*. The countless translations of her work subsequently appear on screen. Schwarzer claims that *The Second Sex* was a vital book in the process of women's emerging awareness, in the late 1960s, of the hopeless situation for women in general and in particular for themselves.

Schwarzer explains that, following American journalists, de Beauvoir is generally pictured as the mother of feminism. Schwarzer seeks to discard this image in her documentary and wonders who de Beauvoir *really* is: is she the intellectual, emancipated woman who is just as capable as men; or is she first and foremost the close friend and lover of the philosopher Jean-Paul Sartre (1905–1980) and is her fame merely built on her relationship with this existentialist; or is she perhaps a woman who claims happiness while not being able to escape women's second-class citizenship?

From the way the documentary is set up, it appears that Schwarzer wishes to tell the 'truth' about de Beauvoir. However, since the advent of postmodernism, such a naive truth concept no longer holds, as is testified in several of this book's chapters. Rosi Braidotti shows that feminists began to criticize the alleged universal validity attributed to ideas on truth in the 1970s; Sarah Bracke and María Puig de la Bellacasa examine the ways in which the construction of situated (feminist) knowledge claims actually function; and Rosemarie Buikema subsequently demonstrates the impossibility of an unequivocal answer to the question of the meaning of a work of art. It is therefore legitimate to wonder what image of de Beauvoir was created by Schwarzer and how this image relates to other stories about her.

Although the documentary mentions de Beauvoir's initial aversion to feminism, the emphasis is on her role in feminism in the 1960s and 1970s. In a number of takes, de Beauvoir spells out the feminist list of demands: find a job, don't get married, don't have children, bisexuality for all, abortion legalized (abortion as well as contraceptives were still prohibited in France when *Le deuxième sexe* came out in 1949). The documentary ends with images of a festive dinner party in de Beauvoir's apartment, organized by a group of feminists in honour of Schwarzer's fortnight in Paris.

Both the manner of filming the 'list of demands' and the farewell dinner party serve yet again to frame de Beauvoir as the mother of feminism. Although the documentary features a variety of feminists, it is de Beauvoir who states the feminist demands and who thus becomes the representative of French feminism *par excellence*. Moreover, she is clearly exalted by the feminists present at the dinner party, all of whom are of another, younger generation. Schwarzer sought to abandon the standard image of de Beauvoir, but it is, in fact, reaffirmed. The image of the mother of feminism appears to be firmly glued to de Beauvoir (cf. Sara Ahmed's notion of 'sticky signs' in Ahmed 2004: 92).

This mother role also comes to the fore in the way de Beauvoir's relationships and affairs are portrayed. A kind of collage of photographs of (young) female and male (ex-) lovers is used to emphasize that she did not have a monogamous lifestyle. The view given is rather one-sided, however. The suggestion is that her daily rhythm is determined by her friendship with Sartre: they have lunch together, they work together, and after dinner they play a game of draughts and listen to music. Sylvie le Bon only plays the part of intimate younger friend and adopted daughter. For example, the documentary shows that Simone de Beauvoir administers some motherly advice to Le Bon, on teaching philosophy. In reality, both appear to have abhorred the idea of a mother-daughter relationship, both in theory and in practice, even though Le Bon was indeed adopted by de Beauvoir in 1980 – a formal decision instigated by the necessity to manage de Beauvoir's (literary) estate (Kaufmann, 1986: 127; Bair, 1996: 600 ff). However, they felt that a one-sided emphasis on the mother-daughter relationship, as the only possible relationship between women of unequal age, prolonged an oppressive stereotype. Deirdre Bair, de Beauvoir's biographer, even suggests that de Beauvoir once again turned away from feminism towards the end of her life because it would focus too much, in her view, on mother-daughter models. The documentary filmed by Schwarzer leaves no room for any alternative to such positioning. This raises the question of whether it is effectively true that the only way to think about feminism is in terms of mothers and daughters.

Waves and generations

Simone de Beauvoir is an important figure in the history of feminism, a history that is often characterized as a succession of metaphorical 'waves'. The first feminist wave crested around 1900 and was mainly concerned with women's right to vote. The second wave shook the world between 1965 and 1980, with radical positions on, mostly, the female body, sexuality, and relationships. The wave metaphor aptly encompasses the heyday of feminism as well as its (temporary) submergence. Continuously in motion, waves have neither an end nor a beginning; yet the wave's crest will inevitably disappear into the undercurrent. By suggesting both continuity and discontinuity, the wave metaphor is therefore eminently suitable for characterizing developments in feminism. Still, within gender studies, there is also critique on this metaphorical usage. For example, who can identify the crest or decide its moment? And if it turns out that the heyday of black or non-Western or lesbian feminism is not ever described in terms of a crest, should the conclusion then be that the wave metaphor is racist, Eurocentric, or heteronormative?

Another reason for being circumspect about the wave metaphor becomes apparent once we realize that the crests of feminist waves are generationally delimited. The historiography of feminism suggests that the second feminist wave was predominantly due to baby boomers, a generation born just after World War II, with a liberal sexual morality and radical political positions. They were hippies; they were opposed to the war in Vietnam; and they fuelled the battle for democratizing European universities in May 1968. Moreover, baby boomers did not go along with the general 1960s belief that women's emancipation had been accomplished (Meijer, 1996: 26). In addition, they were critical of the first feminist wave. In their view, first-wave feminists had not been radical enough; the important achievement of women's right to vote was seen as a form of emancipation on paper that was not matched by real life liberation. Moreover, baby boomers were critical of the type of woman they associated with first-wave feminism, to wit upper middle-class bluestockings. In other words, first-wave feminists allegedly defended the interests of a limited group. Or worse, they defended only their own interests.

What the waves in feminism have in common – that is, a radical position with respect to inequality between men and women – fades away when waves are primarily seen in generational terms. The dualist mechanism of one generation succeeding another then becomes the central issue. The dynamic of generations is habitually seen in dualist terms: each new generation is opposed to its predecessors and is not necessarily motivated by historically accurate information in doing so. This pattern also emerges in the historiography of feminism. We now know that first-wave feminists did carry out radical acts – especially the suffragettes in Britain, who chained themselves to railings and ran out in front of police horses in order to make their objectives (the admittance of women into masculine domains) known to politicians.

The second feminist wave, in turn, was criticized by members of the so-called 'generation X'. These 'post feminists', as they called themselves, distanced themselves from what they felt were 'moaning feminists', who publicly denounced their own unsatisfactory sexual and/or professional lives (consider for instance the 'glass ceiling').

Apart from questioning the idea that there was no continuity, as the wave metaphor appears to suggest, gender studies has also sought to reconsider the model of generational dialectics for describing the developments in feminism. Second-wave feminism did not just present itself as different from first-wave feminism, but as more advanced. Feminists of the 1970s opted for emphasizing the differences between men and women, which involved a revaluation and/or stimulation of the feminine. The strategy which was important to feminists around 1900, that is, the struggle for access into the masculine domain, was consequently written off as inferior, as this strategy presupposed that those masculine domains need not change – it was merely necessary to include women.

There are at least two reasons for disputing the low merit awarded to the strategy of first-wave feminism. First, the first-wave notion of equality is still in use as the most efficient way to effectuate a solution for certain problems (think of equal rights and equal opportunities commissions or the campaign instigated by Amnesty International, 'women's rights are human rights'). The claim that the equality strategy is inferior by definition therefore simply does not hold. Second, radical thoughts are not necessarily mutually exclusive to thinking in terms of equality. Domains are connoted either in a masculine or in a feminine way, which implies that it is not facile to simply admit women to the masculine domain because a form of transgression is always involved. As is explained in this book by Buikema, the presence of women in masculine domains raises certain questions about those domains and about the demarcation between feminine and masculine domains – precisely the topic of second-wave feminism.

In other words, it is a mistake to believe that one wave's strategy is better than the other, because equality did not disappear from the scene when the first wave came to an end and because there is a radical variant in line with the 'new' notions of the 1970s. In summary, the idea of generational dialectics is founded on generalizations that ignore the complexities of history.

Another reason for reconsidering the suitability of generational dialectics within gender studies is because it keeps women enthralled in the position of mother or rebellious daughter and subjects them both to the Law of the Father. It is a critique derived from Freudian psychoanalysis – discussed by Rosi Braidotti, Anneke Smelik, and Maaike Bleeker in these pages – and Claude Lévi-Strauss's anthropological concepts. Sigmund Freud (1856–1939) described the conflict which necessarily arises between mother and daughter because both want to be the father's lover, meaning that they are in competition with one another. Lévi-Strauss showed that this pattern of the male controlling inter-female relationships, forms society's foundational structure, based on the principle of women being exchanged by men. Because of this custom of exchanging women between families (or 'tribes'), family ties are not secured in unity, but rather in rivalry between (powerful) families. The explicatory models of Freud and Lévi-Strauss present the type of relationships between women of unequal age – antagonistic, competitive – as universally valid.

However, Freudian feminist criticism maintains that the generational dialectics model does not explain the wave-like development of feminism, but merely (re)affirms discontinuity by adopting a model of inter-female relations which is condoned by patriarchal culture (Stacey, 1993: 58–90; Buikema, 1995: 90–106; Roof, 1997). In other words, de Beauvoir and Le Bon do not find themselves alone in considering that the mother-daughter prototype for a relationship between women of unequal age is, in fact, an oppressive stereotype.

The notion of 'generationality' occupies a central position in the fundamental debates within gender studies, just as with the debates on biological determinism (discussed in the chapter by Cecilia Åsberg), on queer (see the chapters by renée hoogland and Bleeker), post colonialism (the chapter by Sandra Ponzanesi), interdisciplinarity (consult the chapter by Gloria Wekker), and representation (discussed in the chapter by Buikema). The present chapter aims to clarify the (generational) battle for feminism on the one hand; and on the other, it will attempt to present the generational dimension of the phenomenon of feminism in a different light. It is important for a textbook on gender studies to create an insight into the battle for feminism, because the term 'feminism' and its (generational) connotations may keep students and other potentially interested people from engaging themselves with this discipline. Such initial hesitations may be overcome with the realization that feminism has no essence but is not an empty vessel either.

Woman as historical Other to Man

Apart from the probing insight into so-called second-class citizenship, *The Second Sex* also offers an explanation for the unequal relations of men and women and signposts some routes to change these. Binary oppositions are at the core of de Beauvoir's discourse, and *The Second Sex* is packed with dozens of oppositions. De Beauvoir demonstrates that social structures, psychological processes, moral values, and representations are structured according to these mutually exclusive oppositions. Then she goes on to show that each such binary opposition is, in fact, gendered. Within this context, the term 'gendered' implies that gender neutral phenomena principally acquire gender. Paid out-of-doors work therefore acquired masculine connotations, whereas feminine connotations are reserved for running a house and caring for a family. Fairytales, literature, past and present events – they will always position the subject as a token of masculinity, with a host of connotations in its wake: what is active and free, the rational, consciousness, mind, culture, self-determination, responsibility, and being. Conversely, the object, the passive and unfree, the irrational, the unconscious, body, nature, *being* determined, being unaccountable, and nothingness will time and again signify femininity. The third step in de Beauvoir's argument then consists of showing that gender-specific connotations are not simply structured as binary oppositions, but are organized hierarchically. Masculinity, de Beauvoir sustains, is always valued higher.

The scheme of gendered oppositions constitutes a universal truth in de Beauvoir's discourse; *The Second Sex* suggests that the validity of this analysis is applicable to all times and places. Although this scheme was somewhat adapted and refined under the influence of poststructuralism and poststructuralist feminism (i.e. by introducing the possibility of 'hybridity', as discussed in the chapter by Ponzanesi) and was some-what stripped of its universal validity, it still forms one of the pillars of contemporary feminism and of gender studies as a discipline. We are still operating within the paradigm that images, terms, and phenomena are related to one another in gendered and hierarchical ways. The binary oppositions scheme, which was advanced by de Beauvoir, furnishes both the source of our analytical tools and the target of what we seek to deconstruct or change.

The Second Sex employs the conceptual term 'the situation of woman' in referring to the above-mentioned second-class citizenship. In using 'situation', de Beauvoir refers to her thesis that 'one is not born a woman, one becomes one'. She wishes to show that second-class citizenship does not constitute a woman's essence, but that it is a situation which can be changed. She wonders:

How can a human being in situation attain fulfilment? What roads are open to her? Which are blocked? How can independence be recovered in a state of dependency? What circumstances limit woman's liberty and how can they be overcome?

(de Beauvoir, 1988 [1949]: 29)

The Second Sex begins with the statement that the equality between men and women achieved by first-wave feminism is merely equality on paper:

The terms *masculine* and *feminine* are used symmetrically only as a matter of form, as on legal papers. In actuality the relation of the two sexes is not quite like that of two electrical poles, for man represents both the positive and the neutral [. . .]; whereas woman represents only the negative, defined by limiting criteria, without reciprocity.

(ibid.: 15)

In order to understand what she means to say here, consider the word 'doctor'. In theory, this term refers to both male and female physicians, yet we all too often come across 'female doctors'. The 'female' adjective designates 'doctor' as a masculine or ostentatiously neutral term. The fact that it is important to add 'female' when speaking of female physicians implies that they cannot be 'real' doctors for certain.

De Beauvoir explains the absence of reciprocality between men and women by following the philosopher Hegel (1770–1831) in maintaining that the duality of Self and Other is fundamental to human thought and actions. However, in the case of man (Self) and woman (Other), there is no reciprocality, whereas normally each duality has a reciprocal aspect. The woman question is, in other words, a *specific* question. She draws a comparison, for example, between women and people of the working classes, but she emphasizes that this comparison does not hold water. In her words, the woman question is a *specific* question due to the absence of any form of reciprocality between men and women:

[. . .] proletarians have not always existed, whereas there have always been women. They are women in virtue of their anatomy and physiology. Throughout history they have always been subordinated to men, and hence their independency is not the result of a historical event or a social change – it was not something that *occurred*. The reason why otherness in this case seems to be an absolute is in part that it lacks the contingent or incidental nature of historical facts.

(ibid.: 18)

What she shows here is that woman is the *historical Other* to men. She also clarifies the fact that women – all women in any situation – are the negative and non-essential with respect to men who are manifested as the neutral (or positive) and the essential, a situation which is perceived as natural.

In using terms such as 'Self' and 'Other', de Beauvoir betrays her debt to existentialism, the Sartrean philosophy.[1] Sartre and de Beauvoir were not just partners for life, both had actually been star students in philosophy at the Sorbonne and when they met

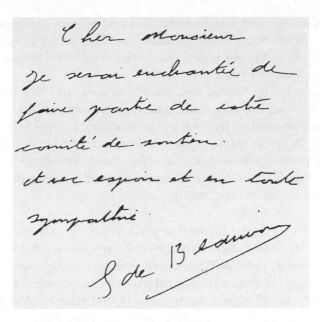

1.2 Note written by Simone de Beauvoir.

they were reading at the prestigious *École Normale Supérieure* in Paris. Since their time at university, they belonged to more or less the same circles of friends. Together they set up the leftist periodical *Les temps modernes*; they had joint publications and read each other's work before it went to the printers.

Existentialism provides the foundation for an ontology of being. There are two types of being in this philosophy: in oneself or itself *(en-soi)* and for oneself (*pour-soi*). 'Things' are not included in this duality, they are of necessity *en-soi*. People are *pour-soi*, in the sense that they can allocate place and purpose to things; they can read and interpret; they can assume responsibility and make certain choices. One such a choice is to opt for being *en-soi* rather than *pour-soi*. That should not really happen within the perspective of existentialism, because human beings are assigned to be *pour-soi*. But it is also important to realize that when two people meet, only one can be *pour-soi,* although (ideally) it is the aim of both. According to existentialism, there is always a conflict when two people meet. One becomes *pour-soi* and classifies the other as *en-soi*. The first transforms to the transcental subject, the second to the immanent object.

This occurs in love too, as Sartre argues, which turns love into an impossible enterprise. In the eyes of de Beauvoir, however, two people can merge in love – or in carnal love – and they should continuously aim for such blending (Vintges, 1992: 36–69, 70–96). This implies that, to de Beauvoir, there is not just the subject or the Self which exists thanks to the negation of an object or the Other.

The point of this brief survey is to show how *The Second Sex* effectively argues that Sartre's existentialism is gendered. Woman is the Other to man for historical and not for biological reasons. Time and again man has assigned himself the part of Self, at the expense of woman who is made Other. The critical point in this process is formed by reproduction. When reproducing, women affirm the subjectivity of men because they lock themselves in: in their bodies (temporarily) and their homes (forever) – thus blocking the road towards transcendence.

The conclusion to *The Second Sex*, titled 'The Road to Liberation,' states that it does not suffice to change the economic situation for women if the moral, social, and cultural consequences entailed by such a change are not accepted (de Beauvoir, 1988 [1949]: 734). De Beauvoir wants women to have access to masculine domains, but realizes that the presence of women will affect those domains. Her objective is an 'androgynous world' (ibid.: 735), where women can fully realize their potential. This emphatically does not lead to uniformity:

> New relationships of flesh and sentiment of which we have no conception will arise between the sexes; already, indeed, there have appeared between men and women friendships, rivalries, complicities, comradeships – chaste or sensual – which past centuries could not have conceived [. . .] I fail to see [. . .] that liberty ever creates uniformity. [. . .] her relations to her own body, to that of the male, to the child, will never be identical with those the male bears to his own body, to that of the female, and to the child.
>
> (ibid.: 740)

She puts her bets on communism in *The Second Sex*, to realize the swing towards full reciprocity between men and women (ibid.: 733, 741).

The female line of thought

Although de Beauvoir puts her stakes on the communist rather than feminist revolution, *The Second Sex* is generally seen as the bible of second-wave feminism. It is believed to have acted like a starting shot; it set the movement in motion because women became conscious of their own situation when reading *The Second Sex* and many decided to become active in the practice of women's emancipation, which resulted in a transnational women's liberation. We now know that this narrative does not represent historical reality, but is part and parcel of the mystification which surrounds *The Second Sex*.

De Beauvoir wrote this book just after World War II. She worked alone. In attempting to readdress the woman question from a new perspective, which entailed arguing why there was not a case of a 'man question', she extensively researched the sources held by the *Bibliothèque Nationale de France* in Paris. The book was not received with much enthusiasm in post-war, conservative France. A small number of women read the book but it certainly did not result in an instant large-scale women's movement, such as the later *Mouvement de Libération des Femmes* or *MLF* (Rodgers, 1998: 15–22). In fact, in the *MLF*'s first publications, which appeared around 1970, *The Second Sex* is only met with disapproval (Vintges, 1992: 253, note 19). A transatlantic journey of *The Second Sex* by way of an English translation and publication in the US was necessary for the book to be recognized *en masse* by feminists in France and Europe.[2] American feminists turned de Beauvoir into the icon of Women's Lib, as is testified, for instance, by the dedication to Simone de Beauvoir 'who endured' in Shulamith Firestone's *The Dialectic of Sex* (1971). Firestone appears to be saying that de Beauvoir's analysis of the situation of women was probably complete and pervasive (Firestone, 1971: 7).

It seems that the book appeared just a little too soon in France. It was too radical for those who were in charge of feminism after World War II, and the women who would later become *MLF* militants were too young to appreciate it when it came out and could not dispose of a feminist context or a group of friends to help interpret the book (Rodgers, 1998: 17, 21–22). In other words, the book needed to travel in order to become influential and perhaps the timing was in any case better when it was launched in the United States, as it took a while before *The Second Sex* was translated. That translation, incidentally, was neither accurate nor complete. Thus, *The Second Sex* became a feminist text in the United States first; European feminists followed suit because at the time they were being inspired and influenced by feminist publications from the States.

Even so, the initial reactions of new-baked feminists were at best lukewarm at the text's return to continental Europe, as can be illustrated by the history of *The Second Sex* in the Netherlands. A Dutch translation was available when the second wave flooded the Netherlands too in the 1960s, but this was only read by a small circle of non-feminist intellectuals (Meijer, 1996: 26). An essay by Joke Kool-Smit (1933–1981) was published in the prestigious journal *De Gids* in 1967. Entitled 'Discontent of Women', in retrospect this essay appears to have launched the second wave in the Netherlands. It refers to *The Second Sex* with a mixture of praise and criticism:

> Men are having a good time, women are miserly. This is what remains after reading the otherwise excellent study by Simone de Beauvoir, *The Second Sex*. But this residue misrepresents reality. If there is a second sex at all, then most men belong to it too, because top dogs are simply rather rare. One could even say that most women have a much easier life than men, as it is less frustrating to do routine work while running a one-person company than having to obey orders.
>
> (Kool-Smit, 1967: 267)

This influential essay was founded on a partial reading of *The Second Sex*, as de Beauvoir does not restrict her discussion of women to their economic position alone, but refers to society as a whole. According to de Beauvoir, women are by definition worse off than men (even when compared to the lowest in rank), because men, whatever their job or function, allegedly are neutral or positive and women negative.

There is then no historical reason for the picture painted by Schwarzer and her predecessors: de Beauvoir is not the unproblematic 'mother' of feminism who single-handedly engendered second-wave feminism. Rather, the book was picked up and made into the standard work of the movement by feminists of the baby boom generation in the late 1960s and early 1970s. Eventually de Beauvoir, who despised mothers, was declared the mother of second-wave feminism in Europe. In the US, this part was reserved for Betty Friedan.

Considering this, how can it be explained that women keep positioning *The Second Sex* as the origin and cause of second-wave feminism? Perhaps this is because the above-mentioned antagonistic and competitive relationship between women, due to their subjection to men who control and determine relations in society, is often consciously reversed by feminists. It is therefore a feminist *position* to ascribe such prominent propelling force to *The Second Sex*. Historical reality is subordinate to theoretical points such as made by the feminist Adrienne Rich, who stated that continuity between women is central and who questioned the alleged psychoanalytical inevitability of rivalry between women.

Rich addressed the institution and experience of motherhood in her influential treatise *Of Woman Born: Motherhood as Experience and Institution* (1976). Writing about the mother-daughter relationship, she argues that in patriarchy this has become a relationship of mutual exclusion which ignores the fact that each mother is a daughter too, and each daughter may become a mother. This is in fact true in a figurative sense as well, she says: all women are mother and daughter alike, because even when they do not bear children of the female sex, women act to type in relating to other women. There are mothers, or 'eternal givers', and daughters, or 'free spirits'. Rich goes on to say that the mutual exclusion engendered by patriarchy entails a hierarchical order as well, with motherhood representing the negative and daughterhood the positive. She writes that 'patriarchal attitudes have encouraged us to split, to polarize, these images, and to project all unwanted guilt, anger, shame, power, freedom, onto the "other" woman' (Rich, 1976: 253). Having unravelled the question of rivalry between women, Rich subsequently argues that this pattern should be subverted, because 'any radical vision of sisterhood demands that we reintegrate them' (cf. ibid.: 246).

Contrary to de Beauvoir, who puts the blame on reproduction when explaining the situation, Rich argues that reproduction is the source of potential:

> This cathexis between mother and daughter – essential, distorted, misused – is the great unwritten story. Probably there is nothing in human nature more resonant with charges than the flow of energy between two biologically alike bodies, one of which has lain in amniotic bliss inside the other, one of which has laboured to give birth to the other. The materials are here for the deepest mutuality and the most painful estrangement.
>
> (ibid.: 225–226)

She locates the 'most painful estrangement' in the anger daughters feel with regard to their mothers: their mothers have set them loose in a male-dominated world (ibid.: 225). There might have been the 'deepest mutuality' between mother and daughter if patriarchy had not intervened (ibid.: 245–246).

Rich believes that feminism will provide the impulse for restoring reciprocality between women. Note that Rich's agenda involves reciprocality of women only and not, as with de Beauvoir, the (exclusive) search for reciprocality between men and women. It signifies both a personal quest and an artistic and academic process:

Without the unacclaimed research and scholarship of 'childless' women, without Charlotte Brontë (who died in her first pregnancy), Margaret Fuller (whose major work was done before her child was born), without George Eloit, Emily Brontë, Emily Dickinson, Christina Rossetti, Virginia Woolf, Simone de Beauvoir – we would all today be suffering from spiritual malnutrition as women.

(ibid.: 252)

Rich wishes to reinstall a female continuity which has been dismantled by patriarchy. In other words, she seeks to fortify the female rather than the male line.

Thinking in the female line – symbolized by the term 'sisterhood' in Rich's treatise – is also referred to as *thinking difference* (see the guides to key concepts by Andermahr, *et al.*, 2000; Pilcher and Whelehan, 2004). Thinking difference elaborates on the radical branch of thinking equality. In radical forms of thinking equality, it is argued that domains which are coded in a masculine way are subjected to critique when women are admitted. Difference thinkers are focused on female coded domains which have remained underexposed, both in society and in feminism. They wish to reassess these allegedly nonessential domains and help them to flourish, although they believe that this can only ultimately happen from within the domain itself. For example, difference thinkers will question what has been written by men about women, because such writings tend to keep women trapped in the negative and nonessential. In other words, in defining women, such writings prolong and entrench the hierarchical relation between men and women.

Thinking difference seeks to design a *female* standard based on horizontal/reciprocal relationships, instead of vertical/hierarchical relationships. Thinking difference involves reappraising femininity. For instance, a female canon is proposed, or a female aesthetics. The general standards for literariness, the poetical (see the chapter by Maaike Meijer), or beauty (see the chapters by Ann-Sophie Lehmann and Marta Zarzycka) which are coded by masculinity can thus be abandoned in favour of a new standard based on the work of women. This creates an understanding for the difficulty in defining such works in masculine terms. Still more radical differential thinking rejects the linguistic system as masculine and hierarchically organized in its entirety. French poststructuralist feminists, such as Hélène Cixous, developed the notion of feminine writing (*écriture feminine*) with the idea of reciprocality between women at its core.

The question of the 'essence' of woman arises again within the context of thinking difference. De Beauvoir rejected this notion, but within gender studies there has been some debate among difference thinkers about reintroducing the idea of essence. In the end, the conclusion is that the emphasis on the feminine does not necessarily entail erasing differences between women. However, one should remain alert, because the risk of ignoring power differences between women, or other types of differences, lurks in the prevalence of white ethnicity and heterosexuality. As is variously explained in this book by Braidotti and by Bracke and Puig de la Bellacasa, Rich used her 'politics of location' concept to design a methodology which was alert on differences, arguing that thinking should occur from the concretely physical and, on occasion, fragmented locations (Rich, 1985c). In addition to gender, her work systematically addresses issues of ethnicity and sexuality too. One such location from which Rich's own thinking departs is her Jewish descent. She writes that being both a woman and a Jew implies that she is 'white' in some situations and 'non-white' in others, an observation which serves as a starting point for her analysis of power differences between white and black women. Rich's own lesbian sexuality informs her famous essay 'Compulsory Heterosexuality and Lesbian Existence' (1981), which reflects on both the differences and similarities between heterosexual and lesbian women (consult the chapter by hoogland).

The work of Teresa de Lauretis offers a good illustration of the way in which thinking in the female line can be further developed and deployed within gender studies. This notion informs her article 'Feminist Genealogies' (1993), about the hidden connections between Elena Lucrezia (1646–1684), Belle van Zuylen (1740–1805), and Virginia Woolf (1882–1941). On the face of it, these women appear to have nothing in common, if it were not for the fact that all three were female and that each of them had an impact on the thoughts of de Lauretis. They each resisted being gagged by misogynous circumstances and in resisting they spoke up for all women, giving vent to silenced voices. Thinking up and describing such 'genealogies' is an important part of feminist theory. In contrast to de Beauvoir and early second-wave feminists, who mainly denounced their predecessors and therefore effectively gagged them once again, difference thinkers wish to surmount rivalry between women by imagining a more affirmative inter-female relationship.

De Lauretis' genealogy (Lucrezia–van Zuylen–Woolf) clearly is not necessarily valid for all (academic) feminists. This is an important aspect of de Lauretis' work, which is attentive to the partial dimensions of her efforts, and in line with poststructuralist tendencies in feminist theory. Poststructuralist feminists question the single and undivided assumption of the idea of women's writing or female literariness or aesthetics. They represent a mode of feminist thought which is focused on context-dependent research. The feminist genealogies of de Lauretis – note the plural – then explicitly do not pretend to represent general truths (there are always other connections that can be drawn), but are narratives which can be located specifically in time and place. They claim that the loss of the comfortable suggestion of a single Truth is balanced, if not improved, by the exactitude of narratives which account for the politics of location.

Dis-identification

So it was only subsequent to the beginning of a transnational women's movement that de Beauvoir came to present herself as a feminist. She was not the source of second-wave feminism, but was rather *made* into the mother of feminism. In feminism and by feminism, de Beauvoir became a feminist and *The Second Sex* a feminist tract: One is not born a feminist, one becomes one. She too had no essence but acquired one through interacting with a transnational feminist movement.

On the flip side of the coin, there is no essence to *feminism* either. There is no single origin or aim. There are different feminist actions which each inform 'feminism' and create (new) feminist heroines and fundamental publications. A feminist genealogy, in short, is continually revised and reshaped. For example, the brand of feminism which inked in, as it were, de Beauvoir and *The Second Sex* in the 1970s, is a specific kind of feminism that does not necessarily have an eye for non-Western forms of feminism or for feminisms less focused on propagating the slogan that 'the personal is political'. It is a pity that, in general, there is only a single ostentatiously true story about the history of feminism. This hackneyed narrative excludes certain forms of feminisms or fails to qualify these as feminisms and also classifies some feminists as more feminist than others.

Present-day feminist theory is attentive to the ways in which the history of feminism is (re)told and in this context often reconsiders the generational dimension of (stories about) feminism (Hemmings, 2005a). De Lauretis' proposal to devise partial genealogies for feminism, rather than the alleged truth of a single feminist historiography, has become common practice within gender studies. Female continuity acquires specific significance with this gesture. Recently, this debate was enriched by a term introduced by Astrid Henry, which encompasses both continuity and rivalry between women. She argues that the binary opposition of continuity versus rivalry masks the *ambivalent* relationship between (generations of) women. Feminists of the past are neither necessarily our arch rivals, nor unproblematically our sisters. They are, or should be at best, both. Henry explains in her book *Not My Mother's Sister* (2004) that there is a new generation of third-wave feminists who relate to second-wave feminism according to a pattern of so-called 'dis-identification' (Henry, 2004: 7).[3]

Dis-identification immediately signifies the identification *against* something or somebody and the intimate concentration on otherness or the other person. If, as a feminist, you wish to identify *against* de Beauvoir, you will need to know her work intimately, you will need to know it by heart. Henry explains that dis-identification does not involve refusal (I refuse to relate to de Beauvoir's work) but rather a resistance to an identification which has already been made (I don't *want* to identify with de Beauvoir because she claims universal rather than specific validity for her statements about women and because she was opposed to having children). De Beauvoir's feminism is then acknowledged but not accepted as the desired type of feminism for third-wave feminism. The concept of dis-identification then offers the opportunity to understand the work of American feminists and their references to de Beauvoir in the following terms: they did not all wholly agree with de Beauvoir, but in carving out their own position in feminism, they could not do otherwise than take in *The Second Sex* because this was a text that was at their disposition. Because feminism in the tradition of difference initially subverted and glorified the mother-daughter relationship, de Beauvoir was automatically converted into the symbolical mother of second-wave feminism. When European feminists began reading work by American feminists, they also began to take account of de Beauvoir.

The concept of dis-identification helps to think through generationality as a notion which involves neither sheer rivalry nor continuity. It accounts for both continuity between women and for specific cases of inequality between women (based, for instance, on nation, ethnicity, or sexuality). The notion also makes clear that a feminist 'wave' or generation is neither wholly new nor entirely the same and so a simple copy or repetition. Because of dis-identification, you can immediately think of and talk about continuity and change in feminist thoughts. It allows for waves or generational positioning, while making clear that the stale pattern of rivalry between women is not repeated.

The history of *The Second Sex* teaches us that, in thinking about feminism, the dimensions of (national) location and generation should always be taken into consideration. However, at the same time, analysis of this history proves that neither location nor generation are stable concepts. In discussing feminist thought, one should allow for the possibility that certain texts or images have made a (trans-Atlantic) *journey* and also account for generational disidentification or *transposition*. The latter implies that early feminist works are neither mechanically rejected nor automatically accepted. In retelling the history of feminism, we should consider *where* feminist theory originates (and such a location can imply plurality or motion) and *who* were involved in constituting feminist thoughts.

Notes

1   There is some speculation among de Beauvoir scholars about the share of de Beauvoir in Sartrean existentialism. They wonder, for example, about the contents of her dissertation, inaccessibly guarded by Le Bon in a vault. It has been suggested that it possibly contains the earliest formulations of existentialism (Fullbrook and Fullbrook, 2008).
2   Sarah Glazer (2004), as well as Karen Vintges (1992), nicely sum up the debate on the American translation of *Le deuxième sexe*, which suffers from mistranslated philosophical concepts, the omission of important sections, biologisms, etc.
3   The term I use for this pattern is 'jumping generations' (van der Tuin, 2009).

Questions for further research

1   Is feminism considered in the study you are enrolled in? If the answer is negative, why should this be so? If positive, then what is feminism associated with? In answering the question, refer to a textbook for an introductory course in your first year.

2   What famous feminists can you mention? Where did you come across these women, and what does that tell you about their place in, for instance, the literary or philosophical canon and in popular culture?

3   What do you think is the reason for founding special libraries and archives for women and the women's movement? Think of The Women's Library in London (www.londonmet.ac. uk/thewomenslibrary) or the Bibliothèque Marguerite Durand in Paris (www.annuaire-au-feminin.net/assBIBmargDURAND.html) or The International Information Centre and Archives for the Women's Movement (IIAV) in Amsterdam (www.iiav.nl/eng). Visit these websites and describe how these libraries mediate libraries and archives in general, on the one hand, and the women's movement, on the other.

4   Is feminism strictly a women's topic? Argue why (not).

5   Is it possible to see women's lib as disconnected from fighting racism or homophobia or ageism? Argue why (not).

6   Is the base of feminism destroyed in acknowledging the differences between women? Try and argue both a negative and a positive position in relation to this question.

The arena of the body: The cyborg and feminist views on biology

2

Cecilia Åsberg

2.1 Lynn Randolph's Cyborg *(1989)*

The woman warrior described in this chapter is a dubious type. She is not entirely human and it is not even clear if she is a woman at all: the woman warrior of feminist science is the hybrid figuration of the cyborg. The term cyborg is short for *cyb*ernetic *org*anism. A hybrid of body and technology, of flesh and steel, the cyborg of contemporary popular culture often is depicted as the highly gendered incarnation of either the sexy femme-bot or the hard-boiled masculine terminator. The latter is the preferred version in science fiction, where cyborgs figure as ultra-gendered fighters, in films such as *Terminator, Bionic Woman, Robocop, The Matrix* and *Ghost in the Shell*. Cyborg bodies are simultaneously biological and technological. They seem like a combination of human organs infused with visible implants. There obviously is not anything purely natural about them.

The cyborg is the curious offspring of neo-colonial science and super-power Cold War militarism. The men who coined the very term cyborg had far-reaching visions. Nathan Kline and Manfred Clynes, scientists contracted by NASA, published a radical article, 'Cyborgs and Space', in the scientific journal *Astronautics* (1960). This article sketched the potential of enhancing the human body for space exploration. The body could be modified to endure the hostile environment of outer space with the help of, for instance, self-regulatory devices such as adrenaline pumps inserted directly in the heart, exoskeleton space suits, and even long-term genetic engineering to augment the oxygen and breathing capacity of humans. Kline and Clynes imagined that cyborgs would drastically improve the position of the United States in the space race with the Soviet Union. The space race was part of the Cold War, the period during which the world was strictly divided, in military and political terms, into West and East, or NATO versus the Warsaw Pact. The cyborg was the answer to such global controversies.

At a historical conjunction, when every inch of the globe was to be claimed, colonized, and meticulously monitored by military satellites, the idea of the cyborg offered the opportunity of a twofold territorial conquest: outer space and the inner space of the body. Some of these initial ideas would be implemented in the long run, such as in the plan for identifying all human genes, the so-called Human Genome Project. Medical technologies, such as ultra-sound and computer tomography (CT scans), are military spinoffs that enabled new insights into and cartographies of the body. Cyborgs were to operate according to the military logic of C3I: command-control-communication-intelligence. C3I was designed to replace brute force by deploying smart technologies for effective regulation, guidance, and steering (Haraway, 1991a: 164). Cybernetics, the science of feedback and regulation, of engineered control and communication in living organisms as well as in stealth airplanes, was applied to the human body and to society in general. The term cybernetics is derived from the Greek word for pilot, rudder, or steersman: *kybernetes*. The term 'government' is also rooted in *kybernetes*. Cybernetics then is about steering genetic or computer generated information. Kline and Clynes envisaged the cyborg as a body containing an integrated artificial feedback system. The feedback system was the key to controlling these cyborgs, these man-machines or animal-machines that incarnated the super-enhanced hybridity of flesh and technology. The cyborg was thus initially conceptualized in relation to war and imperialism. It was a science fantasy of man-made generations of hyper-masculine warriors that would resonate in popular culture. Think for instance of Hollywood productions such as the *Terminator* films or science fiction TV series such as *The Six-Million-Dollar-Man* or *Star Trek*. However, in the era of the Cold War, cyborgs soon enough evolved from fiction to fact. Osmotic pumps distributing the exact dose of a substance for medical trials were implanted in laboratory rats, and before long human patients followed suit with the implantation of pacemakers, artificial organs, and other prosthetic devices. Cyborg practices proliferated as foetal development began to be carefully monitored inside the womb and combat pilots were sensorially attached to the interface of their aircraft. Indeed, any woman on the pill (regulating her internal hormonal levels) embodies an example of cyborg engineering. In short, cyborg technology is life-prolonging and maintains the rickety structure of the human body. More than that, it is used to enhance the body and create a superman in the case, for instance, of the cyborg pilot or the formula-one racing driver. Today, the enormous variety of human-machine couplings defies definition and ranges from disabled patients who can rely on high-tech equipment or the vaccination of newborns to the creation of effective human killing machines. Both in their life-prolonging and life-threatening functions, cyborgs have become a symbol of the ambivalences of high modernity.

In this context, the cyborg is a figuration containing both promises and threats with respect to the future of our bodies and our sense of self. It symbolizes the destructive as well as the reproductive powers of modern science. Modern scientists did not just invent atom bombs or contribute to biochemical warfare; they also developed techniques for artificial insemination and fertilization that helped childless couples at fertility clinics. The cyborg vision has led to a radical redefinition of bodies, identities, and the scientific discourse of biology in general. Feminists have high stakes in such changes and the cyborg, consequently, came to represent a gamut of possibilities in academic feminist writing.

The trouble with biology

In the 1970s, the discipline of biology, as with other fields of scientific inquiry, appeared to be in urgent need of critical inquiry from a feminist perspective. Such appraisals did not just concern gender inequality in academia, but especially focused on the deeply entrenched androcentrism that had characterized the discipline. In socio-biologist arguments from the late 1970s, the solution to the social problems of aggression, territoriality, racism, and male supremacy was reduced to a matter of genetic programming. Thus famous male sociobiologists, such as Richard Dawkins and E.O. Wilson, maintained that so-called biological facts, such as male heterosexual philandering and female coyness, and even the genetic determination of the 'inevitability of patriarchy,' selfishness, and capitalism, formed inextricable and insurmountable impediments to feminist demands. Feminism, in their eyes, just went against the laws of nature.

In fact, the biologist's idea that the options for social change are slim due to the laws of nature, admonishes women to accept their fate. Feminist theorists, ranging from Simone de Beauvoir to Judith Butler, reject such biological explanations for the social position of women and argue instead that scientific authority is used as a powerful weapon for consolidating social norms rather than the ostentatious biological facts.

They advanced the notion of gender as a social construction in order to counter the blatant biological determinism that held sway. In de Beauvoir's famous words, 'One is not born a woman, one becomes one' (1988 [1949]). As Donna Haraway observed, 'all the modern feminist meanings of gender have [their] roots' in this famous phrase (Haraway, 1991b: 131). The separation between socially constructed gender and biological sex thus enabled feminists to contest the belief that social inequalities of women were rooted in and hence justified by biology (Butler, 1990).

The distinction between (biological) sex and (socially constructed) gender allowed for a torrent of studies on the variety of constructions imbued in power and gender that underpin the disciplines of history, social sciences, medicine, and the natural sciences. Gender became the touchstone for feminist research and scholarship. A social construction as opposed to biological sex, gender was deployed to explore the mechanisms of sexual difference and debunk Freud's idea that 'anatomy is destiny' (Freud, 1931). Lynda Birke, a biologist and feminist science scholar, succinctly summarizes the feminist problem with biology as follows: '(We) women have long been defined by our biology. It is a familiar story; anatomy is destiny, our hormones make us mad or bad, genes determine who we are' (Birke, 2000: 1). However, the problem of the distinction between sex and gender in feminist scholarship is that it appears to reproduce the nature/culture dichotomy. This problem is tackled in many different ways. For example, feminist scientist Ruth Hubbard (1990) argues that women's bodies, more than men's, are socially constructed in biological discourse, for the politically motivated reasons of endorsing domination. She also maintains that nature is not just interpreted through the cultural lens of patriarchy, but that physical bodies are actually in part shaped by culture. In that sense it is difficult to tell apart nature from culture, or sex from gender (Hubbard, 1990). In short, the vast area of feminist research includes diverse and at times even contradictory approaches to biology and the body.

However, the most fundamental critique in feminist approaches to biology is concerned with gendered interpretations of the body and nature. Western science consequently divides the world into the two opposites of nature and culture. Culture then is perceived as representing the changes brought about by humans in the course of time, while nature stands for the given of the unchanging true world untouched by human intervention. But just as science, including biology, has a history, so does nature – in the form of evolution. Throughout the Western history of science, scientists have been occupied with the question of the 'nature' of Nature. That fundamental scientific question was in many ways symbolically linked to the question of the nature of 'woman' and 'native' as opposed to 'civilized man' (Bryld and Lykke, 2000). Sex and 'race' were defined in terms of difference to an implied norm. In other words, physiognomic differences and variations were taken to imply natural hierarchies that indicated the optimal order of society. The role of biology then was to determine and classify the questions of difference and settle the matter once and for all. Sustained by the immanent social authority of the sciences, therefore, the discipline of biology was pre-eminently apt to gather knowledge about society.

Feminists critiqued this widely ramified belief system and queried the notion of 'the natural', exposing how it operated as a foil for dominant ideologies. They pointed out that the very institutions of science had a stake in producing knowledge about nature. Rather, they argued, science was a cultural phenomenon, subject to historical changes and part of a gender divided society. Science historians exposed the normative role of implicit gender concepts in constructing past truths, scientific facts, and the ways of understanding nature.

Carolyn Merchant's *The Death of Nature: Women, Ecology, and the Scientific Revolution* was published in 1980. Relating environmental history to feminist theory and the history of science, Merchant described science as a specific culture with a social history of its own. In this perspective, the distinct issues of our current ecological crisis, the domination of nature, and the devaluation of women in the production of scientific knowledge are shown to be interrelated: their common roots are traced to the beginnings of modern science in the seventeenth century. Other studies have shown that the formal exclusion of women from fame or top-ranking positions in the past has given way to an implicit, tacit, and tradition-bound set of motifs that keeps women from acquiring secure and important positions in the sciences. The culture of modern science that originated in seventeenth-century Europe did not simply exclude women as subjects of knowledge production in research, it was *defined in defiance of women* (Noble, 1992: xiv).

The history of science exhibits many examples of the projection of social inequalities, such as 'race', class, and gender on nature, with the result that, in turn, the cultural assumptions about societal divisions and hierarchies appear to be illustrated by nature (Merchant, 1980; Jordanova, 1989; Fausto-Sterling, 1992; Schiebinger 1993). In biology, such societal differences have been inscribed in different subject areas ranging from blood, genes, and hormones to the foetus, the genitals, the brain, or the bones (Mol, 1989; Lacquer, 1990; Oudshoorn, 1994; Haraway, 1997; Klinge, 1997). However, it is important to note in this respect that the feminist stance regarding the sciences and biology is not necessarily oppositional. Science may offer some opportunities too. Thus, Shulamith Firestone, one of the pioneers of the Redstockings, a New York based feminist caucus in the 1970s, maintained in her programmatic *The Dialectic of Sex* (1971) that the appropriation of medicine and reproduction techniques would pave the way for women's emancipation. Women would be freed from work and childbearing by science and technology, and thus cease to act as the indispensable agents in production and reproduction, those cornerstones of the capitalist society that Firestone wanted to revolutionize. Firestone utopically envisaged that, apart from the recourse to abortion, reproductive technologies such as artificial insemination and gestation outside the womb (this so-called *ectogenesis* still is a fictive technology to date) would free women from the drags of pregnancy, childbirth, and nurturance, which she considered to be the major obstacles for women's liberation. The control of and power over women's bodies, especially with respect to fertility and sexuality, was a fundamental issue in Firestone's thinking. The problem was located *within women's own bodies* and the application of a neutral technology would bring an end to biological motherhood. Sexual equality would become a real possibility.

Firestone's technophilia, her strong belief in the power of science, was mitigated by the critical attention she paid to the contemporary state of affairs where science, medicine, and technology in fact facilitated oppression, marginalization, and exclusion

(Lykke, 1996: 2).[1] There were other critical voices too, in the early days of second-wave feminism. Firestone's enthusiastic endorsement of the idea of developing artificial wombs was countered by a growing feminist resistance to the misogynist application of genetics and reproductive engineering (such as embryo screening and sex selection resulting in the abortion of female foetuses). The most vociferous protest came from a group of radical feminists called FINRRAGE, short for Feminist International Network of Resistance to Reproductive and Genetic Engineering (Arditti, *et al.*, 1984; Corea, *et al.*, 1985). This group argued that the development of reproductive technologies was a form of patriarchal exploitation of women's bodies. FINRRAGE saw an inextricable link between reproductive technologies and the fields of genetic engineering, that is, manufacturing so-called 'designer babies' and eugenics. Women's unique source of power was in danger, in other words, and women risked being reduced to birth machines in what one spokeswomen, Gena Corea (1985), foresaw as 'reproductive brothels', comparable to the breeding of animals in batteries and the like. In radical opposition to Firestone, FINRRAGE maintained that biological motherhood and maternal thinking should rather be reclaimed in order to resist the complacent destructive orientation of men, for whom reproductive and genetic technologies were all about conquering the last frontier, about gaining power over 'life itself' and hence acquiring the ultimate control over nature. The feminist opposition to such views is comparable to eco-feminism, a movement that considers biological warfare, imperialist biopiracy, and the ecological effects of modern technologies to be the products of a violent, racist, and patriarchal Western culture (Shiva and Moser, 1995).

Feminists thus tend to approach the sciences either as a determining force (eco-feminists and FINRRAGE) or as neutral and value-free (Firestone). Consequently, their view on the implications for women tends to be either over-pessimistic or over-enthusiastic. Either science is patriarchal and capitalist, that is, it exploits nature and indigenous peoples and subjects women to masculine technologies that serve the desire of men to control women's biology. Or, conversely, science and technology are purely neutral, which creates a basis for the opposite political conclusions that women who are trapped in their reproductive bodies can be liberated by science and technology. The latter vision did not stop with Firestone: the techno-enthusiasm of some of the early 1990s *cyberfeminists* appears to share Firestone's optimism by welcoming electronic media and the Internet as a space where bodies are redundant and feminism prospers subversively like a virus (Plant, 1997; and for a critique of such disembodying cyberfeminism, see Braidotti, 1996).

The body has always been central to the early second-wave feminism analyses of patriarchal power relations (Firestone, 1970; Mitchell, 1970; MacKinnon, 1982), and it is turned in an important topic for scholarship by feminisms of different kinds (Bordo, 1993; Braidotti, 1994). Developing in various ways, these approaches led among others to the rise of the new field of Body Studies (Davis, 1997; Fraser and Greco, 2005). The various orientations within Body Studies owe a great deal to feminist research. To take an example, a 'Cartesian dualism' is disclosed that underpins the feminization and racialization of the body: the unmarked given or *a priori* category is reserved for the mind and for disembodied white masculinity as soon as body matters arise. As a philosophical move, such distinctions – between man/mind/culture/white centre and woman/body/nature/exotic other – are anything but neutral, since it implies an asymmetrical hierarchical pattern.

However, Lynda Birke (2000) suggests that feminist studies have neglected the biological body, that is, the materially real and fleshy dimensions of the body, through favouring instead the idea of the body as a cultural entity. Although she acknowledges sociological and feminist theories for their cultural inscriptions on the body, Birke argues that the somewhat ironic effect of such thinking is that the actual body recedes into the background. The preference for social and psychoanalytical explanations, rather than a physiological understanding of inner bodily processes, has effectively led to leaving the body's interior mechanisms to the devices of traditional biomedical experts and authorities. As a trained biologist, Lynda Birke engages with feminist health issues and animal rights activism. She argues for bridging the gap between the natural sciences and cultural research on the body, since the biological sciences have a lot more on offer than deterministic narratives on the workings of nature. She maintains that the analytical tools from the social and cultural sciences are inept for dealing with some pertinent biological issues. Birke urges to problematize the assumption that the natural body is fixed and unchanging and argues for developing a feminist practice of natural sciences, just as she also advocates stimulating feminist scholarly research on the disciplines of natural sciences and technology.

Feminist re-visions of biology

Much like the way women's studies grew out of the women's movement, feminist science and technology studies evolved from health activist movements and from women's engagement with medical, ecological, and scientific issues. This field has specific roots of its own and cannot be seen as just another chapter in the history of mainstream science and technology studies (Lykke, 2002: 140). One root can be traced to the feminist medical self-help movement and the famous book *Our Bodies, Ourselves*. This book was first published by the Boston Women's Health Book Collective (1971). That first publication was followed by many editions all over the world, as it was updated and rewritten by different women's communities on a global scale (Davis, 2002). Medical discourse also is thoroughly investigated by feminists. Such studies range from prizing apart the former notions of hysteria and nymphomania to critically evaluating contemporary ideas on PMS, post-natal depression, and anorexia. One of the most important conclusions of these studies is that the entire discourse on medicine, down to the letter of scientific articles on cells, has imagined the female body as more susceptible to pathologies and ailments than the male body. Two classical publications in this regard were provided by the feminist anthropologist of science, Emily Martin: *The Woman in the Body: A Cultural Analysis of Reproduction* (1987) and the article 'The Egg and the Sperm: How Science Has Constructed a Romance Based on Stereotypical Male-Female Roles' (1991).

Apart from the orientation on medical and reproductive discourses, the focus of feminist scholarship on the body also resulted in studies on sexuality, sexual desires, and sexual violence, as is shown, for instance, by Kathy Davis, a feminist sociologist and body scholar (Davis, 1997: 6). The constitutive role of beauty and fashion, as well as cosmetic surgery in women's *embodied experiences*, is also explored (Bordo, 1993; Davis, 1995). Remarkably little feminist work is carried out on *male embodiment* and men's experiences with, for example, the effect of changing their bodies with Viagra, body building hormones, and penile implants (Åsberg and Johnson, 2009).

The links between racism, science, and the body are variously explored in the work of science studies scholars (Gilman, 1985; Hill Collins, 1990; hooks, 1990; Hammonds, 2000; Mulinari, 2004). The 'racial types' of the modern period, that today's biologist mostly discard as overtly racist, was constructed by science to justify European colonial rule and slavery. Anne McClintock (1995), Londa Schiebinger (1993), and Anne Fausto-Sterling (1995) have pointed to the distinct role of African women's bodies in the minds of male European scientists. Black women's bodies were taken to be more untamed, sexually more excessive, and closer to animals (to the degree of using them as biological test-subjects similar to today's laboratory animals). In sharp contrast, the over-idealized image of white women of class was shaped with respect to the ideal of a marriage- and breed-worthy representative of the European nation, whose bodily integrity and fragile purity was to be defended from alien influences at all costs. The image of African women that originated in colonial science held sway for a long time and was noticeable in popular culture too. This is exemplified in the commodification of Josephine Baker in the 1920s or Grace Jones in the 1980s, who were both portrayed as animal-like and exotic.[2]

The alleged feminist neglect of the physical body now made way for an idea of the body as *both* a physical and a sociocultural entity. The body was re-introduced on the research agenda by feminist biologists or natural scientists such as Ruth Hubbard, Ruth Bleier, Lynda Birke, Evelynn Hammonds, Pat Spallone, Anne Fausto-Sterling, Evelyn Fox-Keller, Karen Barad, and Donna Haraway.[3] Such authors formed a feminist faction in the diverse research field of science and technology studies (STS).[4] While often not properly acknowledged by their 'malestream' peers, they started making interventions in the very practices and discourses of science (Haraway, 1997).

To feminist science studies, the problem of the biological body is hinged on four different perspectives or approaches (Mol, 1989). First, there is the problem of *determinism* or the idea that 'anatomy is destiny': biological facts about the body are used for the causal explanation and, implicitly, the justification of societal power differences. The twofold feminist tactics for countering biological determinism was to make a strategic distinction between sex and gender and to expose both the social construction of biology and the historical wrongs resulting from alleged biological facts, especially 'race', as a distinct biological category relevant to humans was successfully problematized. Second, the problematics involved in *scientism* were laid bare. The authority of science as such and the implicit masculine gendering of expertise was problematized in feminist historical studies on the practices and traditional knowledge of midwifes. These studies showed, for instance, that such traditional lore was actively suppressed by the emerging profession of male doctors and gynaecologists. Third, there was a feminist concern with the *objectification* of the body, or the intractable idea that bodies can objectively be observed. They are an exterior, looked at from an apparent distance, as if the perspective of the observer does not inhabit a body of his/her own. It is a problem of nature and bodies being treated as passsive resources, disassociated from any subjectivity or agency. This relates to the fourth feminist concern with the biological body: the idea of the *disembodiment* of science that prioritizes the mind and rational thought as if the mind were not embodied, as if the process of thinking takes place on a plane that has nothing to do with a body, indeed as if the body is uninhabited by thought. The latter two problems are addressed by feminists who study science as a cultural and social practice. Scientists are shown to be embodied and gendered, possessing a set of standards and values. In addition, there is a range of material practices to consider. Costly equipment and instruments, for example, will also contribute to the shape knowledge takes.

As a result of these feminist discussions on gender in the sciences, Sandra Harding's pioneering book *The Science Question in Feminism* (1986) announced a turn away from the problems of representing gender in the sciences and advanced instead the science question of feminist theory. She focused on the question of what kind of science feminist approaches would generate. This inspired the feminist ambition to engage explicitly with the reality producing potential of science. The problematic of gender in science shifted from the equality question towards a concern with funda- mental changes within the sciences. From the vantage point of complicity, feminists in the sciences embarked on the project of changing science, recalibrating its 'thinking tools', models, and figures, to less oppressive ends.

Haraway's cyborg

It is as such a recalibrated 'thinking tool' that the cyborg has become a promising and important figuration in feminist science studies. It was first deployed for feminist objectives in a famous and most controversial article from 1985: 'A manifesto for cyborgs', by Donna Haraway. Haraway's cyborg signals more than just the joint merg- ing of biology and technology. The cyborg bridges the illusive distinction between the human body and other biological organisms, between the virtual and the real (Haraway, 1991a; 1992). It is an imploded node of fact and fiction, embodied and embedded in the networks of 'technoscience'. An implosion, in contrast to an explosion, concentrates matter. As a materialized metaphor for contemporary technoscience, the cyborg embodies the deconstruction of the very modern dichotomies it was built on. The nature/culture division, for instance, collapses into the cyborg.

Haraway re-read the cyborg as *a political myth*, an ironic parable of processes already set in motion that not necessarily needed to end badly (with self-destruction). There was a potential in the figuration of the cyborg. Haraway held that it was impossible to sustain the nature/culture dichotomy, due to the cyborgian nature of lived everyday reality. Other dichotomies, such as the feminist sex and gender distinction, would collapse along with it. In that sense, Haraway's cyborg signalled an immense feminist challenge, because it provoked social constructivist assumptions about gender. It was a call for the feminist engagement with the material processes of embodiment as well as with biology as a high-tech science discourse generating sexual difference. Haraway's cyborg brought on a merge of 'hard' science and 'soft' scholarship and thus became the mascot of interdisciplinary alliances in interdisciplinary feminist scholarship and the feminist critique on science.

Originally a historian of science, Haraway also received a Ph.D in biology and she currently holds the chair of History of Consciousness at the University of California in Santa Cruz. She is widely regarded as a leading thinker about the relationship between technology and information, on the one hand, and bodies and the natural sciences, on the other. Her work has become essential reading in feminist classes. Reading Haraway means engaging with a long tradition of feminist struggles with issues of the body and the biological sciences. A pivotal figure in interdisciplinary feminist science and cultural studies, Haraway has changed and influenced the fields of primatology, evolutionary biology, and informatics as well as feminist theory, cultural studies, and science and technology studies (STS).

Haraway is a key contemporary theorist, but one with a remarkable knack for unexpected empirical examples and twisted cases drawn from lived experience, our collective imagination, and a variety of scholarly areas. Beside her cyborg manifesto, publications such as *Primate Visions. Gender, Race and Nature in the World of Modern Science* (1989); *Simians, Cyborgs, and Women: the Re-invention of Nature* (1991); *Modest_Witness@Second_Millennium.FemaleMan©_Meets_OncoMouse™* (1997); and *When Species Meet* (2008) have established her as one of the most evocative and challenging feminist writers of our time. None of Haraway's publications can easily be said to fit either social constructivist or naturalist-biologist takes on biology. She makes use of her biological knowledge but shuns biological determinism; she deploys cultural theory abundantly but rejects the pure culturalist view on the body as the blank space for social inscription. Referring neither to nature nor to culture as purely separate domains, she wields instead the very specific constellation of impure and messy *natureculture* (Haraway, 2003). Her work is a serious effort to move beyond assumed disciplinary distinctions in order to deal with hybrids, complexities, and border zones.

Haraway's work reads like poetry; it is associative and compelling. She practises what she preaches, that is, science as story telling (Haraway, 1989: 4). She will always implicate herself in the stories she tells and the critiques she makes, by drawing on her own upbringing and interdisciplinary education in the USA and situating herself in the midst of a complex society and complicated disciplinary relations.[5] She positions her knowledge and herself as knowledge producer by drawing on a wide plethora of sources.

A passionate reader of science fiction, Haraway recognizes the feminist potential of this genre that is inhabited by all kinds of cyborgs. The attraction of science fiction is not just in the implicit reflections and comments on an already existing society through the story's setting in an imagined time-space. To Haraway, the utopian potential of science fiction in imagining a possibly different world constitutes the true attraction of the genre. Imagination is reality production in process. She was raised in a world profoundly shaped by the narratives of evolutionary theory and Christianity; narratives that in turn shaped her too. When asked about the origins of her thinking she said:

The whole thing came out of other places, and it came out of having been a biology graduate student at Yale, having been overwhelmingly against what I perceived as genetic reductionism; and being much more interested in the way in which the organism was a poem – my commitments to the notion of organic form, and my Catholic sensibilities.

(Haraway in Schneider, 2005: 126–127)

Haraway's work is characterized by a passion for biology that is paired with a sense of frustration. Other features include an interest in *figural realism* and an unusual form of analysis or reading strategy, exemplified for instance by reading the organism as a poem. She is also inspired by the practices of Catholicism that were part of her upbringing, such as the Eucharist (the sacrament of turning ceremonial wine and bread into the flesh and blood of Christ). Decades later, as a devoted atheist, Haraway adapts this sacred ritual to the 'worldly practice' of studying symbolic entities whose existence is quite real and connected to our everyday life (Haraway, 2004). She brought this 'figural realism' to her scholarly work as a way of insisting on the worldly and material and as an act of faith, in an attempt to resist the separation of the material and the semiotic (Haraway, 1997: 11).

The separation between nature and culture, between the real and the meaning we attribute to it, is fundamental for our conventional thought tradition. That is why Haraway's cyborg was such a controversial example in the concept of figural realism. The cyborg was a feminist science fiction character that, like Haraway herself, was forged in the heat of worlds at war (Haraway, 2004). After all, as Haraway often notes, she is the child of the Cold War, the Sputnik, and American post-World War II militarism; as well as the privileged white daughter of the Vietnam War, 1960s student movements, and the Civil Rights, Women's Rights, and Gay Rights movements that swept Europe and the USA somewhat later. In the 1990s, she came to inherit the battle between interdisciplinary scholars on the one hand and defendants of 'science proper' on the other, the so-called *science wars*. No wonder she was attracted to the warped warrior figure of the cyborg. In deviation from previous feminist approaches to the body, the cyborg was neither sexually pure nor innocent but instead irreverent and promiscuous. In an act of subversive resistance, Haraway deployed the cyborg as a tool for feminism and described it as female. At the same time she characterized it as 'post-gender' in relation to the biological complexities of sex, although she would later reject this term (Haraway in Lykke, *et al.*, 2004a: 321–332). For Haraway the cyborg was not so much about the visible technological appendixes of a body, as about the way in which science and technology had managed to become such an intricate part of the way we live and make sense of our lives. The cyborg provided the possibility of getting around romantic ideas about the natural and women's alleged relationship to nature as an unquestioned given, a stance that was defended by ecofeminists and other feminist communities at the time that Haraway wrote her ironic manifesto. In the midst of President Reagan's Star Wars, she controversially celebrated the cyborg, rather than the nature goddess, as a more accurate reflection of women's real life experiences.

Haraway famously ended the manifesto with 'I would rather be a cyborg than a goddess', which surely suggested a provocation to spiritual ecofeminism as much as a call to engage with science and technology (Haraway, 1991a: 181). Although partly fictional and partly the factual offspring of militarism, the cyborg was about developing a realistic outlook on the unexpected promises (of undoing gender and dualisms, such as culture versus nature) and threats (of extinguishing both human and non-human animals from the surface of the Earth) of technoscience. As Haraway exclaims: 'Cyborgs for earthly survival!' The cyborg thus became a figuration for describing not so much individuals as such, but the whole spectrum of techno-saturated life, culture, and society. If the previous focus on women's bodies entailed the risk of re-enforcing the traditional woman/body/nature and man/mind/culture symbolism, the cyborg managed to twist things around: the cyborg emphasizes the connection between technology and women as *already made*. Technology in this respect is understood to encompass more than just hardware and metallic machinery: it also includes the discursive modes of production and complicated ways of living.

A socialist feminist to the core, Haraway pointed out that women all over the world were part of an integrated circuit of capitalist society, whether they were working under poor and extreme conditions in exploitative settings such as the electronic industry sweat shops, or whether rich enough to subject themselves to body-enhancing cosmetic surgery. With her understanding of the cyborg it became clear to what extent women, who were otherwise seldom associated with technology, were in effect an intrinsic part of the machinery of society. We are all implicated in this, and more than that, according to Haraway, we are all complicit because we are all already non-innocent cyborgs: we cannot simply step outside that frame. In fighting against racism, capitalism, and sexism we are all already structured into these 'isms' and part of how they work. She signalled the *complicity* with the cyborg as a resourceful way for changing research and society from within. Thus, in re-interpreting the figuration of the cyborg, Haraway clearly did not celebrate scientific innocence, but proposed instead a critical tool for analysis that took both scholarship and science to task. Departing from the reality producing potential of scientific visions, such as those of Clynes and Kline, Haraway took a leap into the realm of the futures that are sketched in science fiction in order to envision alternatives for sustainable survival of the diverse and connected inhabitants of the planet.

There is a scary and promising ambivalence to Technoscience, which is also an important part of Haraway's cyborg. It is no use to either demonize science or simply celebrate it. We need to move beyond good and evil and engage in new, 'incurably informed' and concrete manners with the material, the organic, and the biological (Balsamo, 1997: 133). With a renewed feminist interest in the material and fleshy body, much pioneered by Haraway, the many slippery meanings attached to the term 'biology' can be dissected. Biology signifies both a field of science and the physical processes within or between bodies. Furthermore, biology has been taken to mean something like the nature of Nature; a portmanteau concept for everything beyond human control. Importantly, Haraway's cyborg prompts a crucial shift in the feminist attention to biology as 'a political discourse, which we should engage in at every level'.

Furthermore, 'biology is a source of intense intellectual, emotional, and physical pleasure. Nothing like that should be given up lightly – or approached only in a scolding or celebratory mode' (Haraway, 2004: 203). As it was the tendency in biology to conceive of the body as an unchanging source of naturalness, we should rather approach it as a social discourse open to intervention (Haraway, 1991: 134). The figuration of the cyborg forms an intervention in this discourse. It is an example of a type of feminist analysis whose end result is not given or known beforehand. Such an open yet accountable approach means that one has to learn to live with ambiguities, even in the very material practice of knowledge production and scholarly writing.

The proliferation of post-cyborg feminisms

Haraway's ironic style in the manifesto masked a large dose of anger and frustration. The cyborg was a way of playing out the ambiguity between the literal and the figural, that specific facticity of the effects of our technosociety on our bodies and our selves (Haraway, 2004). Her cyborg manifesto was sometimes hard to digest, even for fellow feminists, and her ironic approach and rummaging, suggestive writing style also meant that the manifesto was open to different interpretations and several misunderstandings. Critical questions were raised regarding the usability of the cyborg as a descriptive metaphor. What does it really provide us with, besides a playful space for thinking beyond dualities? In popular culture, cyborgs actually rarely challenge the traditional stereotypes of 'race' and gender. Instead, cyborgs seem to be excessively gendered, and very traditionally too. In other words, cyborg imagery is hardly post-gender, as was contended by the feminist cyborg scholar Anne Balsamo (2000). She pointed out that cyborgs could also re-insert us into the traditional bourgeois notions of humanity, the machine, and femininity. Haraway's oppositional division between the goddess and the cyborg likewise met with criticism, although it also provoked responses that led to new kinds of hybrids (Lykke, 2000).

Haraway's writing style too was targeted by feminist criticism, as some readers felt excluded by it. This is unfortunate, given that an important theme of her work precisely is the extent to which women are excluded by scientific discourse. Moreover, some readers argued that the reconfiguration of science and technology in mere writing did not really provide clear guidelines for how feminists could practically act to change them in political terms (McNeil, 2000: 230; Wajcman, 2004: 95). This said, the cyborg manifesto is nonetheless one of few feminist texts to have reached an exceptionally large and diverse audience (Kunzru, 1997).

In spite of such feminist criticism, it must be emphasized here that new writing styles and innovative ways of thinking are much needed, since the old ones clearly are not doing the job. One cannot afford to lie back comfortably, if one is intent on changing our complex world for the better. Rather, one must learn to account for the way complex realities and intricate power relations come about. This is what Haraway's cyborg hands down to us as an interdisciplinary challenge. In the post-cyborg era, what counts as biological kind disrupts the established categories of organism. The technological and the textual are integral to the organic and vice versa in irreversible ways (Haraway, 2003: 15). In the 'cyborg manifesto', Haraway provides a tentative trope, a literal figure, for doing justice to the practices of our contemporary technoculture 'without losing touch with the permanent war apparatus of a non-optional, post-nuclear world and its transcendent, very material lies' (Haraway, 2003: 11). Importantly, the cyborg hardly exhausts the figural potential for bringing insight to our complex world and engendering change. Haraway herself has shifted her attention to other figures. Cyborgs now are for her and other feminists the junior siblings in a much bigger, curious family of companion species such as transgenic lab animals, pet dogs and coyotes, and primates (Haraway, 1989; 1997; 2003).

Certainly, the cyborg took on a life of its own after Kline and Clynes conceptualized it. One of the most influential feminist scholars of the body and the natural sciences in our time, Haraway, uses the cyborg to herald a crucial shift in the feminist modes of attention towards the body and biology as a scientific discipline. Conventionally, scientists should deal with real nature and scholars with culture. But feminists such as Haraway mess things up – to the dismay of both traditional scientists and disciplinarity puritans in the humanities. Modern society has not solved the complicated issues of life and healing, death and suffering, of who gets to live, who gets to die, and who gets to decide. The woman cyborg proposed by Haraway is a way of unpacking and holding up for inspection some of the intricate details that in everyday life effectuate all kinds of feminist politics and democratic science issues. The cyborg is a tool for thinking through such complex issues. With respect to the relationship between science, the biological body, and feminism, Haraway's cyborg manifesto must be read as a declaration of alliance as much as a call to arms. Most effectively, the figuration of the cyborg describes interdisciplinary alliances and complex relations such as those between feminist theory, cultural studies, and science and technology studies. Nina Lykke tracks these interdisciplinary connections across national borders and describes the North European hybrid of feminist cultural studies and technoscience as *cyborg studies* (2002). Thus, Haraway's cyborg feminism has proliferated beyond the time and place of the dubious origins of this figuration.

Notes

1   Technophilia is the opposite of technophobia. Technophilia signifies a strong enthusiasm for scientific and technological progress in relation to societal development while technophobia signifies the fear that societal reliance on technology might lead to dehumanization. Both these extreme positions share an immense belief in the transformative powers of science and technology.
2   Women's bodies have functioned as metaphors for the nation, just as 'Marianne' represents post-revolutionary France. This works to sustain the symbolic distinctions between 'us' and 'them' to the effect that the mass rape of women of the enemy nation became a devastating war tactic (Cockburn, 1998).
3   The feminist forays into the natural sciences of the late 1980s and early 1990s ranged from deep-rooted close readings and critiques of fundamental concepts and practices in the sciences to the epistemological reconsiderations of making and judging knowledge claims (cf. Evelyn Fox-Keller, 1992).

4   Science and technology studies (STS) encompasses a gamut of approaches to science and technology as social phenomena. It is an interdisciplinary field of critical studies of science and technology in a historical, philosophical, economical, and practical context. Initially, STS dealt with the question of how social factors intruded upon science (so that science, if done correctly, might be free of anything 'social'). It changed into the sociology of science when the attention was shifted to the products of science and the very process of doing science. Truth claims, for instance, are affected by social factors. The prime target became the positivist notion of science as a self-developing entity that transposed into a logical series of technological applications that determine societal development, or *technological determinism* (Lykke, 2002: 139).

5   As with many other high school graduates, Haraway went to a nearby college in Colorado, but unlike many others, she pursued a triple major in zoology, philosophy, and English literature (Haraway in Goodeve, 2000: 13). Later, she tried to excel in the laboratory like the other Ph.D students in biology at Yale University, but hers was a different path. She found a professor who allowed for a wider range of projects to be pursued by his graduate students and who supported differently thinking or 'heterodox' women (Haraway in ibid.: 19). Here she developed much of the thinking that would return in her work for decades to come. She dedicated herself to the historical and philosophical study of biology and embryology as practices of knowing about the world through a set of detailed organic metaphors. Fascinated by how these metaphors of biology open up and enable certain modes of thinking about nature and society that is both very concrete and figural, she resisted reductionist and purist arguments in her dissertation, as she would in her later work.

Questions for further research

1   What has been the influence of the scientific discipline of biology on ideas concerning women's legal capacity? The concept 'biological determinism' should be used in answering this question. In comparison, in what ways has biology influenced the way we think about men and masculinity?

2   Since the 1970s, the accepted interpretations of the body have been subjected to feminist critique. What did this critique consist of? Today, music clips receive much attention in feminist judgements on representing the female body. Watch MTV or TMF for a while and report your findings.

3   In what way is the nature/culture dichotomy deconstructed by the figuration of the cyborg? Why is this important in antiracist feminist theory formation?

4   Show how the cyborg commentates on early feminist approaches of biology. What might be the foundation for the argument that the emphasis on culture *instead of* nature is just as rigid as biological determinism?

5   What is to be gained from approaching biology in various interdisciplinary feminist ways? You can make use of Chapter 4 for an idea of interdisciplinarity.

6   Can you determine some of the ways in which the cyborg challenges feminist cultural studies? In your reply, give a definition of 'figuration' as an analytical tool. Consult also Part III.

The arena of knowledge: Antigone and feminist standpoint theory

3

Sarah Bracke and María Puig de la Bellacasa

3.1 Antigone burying the body of Polinices.

We live with the crushing presence of war. Not a single moment in the histories we remember has been devoid of war in the guise of its many qualifying names – economic, religious, civil, genocidal, national, colonial, and imperial; world and regional; wars over land, oil, water – and its long shadows of pain and reconstruction.

And the actual spilling of blood comes with belligerent imaginaries and declarations, such as the proclamation of a 'clash of civilisations', new political demarcation lines, and epistemological norms.

In this chapter we engage with feminist discussions where political struggle and knowledge production are intricately and intimately related. First, because knowledge is deeply affected by the conflicts and power relations of the time and place in which it is produced, and second because political action and struggle are crucial sites of knowledge production. The recognition that knowledge and politics are interdependent lies at the heart of academic debates concerned with epistemological transformations, and not only in feminist, gender, or women's studies. In contemporary feminism, the contestation of established knowledge is historically related to a political gesture: reclaiming (women's) silenced voices and experiences. A gesture that is far from straightforward.

Antigone is the heroine who will accompany us in the task we have set ourselves. Sophocles' ancient Greek tragedy that carries her name is set in Thebes at a time when the city is exhausted with warfare. The opening scene takes us to the morning after a struggle for succession by two brothers of the ruling family, Eteocles and Polinices, sons of Oedipus, which ended in mutual fratricide. Antigone summons her sister Ismene outside the gates of the city to inform her of the adjudication by Creon, their uncle and ruler of the city, that Eteocles, the hero, should be honoured by the citizens of Thebes while the body of Polinices should be left unburied and prey to dogs and vultures, in order to provide a spectacle that should remind citizens of a traitor's fate. The truth of this fratricide, it is suggested, was far messier, but Creon's act is a political one, inspired less by a need for justice and truth than for law and order. Determined to give Polinices proper burial rites, Antigone seeks Ismene's assistance. When her sister refuses, Antigone sets off to perform her deed alone.

In the dawn following Creon's decree, guards find Polinices' body covered by a thin layer of earth. The perpetrator is to be stoned to death, yet when the guards bring the perpetrator in front of Creon, he is struck by surprise: it is a young woman, his very own niece. Both kinship ties and the fact of political hierarchy put the young woman under Creon's authority. Yet Antigone rejects his authority – both through her act of burial and in her speech, which she grounds in a realm where Creon's proclamations have no jurisdiction, a realm where the duty of giving her brother a burial is sacred. Her defiance infuriates Creon, and while the choir compels him to reconsider and to show mercy, the king is caught in a posture of stubbornness and hubris, driven by pride and an urge to maintain his position of power and show no feebleness. In the *polemos* that unfolds between them, Antigone's death is inevitable. To avoid actual blood on his hands, Creon sends her to a cave where she is left to die, and where she takes her own life. Her death sets a chain of death in motion. Haemon, Creon's son, kills himself out of love for Antigone. Euridyce, Creon's wife, puts a sword through her chest, crying out that her husband murdered their son. Death accompanies the reconstruction of order in the polis and exposes the destructive and cynical nature of the power of the patriarch, who finds himself ruling a desert, alone.

In the *polemos* between the patriarch and the young woman, the figure of Antigone embodies an (other) ethical consciousness and experiential knowledge, oppressed in the face of hegemonic political rule. As a figure defying patriarchal and state authority, refusing to submit to the law of the city, the sovereign, and the man of the family, Antigone's compelling force on feminist imaginaries does not come as a surprise. Her influence can be illustrated by three feminist engagements with Antigone upon which we rely for our own reading of the tragedy.

In *Three Guineas*, Virginia Woolf's unforgettable essay on women, war, and (academic) knowledge, first published in 1938, Antigone appears as a heroine for women who espouse disobedient pacifism in face of the wars of men. Woolf stands for the refusal of the stupidity of war, but her essay is also concerned with how politics of war and politics of knowledge share at least some threads of the same cultural tissues. Comparing the parades of militaries to the parades of academics, the power of patriarchs, professors, and leaders, Woolf provokes us to understand and resist the deadly paths into which Western patriarchal patterns of domination lead us. One of the cultural convictions Woolf sought to destabilize was the idea that the defence of *disinterested knowledge* in academic realms could serve as a means of avoiding war. Contesting a tradition of excluding women from the temples of knowledge, Woolf asserts that there is nothing *disinterested* about the way the academy has built its temples. She instigates women not to listen to the voice of 'the fathers' but rather to seek for other ways of thinking, 'other methods', because those she knew in her time had been constructed in the absence of women and had miserably failed to counter the build-up to what would become World War II. Woolf's essay is a precursor of the collective questionings of established educational orders triggered off by feminist movements in the 1970s. However, in her own time, Woolf did not have much reason to be optimistic about the possibilities of transforming the order of the day; no wonder that the Antigone of *Three Guineas* is a figure of a female resistant condemned to die, for confronting a patriarch's rule in times of war.

Readings of what became known as feminism's second wave focused on the relationship between Antigone and her sister Ismene. In 1967, *The Living Theatre* staged an anarcho-pacifist adaptation of the play in Germany, with a blonde sensuous Ismene and an ascetic dark Antigone dividing the spectrum of available politics: acceptance or negation of the hegemony (Steiner, 1984). The message of the play coincided with that of second-wave feminism: it was time for women to get together in solidarity; time to act, and expose the conventions of death as they are enacted in warfare, capitalism, and male-dominated reality-principles. Only women's authentic liberation, the utter refusal of Ismene's classic femininity, would break the infernal circle. Ismene begs her sister not to put her life at stake as 'it is wrong to hunt for what is impossible'. Her refusal to share her sister's act is grounded in fear as she reminds Antigone of their condition as women 'who cannot fight against men' (Sophocles, 1994). Yet, when Antigone is condemned to death, Ismene seeks to join her. In many ways it is too late – and her will to die is driven by the shattering despair about her sister's death rather than by desire to associate with the vision Antigone sought to defend. Antigone's act is thus represented as one of lucid resistance, while Ismene's ways are those of submission to the order that defines what is possible and what not. If Antigone's resistance leads her to death, the politics of acceptance turn out to be lifeless.

In *Speculum, de l'autre femme* (1974), Luce Irigaray turns to Antigone to think through (some of the stakes of) sexual difference. Irigaray's engagement with Antigone is mediated through Hegel. For Hegel, Antigone represents the highest kind of ethical consciousness women are capable of: an intuitive 'pure love', embodied *par excellence* in the love of a sister for her brother. This ethical consciousness places Antigone, whose actions are driven by love or instinct, outside the public sphere of civic reason. But Hegel, Irigaray insists, misses out what is most significant: in order to embody the paradigmatic womanhood that Antigone is taken to represent, she has to enter the political realm which is a realm women are traditionally excluded from. Irigaray's inquiry into Antigone's act reveals a pattern of sexual difference which revolves around the connections between womb and tomb: it is woman who bears man, but also bears him to his grave. By providing her brother with burial rites, a political act *par excellence*, Antigone ensures his humanity, and her own in the process. But while his humanity is of a universal kind, she becomes the guardian of blood ties, and thus instrumental for his universal universality.

Hegel's Antigone is a paradigmatic figure of womanhood within the logic of oppositions consolidated in his *Phenomenology of Spirit*, a logic in which, at the time of the birth of the modern state, questions of the political-civic and the religious-ritual are condensed into what Genevieve Lloyd (1985) characterizes as an enriched public-private distinction (Hegel, 1977). However, her paradigmatic womanhood remains unsettled and unsettling, as its ethical consciousness depletes the universality of the public sphere through its intimate ties with the particular. As such, her actions always contain a threat to undo the public sphere, and Hegel has subsequently qualified Antigone as 'the eternal irony of the community. Irigaray then takes up her ironic quality, yet displaces the irony. From a figure outside the public forum, who represents an eternal threat of disruption, Antigone becomes the guardian of the social and symbolic order. If Antigone is to be considered outside the terms of the (metaphorical) polis, where Hegel locates her, Irigaray makes clear that this is an outside without which the polis could not exist, thus uncovering a logic that both expulses her from the public sphere and renders her a constitutive part of it. The irony which Irigaray ascribes to Antigone undermines the idea of a pure opposition to power; in the end, she finds herself caught in a culture written by men, which sentences her to death (Irigaray, 1984).

Antigone's resistance offers a powerful, multilayered, and complex legacy for feminism, as these brief accounts illustrate. Her figure has been mostly mobilized in discussions on female defiance of the state, the relation between realms of kinship (the private) and the state (the public), and ethics. In this chapter, we will take Antigone's act as a way to think through the feminist gesture of reclaiming silenced and under-valued women's voices and experiences. We focus on feminist standpoint theory which considers the experiences of women to be a source of knowledge which can be deployed in transforming the public realm which excludes them.

Standpoint feminism: The construction of a theoretical category

The recognition of women as knowing subjects, and their neglected voices and experiences as resources of knowledge, can be considered as feminism's beating pulse; it was notably the driving force of 'consciousness raising' groups which became a characterizing trait of 1970s feminism and continues to be a widespread practice of women's movements all over the world. Consciousness raising is grounded in the recognition that one can become a knowing subject of one's oppression through a process that starts from one's own life experiences and opens them up to a political re-interpretation which takes place in a collective way. Making the structural character of experience visible beyond the merely personal allowed women in consciousness raising groups or other collectives to consider their experiences as a source of knowledge. The facts obtained through this process are considered to unveil different aspects of reality than those proposed in hegemonic visions. In the same vein, standpoint theory claims that knowledge produced in the margins and articulated collectively is potentially better and can enhance the objectivity of traditional knowledge.

The emphasis on recognizing women as knowledge subjects has profoundly influenced the transformations introduced by Women's Studies in the academy. It is a crucial feminist stake, which does not belong to one theoretical vision in particular. Here, we engage with one particular way to think of this basic feminist practice: what became known as *feminist standpoint theory*. One of the earliest and most influential developments of the notion of 'a feminist standpoint' appeared in a paper entitled 'The Feminist Standpoint: Developing the Ground for a Specifically Feminist Historical Materialism' (1987), by social scientist Nancy Hartsock. However, standpoint theory or standpoint epistemology became recognized around the mid-1980s as a strand of feminist analysis through the work of the feminist philosopher of science Sandra Harding – in her now classic *The Science Question in Feminism* and throughout her subsequent work. Harding used the notion to identify common issues in the early writings of Patricia Hill Collins (1986), Nancy Hartsock (1987), Hilary Rose (1983), and Dorothy Smith (1974), who therefore came to be associated with standpoint feminism. Although these authors' work is specific in different ways, according to their projects, disciplinary backgrounds, and interests, they were all seeking, in the words of Dorothy Smith, a 'break with existing disciplines through locating knowledge or inquiry in women's standpoint or in women's experience' (Smith, 1997: 392). In this sense, the impulse of standpoint theories is inextricably fostered by political commit-ment and epistemological investigation.

We want to highlight three threads of thought that inform the early formulations of feminist standpoint thinking, as well as our understanding thereof as inheritors of a conversation which has been going on for more than thirty years (Harding, 2003). The first thread concerns a critical feminist re-appropriation of the classic Marxist claim that when knowledge is grounded in the lives of those who suffer from exploitation (i.e. the working classes), it will produce different *and* better accounts of the world than when it is grounded in the lives of dominant groups (i.e. the bourgeoisie) who benefit from the products of that labour, but remain absent from the processes and mediations that bring them into existence. The construction of a political standpoint which departs from certain experiences of the working classes, consciously affirming them as knowledge, enables a different and more reliable knowledge about the interaction between humans and nature, social and natural relationships, and the workings of capitalism. The workers have a close, daily, and immediate experience of what keeps capitalism running through their work in the factory. The bourgeoisie lacks such direct experience of production. The emergence of the 'proletarian' subject was seen as a new epistemological possibility that Marxist theory was both to explain *and* nurture.

In a reworked manner, feminist standpoint draws on women's lives as enabling a particular and epistemologically privileged vantage point on the workings of male supremacy and its interaction with the social relationships of capitalism – a standpoint which, before feminist interventions, was largely ignored by social and political theories and movements. For instance, paying due attention to the devaluated work of 'care' done mainly by women in most cultural contexts – reproductive and affective labour, care for the young, the elderly and the sick – Marxist and socialist standpoint feminists point to the blindness that results from ignoring the most basic activities and knowledges that sustain our world.

The second thread concerns Black thought and its feminist articulations which are committed to valuing knowledge produced from African-American women's perspectives and lives. This emerged in a context of Black oppositional struggles against institutions of white supremacy – including institutions of knowledge production. With respect to the marginalized position of Black Americans in the small Kentucky town where she grew up, bell hooks (1984) writes of an 'oppositional worldview', that is, 'a mode of seeing unknown to most of our oppressors, that sustained us, aided us in our struggle to transcend poverty and despair, strengthened our sense of self and our solidarity'. Patricia Hill Collins (1990) theorized the position of the 'outsider-within', that is, 'a peculiar marginality that stimulated a special African-American women's perspective'. This refers to women belonging to black communities, who are therefore, traditionally, 'outsiders' to the world of dominant academic knowledge, but who have, nevertheless, obtained access to it and therefore work 'within' the privileged spheres of academic intellectual production. In this sense we can note the importance of W.E.B. DuBois' notion of a 'bifurcated consciousness', which refers to the ability to see things from the perspective of both the dominant and the oppressed (DuBois, 1995). Collins advocates the exploration of a black feminist standpoint as a device for gaining better knowledge based on the silenced experiences of African-American women and committed to transform their living conditions.

The last strand concerns feminist critiques and reconstructions of the meanings of knowledge, science, and epistemology (see Cecilia Åsberg's chapter in this volume). Since the early 1980s, scholars across the academic disciplinary spectrum acknowledge the importance of their feminist commitments in shaping the knowledge they produced and in their enhanced awareness of sexist flaws in the inherited traditions of their disciplines. Harding played a significant role in linking this awareness to feminist standpoints understood as epistemic devices. Standpoint epistemology could work as a 'justificatory strategy' to account for the proliferation of research within a situation that was otherwise, with the available epistemological standards, inexplicable: that 'politicized research' could increase 'the objectivity of inquiry', with *better* facts and theories (Harding, 1986: 24).[1] Indeed, the very fact of academic and scientific knowledge being produced *from* committed feminist standpoints disrupts epistemologies and theories of knowledge construction which hold that, if knowledge is to be legitimate, especially according to academic and scientific standards, it should be *disinterested*, unpolluted by political concerns (see the chapter by Gloria Wekker). Though feminist discussions and controversies on the meanings of science and objectivity fall beyond the scope of this chapter, it must be noted that the notion of standpoints starting from dismissed experiences is crucial in Harding's crafting of a notion of 'strong objectivity', which involves 'to take into account the position of those who are not "at home" in dominant positions and to "value the Other's position" in order to look to our own locations in a more critical way' (Harding, 1991: 151). Moreover, Donna Haraway's engagement with standpoint feminism's ideas was crucial in consolidating this double gesture as a vital tool for feminist knowledge politics and science studies. 'Feminist objectivity means quite simply situated knowledges', she affirmed, while simultaneously calling for accountability for the situatedness of meanings constructed by feminists – 'our own semiotic technologies' (Haraway, 1991b). In other words, objectivity and 'better' knowledge are associated with the accountable inclusion of situated subjectivities and oppositional consciousness (Sandoval, 2000), rather than with their presumed value-free exclusion.

Standpoint feminism is a lively terrain, open to re-appropriation (Harding, 2003), which resonates with a wide array of feminist scholarship posing related questions (Rich, 1985c; Stanley and Wise, 1993; and many others). As a theoretical category related to a specific epistemic logic, it plays a crucial part in the composition of a polyvocal discussion regarding the value of oppressed knowledge and the political and situated character of the construction of knowledge. The construction of theoretical categories such as feminist standpoint theory, however, is never neutral; it is a material process involving an intricate and diverse web of relations and power – access to patterns of publication, networks, friendships, random encounters . . . and indeed the very question of *what counts* as theory (Christian, 1990). It is, therefore, crucial not to take inherited categories for granted, crucial to unfold and rework those categories, as well as the works of authors we associate with them, according to the questions, constraints, and contingencies which compel us in (our) political and disciplinary settings.

Feminist standpoints: An open terrain of knowledge politics

We understand feminist standpoints as positionings open to inclusion of and connection between knowledges generated in different settings of oppression and struggle.

The very possibility of this understanding is an *achievement* of political and theoretical work, of the very debates about standpoint thinking involved in the constant collective reworking of feminist positions and alliances. Having mapped this unsettled terrain, we now pause to think briefly upon three matters raised by the question of *how* to think from women's lives.

The first matter concerns the legitimacy of *experience as a foundation for knowledge.* In an essay questioning the role of experience in feminist thought, Joan Scott (1992) draws attention to the fact that experiences are not raw material scholars uncritically work with, but rather that experiences are always mediated and thus require interpretation. Experience is not an equivalent of knowledge, rather knowledge is constructed in the effort to explain and understand experience, Scott argues. In response to Scott, Paula Moya (1997) argues that the fact of having been born into certain given social relations and conditions or of having suffered the effects of oppression and economic deprivation, does not in and of itself yield a better understanding or knowledge. The epistemic privilege of oppressed groups, she asserts, does not imply that social locations, and indeed experiences, would have epistemic or political meaning in a self-evident way. And indeed, the historical possibility for women to voice their experiences as knowledge was not 'given' within the existing social, political, and epistemological frameworks that various feminisms had come to contest. It is precisely through attending to the mediated character of experience, we would argue, that we can understand the (ever open) possibility of new knowledge emerging from previously ignored lives and experiences.

The second question is concerned with the fact that an epistemic device such as thinking from women's lives begs the question of *whose women's lives* should be thought from. It raises, in other words, the issue of structural power relations between different women's lives. When ignored, a dominant white, middle-class, heterosexual account of 'women's lives' is likely to be reproduced, as critiques developed within minoritarian feminisms sharply make clear. The principle of thinking from women's lives, as we see it, in fact involves a constant reformulation of Sojourner Truth's famous question 'Ain't I a woman?' What is included in the notion of 'women's experience' is indeed a contested matter which does not only concern standpoint theories, but more largely 'woman as an analytical category', in the words of Chandra Talpade Mohanty (1988), that is, 'the crucial assumption that we belong to the same gender across classes and cultures'. An assumption which does not only rely on 'biological essentials', but is established through anthropological and sociological universals, and takes for granted the sameness of 'our' oppression. Mohanty shows how analyses of women's labour or notions of family or religion in Women's Studies scholarship tend to create a unity throughout women's activities which masks the power differences between women. They do so through presuming the universality of women's experiences, while simultaneously unifying the knowledges grounded in different women's experiences.

Taking into account the differences between women along the power axes of 'race'/ethnicity, class, and sexual preference, however, does not necessarily undermine the notion of a feminist standpoint itself. As Collins puts it:

What we now have is increasing sophistication about how to discuss group location, not in the singular social class framework proposed by Marx, nor in the early feminist frameworks arguing the primacy of gender, but within constructs of multiplicity residing in social structures themselves and not in individual women.

(Hill Collins, 1997: 377)

For Collins, this 'new lens' can 'deepen understanding of how the actual mechanism of institutional power can change dramatically, while continuing to reproduce longstanding inequalities'. Collins' point joins an impulse that runs through, to name a few, the Combahee River Collective Statement (1986) and the work of bell hooks (1990), Angela Davis (1981), and Audre Lorde (1984) and has been re-articulated in the 1990s around a term coined by Kimberlé Crenshaw (1989): intersectionality. Intersectional analysis looks at how multiple forms of domination and oppression simultaneously, albeit not analogously, shape the lives of *all* human beings.[2]

A third crucial matter addresses perhaps more explicitly the question of how to conceive of the process of constructing standpoints. We refer here to a *feminist standpoint as a collective achievement* of description, analysis, and political struggle, occurring in a particular historical space and in relation to particular situations of oppression (Hartsock, 1998). Jacqui Alexander and Chandra Mohanty (1997: xi) continue Moya's argument against the self-evidence of the epistemic meaning of social locations:

> Thus, the experience of repression can be, but is not necessarily, a catalyst for organizing. It is, in fact, the *interpretation* of that experience within a *collective* context that marks the moment of transformation from perceived contradictions and material disenfranchisement to participation in women's movements.

Standpoints involve looking for grounds for knowledge claims on the basis of silenced lives, *articulated collectively as a position* for understanding the world in order to transform it.[3]

This reading of standpoint theory resonates with (poststructuralist) sensitivities such as Laclau and Mouffe's (1985) refusal to see the political process as the gathering or mobilizing of already existent actors, considering it instead in terms of the formation of new political subjects. The refusal to assume a preconceived notion of the subject is not the same as negating or dispensing with such a notion (Butler, 1992); rather it is to query the process of its construction and the situated roles we play within the process. In the light of such contextualized and historicized practices of re-constructing political subjectivities, we consider that standpoint theory involves continuous inquiries into the process of subjectivity construction itself and the possible connections between different oppositional struggles.

In a sense, we could argue that such theoretical and political commitments displace the discussion about the legitimacy of 'women's experience' as a ground for knowledge. The effort of constructing standpoints, we believe, refers less to the consolidation of experience as a foundation, than to a process of *transforming* experience

(Puig, 2004). It is in this vein that we understand Haraway's assertion (1985: 149) that 'The international women's movements have constructed "women's experience", as well as uncovered or discovered this crucial collective object [. . .] Liberation rests on the construction of the consciousness, the imaginative apprehension, of oppression, and so of possibility.' The *process* that standpoint thinking seeks to theorize, we insist, cannot be reduced to an epistemological quest, to the search of a theory that could describe, found, and orient what knowledge is more valid (or more true or scientific). Here we recall Collins' critique (1997) of the depoliticizing effect of detaching feminist standpoint from its original moorings in a knowledge/power inquiry, in order to reframe the discussion in terms of feminist truth and method. Epistemological (and methodological) debates have a situated specificity and interest, and there is no doubt that the transformation of experience through collective action has epistemo-logical implications, as it involves the constitution of new subjectivities contesting the legitimacy of established knowledge by expressing other than the dominant visions of the world. The ongoing history of the (re)construction of what counts as feminist standpoints indeed teaches us that no *foundation* can be taken for settled, that all foundations are 'contingent' (Butler, 1992). The openness to new standpoints and possible intersectional solidarities between women is therefore not given; it is a political effort.

Antigone's act: A complex legacy

Guided by our appropriation of feminist standpoint thinking, it is time to return to Antigone and introduce concerns and questions which do not only serve as a route into the richness of Antigone's legacy, but also allow us to probe further our understanding of standpoint theory further. Antigone's posture is, by all means, one of opposition and resistance, anchored in multiple positions and relationships. The *polemos* between Antigone and Creon is, as Steiner puts it, dense with some constants of antagonism or confrontation: between men and women, age and youth, society and the individual, the living and the dead, and men and gods (Steiner, 1984). Yet the answer to the question about the nature of opposition represented by Antigone's act is notoriously difficult and evasive. For millennia we have been hoping to catch her in the act, Carol Jacobs writes, to say plainly and clearly what she is about – 'Yet no vigilance could be adequate to the task' (Jacobs, 1996). Time and time again, she fails to represent: her act and her claims continue to escape even the logic that she herself invokes, and ultimately she fails to leave a trace. Thinking along and about the un-settling figure of Antigone, we would like to raise three points which interpellate feminist politics and epistemological frameworks, by engaging them, and challenging them, through an involvement with the changing conjunctures of women's lives.

We begin by noting Antigone's attachment to the gods. Many discussions of Antigone gravitate around the relation between the realms of kinship and the state, and yet it strikes us that Antigone's references to kinship are matched by those to the gods (including Justice, who resides among them). At the very outset of the polemos, when Creon inquires whether she was aware of his edict and thus knowingly transgressed the law, Antigone asserts:

> Yes, for it was not Zeus who made this proclamation, nor was it Justice who lives with the gods below that established such laws among men, nor did I think your proclamations strong enough to have power to overrule, mortal as they were, the unwritten and unfailing ordinances of the gods.

(Sophocles, 1994)

The divine power she aligns herself to is not the power of a monotheistic God, nor is it a divinity that stands apart from life as such, despite Creon's attempt to assert an autonomous political order. Rather, it is the divinity of a pagan world in which man and gods cohabit, in ways that elude secular readings of the play. Indeed, the very autonomy of the realm of men vis-à-vis those of the gods, and the autonomy of the political vis-à-vis the sphere of kinship and family are the *effects* of the process of secularization – effects that secular frameworks tend to take as normative. In our argument, insisting on Antigone's attachment to the gods becomes a way of inquiring into hegemonic secular frameworks. It allows us to gain insight in the tension between the realms of men and gods invoked by the ancient tragedy, and makes Sophocles' play relevant in light of contemporary debates in Europe about religious claims in a modern nation-state.

Let us make a speculative move at this point, and propose a figure of Antigone which speaks to contemporary urgencies in Europe: a French Antigone of Maghrebin origin who confronts the patriarch's law demanding her to take off her headscarf for the sake of keeping civic order. While by no means disconnected from other European secular regimes, French Republicanism stands out in various respects. It is perhaps significant that reworkings of, and commentaries on, Sophocles' ancient tragedy favouring Creon have found a particularly fertile soil in France (Steiner, 1984). Such readings render Creon as a lone hero guarding the civic order, while Antigone is accused of the fault of individualism (see Bernard-Henri Lévy's discussion of Antigone in 1979). To position as 'individual' or merely 'personal' an act which is claimed again and again in relation to kinship and the gods, requires a radical erasure of the communal grounds of Antigone's motives. Indeed, those practices, experiences, knowledges, ethics, and epistemes, which are neither aligned with nor recognized within an established public civic order, are pushed into the realm of the private or individual, which is conceived of in opposition to the public realm. This is in fact how Talal Asad (2003) understands the construction of secular space, that is, as the transcendence, through a political medium of citizenship, of particular and differentiating embodied practices of the self which are articulated through class, gender, and religion. Secularism, in other words, is understood as the transcendent mediation of different identities considered to be 'particular' (class, gender, religion) and the replacing of conflicting perspectives by a unifying experience aimed at creating a 'universal' subject.

If Antigone's legacy already is a challenging one, the image of Antigone's resistance grounded in her desire to serve the laws of kinship and gods (against the patriarchal rule of man) renders the matter more complex. We invoke a French Antigone of Maghrebin origin who dons the headscarf and who embodies an ethical and moral consciousness at stake with French *laicité*, to address the challenges which the experience of contemporary Muslim women's piety poses to European secular ways of thinking. Such ways of thinking profoundly mark European feminisms, which by far and large remain ill equipped to respond to the present conjuncture of a 'return of religion'.[4] Feminists in Europe have found themselves paralyzed and divided by the claims of pious, and in particular Muslim, women against increasingly rigid and repressive secular states. In the language of the speculative image we invoked, we would argue that some feminists have found themselves heirs to Creon, as they (sometimes vigorously) defend the civic order of the day, with a surprising sense of belonging to that order. Drawing upon the legacy of feminist standpoint theory, we suggest that such a positioning depends on, and is sustained through, the dismissal and exclusion of an entire spectrum of women's voices and experiences, and undermines possibilities to reshape feminist alliances.

A second set of issues relates more specifically to the challenges that the contemporary figure of the pious (Muslim) woman poses for (feminist) theoretical frameworks (Bracke, 2004). Here we note that the rather exhausted mode of thought of 'false consciousness' – i.e. the failure to recognize the conditions and instruments of one's oppression and exploitation – is resurrected, in particular in relation to Muslim women. In response, a growing number of studies on women and religious movements seek to recognize pious (Muslim) women's voices and attempt to *think from* their experiences and lives along the lines of standpoint feminism. This generates accounts that put agency, or the capacity (of subjects) to act upon the world, as central. An emphasis on women's experiences, often through ethnographic accounts, thus serves to focus on the various kinds of negotiations which women engage in vis-à-vis structural realities and power, and the ways in which they are empowered. In this respect we can observe how women's experiences are framed through a 'metaphor of agency' (Bauer, 1997), often at the expense of accounting for the ways in which structural realities shape subjectivities.

This emphasis on agency, in particular when it seeks to 'give voice to an oppressed other', brings forth a number of questions. A first line of questioning investigates the ways in which the emphasis on agency can function to counter the reduction to 'false consciousness' of women's experiences that are not easily recognized within existing feminist frameworks. In *Politics of Piety*, Saba Mahmood develops an argument for the need to explore the meaning of agency within the grammar of concepts in which it resides. The notion of agency, she argues, serves 'to describe a whole range of human activities, including those which may be socially, ethically, or politically indifferent to the goal of opposing hegemonic norms' (Mahmood, 2005: 9). Her ethnographic study of pious women in Cairo leads Mahmood to conceptualize pious subjectivities in terms of an ethical formation of body and mind, and to emphasize the disciplining that such a formation requires. Mahmood makes a case for de-linking an understanding of agency from a teleology of progressive and emancipatory politics which inherently ascribes resistance to agency. We read this approach as an invitation to carefully investigate the liberal secular assumptions which inform our (feminist) notions of (female) subjectivity, freedom, and oppression, and therefore also our understandings of opposition and resistance. Taking this line of questioning seriously, we argue, enables to complexify and rethink the matters of oppression and women's voices which preoccupy feminist standpoint thinking.

Another line of questioning pertains to the kind of work that needs to be done to 'hear' voices based in experiences and forms of oppositional agency that are not easily recognized within the established epistemological and political frameworks. In her celebrated essay 'Can the Subaltern Speak?', Gayatri Spivak (1985a) interrogates the academic effort to give a voice to the gendered subaltern, by drawing attention to how elites reproduce the construction of the subaltern. What is at stake, Spivak asks, when we insist that the subaltern speaks? (see Sandra Ponzanesi's chapter in this volume). If the subaltern cannot speak, Butler comments, it is not because she would not 'express her desires, form political alliances or make culturally and politically significant effects', but because her agency remains illegible in the context of European epistemic regimes, the deep-rooted exclusions they are based upon, and how they conceptualize agency (Butler, 2000). In other words, the point is not to build standpoints on behalf of 'other' women's experiences, neither to trap women's narratives into categories that are not their own. Rather, feminist standpoints and the knowledges they generate are born out of an ongoing collective process that involves the construction of new alliances. Such alliances require both the recognition of other economies of knowledge and experiences, and the openness to question and situate one's own.

The question of new alliances brings this chapter to an end, taking us back to the understanding of the construction of a standpoint as a collective endeavour. Antigone stands alone in the face of the political power of the day; she finds herself in an isolated 'oppositional' position. Despite her compelling force on feminist imaginaries, we cannot take for granted that her position represents a feminist standpoint. Feminism as a social movement and a frame of analysis offers women (and men who refuse the dominant gendered order) the possibility of opposition as a *collective* act. Yet we could reclaim the force of Antigone's act by re-imagining it within the possibility of the collective, upon which standpoint theorists dwell. Here we would like to make a second speculative move irrupting in a moment in which the plot could have taken a different turn. The prologue of the plot figures a dialogue between two figures of femininity, Antigone and her sister Ismene. Antigone solicits Ismene's solidarity and assistance: *sister, will you join my act?* Let's imagine for a moment that Ismene would have answered positively. In the act of constructing their vision and action together, a different plot would have been conspired. And then we could begin to imagine the dawn of a construction of a collective standpoint, in which analysis and action would be shared by Antigone, Ismene, Euridyce. . . and, indeed, most likely Haemon.

If these possible solidarities belong to an imagined past, the current challenges posed by the figure of a Maghrebin pious Antigone are quite tangible. And although we do not pretend to answer the questions and concerns we touched upon ever too briefly, we do rely on the very tradition of standpoint feminism to seek the political and theoretical imaginations required for resisting the belligerent mobilizations of our times. While the proclamation of a 'clash of civilizations' exhorts us, as often in times of war, to take sides – *either you are with us, or you are against us*[5] – our connection to a legacy of standpoint feminisms shows us how hegemonic positions can be refused and new collective grounds for knowledge can be created. Through refusing the severing of certain experiences from the realm of politics by confining them to the individual or the private; through collective sharing, thinking, and organizing alliances between dismissed and atomized experiences; and precisely through acknowledging that such experiences cannot be taken as self-evident, they can become available resources of transformative knowledge and action.

Notes

1   Harding (1986) included standpoint theory in her influential mapping of feminist ways to tackle problems related to science, such as the place of women as knowers and scientists, the re-interrogation of existing practices of knowledge in terms of sexist and racist contents, as well as existing methodologies and assumed epistemologies. It is in relation to this latter field of inquiry that standpoint theory is often associated with re-evaluations of the meanings of 'objectivity' as a measuring category for what will be considered 'scientific' or not – for example because it is, putatively, 'biased'.

2   For a recent discussion on intersectionality in a European context, see Phoenix and Pattynama, 2006.

3   Hartsock (1998: 79) refers to her project as an effort to develop the idea of a feminist standpoint in contrast to a 'women's viewpoint'. She writes: 'Groups must not be seen as formed unproblematically by their subjection, that is, by existing in a particular social location and therefore coming to (being forced to) see the world in a particular way.'

4   With the 'return of religion' in a European context, we are referring to a particular dense conjuncture in which we see the emergence of a new set of religious claims vis à vis the state, as well as the state's involvement in redefining the contours of secularism as to strengthen the connection with a Christian heritage, and a new hegemonic geopolitical situation in which antagonism and conflict is re-articulated along 'civilization' and religious lines, with a global abject 'other' or enemy called Islam.

5   For an example of a feminist articulation in the wake of 'headscarf debates' in France and in many other European countries, which refuses the (ab)use of women's emancipation in the belligerent and performative claims of a 'clash of civilizations' seeking feminism's alignment with the West against Islam, see the 'Not in our names!' statement by the NextGenderation network: www.nextgenderation. net/projects/notinournames.

Questions for further research

1   How does knowledge produced from standpoints of oppressed or oppositional subjects allow for more reliable accounts of the world? What conditions are required by such processes of knowledge production?

2   Explain why standpoints cannot be reduced to experiences. What do you understand by the mediated character of experience? How would you describe the relation between standpoint and experience?

3   Think through the different feminist readings of the figure of Antigone. Can Antigone be a feminist heroine after all? Why or why not? What makes the work of interpreting her so difficult and unstable?

4   How can feminist standpoint theories contribute to contemporary debates on religion and pious subjectivities?

The arena of disciplines:
Gloria Anzaldúa and
interdisciplinarity

4

Gloria Wekker

4.1 *Gloria Anzaldúa.*

> My whole struggle is to change the disciplines, to change the genres, to change
> how people look at a poem, at theory, or at children's books.
>
> (Anzaldúa in Ikas, 1999: 232)

Gloria Anzaldúa (1942–2004) was a Chicana lesbian, feminist, theoretician, poet,
author of children's books and fiction, as well as an activist. She was born as the eldest
daughter of *campesinos*, subsistence farmers, in the Rio Grande Valley of Southern

Texas and only began to attend school regularly when she was eleven years old. Chicanos are a culturally hybrid population, the inhabitants of the border area of Mexico and the United States, featuring the mixed strands of Mexican, American Indian, and Anglo-American culture. Originally they are of Mexican descent, but Chicanos have lived in the United States for generations, since the time this imperialist power appropriated Northern Mexico in 1848.[1]

The children of the Anzaldúa family were supposed to help with work in the fields and together with her mother and sister, Gloria was engaged in collecting the eggs at a chicken farm (Anzaldúa, 1987). While her mother raised Gloria to become an obedient and docile wife, who would bear children and generally behave as a second-class citizen, her father urged her to read and study. From her earliest childhood she created her own world by reading just about everything she could lay her hands on in the local library – encyclopaedias, dictionaries, Aesop's fables, philosophy (Smuckler, 2000 [1982]: 25) – and failing that she would read the labels on food tins. At the time of her father's death, when she was twelve years old, her mother began to rely on her to help raise and educate the younger children and she had to return to the fields again during weekends and summers. Her experiences as a Spanish speaking brown girl in a dominant culture preferring English speaking white or light coloured boys has been of lasting influence on her life and thought (Keating, 2000: 2). Still she managed to attend university to study English and pedagogics, meanwhile teaching Chicano children at primary and secondary school. Later she would teach creative writing, Chicano studies, and feminist studies at, among others, the University of Santa Cruz in California (Anzaldúa, 1987).

In the mid-1970s she moved to San Francisco, where she got in touch with the flourishing feminist movement. With Cherríe Moraga, another Chicana feminist, she edited *This Bridge Called my Back: Writings of Radical Women of Color* (1981), an impressive radical statement made by American women who branded themselves with the novel term 'of color'. They formulated a type of feminism that met with general recognition around the world. It amply accommodated the differences among women: gender was not the only factor making a difference, but was considered as socially significant in connection with 'race'/ethnicity, class, sexuality, and other important personal, institutional, and symbolical axes of signification.

Her most important work is *Borderlands/La Frontera: The New Mestiza* (1987), a path breaking feminist exploration of identity, politics, language, history, and the subject of feminism. It is written from an acute awareness of a politics of location, a concept that was developed by the famous feminist Adrienne Rich (Rich, 1985b). Rich had formulated this concept in a series of essays, as a result of discussions with black feminists such as Audre Lorde, Barbara Smith, and Michelle Cliff.

Rich argues that the unproblematized feminist 'we' should be deconstructed. White feminists especially should be accountable for the significance of their ethnic and class positionings and should not depart from the notion of 'the faceless, raceless, class-less category of "all women". "All women" is a creation of white, Western self-centeredness' (Rich, 1985b: 321).[2] Rich particularly addresses white women, because 'women of colour' usually have not been able to permit themselves such blind spots.

It is about 'recognizing our location, having to name the ground we're coming from, the conditions we have taken for granted' (ibid.), in order to make sure that with the awareness that 'women' are excluded, the insight is gained that 'women' exclude other women – for example, as in white and Western theoreticians who are not accountable for their own situatedness. Accepting responsibility for one's embedded positionings forms the core of Rich's argumentation. It demands a type of reflection that accounts for the way that knowledge that one produces is indissolubly intertwined with those positionings. Like no other, Anzaldúa has made her politics of location explicit, while refusing to be resigned to the limitations brought about by her own positioning. An analysis of her politics of location and the knowledge production it entailed offers an opportunity for understanding the layeredness and complexity of her work.

It should be noted that the notion of 'a politics of location' has become canonically associated with Rich, even though she indicated clearly and without any desire to belittle the importance of this intervention, that her insights were gained as a result of her encounters with women of colour. We are dealing with a different kind of politics here. This is an example of the so-called *politics of citation*; the politics of who is cited and canonized and of the power relations which ensure these mechanisms. Just as white women during the feminist wave were upset about the fact that men had appropriated all kinds of 'typically female' knowledge (consider, for example, the knowledge of midwives) so feminists of colour have pointed out that a lot of their knowledge was only validated once a white feminist had given her approval (Spivak, 1985b; Sandoval, 1991).[3] Rich's voice has facilitated the articulation of the voices of feminists of colour – but it is worth pointing out that, at that point in the history of feminist scholarship, her mediation was apparently necessary to make these voices heard.

Let us return to our woman warrior. The title of her third and last important work, *This Bridge We Call Home: Radical Visions for Transformations* (Anzaldúa and Keating, 2002), marks the point of arrival for the intellectual trajectory covered by Anzaldúa. Published at the twentieth anniversary of *This Bridge Called my Back*, Anzaldúa puts the insights gained in the process of that trajectory to practise in this new text. The metaphor of the bridge has changed meaning from a temporal transition point to a permanent and coveted dwelling place. Now, the bridge signifies the abandonment of thinking in terms of binary oppositions. Different universes are united by the bridge, which thus becomes a symbol for a consciousness that is always in flux. The book contains reflections about transformations by women of colour, but also by white women, transgender people, and men. In addition, spirituality has acquired a much more prominent position.[4]

4.2 Signature of Gloria Anzaldúa.

Anzaldúa has managed to compose an oeuvre from a strongly underprivileged background, which is multi-faceted and eloquently speaks to people both within and outside academia. She became a prominent theoretician who introduced the notion of 'the Borderlands' in gender studies and elaborated this concept into a figuration for a specific research practice. This figuration is therefore not so much characterized by geographical location, but by abandoning the habit of thinking in terms of binary positions in order to attempt to conceptualize a state of in-betweenness, of *mestizaje*. She redefines herself as 'the New Mestiza' or 'the new woman who lives in the borderlands, one who cannot hold concepts or ideas in rigid boundaries' (Anzaldúa, 1987: 101). Her experience as a marginalized subject is thus bent into a surplus: she was able to develop into a person with a great deal of tolerance for ambiguity and contradictions, contrary to those who live in the shelter of the centre and therefore lack experiences to broaden the mind.

There are two reasons for choosing her as the heroine for this chapter. First, because studying the reception of her work in dominant circles within gender studies yields important information about power relations within this discipline. Gayatri Spivak (1985a) has characterized these circles by means of the term *hegemonic feminist theory*. The term signals that the terrain of gender studies is varied and characterized by different currents, each with characteristic approaches and viewpoints, but also that this discipline is no different from others in that it is marked by power relations. Difference should therefore not be mistaken for benign variation, but entails, according to Chandra Mohanty, 'the acknowledgement that knowledge systems are produced in histories that are shot through with differentially constituted power relations' (Mohanty, 1990: 181). This notion will be addressed towards the end of this chapter. Second, Anzaldúa presides as a woman warrior over this chapter because, from her specific situatedness she systematically exposes, interrogates, and transgresses all sorts of boundaries or *borders* contained in our thoughts and acts. Three themes in her work will be dealth with to illustrate this:

- First, Anzaldúa is not only conscious of the way gender works, but also of the simultaneous influence of other grammars of difference, such as 'race'/ethnicity, class, sexuality, age, and spirituality. This border crossing, this inclusive pattern of thought is also referred to as '*intersectionality*.' Intersectional thought is a school within gender studies, the impact of which has become more noticeable during the last two decades.
- Second, she was among the first Chicana authors to use '*code switching*' in written texts as an approximation of Chicano speech. Code switching involves moving to and fro between different linguistic modes, in this case English and Spanish, the North-Mexican dialect, Tex-Mex, and a snuff of Nahuatl. Anzaldúa deployed this code switching, this Spanglish, both in her fiction and in her theoretical work; and other Chicana authors followed in her steps.
- Third, she rewrote the history of the southwest of the United States, a history largely repressed in dominant historiography, from a feminist and female oriented perspective. All sorts of genres are mixed in her new historiography. In a series of

interviews (Ikas, 1999), Anzaldúa makes it clear that her struggle consists of the continuous search for borders in order to show that other realities do exist. She consciously avoids the trap of being incarcerated by the imaginary and arbitrary boundaries of a single discipline, core concept, language, or genre and instead appropriates elements of diverse variants of each of these. This has led to a new synthesis of knowledge and her most fundamental contribution to the field of gender studies. Anzaldúa's intrinsic interdisciplinarity forms the true subject of this chapter.

As a relatively new discipline, which began to take shape in the late 1960s, gender studies provides a prime example of interdisciplinary scholarship, yet it presents itself as a discipline. How can these apparent contradictions that characterize gender studies be reconciled? In order to understand this better, it is necessary to critically examine the history of the university, as an organization partitioned into different disciplines, as the most appropriate form for producing allegedly superior, neutral, and objective forms of knowledge. Below, this history will first be explored, as well as a number of core concepts such as disciplinarity, multidisciplinarity, and interdisciplinarity. The subsequent return to Anzaldúa's case will involve locating the marked features of her work – intersectionality, code switching, and her new historiography – within the context of border crossings. This will help in identifying the significance of her work for gender studies, as it shows the necessity of being continuously alert to core concepts, classifications, canons, and boundaries that are valid within a discipline. They appear to have a 'natural' or logical status, but in reality they result from struggle, inviting us to pose some critical questions: How did these core concepts, classifications, canons, and boundaries come about and what mechanisms of inclusion and exclusion do they contain?

(Inter)disciplinarity

In examining gender studies as a form of (inter)disciplinary scholarship, it is essential to pay attention to the evolution of the sciences in the modern era, which will involve considering different academic practices – disciplinary, cross-disciplinary, or even anti- or post-disciplinary. The practice of the 'borderless' acquisition and production of knowledge as emblematized by Philosophy used to be a scientific ideal up to the nineteenth century. However, during the course of the last two hundred years, working within separate disciplines gradually gained influence as the most 'natural' and optimal form of doing science (Moran, 2002). The kind of university we know at present is usually subdivided into humanities, social sciences, and natural sciences. The historical evolution into such partitioning is usually represented as the outcome of a rational, natural process that increasingly approximates reality. The standard explanation of this course of events runs as follows: the division of labour between disciplines and the 'natural' hierarchy of the sciences that supports it, with the natural sciences as the model for other sciences, guarantees that knowledge production will take place in the most rational and efficient possible manner.

The concept of discipline has two meanings. The first traditional meaning refers to discipline as a field of intellectual research where knowledge is produced and its truth value is tested (Kuhn, 1962). In this respect, disciplines are like nations (Lykke, 2004b) or academic 'tribes' in the conventionally anthropological sense:

> [. . .] academic 'tribes,' like others, have their traditions and taboos, their territories and boundaries, their fields of competition and their pecking orders within and between them, their tacit knowledge and hidden assumptions, and their specific patterns of communication, publication, division of labour, hierarchies and careers.
>
> (Becher, 1989, quoted in Griffin, *et al.*, 2005: 26)

Common features of nations and academic 'tribes' are a characteristic history, specific linguistic conventions, typical traditions, and a shared consciousness about what unmistakably constitutes their unique identity. This obviously hampers cross-border communication. A discipline's unity is the result of shared socialization with respect to the questions posed and the theories, concepts, and methods that are characteristic of that discipline. Students who aspire to a career in the sciences learn to develop a type of scientific argumentation which is specific to their discipline (Griffin, *et al.*, 2005: 24). The 'hidden curriculum' partly consists of learning the discourses, narratives, and styles, and often forms the unspoken condition for academic success. According to Marjorie Pryse, the ongoing project of forging and maintaining a disciplinary identity requires a disciplinary socialization and methodology which are less easily relinquished than general cultural biases or attitudes, even with scholars in gender studies (Pryse, 2000).

For a long time the consensus was that progress in the sciences involved a gradual but inexorable and evermore precise approach of reality. Such progress was and continues to be conceptualized as a question of posing ever more lucid questions, using more advanced methods and instruments, a system of feedback between results and new questions, and an ever sharper delimitation of the object of research in a certain discipline. Thomas Kuhn, a historian of the natural sciences and a precursor of a new and more critical scientific outlook, abandoned this classic model in *The Structure of Scientific Revolutions* (1962) and demonstrated instead that developments in the sciences were not gradual but abrupt. They take place with revolutionary eruptions. According to Kuhn, disciplines are regulated by systematic, theoretical, and epistemological assumptions and further by methodological instruments and predetermined objects of research. Scientists and scholars within a discipline agree on these *paradigms* during periods of *normal science*. Legitimate research questions and answers are formulated within the current paradigm and researchers spend a large part of their time on solving puzzles within the current paradigm. However, there comes a moment when this paradigm can no longer satisfactorily answer all questions that arise in the discipline. As it weakens, new paradigms are launched and a battle for dominance ensues. Those who are entrenched in all sorts of key positions inside the discipline, the so-called gatekeepers, act as *guardians* of the current paradigm, but are gradually losing ground and have to make way for the representatives of the new paradigm. The 'heroic' science myth is subverted by Kuhn, as he shows that progress in the sciences is not at all irreversibly making progress. Gender relations are not his concern, but feminist scholars have deployed his insights to make it clear that the traditional concept of science is highly gendered: the lonely masculine genius finding solutions for intricate problems.

The explanation for arriving at optimal results in the sciences, as sketched out in the previous paragraph, is usually associated with a so-called *internalist* epistemology (Harding, 1998), the idea that science is driven by an internal, inexorable course towards 'the truth', without interference of external factors. It is an explanation which seamlessly fits in a *positivist* concept of science. Positivism constitutes a philosophical position founded on the idea that phenomena exist in the world, independently from our ideas, feelings, or attitudes concerning them and unaffected by language and other systems of representation (Sturken and Cartwright, 2001). Positivism had a key role in the rise of the natural sciences. Its fundamental notion is that the true, factual nature of things can be determined by the experimental method. Thus, the laws of nature can be unveiled. There is only one, universal science in this view, the key characteristics of which are objectivity, rationality, neutrality, and value-freeness. These assumptions about scientific knowledge still prevail and continue to be disseminated in the media, for instance in the science sections of the daily papers or science quizzes on television. If scientific investigation is guided by these characteristics, a superior kind of knowledge will ensue – this, anyway, is the assumption of adherents to the positivist concept of science.

Internalist epistemology is increasingly being viewed as a remnant of Western 'folk belief' in critical academic circles (Harding, 1998). The internalist approach has no eye for the social-historical context in which science evolves and masks struggles for hierarchy between different disciplines and within a single discipline. The second meaning of discipline comes into view here, as the term also implies maintaining order and control. From its earliest usages in antiquity, the term has, in fact, been implied in questions of power/knowledge (Foucault, 1980; Moran, 2002).

The division into humanities, social sciences, and natural sciences is increasingly being explained on other, *discursive* and *constructivist* grounds and stripped of its alleged inevitability. Scientific *discourse* (Foucault, 1980) is a localized, historically constructed knowledge formation, defining and delimiting what can be said and thought about a specific subject. The *constructivist* approach departs from the idea that science and society evolve together, reacting and relating to one another (Harding, 1998). Certain questions then become pertinent: how do the demarcations between disciplines come about? What power relations are implied in the division of labour between disciplines? Who does and who does not dispose of legitimate knowledge? What part is played in this by factors such as gender and 'race'/ethnicity? The rise of separate disciplines then no longer has the aura of rational and universal inevitability, but from a historical perspective this division turns out to be the outcome of cultural historical processes, of a struggle for territory and disciplinary borders (Lykke, 2004b). In other words, disciplines are constructions. Their coming about and maintenance is subject to determinate power relations, processes of inclusion and exclusion, and specific concepts about knowledge and the nature of science. In this view the idea is that science bears the traces of gendered and 'racial' relations in a given period, but also contributes to those relations.

Arguments to prise the hegemonic position of separate disciplines apart and to study phenomena from a more multi- or interdisciplinary perspective have arisen from various critical science formations during the final decades of the twentieth century. A number of concepts are in circulation to grasp the desire to surpass discipline, but the precise meaning of these concepts in different European countries remains a little unclear. In general, multidisciplinarity is understood as a process of addition: knowledge is assembled from various disciplines, but these can each be identified and continue to exist separately. *Multidisciplinarity* occurs often, for instance in the case of juridical procedures such as when both prosecutor and psychiatrist are involved in identifying motives for a criminal offence. *Interdisciplinarity* is a step beyond this and involves the integration of separate knowledge domains, resulting in a new synthetic field. It is a possibility, though no prerequisite, for interdisciplinarity to remain critical of traditional disciplinary boundaries. Finally, *post- or antidisciplinarity* embodies the most radical position characterized by a striving to be unaffected by any disciplinary process, because of the inevitable association with positivism (Lykke, 2004b).

Interdisciplinary disciplines such as gender studies, postcolonial studies, environment studies, and science and technology studies are of recent origin. The call for interdisciplinarity has several explanations. For example, Bruno Latour, a sociologist of the sciences, argues in *We Have Never Been Modern* (1993) that some phenomena of late modern societies are simply too complex to be researched with the help of a single discipline. Issues such as ozone depletion, HIV, or the question of emotional well-being each require input from the natural sciences, but also from social sciences and the humanities. Latour reasons that the disciplinary subdivision of the sciences has a fictional, rather than a rational cause.

In addition, national and international research funding bodies acknowledge the challenges that sciences are facing in the twenty-first century. These bodies have signalled a lack of 'global competitive power' in the European Academy, an organization still burdened by its disciplinary order (Griffin, *et al.*, 2005).[5]

This so-called 'post-Kuhnian revolution' (Harding, 1998), which interprets the evolution of the sciences within its social-historical context, has led to a novel way of looking at knowledge and knowledge production. In that perspective, doing science is a social activity performed by a specific group (largely white middle-class males). This view on scientific activities then also paves the way for a critical stance vis à vis the sciences, with respect to the knowledge produced about, for example, women or peoples of colour.

Feminists and other critically-minded scholars and scientists locate the beginning of modern scholarship in the context of the mid-nineteenth century, when nation building, industrialization, colonial expansion, and delimitative, disqualifying notions about women and peoples of colour formed a 'determining horizon' (Said, 2002). There is a plethora of examples drawing (the) connections between these specific circumstances and the content of science. Here, only the last two factors will be singled out in order to examine the underlying ideas regarding gender and 'race'.

Linda Gordon, for instance, argues in *Woman's Body, Woman's Right* (1976) that the link between science on the one hand and truth and objectivity on the other was established by disassociating science from 'magic'. Both forms of knowledge are rooted in the desire to control and explain one's surroundings. However, magic was associated with women's healing practices; and with the rise of science, women, and the knowledge they had of surroundings and people (again, midwives!), were discredited. At the same time the association between science and 'hard' (masculine) practice was reinforced. At a stroke, women were disqualified as legitimate producers of knowledge and the hierarchical position of the natural sciences with respect to social sciences and the humanities was firmly established.

The course of practically all scientific subdivisions – geography, anthropology, linguistics, medicine, astronomy, naval architecture, mechanical engineering – was propelled by questions engendered by the Western project of colonization, as Sandra Harding argues (1993; 1998). This included delivering 'scientific evidence' for the *sine qua non* of that project: 'proving' the inferiority of peoples of colour, who were/are differently envisioned according to gender.

This concise outline of the history of science serves to frame the origin and development of women's studies or gender studies, a discipline which emerged in the late 1960s in response to the complete absence of any orientation on women in the academy. The first department of women's studies was established in San Diego in 1969. The first academic feminist-socialist study groups in the Netherlands emerged in 1974. These academic seminars sought to supply a theoretical foundation for the understandings of the women's movement (Brouns, 1988). Female professors were severely under-represented in various countries and there was a general lack of gender perspectives in curricula or research fields, which led to a supportive network of interdisciplinary collaboration (Widerberg and Hirsch, 2005). 'Gender' was not felt to belong to a sole discipline and disciplinary borders might even frustrate acquiring insight into and understanding of gender. There was therefore a strongly felt necessity for new approaches, methods, and questions.

The problematics forming the object of research in gender studies is necessarily layered. It is about the part played by (biological) sex, later gender, in ordering reality, that is, in the way cultural artefacts and social, psychological, historical, economical, and political phenomena are functioning. It permeates knowledge, history, and the world. Gender is a complex category because it is operative at three different levels at the same time, whether it is taken in its singular meaning or in the intersectional sense: at personal, institutional, and symbolic level (Scott, 1986). In order to respect the complex way that gender behaves, it is essential that scholars within a discipline employ the findings and methods of other disciplines. Gender studies has therefore evolved as an interdisciplinary domain right from the very start.

Despite various social developments and the theoretical awareness that clearly indicate a course towards interdisciplinarity, certain processes still contribute to the perpetuation of disciplinarity. When considering staff appointments, possibilities for publication and funding, or conferences and professional associations, it is apparent that the academic universe largely remains organized according to discipline. There is great pressure from several sides to operate within a discipline. A disciplinary back-ground is still thought to warrant quality. A researcher carrying no disciplinary 'passport' is often taken to be intellectually stateless and is consequently treated with suspicion (Leezenberg and de Vries, 2001).

Interdisciplinarity is therefore certainly no easy or self-evident option. Never-theless, it is vital to acknowledge that the organization of academic disciplines, no matter how 'natural' it may appear to us and notwithstanding institutional entrench-ment, is the result of a historical path characterized by the struggle for borders and territory. In other words, the partitioning into disciplines is arbitrary and the opposition of disciplinarity versus interdisciplinarity is constructed. It is just as important to understand that such a partitioning and the choice for one particular core concept has an impact on the kind of knowledge that will be produced.

Gender studies has opted for the twofold strategy of actively seeking to mould a new discipline and presenting itself as such because of the conventional academic structures, combined with more or less fundamentally making an issue of these disciplines' *raison être*. Despite the growing clamour for interdisciplinarity, the as yet dominant disciplinary order of academia hampers stepping off the beaten tracks of disciplinarity. The young discipline of gender studies is very aware indeed of the various dilemma's inherent to that positioning as, on the one hand, an autonomous discipline and, on the other hand, an interdiscipline. Gender studies therefore targets both the autonomous development of the discipline proper and gender awareness in other disciplines.

Intersectionality

Let us now return to the three characteristics of Anzaldúa's work. She crossed the border in more than one sense and refused to be guided by the conventionally ensured limitations to her knowledge production. The term 'intersectionality' was coined by the feminist law professor Kimberlé Crenshaw in 1989. The term was meant to indicate a manner of thinking within gender studies that was predominantly, though not exclusively, developed by North-American feminists of colour, which involved a mutual co-construction and simultaneous operation of gender, 'race'/ethnicity, class, sexuality, and other axes of signification, such as age, nationality, and religion (Anthias and Yuval-Davis, 1992). Gender is not the only or most important object for research in this theoretical perspective, but is always investigated in conjunction with other grammars of difference. The intersectional approach, in other words, entails that gender is always furnished with ethnic and class significance and that 'race'/ethnicity always already has a gendered and class content (Crenshaw, 1989; Botman, *et al.*, 2001; McCall, 2005; Phoenix and Pattynama, 2006).

Feminists of colour in the United States, Great Britain, and the Netherlands – where the terms 'black, migrant, and refugee feminists' are commonly used – long ago under-stood that the interaction between social and symbolical (stratifications of) categories in different classes and ethnic groups produce different genders from those in the dominant class and ethnic group (Sandoval, 1991). Another way of succinctly summarizing this inclusive manner of thinking is to say that 'race'/ethnicity, culture, or class influence the constitution of gender. It is the prerogative of those belonging to the dominant ethnic group, class, or sexual positioning to erase the significance and privileges of such a prime position and represent them as universal.

Intersectionality has gained influence during the past two decades, both within the discipline of gender studies, as well as in national and international policy institutions geared to abolishing the unfair differences in opportunities for people, such as the UN, the EU, or the Dutch national expertise centre E-Quality and other local diversity programmes.

Long before the term intersectionality was more widely disseminated, the manner of thinking indicated by this concept was already being practised. There is the telling example of Sojourner Truth (1797–1883), a former slave. She was born as the property of a Dutch slave owner in the state of New York and later became known as an abolitionist. She also struggled for the right to vote for blacks, and addressed an audience campaigning for the vote for women at a convention in Akron, Ohio, in 1854. The vote for women was a white women's privilege – a manner of thinking that Truth combated in her speech by presenting the congregation of white women with the narrative of her life story, larded with the rhetorical interjection 'and ain't I a woman?' (Lerner, 1977). In this way, Truth effectively deconstructed the dominant current conceptualization of 'women' and revealed the privilege of whiteness and class behind it.

There are countless fine examples of intersectional analysis in Anzaldúa's work. Her complex positioning as a Chicana lesbian in a strict Roman Catholic and patriarchal milieu, where women had little option other than to get married and offer their bodies to men, caused her to express the following forceful statement:

> As a *mestiza* I have no country, my homeland cast me out; yet all countries are mine because I am every woman's sister or potential lover. (As a lesbian I have no race, my own people disclaim me, but I am all races because there is the queer of me in all races.) I am cultureless because, as a feminist, I challenge the collective cultural/religious male-derived beliefs of Indo-Hispanics and Anglos; yet I am cultured because I am participating in the creation of yet another culture, a new story to explain the world and our participation in it, a new value system with images and symbols that connect us to each other and to the planet.
>
> (Anzaldúa, 1987: 102–103)

The first sentence contains a reference to Virginia Woolf, who famously said that 'As a woman I have no country. As a woman I want no country. As a woman my country is the whole world' (Woolf, 1978 [1936, 1938]). However, Anzaldúa immediately complicates this statement. Woolf was often rebuked for being blind to the kind of privileges that actually permit such a statement, whereas Anzaldúa here exposes her politics of location – *mestiza*, feminist, rejected by her own country and culture, disinherited by a male-dominated religion, and lesbian. Existent categories for identity are strikingly not dealt with in separate or mutually exclusive terms, but are always referred to in relation to one another. She draws being a lesbian within the category of 'race'; she understands nationhood in terms of family and sexuality; she connects culture to feminism, and gender to religion. This inclusive manner of thought, which reaches out to all sorts of marginalized groups and tries to define a common ground, is deployed to represent the intersectional, heterogeneous plurality of her identity. This identity is irreducible to the single pole of modernist binary axes constructing the Western subject (Grewal, 1994). Instead, a new, postmodern concept of identity is advanced, one that is always in flux, open, fragmentary, in process.

Code switching and autohistory

Chicanos developed a language of their own during the course of 250 years of Spanish and Anglo-American colonisation, called either Tex-Mex or Spanglish. Because Chicanos were linguistically secluded from other Hispanophones in the Valley of Southern Texas for hundreds of years, their language contains archaic elements from medieval Spanish – remnants from the era of coloniser Hernán Cortés – and many Anglicisms or English words adapted to Spanish linguistic conventions, such as *cookiar* for cook or *watchar* for watch (Anzaldúa, 1987: 79). This language does not rank highly within the hierarchical relations of different US populations and is considered to be deficient and incorrect. It is seen as a 'bastard language', a negative judgement internalized by many Chicanos:

> *Deslenguadas. Somos los del español deficiente.* We are your linguistic nightmare, your linguistic aberration, your linguistic mestizaje, the subject of your *burla*. Because we speak with tongues of fire we are culturally crucified. Racially, culturally and linguistically *somos huérfanos* – we speak an orphan tongue.
>
> (ibid.: 80)

Chicanos dispose of a number of additional languages for daily usage, which they speak according to circumstances: standard English, working-class English, and slang; standard Spanish, standard Mexican Spanish, North-American Spanish dialect; and regional dialects of Chicano Spanish and Pachucco (ibid.: 77). In linguistics, the term code switching is used for transferring from one language to another within a single linguistic utterance. It is characteristic of Anzaldúa's writing, her theoretical work, as well as her children's books and poetry.

She calls it an orphan tongue in the quotation above, a language with no family, no parents. Other pertinent and moving images also serve to describe the language of Chicanos: 'a language with terms that are neither *español ni inglés*, but both. We speak a patois, a forked tongue, a variation of two languages' (ibid.: 77). When she stops being ashamed of her language, she 'will have my serpent's tongue – my woman's voice, my sexual voice, my poet's voice. I will overcome the tradition of silence' (ibid.: 81).

With such descriptions, Anzaldúa is at the heart of postcolonial debates on the influence of colonial discourse on the language/languages of formerly colonized peoples. What language should they use to represent their truths in literature? Should they appropriate the languages of the former colonizer and change them from within, strip them of harmful images and design as yet inexistent subject positions for the colonized in these languages? Or should they distance themselves from colonial discourse and employ their own – African, Indian, other – languages? (Williams and Chrisman, 1994; Hoving, 1995). The tropes of the forked serpent's tongue indicate that for Anzaldúa, English or Spanish have long ceased to be the colonizer's exclusive languages, but that Chicanos can claim ownership just as well. At the same time, these descriptions imply that hybridity is accepted. There is no preference for one language or the other. In fact, both are used to undermine and resist boundaries. The language she speaks, the culture she partakes of, her identity: they are all hybrid and plural.

A single language, whether Spanish or English, is therefore not capable of doing the kind of work Anzaldúa wishes to realize. In this respect too she is transgressive, crossing the borders of the various languages she disposes of. What she prefers is a language that matches her way of being, of situating herself in the world as a Chicana. It is a preference steeped in power relations:

> Until I am free to write bilingually and to switch codes without having always to translate, while I still have to speak English or Spanish – when I would rather speak Spanglish, and as long as I have to accommodate the English speakers rather than having them accommodate me, my tongue will be illegitimate.

> (Anzaldúa, 1987: 81)

Borderlands is not exclusively concerned with language, but also addresses the history of the border territory of Mexico and the United States. This local history is rewritten from a feminist perspective. The style of her rewriting is, in Anzaldúa's words, a form of 'autohistory', which means that 'in telling the writer/artist's personal story, it also includes the artist's cultural history' (Saldívar-Hull, 1999). A history erased or banned from the official archives is retrieved and represented by Anzaldúa in different literary registers. Saldívar-Hull characterizes the result as follows:

> . . . in this new genre, a moving personal narrative about her grandmother's dispossession occupies the same discursive space as a dry recitation of historical fact, while lyrics from a *corrido* about 'the lost land' butt up against a poetic rendition of an ethnocentric historian's vision of US domination over Mexico.

> (Saldívar-Hull, 1999: 3)

She links these elements to contemporary tales of female *sans-papiers* looking for employment in illegal border factories, the so-called maquiladoras.

Anzaldúa does not limit herself to exposing the Anglo-centric orientation of dominant historiography, but also combats the male-dominated Chicano narratives.

She achieves this by giving a voice to women and by rehabilitating women who were traditionally jeered as traitors and temptresses, such as *Malantzín* and *la Llorona*. In describing herself as both a man and a woman, she ponders the theoretical question of why it is pre-eminently in the sexual arena that Chicanas give shape to their rebellion.

Borderlands thus consists of a generic mixture normally not seen in traditional historiography. Autobiographical narratives, *testimonios*, poetry, lyrics, and feminist theory are interwoven with traditional historiography. In the process of writing, Anzaldúa produces herself as the activist subject that inscribes herself in a specific geopolitical history.

Gloria Anzaldúa and (inter)disciplinarity revisited

This chapter began by introducing Gloria Anzaldúa as a situated theoretician whose work is hallmarked by countless transgressive moves. Subsequently, the organization of the sciences as a hierarchy of disciplines was discussed, as well as the more recent developments in the field of interdisciplinarity. Finally, the kind of knowledge produced by Anzaldúa's interdisciplinary manner of thinking was addressed. Disciplinary transgressions are vital to her work, because it is only by crossing borders that the constructed aspect of disciplines, categories, key concepts, and the knowledge coming forth from these constructs can be brought to the fore and problematized. Her transgressive work exposes the silent contracts framing the production of knowledge in a particular discipline, what concepts, assumptions, and methods endorse this production, and what a discipline's boundaries actually are. As remarked above, scholars or scientists who systematically ignore boundaries are not easily canonized, as their place is hard to define for lack of suitable categories. There is even more to say in Anzaldúa's case.

When critically evaluating gender studies as a young, interdisciplinary science from a social-historical perspective, the conclusion is that this (inter)discipline does not fully escape the disciplinary force of dominant thought in society as a whole. In the context of the European legacy of ascribing 'race' and the counter category of ethnicity solely to the non-European Other – largely vacating the term where the dominant group is concerned – it is not an innocent gesture to privilege gender, dissociated from ethnicity, class, or other axes of signification, as the key concept of the discipline. Inside the discipline, the concern with the dominant core concept has a disciplinary effect too. If, however, the discipline is taken to be focused on 'the power pervaded intersections of gender, ethnicity, sexuality, age, class, etc.' (Lykke, 2004b), gender systematically becomes operative in other grammars of difference, while at the same time the boundaries of the discipline are removed and favourable conditions are created for further developing inter- and antidisciplinary work. In that sense, intersectionality (and other transgressions) and interdisciplinarity facilitate one another. A limited and delimitative concept of gender unduly influenced Anzaldúa's reception for a long time.

Today, however, we can say that Anzaldúa has indeed been canonized as a heroine of gender studies. This becomes apparent, among others, from the boost her work gives to the development of a new discipline, *border studies*; or from the fact that her work is taught in a wide range of disciplines: apart from gender studies, also in literary studies (English, Spanish, Chicano), American studies, ethnic studies, history, cultural studies, cultural anthropology and political sciences, composition studies, queer theory, and postcolonial theory (Saldívar-Hull, 1999: 13). What is remarkable about this list of areas in scholarship, where her work has found an entry, is that these are mostly young disciplines which are, just like her work, characterized by interdisciplinarity. Her most important work, *Borderlands/La Frontera: The New Mestiza* (1987) was branded as belonging to the 'alternative canon' in 1998 and was listed among the one hundred most influential works of the twentieth century.[6] In the US, Ph.D candidates in gender studies mention Anzaldúa as the theoretician who has influenced them most (Anzaldúa and Keating, 2002).

Yet, it should be remarked that she did not have this status for the larger part of her life. She did not live to witness her successes, either at a personal or at a professional level. She was still bringing her Ph.D dissertation to a close towards the end of her life and never acquired tenure at a university. She was alone and uninsured when she died in May 2004 from the effects of neglected diabetes (Alexander, 2005: 285). Moreover, her work met the same fate as that of other women of colour: for a long time leading white feminists in the field marginalized it as sheerly descriptive, as interesting material for illustrating certain arguments, as 'the special force of the poetic' – but not as theoretically pertinent (Sandoval, 1991). Anzaldúa fell victim to the tragic mechanisms that determine the fate of those who are ahead of their time.

Notes

1 In 1848, the Treaty of Guadeloupe Hidalgo ended the US-Mexican war. The northern part of Mexico was incorporated into the US (this included the territory of the states currently known as Texas, California, Arizona, New Mexico, and Colorado). The treaty created a new minority group within the USA, Americans of Mexican descent who faced various forms of exclusion.

2 See Kaplan (1994), for a history of the concept of 'politics of location'.

3 As an example, Sandoval (1991) mentions her own work on oppositional consciousness. Haraway acknowledged and discussed it in *A Manifesto for Cyborgs* (1985), which led to a wide critical visibility and subsequent adoption by prominent feminist theoreticians.

4 Her other titles include *Making Face, Making Souls*; *Haciendo Caras* (Anzaldúa (ed.) 1990); and books for children: *Friends from the Other Side/Amigos del Otro Lado* (1993) and *Prietita and the Ghost Woman/Prietita y La Llorona* (1996).

5 NWO is the acronym of the Dutch Scientific Research Council. It is the most important organization in the Netherlands that stimulates and funds scientific research.

6 *Borderlands/La Frontera* was selected by the *Utne Reader* for the alternative canon; the *Hungry Mind Review* listed it among the one hundred most important American books of the twentieth century. The *Utne Reader* is a bimonthly publication, with the mission to be 'the best of the alternative press'. The *Hungry Mind Review* advanced a counter canon with a better 'gender and race balance' than the Modern Library's one hundred best novels since 1900. The Modern Library's selection only includes six titles written by non-whites and nine by women. The majority of the titles are pre-1960.

Questions for further research

1   Reread the quote by Anzaldúa that begins with 'As a *mestiza* I have no country' and compare it to the saying by Woolf quoted below on the same page. Discuss the most important differences and possible similarities between these two utterances.

2   Can the concepts of 'a politics of location' and 'a politics of citation' be related to one another? If so, in what sense(s)?

3   What is the so-called post-Kuhnian revolution and how does it relate to positivism?

4   What scholarly/scientific premises (positivist, constructivist, etc.) are dominant in the discipline you are most familiar with? How can you tell?

5   Can we speak of a singular paradigm or various paradigms within gender studies? In arguing your point, pay attention to the differences between possible paradigms.

6   Create different examples of a disciplinary, a multidisciplinary, an interdisciplinary, and a postdisciplinary research project.

The arena of imaginings: Sarah Bartmann and the ethics of representation

5

Rosemarie Buikema

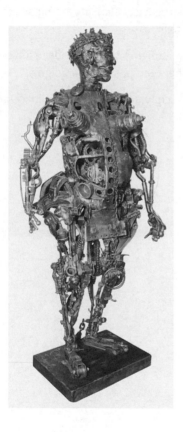

5.1 *Willie Bester's sculpture of Sarah Bartmann.*

There is a sculpture, larger than life, in the library of the University of Cape Town's Science and Engineering Department. Set on a low plinth, it is made of odds and ends of scrap iron. Pliers, skateboard undercarriages, shock absorbers, cylinders, screws, nuts, and other machine parts have been welded together in such a way that the shape of a woman's body is unmistakable. The proud breasts are formed by two tangentially pointed cylinders; an iron dog-collar around the neck, a bike lock, and a sort of dog chain can be discerned; a diadem from which nickel coins are hung adorns the head; the face is welded from molten scrap iron and is averted from the viewer.

This monumental statue pays tribute to Sarah Bartmann, a South African Khoikhoi woman whom people in nineteenth-century Europe came to look, for a fee, at freak shows and fairs. The statue was crafted by Willie Bester, a South African artist who is known for often working with recycled material. He uses his art to persistently criticize the colonial and totalitarian history of his country. He made this sculpture in the late 1990s, prompted by a poem read by a poet friend, Diana Ferrus. The poem was titled *A Tribute to Sarah Bartmann*:

I've come to take you home
home, remember the veld?
the lush green grass beneath the big oak trees
the air is cool there and the sun does not burn.
I have made your bed at the foot of the hill,
your blankets are covered in buchu and mint,
the proteas stand in yellow and white
and the water in the stream chuckle sing-songs
as it hobbles along over little stones.

I have come to wretch you away
away from the poking eyes
of the man-made monster
who lives in the dark
with his clutches of imperialism
who dissects your body bit by bit
who likens your soul to that of Satan
and declares himself the ultimate god!

I have come to soothe your heavy heart
I offer my bosom to your weary soul
I will cover your face with the palms of my hands
I will run my lips over lines in your neck
I will feast my eyes on the beauty of you
and I will sing for you
for I have come to bring you peace.

I have come to take you home
where the ancient mountains shout your name.
I have made your bed at the foot of the hill,
your blankets are covered in buchu and mint,
the proteas stand in yellow and white -
I have come to take you home
where I will sing for you
for you have brought me peace.

(Ferrus, 2003)

At the unveiling of the statue, Ferrus again read her poem to the audience. However, when the University of Cape Town acquired this work of art and placed it in the library, a fierce controversy arose, both in the corridors of the university and in university bulletins. It turned out that many students were offended by the exhibition of Sarah Bartmann in a Science and Engineering Department. It was as if history was repeated once again: after her dramatic wanderings in colonial Europe, Sarah Bartmann had been put on display yet again, her nakedness once more subject to scientific interrogation. And this in her native country to boot, a South Africa that had become postcolonial!

Two forms of representation

Whenever an image of Sarah Bartmann appears or a story about her is told, emotions invariably flare up, followed by heated debate. The ethics of representation are indissolubly interwoven with this figuration. It is this interwovenness that this chapter aims to unravel, analyze, and interpret. In other words, in exploring the historical and geopolitical dimensions of Sarah Bartmann's life, the political, pragmatic, and technical aspects of representation – such a central concept to gender studies – will be spotlighted in these pages. The concept of representation is taken to refer to the act of making present what is absent in reality or in language and culture, that is, the symbolic order.

In the first as well as the second feminist wave, the efforts of feminist politics and sciences were geared towards effectuating an adequate representation of women in the public sphere and in art and culture. In this respect, the concept of representation refers to ensuring that women are present both in political and in other public bodies, as well as in historiography, literary history, art criticism, etc. It concerns the struggle for the vote, the admission to higher education, or the right to work, and can involve lobbying for appointing female mayors, commissioners, professors, and ministers; but it also concerns the search for forgotten female authors, painters, composers, or those female historical personages who are not mentioned in historical records or in history books. At this level, representation is concerned with *presence*. Representation, however, is operative both concretely and at a symbolical level. Language can be a means of making present whatever is absent. Female historical personages, authors, composers, painters, film directors, or photographers can be added to the historiography of culture. But how is this achieved? What language or what scenarios are at our disposal to tell about women? How can it be avoided that we speak of women and their lives in the same sexist and stereotypical way as has been (and continues to be) common practice in history, literature, theology, film, journalism, popular culture, and so on? How can we develop narratives and images that create new perspectives on the significance of being female, or male for that matter, in a given historical and geo-political context? Gender sensitive research in the area of representation thus involves both the level for which the feminist slogan 'a woman should be in' is emblematic and the level of analyzing sexism and racism and thinking about alternatives to these in word and image. When the woman is 'in', how do we want her to be addressed, discussed, or represented?

In the past decades, Sarah Bartmann gradually became an icon for the South African nation. She had not in the least been forgotten, but in order to understand why placing a sculpture of her likeness in 2002 has given rise to such commotion, it is important to consider the various aspects implied by this icon. This is the precondition for narrating her story and representing her in a manner conscious of the semiotic principle that, in the evocative words of the Russian formalist Bakhtin, 'the word does not forget its own path' (1982). Each text and every sign we use for signifying what we mean and intend has been used before, has figured in another context. On the one hand, it is the prerequisite for making ourselves understood; on the other hand, the connotations of that former usage are brought along in the linguistic sign. Because of all those intended and unintended connotations, we usually say more, by means of words and images, than we are aware of. The iron statue of Sarah Bartmann evoked a range of significances with the students of the University of Cape Town, who expressed their indignation and outrage in more or less qualified terms. In order to locate and understand this indignation, it is necessary to track some of the connotations that constitute the meaning of this sculpture. This involves, first of all, knowledge of the relevant elements that have constituted the history of Sarah Bartmann as a historical personage. Next, the description of such elements will be contextualized by situating the history of Sarah Bartmann against the backdrop of the dominant issues of her era, the nineteenth century. Subsequently, an evaluation of the way the new image relates to the old story will lead to questions about the way the sculpture is made up, what it constitutes, what knowledge about the narrative and visual technique we can implement in order to assign meaning to the sculpture. Can we say that it is really innovative or are the students right in asserting that it is a case of new wine in old bottles?

The history of Sarah Bartmann

Sarah Bartmann was born at the end of the eighteenth century (most sources state 1789) in the Gamtoos Valley in the Eastern Cape. She belonged to the Khoikhoi, one of the many ethnic groups who had gradually moved southwards from the North of Africa in search of grazing areas for cattle. The Khoikhoi are considered to be the oldest inhabitants of South Africa. They were called 'Hottentots' or 'Bushmen' by the Dutch who encountered them in the seventeenth century and who suspected them of stealing their cattle. Many were killed in the process of land claims by Dutch migrants. Moreover, the Boers used the indigenous population as a cheap labour force (Barend-Van Haeften and Paasman, 2003: 9; Qureshi, 2004: 234).

This colonial context formed a decisive influence on the short life of Sarah Bartmann. A group of African warriors contracted by the British army attacked her native village around 1807. Her lover and father were killed and Sarah was captured and brought to Cape Town. Here she was set to work as a wet nurse and servant in the household of Hendrick Cesars and Anna Catharina Staal, brother and sister-in-law to the man who had brought her down from the Eastern Cape. Sarah's employers were second- or third-generation migrants of (what in the meantime had become) mixed

European-African descent (Holmes, 2007: 30). The Cesars in turn were employed by Alexander Dunlop, a British army surgeon. As the consequence of a conflict with the colonial authorities, Dunlop lost his position and had no option but to return to Europe. The future of the Cesars household, including slaves and servants, was equally uncertain as the result of this dismissal. Cesars and Dunlop then concocted an infamous plan for solving their mutual financial troubles. This is the plan that led to their ill historical repute of villainous, colonial traffickers in women. Cesars and Dunlop envisaged the possibility of making a fortune in Europe by exhibiting Sarah, the 'Hottentot', at freak shows and fairs. On top of that, Dunlop had hopes of establishing his name in medical science because of the stories circulating in Europe about the physical features of Hottentots – he would be able to supply the living proof. Dunlop and Cesars managed to convince Sarah to accompany them to Europe by promising her a share in the profit they expected to make with this ploy. A glowing future of prosperity and wealth was thus dangled before her eyes.

The threesome arrived in London in 1810.[1] An advertisement placed by Cesars in *The Morning Post* heralded the arrival of Sarah: 'Just arrived: the Hottentot Venus. Two Shillings per Head. Piccadilly Street' (Qureshi, 2004). The label of 'Hottentot Venus' was designed to capitalize on two important myths qualifying the female subject: alien and deviant as well as physical, erotic, and arousing. However, even in 1810, the exhibition of persons thought to be physically deviant was not wholly unproblematic, as research in the records of news reports in the London papers has shown. Within a month of her arrival in London, the antislavery movement had started legal proceedings in order to denounce the degrading conditions of Sarah Bartmann's exhibition. It was reported that visitors prodded her buttocks with walking canes in order to check whether they were real. The trial that took place on 28 November 1810 was centred on the question of whether Bartmann had been exhibited against her will or whether she had consented to this lucrative business. The media debate which ensued at that time has a disconcerting contemporary relevance in the sense that the question was transposed to the question of whether those who had been subjected to capitalist and imperialist machinations were able to dispose of a free will at all. However, the outcome of the trial was that Sarah had agreed to each and every condition and promise that had been furnished by Cesars and Dunlop and that she had been properly paid for her services (Schiebinger, 2001; Holmes, 2007: 105).

The debate in the London press at the time, and in the meantime also among present-day historians, is of course concerned with the question of whether or not Sarah Bartmann was pressured into stating her consent. Some historians take the view that Sarah should not be portrayed solely as the victim of circumstances. Instead they emphasize that Sarah had succeeded in making the most of the situation, given the fact that her prospects in South Africa at the time would have been rather bleak. Some sources state she married Dunlop, educated herself in her spare time, and was able to learn new languages (Schiebinger, 2001; Holmes, 2007).

In any case, all the fuss was not good for business, and Sarah Bartmann consequently disappeared into anonymity, away from recorded history. When she surfaced again in 1814, she was in Paris, in the company of Cesars. According to several reports in the Parisian papers, she was now performing as a dancer in a show at the *Rue Neuve des Petits Camps*, a well-known establishment frequented by the upper classes.[2] When her health started to deteriorate and Cesars wished to return to his spouse Anna Catharina, he sold Sarah to a man called Réaux, a Parisian who was known to trade in animals and who had business connections with the Museum for Natural History in Paris. The sum involved in this transaction is unknown, but it is a fact that, at the time of his death in 1841 in Cape Town, Cesars bequeathed a nice little capital to his family.

At the hands of Réaux, Sarah aroused the interest of Henri de Blainville, who was a professor at the Natural History Museum. He and his colleagues, Georges Cuvier and Geoffroy Saint-Hilaire, wanted to examine Sarah Bartmann in order to be able to describe the alleged anomalies of her genitalia as accurately as possible. Thus, Blainville reports, it would be possible to render a detailed comparison between the black human being, who was ranked as the lowest category of the human species, and the orangutan as representative of the highest type of animal species (de Blainville, 1816). At the request of these scientists, Réaux brought Sarah to the nearby museum so that she could be examined, but Sarah Bartmann refused to cooperate and the men did not get a glimpse of what they so fervently desired to inspect: her private parts. However, this was not the end of the story, because when Sarah died a year later in 1816, Réaux alerted Saint-Hilaire who immediately wrote to the Prefect of Police, asking for permission to put her body at the disposal of the museum. Although the law only allowed for human bodies to be examined post-mortem at the University of Paris' medical faculty, her body ended up on the examination table of George Cuvier's staff without much ado (Holmes, 2007).

In 1817, Cuvier published a detailed description of Bartmann's physical characteristics. In this publication, he zoomed in on her genitals in particular, in order to prove his point that the Hottentot belonged to an essentially different type of the human species. At numerous places in the text, Cuvier compares Sarah's body parts, ranging from the shape of her buttocks to the form of her ears, to those of animals – mandrills, orang-utans, and other ape species in particular. The text, titled 'Extraits d'observations faites sur le cadavre d'une femme connue à Paris et à Londres sous le nom de Vénus Hottentot' (Cuvier, 1817) was reprinted several times in medical journals and was very influential in the medical discourse of that era.

Once Cuvier had finished his examination, Sarah Bartmann's genitalia and brains were preserved in formalin. A plaster cast was made of her body. Until 1976, this plaster image of Sarah Bartmann was displayed in the Musée de l'Homme; after that date it was removed to the museum's stockroom. The sculpture crafted by Willie Bester was made to that likeness. And so we have come full circle: we are back where we began, with Sarah's iron likeness in the university library and the student protests in Cape Town. At the moment of the unveiling of Bester's sculpture, Sarah's organs and the plaster cast of her body were still stored at the museum in Paris. It had been Bester's aim to voice an indictment against such forced banishment. Symbolically, his sculpture was designed to bring Sarah home. Her history and bodily shape were once again made present in post-apartheid South Africa, a feat that was also achieved with the poem by Diana Ferrus. So how can the commotion be explained?

The politics of representation

In order to understand why it is of critical importance to be circumspect about the way we make people and histories present and why retrieving such a tragic history as that of Sarah Bartmann, some two hundred years after her death, still touches a raw nerve, it is necessary to return to the European fascination with Sarah Bartmann's body. Although this fascination can be explained in historical and geopolitical terms, it is blatantly racist and sexist in our current perspective. It is obvious that such fascination was subject to the laws of capitalism and the production of ostensibly objective knowledge. It is the merit of theoretical approaches in feminism, Marxism, and postcolonialism that such ostensible scientific objectivity has been redefined in terms of a project that is motivated by specific anxieties and desires. Precisely the intrinsic interconnection of fear of otherness and the desire for control, capital, and knowledge have turned any representation of Sarah Bartmann – although not of her alone – into such an intricately layered object for study.

To begin with, any representation of Sarah Bartmann is invariably associated with the nineteenth-century exhibition practice that she either was or was not forced to participate in. This is what each new representation of Sarah inevitably will have to refer to, if it is to be innovative. Anything that deviated from the ordinary was put on display in the nineteenth century. One could look at the dwarf, the giant, the bearded lady, or a child with hydrocephalus for a fee. Sarah Bartmann would have been considered a curiosity at the time, because she was specified as a Hottentot. The Hottentots had already acquired certain fame in Europe, due to travel writings that described encounters with the Khoikhoi. They held a special fascination for Europeans because of the broad hips and protruding buttocks of female Khoikhoi. A feature of Khoikhoi women is indeed that body fat is stored in thighs and behinds, indeed resulting in a rather imposing bum. This physical characteristic was not simply perceived in terms of physiological difference, but labelled as a deviation for which the term *staetopygia* was coined. The voluminous behind then became the signifier both of what was primitive and of active sexuality. However, there was a second reason why the imagination of Europeans was stirred by the idea of Sarah Bartmann. This had to do with the accounts of travellers that concerned the anatomy of female Khoikhoi genitals. It was customary for Khoikhoi women to mutilate their labia according to a certain ideal of beauty, to the effect that these labia are elongated. The travel books of naturalists such as François Le Vaillant and John Barrow describe this type of mutilation as a distinguishing characteristic of the Khoikhoi woman referred to as the 'Hottentot apron' (Le Vaillant, 1790; Barrow, 1806). It was a matter of form which was not recognized as the result of conventionally inspired manipulation, but instead perceived to indicate intrinsic black voluptuousness and excessive sexuality. To draw such a relation between signifier and signified was in line with the ambition of natural history, the nineteenth-century precursor of biology. The drive to classify people and animals in the nineteenth century was propelled by the desire to relate the visible to the invisible – its deeper cause, in other words. Thus, the distinguishing characteristic within a species was regarded as the visible sign that referred to some hidden depth (Foucault, 2006: 274).

Because of this background of linking physical differences between people to qualities in people, the case of Sarah Bartmann figures in a range of studies with a feminist commitment in the area of representation and interpretation (Gilman, 1985; Fausto-Sterlin, 1995; McClintock, 1995; Hall, 2001; Schiebinger, 2001; Ponzanesi, 2005). Such research specifically calls attention to the colonialist manner in which Sarah Bartmann's body was subjected and appropriated, analogous to the way the colonizer subjected and took possession of the colonized land. Framed against a timeless backdrop, Sarah Bartmann had become a fixed spectacle. Look at her – there she was. And if you looked carefully, you might filch her secret at last. The secret of her strangeness, her primitiveness and, concomitantly, the excessive sexuality that was ascribed to her: the Hottentot Venus. These cultural critics all point out that right up to the present, the tradition of displaying the black female body as a spectacle for the colonial gaze affects the representations of black women in the art of painting, photography, and popular culture – with, as a consequence, all manner of stereotyping effects. Part of the students' objections against placing the likeness of Sarah Bartmann was motivated by such analyses. But there was more.

In exhibiting Sarah Bartmann at fairs and shows, Cesars and Dunlop meant to provide a living sample as an illustration to go with the stories and conjectures that had been circulating in Europe during the course of the eighteenth and nineteenth centuries. However, their main objective was to make a fortune. Cuvier, on the other hand, had a scientific rather than a pecuniary interest. He had a stake in producing knowledge rather than capital. The specific discourse on black people that originated in early eighteenth-century travel literature had also seeped into scientific discourse. To take an example, the French naturalist Louis le Clerc de Buffon describes the black human being as lecherous, ridden with animal sexuality, and afflicted with physical characteristics that are closer to orangutans than to humans (Buffon, 1837). Unchecked observations were thereby adopted by scientific discourse on differences within the human species, in an attempt to distinguish the human race from animals and to control nature by classifying and labelling each of its aspects. Thus the idea had come about that the white European embodied the highest form of the human species and that the Hottentot was its most pronounced antithesis. The excessive sexuality attributed to Khoikhoi women would contribute to their primitiveness and so to their inferiority with respect to civilized Europeans.

Such categorization became unacceptable to late nineteenth-century empiricists, because of the lack of specific case studies which could substantiate such generalizations. Their objections were in no way ethical or political, but purely scientific: any allegation ought to be proven empirically. In analogy to medical science, where it was possible to have a precise description of what was and was not pathological, it should be possible to describe the polygenetic differences between the races in terms of normalcy and deviancy. In any case, it should be possible to make clear that the extent of the differences between Europeans and Khoikhoi was similar to that between Europeans and 'the proverbial orangutan' as Sander Gilman expressed it (Gilman, 1985: 89). It is this scientific discursive context that rankled in situating the statue of

Sarah Bartmann in the Science and Engineering Department. The protest of students was suffused with a sense of history repeating itself. Once again, Sarah Bartmann would be serving science against her will.

Are the students right in this assertion? Is the placing of Bester's statue in the Science and Engineering library indeed similar to what occurred in Cuvier's lab? In order to determine this, the circle will have to be drawn even wider. Studying representation is not only about the referent of text or image, but also concerns the material context in which text or image operates.

The pragmatics of representation

Sarah Bartmann's story is not unique. All over the world, the human remains of Khoikhoi have been kept or put on display in museums for natural history, alongside the skeletons of dinosaurs and other objects of interest. The Utrecht University museum, for example, has a small cabinet of curiosities where the cranium of a hydrocephalus sits next to a sketch of a Khoikhoi woman. And in Cape Town too, a diorama of plaster figures of a group of Khoikhoi – all as good as naked – juxtaposed to the enormous skeletons of the famous South African whale used to be part of the South African Museum's permanent exhibition.

The practice of such a display is a case of visual rhetoric, according to Patricia Davison, the present deputy director of the South African Museum. In her essay on museums as the sites of collective memory and knowledge production, she writes how in one gallery we look at a display of Khoikhoi hunters and gatherers, whereas in the next fossils and stuffed fish and fowl are found on display. As such, Davison argues, the problem is not that the human species is exhibited in a museum for natural history, but that only the ethnic other is classified in this way: such 'spatially encoded classifications embody theoretical concepts that shape both knowledge and memory' (Davison, 1998: 144).

Davison's argument concerns two related points. First, the essentialist approach to the Khoikhoi is revealed by the way the diorama is situated. Because of its location, next to the skeletal remains of whales, in a museum devoted mainly to natural history, it is not the Khoikhoi's cultural historical context that is emphasized, but their biological characteristics. Such a display simply reiterates the colonial representation of non-Western ethnic groups as being different from modernity, congealing them forever in an unchanging tradition. Such dioramas, such essentialist and stereotypical representations of groups of people, obliterate all individual identity and obfuscate history. The diorama neglects to tell about the huge discrimination the Khoikhoi have suffered, not just at the hands of colonialists and Europeans, but other indigenous ethnic groups as well (remember that Cesars was a South African of mixed descent), most recently of course because of the disastrous system of Apartheid. Second, the exhibition of the nearly naked plaster figures in a museum inevitably calls to mind the 'freak shows' where Sarah Bartmann was exhibited and the manner in which her body was expropriated and dishonoured. The setting refuels thoughts about the relation between anatomical characteristics and the degree of cultivation. The display in a showcase irrefutably emphasizes what is deviant and different, if not the thingness of the objects on display. It follows, Davison asserts, that writing history in this manner does not solely emphasize deviancy in certain ethnic groups, but even generates normalcy and deviancy. Each representation acts to normalize some worlds and exclude others.

This is the reason why Davison eventually decided in 2001 to remove the diorama from the museum, because nineteenth-century exhibition practices were not truly commented upon. In 2004 the diorama was returned to its original position in the South African Museum. However, the entire entourage of the plaster figures had been altered according to Davison's philosophy of adequate representation. Before, the plaster figures were placed, without further explication, in an Arcadian setting not unlike the background and trappings that Dunlop and Cesars had furnished Sarah with: a hut, a chain of shells, and ostrich feathers brought in from South Africa for the occasion. However, now the figures sit in a showcase that clearly interacts with the context of a museum. Utensils no longer fade into the painted backdrop of before, but are spot-lighted as the signs of a past culture, with notices bearing cultural historical information. There was no consensus that this was an improvement, as is testified by the vehement debate in South African newspapers, both when the diorama was closed and when it was reinstalled. Many white South Africans felt that a valuable childhood memory had been wrecked, but others cheered the transformation from a colonial to a postcolonial practice of representation. Nonetheless, despite the rearrangement, it is still the question whether a museum for natural history should house a diorama with Khoikhoi.

Hence, it is the question of whether Willie Bester's sculpture in the Science and Engineering library reasserts the colonial exhibition practice or whether it in fact comments on this practice. Finally, settling this question will involve drawing in the materiality of the sculpture, in order to assess how its concrete form relates to the historical, cultural, and geopolitical context provided the focus for our discussion. When I asked Willie Bester about it in an interview, he told me that the sculpture was made with the intent to raise consciousness about the dehumanizing aspects of South African colonial history. Both his sculpture and the poem by Diana Ferrus were inspired by the negotiations that had been going on since Mandela had become president in 1994 and concerned the effort to get a decent burial for Sarah Bartmann's remains, which at the time were still kept in the Musée de l'Homme in Paris. Decent, that is, according to the traditions and principles of the Khoikhoi. Ferrus and Bester both believed that in some cases art could achieve more than politics. The result of the joined efforts of art and politics will become clear in the remainder of this story – let us first, however, take a proper look at the sculpture.

The technique of representation

In the end, when the ethics of representation are at stake, it is the image that has the final say in the matter. Not the artist. Because no matter what was originally intended in shaping this image, if that intention is not brought across to the viewer or reader, or if the viewer or reader has a different reading of the image or text, then only analysis of the work proper will yield the decisive argument for attributing meaning.

As was mentioned at the beginning of this chapter, the feminist analysis of representations makes use of the tools of semiotics, the theory of signs (Hall, 1997; Smelik, *et al.*, 1999). Now that the history and context of the icon of Sarah Bartmann has been explored, the interpretation of Bester's statue will finally be made by means of semiotics, which will conduce to a well-argued position with respect to the ethics of this specific representation. The vocabulary of semiotics was used without much emphasis in the preceding sections in discussing the historical and pragmatic aspects of the icon Sarah Bartmann. Feminist semiotics departs from the poststructuralist concept of language. Briefly, this comes down to the notion that images and texts precede people and things. Not in the sense of cause and effect (first there was the sign and then the object), but in the perspective of the functioning of language and subject formation. A girl is named girl even before she knows that this is what she is. In language, ready-made connotations are just waiting to be picked up: her domain is pink, she is sweet, passive, physical, spontaneous, beautiful, and so on. The boy, on the other hand, is approached with an entirely different set of terms: sturdy, smart, resourceful, etc. Even before they are potty trained it will be absolutely clear which lavatories they will have access to in the future, and which will remain forbidden territory. They have not yet developed the tiniest sense of taste, yet it is already known what clothes are suitable and what is thought to be less fitting. In short, before a boy or a girl has had the opportunity of being someone, she/he has been gendered via the interpretative frames of the symbolic order, that is, the functioning of discursive and visual signs. Rather than experience reflected in the symbolic order as experience, masculinity and femininity are produced in and by the symbolic order. This is the insight the feminist theory of representation owes to semiotics. The turn to semiotics has been of the utmost importance in developing a feminist theory of representation. Semiotics offers the theoretical framework which supports the claim that one is not born but made a woman. One becomes woman in and through language, in and by means of the symbolic order; and not because of some biologically determined destiny. This is not to deny the anatomical differences that distinguish men from women. The brief outline of developments within natural history sketched in these pages demonstrates, however, that thinking in terms of difference has been deployed to support hierarchical concepts. Signification, therefore, involves power and control. The observation that 'a Khoi looks different from a European' acquires, within the European perspective, the connotations that 'a Khoi is ranked closer to animals than a European' and that 'a European is more civilized than a Khoi'. Visible differences thus refer, in this discourse, to an underlying signifying structure. That structure of signification was constituted, as we have seen, on dubious grounds, but has nonetheless stuck to the signifiers of difference. Semiotics does not take the nature of the relation between signifier and signified for granted, but considers it precisely as an object for study.

Feminist semiotics, therefore, maintains that gender differences are historically constituted and have become institutionalized. Those historical differences are then incorporated by individuals as real differences, as essences. The relation between signifier (the body) and signified (attributes, qualities, agency) is fixed for a determined period and place. The feminist analysis of representations will always be oriented on deconstructing that set relation between signifier and signified, on opening it up and making it fluid again, on establishing new relations.

It has, therefore, become evident that the signifiers of masculinity and femininity have altered dramatically during the course of history. Pink, for example, is a colour that was a strong and masculine colour before World War II, whereas blue had soft, sweet, and feminine connotations; but at present the gendering of these two colours is precisely reversed. The same is true for the manner in which the differences between Khoi and Europeans have been signified. Sarah Bartmann's voluminous behind was perceived as the signifier of primitiveness and lust in the nineteenth century, whereas in the twenty-first century, silicone buttock implants for ladies are all the rage in Europe and the Americas, although only affordable to the well off. In other words, there is no intrinsic meaning to words or images or signs – significance is acquired within a context that depends on the time and place. With the tools of semiotics, the genealogy of significations can be traced and the transformation processes that concern the relation between signifier and signified are made visible. Feminist semiotics is first of all associated with the work of the French-Bulgarian linguist and psychoanalyst Julia Kristeva (1981). Important contributions to the development of feminist semiotics were consequently made by Kaja Silverman (1983), Teresa de Lauretis (1984), Mieke Bal (1986), Nancy Armstrong (1987), and Anne McClintock (1994, 1995).[3] McClintock in particular deploys semiotics to historicize and analyze the interconnection of gender and ethnicity.

As we have seen, the influence of this interconnection was characteristic for the fate of Sarah Bartmann and has continued to determine the current debate on the way her image should live on. Sarah Bartmann was exploited as a spectacle. Is it possible to represent her freshly, without reproducing a sexist and racist appropriation? Can she be represented, in other words, in a gender sensitive way? And if so, to what extent has Willy Bester succeeded in doing so? In order to address this question, we will look at the material level of representation for the possible relation between signifiers and signifieds.

As said, the sculpture by Besters is larger than life and is made up of recycled iron matter. The welds in Sarah's face give a sense of her being sown together from different body parts, just like Frankenstein's monster. This patchwork can be taken as a significant sign, by means of which the specific image of Sarah Bartmann simultaneously represents many different bodies and histories. The stories are recast as an icon of imperialism and exploitation. The recycled matter that shapes Sarah's feminine body calls to mind the many contexts in which her body was circulated. Moreover, it is derived from a domain that is traditionally largely masculine, that of the metal industry and motor technology. The various pieces of jewellery that adorn her body are also made from industrial waste. Her head is adorned with a diadem, fabricated by a bike chain from which coins are hung. There is a dog collar around her neck with a lock, and her feet are chained. The most important connotation of all this recycled scrap iron is that there is absolutely nothing natural about this woman's body. It is overtly clear that it has been put together by human hands or machines. Even if something sexual were to be discerned in her fabricated breasts, her behind, or her hips, then still the material constitution of these body parts will have to be considered. These breasts have been elsewhere, have had other uses, other meanings. The sculpture crafted by Bester is very much a sculpture that foregrounds its own functioning *as* representation. It is hard to miss the materiality of this representation and its meaningfulness. All things considered, it is impossible to maintain that this is yet another image of Sarah Bartmann and that Bester is no different from the nature scholars who scrutinized her body and drew pictures of it, or from the cartoonists who took great pleasure in projecting the fears and desires of Europeans on the body of Sarah Bartmann, by giving it monstrous proportions. Bester imposes the technique of sculpture between the object and the process of signification. The sculpture, made up from industrial waste, problematizes the association of Sarah Bartmann's body with primitiveness. Instead of referring to the archaic backdrop of ostrich wings and thatched huts, the paraphernalia which adorn Sarah constitute an index of capitalism, the traffic in women, and slavery.

Final remarks

Let us return, finally, to the intertext to Bester's sculpture, the poem by Diana Ferrus. Ferrus wrote this poem when she was enrolled as an exchange student in the Department of Gender Studies at Utrecht University. Within that programme, we pay attention to the issue of Sarah Bartmann as the epitome of the interconnection of gender, ethnicity, and representation. Far away from home and with the traces of Khoikhoi in her family history, Diana Ferrus was inspired by Sarah's history and wrote her *Tribute to Sarah Bartmann*. Back in Cape Town, she put the poem on the Internet. At that particular moment, negotiations about the return of Sarah's remains had come to a dead end. According to French law (dating back to 1850), all objects in French museums were the property of the state, and so Sarah Bartmann's body belonged to France. Although negotiations between Mitterand and Mandela had started when Mandela came to power in 1994, both had left the political scene before an agreement was reached.

However, a copy of Ferrus' poem was brought to the attention of the French senator Nicolas About, by his secretary Anne Petit, just when he was pondering to propose an amendment of the law once more. He sought contact with Ferrus and asked for permission to translate the poem, adding it to his political document. A change of law was in fact soon implemented, and in 2002 Ferrus and a small committee of representatives were flown from Cape Town to Paris in order to accompany the remains of Sarah Bartmann back to South Africa. On 9 August 2002, the national women's day in South Africa, Sarah Bartmann was buried at the shores of the Gamtoos River.

On this extraordinary occasion, President Mbeki delivered a speech in which the history sketched in these pages received some very critical comments (Mbeki, 2002). He was fiercely critical about the racist and sexist scientific practices of so-called civilized Europe and wondered who the real barbarian was in this story, the Khoi woman or the Parisian scientist. Mbeki cried out that 'we are people with no past, no names, and no identity'. According to Mbeki, it was an act of justice to individualize Sarah Bartmann's history, unravel her fate, and try and understand her soul; and this was a step towards making amends for the loss of dignity that she had to suffer in her lifetime. At the same time, her individual story was an example to others, to all those blacks in Africa who had been made anonymous.

The North American and European artists, scholars, and political activists' interest in her history is evidence of both the specificity and exemplariness of Sarah Bartmann's story. Not only Diana Ferrus and Willie Bester, but also Stephen Gray (1979), Zakes Mda (2000, 2002), Njabulo Ndebele (2003), Ingrid Winterbach (2004), and Candice Breitz (Beccaria, 2005) have re-imagined a vision of the history and identity of the South African in their version of Sarah Bartmann. Also, in Zoë Wicomb's novel *David's Story*, in the charcoal sketches by the artist Penny Siopsis, in the performances by Tracey Rose, or in jazz music and girls' rap and poetry, Sarah Bartmann has inspired the creation of new images and new stories that each make up the many facets of colonialism, sexism, and racism in South African history both current and debatable from a different perspective. The acknowledgement that Sarah Bartmann's history is exemplary for South Africa's national identity is an important reflection of the view that, in South Africa, no one has emerged unharmed from what is, in many respects, a tragic past. At the same time, the continuing commotion with respect to the question of how this history should be represented appeals to the worldwide belief in the power of imagination.

Notes

1   In her biography of Sarah Bartmann, Rachel Holmes mentions that both gentlemen also brought along a giraffe's hide, which they offered for sale in London to museum director Bullock. He accepted the hide but refused the offer of a live Sarah Bartmann in his collection (Holmes, 2007: 57).
2   More than a century later in the Champs Elysées theatre, Josephine Baker, who hailed from Harlem, would explicitly pay tribute to her unfortunate predecessor, being adorned with feathers and other exotic attributes for her *danse sauvage* in La Revue Nègre.
3   The instruments of semiotics are a great deal more refined and diverse than can be outlined here. For different visions and adaptations, see the sources mentioned in this chapter.

Questions for further research

1   The ethics of representation is always operative at the level of 'what' (making what is absent present) as well as at the level of 'how' (in which manner should the absent be made present). Describe the dilemma the feminist historicist faces in describing the legal proceedings that resulted from exhibiting Sarah Bartmann in 1810.

2   In the practice of nineteenth-century natural history, the differences between human characteristics were habitually ascribed to deeper causes. Thus, Cesare Lombroso, the physician from Turin, described the stigmata of the born criminal in 1876 as follows:

receded eyes, protruding brows, fleshy lips, low sloping forehead, disfigurements of the ear, smaller cranium content, etc.) Lombroso had his body put at the disposal of the discipline of criminal anthropology. His bottled brains are still on display in the museum for criminology in Italy. Why does the case of Sarah Bartmann occupy a special position in this nineteenth-century practice? Consult the www.museounito.it/lombroso website and make sure you involve both gender and the pragmatics of representation in your argument.

3   Try to identify with the assertion that Sarah Bartmann has been sufficiently expropriated and appropriated by the colonial and capitalist 'Other'. Defend the view that it is not a good idea to create new images of her because each new image reiterates the past humiliation of her body. Then proceed to argue that only the memory of her fate can prevent its repetition at a concrete or symbolical level.

4   Go and visit an ethnographic museum and write a review on the pragmatics of representation, that is, on the manner of exhibiting objects.

5   One of the strategies for disconnecting the fixed relation between signifier and signified consists in the Irigarayan strategy of mimesis. You appropriate the sign that should repress you. An example is the pink triangle: the stigma for homosexuals during World War II, it is at present appropriated by gay liberation and gay pride movements. In analogy to that strategy, there are action groups in South Africa that have convoked so-called grootgat (big bump) competitions. Go and look for other examples where the distinguishing repressive feature is being repossessed by marginal groups and implemented in the struggle for emancipation.

The arena of the colony: Phoolan Devi and postcolonial critique

6

Sandra Ponzanesi

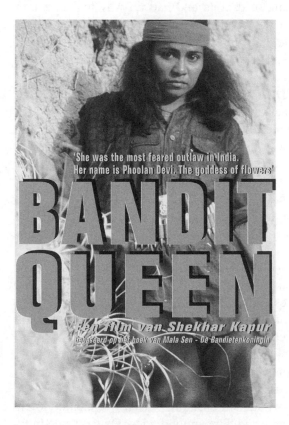

6.1 *Poster of the film* Bandit Queen, *about the life of Phoolan Devi.*

In February 1994, a woman of legendary status, Phoolan Devi, was released from prison under the full mediatic blow of the Indian nation.[1] Better known as the Bandit Queen, the Avenging Angel, or the Rebel of the Ravines, Devi made a remarkable transformation from lower-caste fisherman's daughter (mallah) to member of the Indian Parliament in 1996.

With a red bandana on her head and a rifle in her hand, Phoolan Devi had become the popular embodiment of cruel and bloodthirsty goddesses such as Kali or Durga.

Kali is the goddess of destruction, and the patron of *dacoits* (bandits). She reputedly slaughtered her enemies with her thousand arms and with a smile on her face. Durga is the goddess of war and notorious for her slaughter of demons. Phoolan Devi's larger-than-life image is that of a victim of caste oppression and gender exploitation, who fought back first by resorting to acts of revenge and later by moving on to the political plain. There, she metamorphosized into a phenomenal leader who waged a persistent struggle in the cause of the weak and downtrodden.

Married off at eleven years of age to a man three times her age, Devi ran away after being abused and was consequently abandoned by her family. By the time she was twenty years old she had been subjected to several sexual assaults, both from higher caste men (*thakurs* or landowners) and from police officers during her unexplained arrests. She was then abducted by a gang of dacoits and had no way to return into normal society. She subsequently became the lover of the gang leader, Vikram Mallah, who like herself was from a lower caste, until he was killed by a higher caste rival. Devi was kidnapped and brought to the village of Behmai where she became the victim of a collective rape by higher caste men.

This was a turning point in Phoolan Devi's life, as she then decided to take revenge by forming her own gang of dacoits. She was feared by other gangs, thwarted police attempts to catch her, and raided the ravines of Uttar Pradesh for many years, robbing from the rich and redistributing her loot to the poor. These acts made her become a legendary champion of the oppressed; a female Robin Hood in modern India with its feudal system of caste oppression and female exploitation. In 1981, Phoolan Devi was charged with the murder of twenty-two thakurs in Behmai. She denied any involvement but decided to surrender to the police in the central state of Madhya Pradesh in 1983, after carefully negotiating the terms of her surrender with the then primary minister of India, Indira Gandhi.

When she was released on parole in 1994 (her involvement in the massacre of Behmai still to be determined), she joined the regional Samajwadi Party (Socialist Party), which represents the lower castes that account for about 85 per cent of those eligible to vote in India. Devi, a feisty, blunt speaker who drew large crowds, became a member of the lower house of parliament in 1996, was defeated in the 1998 election, and made a comeback in 1999. A few months before the 2001 election, Phoolan Devi was brutally murdered with six bullets outside her official residence in Delhi in a high security neighbourhood, by two masked men who managed to escape.

The news shocked the nation and beyond as the Bandit Queen's reputation knew no boundaries. The joint reputation of crime and fame embodied by Devi outside India was especially due to the controversy surrounding *The Bandit Queen*, a film based on Phoolan Devi's life that was made by Shekhar Kapur and financed by Channel 4. The film was presented at Cannes in May 1994. Several critics considered the production to be among India's twenty best films of recent years.

The film was meant to overcome the boundaries between East and West and combines the style of European arthouse films with Bollywood escapist entertainment. This hybrid form allows for a revolutionary foregrounding of two aspects that are silenced by Indian politicians. Both the oppression of women and the Indian caste system are denounced. In order to achieve this effect, the filmmaker focused on two aspects of Devi's life: the rape by several higher caste men from the village of Behmai and the revenge she takes on her rapists by killing them a number of years later. The film originally opened with the claim that 'this is a true story' and was based on the biography published by Mala Sen, *India's Bandit Queen: The True Story of Phoolan Devi* (1991). As Leela Fernandes writes, 'the film sparked a contentious and distinctive debate on the politics of authenticity, agency, authority, and responsibility in the representation of the "real" life experience and struggle of an individual' (Fernandes, 1999: 128).

Devi's involvement in the Behmai massacre was still under legal scrutiny when the film premiered in Cannes and the film's claim to truth could have sent her straight back to jail. Phoolan Devi denied both aspects, the rape and the revenge, and threatened to burn herself alive outside the Indian Board of Film Censors if the film was not banned.

While Kapur claims to reflect the reality of rural India, where the rape of lower caste women is not even considered an issue, Devi resisted her objectification in the film as the abused and raped rural woman. In acknowledging the oppression of women in India, the film has a consciousness raising effect; but it also glorifies oppression by playing with too sensationalistic images of violence against the Indian downtrodden woman. Eventually the ban was lifted and the film became a moderate box office success in India, while internationally it received critical recognition and many awards.

The fact-versus-fiction issue was brought again to the attention of the Indian public in a double essay called 'The Great Indian Rape Trick, Part I and II', which was written by one of India's most prominent writers, Arundhati Roy, in 1994. Roy attacked Kapur's claim that the film was a true story (later, the claim was removed from the opening titles). She wrote in defence of former dacoit Phoolan Devi whom she felt had been ruthlessly exploited by Shekhar Kapur's film. Arundhati Roy dismantles Kapur's claim to truth bit by bit, by making a close comparison between the biography written by Mala Sen and the characters, plot, and motives chosen in the film. The biography was based on interviews, newspaper reports, and dictated information by Phoolan Devi in prison.

Roy's major accusation is that Phoolan Devi, the woman, has ceased to be important to the filmmaker. As she is suffering from a case of 'Legenditis' she has become only a caricature of herself in the film. Kapur visualizes rape and oppression in order to tell something about the life of Indian women, but for commercial reasons too. This exploitation of Devi's legacy is, according to Roy, more deathly and disempowering than any assaults endured by Devi during her life.

What can we conclude from this debate? Who was the Bandit Queen? Was she a fraud? A femme fatale? A woman warrior? A politician on the win? The debate unravels the part played by stories and the media in the construction of female identity. Devi can claim to be the only one to have the right to her own true story. However, *because* she had become a legend constructed through many layers of media reports and several cinematographic and printed biographies, it becomes rather complex to ascertain who is entitled to tell whose story and who is entitled to the 'truest' version (see also Devi and Cuny, 1996 and Rambali, 2006).

This case is exemplary in illustrating a series of feminist topics that seems to vex the relation between, on the one hand, Western forms of representation of the Other, and on the other hand, the postcolonial subject's attempts to claim a voice of his/her own and determine moments of agency in his/her own terms. How can we develop a notion of female emancipation beyond the Western ideological framework? And how can we develop a form of solidarity which takes into account diversity without falling into cultural relativism or political correctness?

These are central questions for postcolonial critique. Issues such as those surrounding Phoolan Devi cannot be properly studied without taking into account the insights that emerged from this interdisciplinary field of studies. In order to locate the debate on the Bandit Queen in the context of feminist postcolonial studies, a brief survey of the most pertinent aspects, which have emerged from this discipline, is required.

The postcolonial debate

Postcolonialism is an interdisciplinary field of studies that is not characterized by a cohesive set of theories and methods. However, a definition is possible. The common denominator of postcolonial studies is that it offers critical tools for exposing, studying, and interrogating the ongoing legacies and discursive operations of Empire. Post-colonialism considers the perspectives that were silenced by colonization. Take, for example, the colonial idea that the West brought culture to previously uncivilized societies. Postcolonialism makes a plea for the interrogation of the concept of culture. In the colonial discourse this concept functions mainly as a Western tool for domin-ating, exploiting, and silencing other histories and traditions.

In historical terms, the term postcolonialism refers to the period of independence, so after colonization. The dates of this period are different for the individual nations involved. India, for example, became independent from the British Empire in 1947, Algeria from France in 1962, and Mozambique from Portugal only in 1975. However, more than in chronological terms, postcolonialism should be interpreted as an intellectual movement that re-interprets the relation between the metropolitan centre and the colonial outposts by proposing a reversal of roles. The 'postcolonial' works to shift the object that is scrutinized and spoken for towards a subjective position in which the postcolonial actively represent him/herself from his/her own perspectives and speaks back.

Whether this postcolonial consciousness emerged before or after independence is still subject to debate, along with the question as to whether this colonial hangover will ever belong to the past. We can affirm that postcolonialism comes into being when there is an awareness of oppression that is coupled to the need for articulating resistance to colonial hegemony – a dynamic of power struggle that is still present in today's society.

However, there is agreement on the text that inaugurated the postcolonial critical discourse and brought it to blossoming: *Orientalism* (1978) by Edward Said. A literary scholar of Palestinian origin, Said grew up in Cairo where he attended the American school. He continued his education in the United States, where he lived until his premature death in 2003. In *Orientalism*, Said developed a sophisticated discursive approach that linked Foucault's notion of knowledge and power to Gramsci's concept of hegemony, by combining the analysis of political colonial dynamics with representational issues.

He argued that the most damaging and lasting effect of colonization was not caused by Western military domination or by the violence perpetrated in the colonies, but rather lay in the construction of Western scholarship on the Orient. Such scholarship constituted in truth a 'Western style for dominating, restructuring, and having authority over the Other' (Said, 1978: 3). Said refers here to the ideological use of colonial doctrines such as philology, literature, painting, medicine, ethnography, evolutionary theory (such as social Darwinism), racial theories, and cartography. Together they form the supposedly scientific practice of Orientalism which constructed the 'Orient' as the exotic, irrational, and feminized Other that was fixed in time. The Orient was, therefore, an invention; necessary for defining the West as superior or for projecting Europe's own fears and desires onto the other. According to Said, the 'other' was thus deprived of identity and subjectivity and was submitted to a detailed and differentiated map of representation, according to which no space is left for his/her own voice and desire. It was in order to install and perpetuate hegemony that certain discourses on otherness as racial inferiority had been invented, enforced, and propagated.

The success of postcolonial critique consisted both in the reappraisal of Said's *Orientalism* and in the criticism of this seminal text, which was found to contain a number of deep-rooted contradictions and several shortcomings. Homi Bhabha (1994), for example, problematized Said's rigid dichotomy which fixed the Oriental other into a passive, victimized subject without envisioning any possibility of resistance. Whereas Said focused almost entirely on the colonizer, Bhabha highlights the complex psycho-political dynamics between the colonizer and the colonized. He focuses on the reciprocity of negotiations across the colonial divide and beyond the system of binary oppositions that underlay Said's argument.

For Bhabha, the colonial discourse is never quite as authoritative and unified as it claims to be. Rather, it is in the gaps, contradictions, and slippages of colonial rule that the subjectivity and agency of the colonized subject can be detected. Bhabha integrates postcolonial experience with poststructuralist thought, which is based on the work of Lacan, Derrida, and Foucault and postulates the splitting of the subject and the destabilization of margins and centres. Thus, he is able to articulate the possibility of resistance for postcolonial subjects, minorities, migrants, and subalterns.

Both Said and Bhabha are blind to the gender implications of colonial discourse. Said's book, *Orientalism*, failed to show the interaction between gender and empire in much detail. In reality, gender plays a crucial part in Said's book. The relation between the Occident and the Orient is defined in terms of power and domination and Orientalism is posited as an exclusively male phenomenon, with the Oriental woman a projection of European male fantasy. Nonetheless, Said refrained from exploring the relevant female perspective. Anne McClintock criticizes Bhabha for the same reason in her article 'The Return of the Female Fetishism' (1994: 2). She argues that Bhabha acknowledges female agency only when it is represented by men. The postcolonial debate has therefore been accused, especially in its initial forms, of gender blindness and of upholding masculinist notions of nationalism and resistance.

Gender relations have instead played a crucial part in the operation of colonization and in the rise of nationalist movements. McClintock (1997) extensively discusses the image of woman in the colonial arena as a site of controversy and an object of control, rather than a locatable agency within the conflicting policy of empire. She discusses 'Algeria Unveiled', an influential essay from 1965, in which Franz Fanon argued that the liberation of women was part and parcel of the nationalist project of Algerian liberation (Fanon, 1965). Fanon illustrates in an original way, how during the Algerian War the veil played a pivotal role in the power relations between the Algerians and the French. The veil became a symbol of resistance during the revolution. As Fanon explained, this was due to the colonialist fantasy of unveiling Algeria's women, which meant possessing them and thus, by way of metonymy, possessing Algeria as a country. Fanon was among the first to recognize the 'historical meaning of the veil'. He analyzed how Algerian women veiled, unveiled, and revealed themselves while participating in terrorist activities, in order to reverse the stereotypical colonial expectations of the French army, while simultaneously trespassing the limits of patriarchal traditional roles.

A significant and beautiful illustration of this phenomenon is formed by Gillo Pontecorvo's film *The Battle of Algiers* (1966). The film follows the tactics and strategies of the FLN (*Front de Libération National*) – the armed movement that organized the masses to rebel against French colonization – and visualizes the strategic role played by women as illustrated by Fanon. Pontecorvo shows how women carried weapons and bombs under their veil, deceiving the French military at checkpoints. Once this device was discovered all women were suddenly subjected to severe scrutiny. Militant Algerian women subsequently mimicked the colonial masquerade. They dressed up in Western clothes, cut their hair, and 'unveiled' their faces. Thus, they played with French expectations and stereotypes about the role of women in the Islamic society.

However, it is the question whether women really gained a subject position via this participation in terrorist activities, or whether the strategic unveiling is simply a symptom of their 'designated agency'. This term was coined by McClintock in order to refer to an agency by invitation only: 'female militancy in short is simply a passive offspring of male agency and the structural necessity of the war' (McClintock, 1997: 98). While Fanon deals with the nuances in the Algerian struggle for independence and represents women as taking part in this common effort, he does not fully consider how women's distinct agency should be implicated in the formation of the nation. According to McClintock, Fanon does not go beyond describing women as a kind of arsenal for the male position in combat. In the end, he denies the historical dynamism of the veil, which counters his original position in which he had refused to invest the veil with an essentialist meaning (the sign of women's servitude).

Other feminist critics, such as Assia Djebar (1992), Winifred Woodhull (1993; 2003), and Meyda Yeğenoğlu (2003), also engage with Fanon's article 'Algeria Unveiled'. They read it against the grain and articulate possibilities for female agency in the gaps of dominant historiography. According to Yeğenoğlu, for example, the veil allows women to see without being seen. It creates a position of empowerment and frustrates the Western man's desire to know what is behind the veil. Thus, the veil thwarts the scopophilic pleasure of the Western male gaze and becomes a site of resistance.

Feminist postcolonial theories: 'Can the Subaltern Speak?'

Feminist postcolonial interventions change both the configuration of Western feminism and of postcolonial theories vis à vis gender discourses. This means that crucial postcolonial questions are tackled from a feminist perspective, such as whether the female subaltern has a voice outside Western categories of thought. To answer this question, feminist postcolonial theory proposes a radical rethinking of gender and agency, not just as context-bound concepts but also as categories that need a constant interrogation in order to have operational value.

Gayatri Spivak, the third important postcolonial critic of the 'holy trinity' (Said, Bhabha, and Spivak), is the first to have inflected the analyses of colonial discourse with a feminist agenda. Spivak addresses the epistemological problem of representability for people of the Third World and in particular for subaltern women. Her seminal article 'Can the Subaltern Speak?'[2] (1985a) is informed by feminism, psychoanalysis, Marxism, and deconstructionism. Here, she argues that the category of 'Third World Woman' is an effect of discourse, rather than an existent, identifiable reality. In order to support her argument, Spivak applies her analysis to the Indian case of *sati*, the religious practice of the widow's immolation on her deceased husband's funeral pyre. Spivak dives into the colonial archive and wonders whether it is possible, on the basis of the sources available – the reports of the British colonial administration who wanted to ban sati and the Sanskrit texts that considered it to be part of the Hindu religious tradition – to retrieve the voice and agency of those Hindu women who indeed opted for self-immolation.

Spivak concludes that the 'subaltern cannot speak' (Spivak, 1988: 308). The voice and agency of subaltern women are doubly embedded, in Hindu patriarchal codes of religious and moral conduct, and in the British colonial representation of subaltern women as victims of a barbaric Hindu culture. These voices are impossible to recover. Or, the voice and subjectivity of the female subaltern is erased as she becomes the object of dispute between tradition and emancipation. She can only be represented and spoken for by others, in a distorted or 'interested' fashion. As Spivak succinctly and memorably put it: 'White man [wanted to save] brown women from brown men' (ibid.: 297).

Taking inspiration from Marx's *Eighteen Brumaire of Louis Bonaparte* (1851–1852), Spivak analyses the problem of 'representation' of the oppressed as the subject of knowledge, who 'cannot represent themselves: [but] must be represented' (Spivak, 1994: 71). She refers to the double meaning of representation as it is distinguished in German, where it signifies both *vertreten* or representation as 'speaking for' (as in politics) and *darstellen* or re-presentation as portrayal (as in art or philosophy) (ibid.: 70). The two senses of representation – referring on the one hand to state formation and the law, and on the other to the theory of the subject – are related, according to Spivak, but also irreducibly discontinuous. They should never be conflated. The two related meanings point to the relation between nation-state alliances (domination in geopolitics) and global capitalism (exploitation in economics) (ibid.: 70). Critical theorists, Spivak continues, cannot afford to overlook these two senses in the category of representation:

> They must note how the staging of the world in representation – its scene of writing, its *Darstellung* – dissimulates the choice of and need for 'heroes', paternal proxies, agents of power – *Vertretung*.
>
> (ibid.: 74)

Unless Western intellectuals, including Western feminists, will start taking into account the aesthetic dimension of political representation, the voice of subaltern women will continue to be silenced. As was observed by Ania Loomba, Spivak signals the necessity of adapting the Gramscian maxim 'pessimism of the intellect, optimism of the will' by 'combining a philosophical scepticism about recovering any subaltern agency with a political commitment to making visible the position of the marginalized' (Loomba, 1993: 218). Though often accused of nihilism, Spivak is actually making an important intervention into the issue of representing the subaltern. Postcolonial feminist intellectuals tend to guard them against constructing the Other as an object of knowledge:

> The subaltern cannot speak. There is no virtue in the global laundry lists with 'woman' as a pious item. Representation has not withered away. The female intellectual as intellectual has a circumscribed task which she must not disown with a flourish.
>
> (Spivak, 1988: 308)

Spivak problematizes the validity of Western representations of Third World women; nonetheless she pleads that Western feminists keep being critically involved in order to make the position of marginal women visible.

One of Spivak's most ethical gestures in this regard is to constantly point out the silencing of women's own narratives. In 'Can the Subaltern Speak?' she writes about the suicide of a young Bengali woman, Bhuvaneswari Bhaduri, in 1926. Bhaduri was secretly part of a pro-independence group who had assigned her with a political assassination. She was unable to carry out the mandate and committed suicide to prove her political loyalty. Unwilling to let society interpret her death as proof of illicit love (for why else would a young woman commit suicide?), she waited until the onset of menstruation to hang herself. Because of this decision, her death could fit neither in popular narratives about a women's tragic love affair (she could not be pregnant), nor in hegemonic narratives of freedom fighters such as Durga. Thus, it appeared to have no meaning and became insignificant. According to Spivak, Bhuvaneswari's participation in the anti-colonial resistance struggle is erased by the supplementary narratives that try to re-tell her story. The subaltern woman is always forced into this kind of silence.

Towards an 'enlightened' postcolonial subject?

We can now try to apply Spivak's critique of representation to the specific case of the Bandit Queen. Can we hear her voice without removing the filter of dominant political ideology? According to the critic Bart Moore-Gilbert, the Bandit Queen is one of those clear examples that refute Spivak's dark scenario. In his view, the resistance of subaltern women such as Phoolan Devi is indeed acknowledged and recorded in dominant historiography (Moore-Gilbert, 1997: 107). But what has actually been recorded? Phoolan Devi's 'real' story, by any chance? Or perhaps the story that the Indian government wants to tell in order to exploit the fame of a subaltern woman and effectuate a controlled mobilization of outcasts? Or is it a tale that surpasses the personal and becomes 'representative' of the exploitation of women in India, as Kapur's film illustrates?

According to Arundhati Roy, Phoolan Devi the woman has ceased to be important. She has come to stand for many different things according to the interests at stake in representing her. Is this not a case of the collapse between representation (*Vertretung*) in political terms and re-presentation (*Darstellung*) as in portraying the subject-construction? Does this imply that Phoolan's agency is erased in the clash between elite nationalist politicians and the Western benevolent attempt to speak on her behalf (as if they had direct access to her true self and best interest)? Is Phoolan destined to acquire her political and discursive identity through historically determined systems of political and economic representation?

Phoolan Devi's case is extremely interesting and at the same time problematic for highlighting Spivak's methodological interventions on questions of representation,

6.2 Cartoon depicting numerous versions of Phoolan Devi's story.

self-representation, and representation of the Other. Phoolan personally dictated part of her memoir to Mala Sen and accepted her version, therefore entrusting others with a level of control over the aesthetic re-presentation (*darstellen*) of herself. She also agreed on basing the making of the film on the memoir but disagreed with the result of the transposition. She became a successful politician and therefore could guarantee representation of herself by political proxy (*vertreten*) and act on behalf of many other outcasts who did not have a clear class consciousness.

For the first case, that of aesthetic re-presentation, we need to take into account that the memoir does not offer us any more unmediated access to the truth of Phoolan Devi's life than the film. Autobiographies, along with memoirs or *testimonios*, are situated and negotiated texts that are constructed through particular strategies of representation. The production, commodification, and distribution of Phoolan Devi's life history through film and autobiography take place within the context of a global multinational cultural system. There is a recent rise in consumer demand for the real stories of Third World women in the form of testimonials, autobiographies, and documentary films (Trinh, 1989). This further complicates the analysis of the politics of representation for the subaltern. Oral testimony and visual spectacle function together in the production of an authentic, realist representation of the Third World subaltern woman. However, in doing so, they show forms of collaboration that simultaneously mark and seek to erase the relation of power between First and Third World.[3]

The film *Bandit Queen* is, like Mala Sen's memoir, a collaborative project between First and Third World. A British television company funded and produced the film, but the direction and shooting of the film took place in India, with an all-Indian cast. The script was co-written by Mala Sen, Phoolan Devi's biographer, and Shekhar Kapur. The latter is a filmmaker of Indian origin, supposedly better equipped and informed than other Western intellectuals to tell 'her story'. However, it is not the level of awareness of Kapur in relation to Phoolan's story that matters here, or the cast he selected; there is an additional complication in the audience that he intended to target. This was obviously a Western audience, ready to identify with the many stereotypes about the position of women in the Third World, as depicted in Western popular culture and even in academic scholarship.

Despite the director's best intentions, Kapur's counter-hegemonic strategies of representation may inadvertently work to re/colonize Phoolan Devi. Devi's opposition to the film signals significant paradoxes in the representation of violence against women. There is always the danger of reproducing a paradigm of victimhood involved in such a representation. The film's emphasis on rape shifts Phoolan Devi from a legendary figure in the Indian context – a woman *dacoit*, both heroic and notorious – to the status of rape victim. The film's graphic representation of rape as an explanation for Phoolan's transformation into an outlaw transforms rape into the sole motivation for her subsequent actions.

This is in sharp contrast with the autobiography which deals at length with the complex conception of social justice that motivated Phoolan Devi's numerous raids on various villages. In her vision of justice, resistance was not merely retaliation against her own personal experiences of violence but also against the exploitation of lower-caste villagers by upper-caste landlords. What Devi principally opposed is the form of 'portrayal' of her subjectivity and economic status as the gendered and lower-caste subject (*Darstellung*), which collapses into her political representation. She is being spoken for in distorted ways (*Vertretung*). The consequence was that she had no space left to articulate her own position, which had damaging consequences for her political career at a time (with the upcoming election) when she needed to be portrayed as a strong and independent woman.

A final interesting question is whether Phoolan Devi had become, before her death, an 'enlightened postcolonial subject'. Spivak introduced this term after the attacks of 11 September 2001 on the Twin Towers, in order to discuss the prominent part played by women in the war on terrorism. Take, for example, the CNN representations of empowered US women on aircraft carriers versus the somewhat differently coded representations of the women of Afghanistan. According to Spivak 'the old topos of intervening for the sake of women continues to be deployed. It is to save Afghan women from terror that we must keep the peace by force of arms' (Spivak, 2004: 92). Spivak argues that the liberation of Afghanistan from Taliban rule by the United States did not lead to a corresponding revolution for Afghan women. Rather, Spivak suggests, 'the emancipation of Afghan women needs to come from non-coercive enlightened postcolonial subjects who recognize the particular circumstances and experiences of Afghan women' (Morton, 2003: 168).

It looks as if Spivak seeks to integrate the intransigent and profoundly deconstructive stance she took on the subject of subaltern woman with 'strategic essentialism', as she once called it: the short-term use of essentialism by minority groups to affirm a political identity (i.e. queers, blacks, and Muslims). According to Spivak, one 'has to look at where the group – the person, the persons, or the movement – is situated when one makes claims for or against essentialism. A strategy suits a situation; a strategy is not a theory' (Spivak, 1993: 4). It follows that the 'enlightened postcolonial subject' might be better understood as a *figuration* rather than as a transparent political subject who speaks and acts for herself within specific positions.

The Bandit Queen – in real life and in the stories surrounding this life – has certainly made an intervention, though an ambivalent one, into the debate on the 'enlightened postcolonial subject'. However, the representation of women warriors as 'heroic' and 'fearless', for example in the case of female freedom fighters or suicide bombers, does not necessarily equate female emancipation. When women are shown to carry bombs during the Algerian revolution (analyzed by Fanon and filmed by Pontecorvo), their active role in resistance movements is made visible. The same is true for Palestinian women who prepare or commit suicide bombings for Hamas; or for women active in other political movements such as the Tamil Tigers in Sri Lanka (see *The Terrorist,* a film by Santosh Sivan from 1998) or the Kashmir liberation movement (see the film *Dil Se* by Mani Ratman from 1998). Yet, the representations of these women as heroic freedom fighters are often subordinated to a masculine and nationalist historiography, in a way not dissimilar to the case of Bhuvaneswari Bhaduri.

Women in these texts are interpellated in a male revolutionary rhetoric but they hardly come to share the success of political governance once their revolution overturns colonialism or the oppressive regime. This is corroborated by many stories of nationalistic movements such as the *tegalit* (female combatants of the Eritrean Popular Liberation Front) who, after the victory on Ethiopian occupation in 1991, receded into the background of patriarchal society. Or such as the Women's League, the organization of black South African women founded in 1943, who supported the ANC struggle against Apartheid but who did not gain direct visibility as a return for their contribution to the struggle.[4] As is argued by McClintock, women are often the symbols of nation building – think of the figure of Marianne for France or the *Volksmoeder* in the case of the Afrikaner myth of the South African nation – but never the subject of this process (McClintock, 1997).

On the other hand, female suicide bombers certainly are not recorded in the Western media as 'enlightened postcolonial subjects' but as terrorists who resurrect the figure of a monster, a sexually, racially, and psychologically deviant subject. In their article 'Monster, Terrorist, Fag', Puar and Rai describe how, after the attack on Twin Towers, posters appeared in midtown Manhattan showing a turbaned caricature of Bin Laden being anally penetrated by the Empire State Building. The legend beneath reads: 'The Empire Strikes Back.' Other forms of gendered-based black humour describe the appropriate measure to punish Bin Laden: he undergoes a sex operation and must live as a woman in Afghanistan. These portrayals of American retaliation that promise to emasculate Bin Laden and turn him into a fag entail deeply racist, sexist, and homophobic suggestions. According to Puar and Rai, the US nation-state has experienced both castration and penetration of its capitalist masculinity and offers up a narrative of emasculation as the appropriate punishment for Bin Laden, brown-skinned folks, and men in turbans in general (Puar and Rai, 2002: 126).

Puar and Rai maintain that the monsters that haunt the stories of current counterterrorism have emerged from the pre-modern monsters of Western civilization; from those who in the eighteenth and nineteenth centuries were classified, racialized, and sexualized as the *persona non grata*, the vagrant, the Gypsy, the savage, the Hottentot Venus, or the sexually depraved Oriental. The intent of terrorism studies, they argue, is to reduce complex social, historical, and political dynamics to Western models rooted in the dynamics of the bourgeois heterosexual family. The questions of political economy and the problem of cultural translation are kept out of such studies, as are the attempts to master fear, anxiety, and the uncertainty about a form of political dissent. Instead, these studies resort to the banality of a taxonomy of the terrorist-monster.

Conclusion

Since 11 September 2001, there has been a backlash in the construction of the Other. The uncritical contiguity between premodern and postmodern representations is not only left unchallenged but is, in fact, being reinforced. The new right wing terminology proposes again, and without any critical self-reflection, the dual narrative of enlightened modernity and secularism versus tradition and fundamentalism. This leads to the endless construction of the 'suspicious' Other as the foundation for defining the Self. The collapse between political and aesthetic representation is thus magnified, as the Other does not have access to his/her own awareness – white men are saving brown men/women from brown men; that is, from fundamentalists, fanatics, terrorists – yet needs to be represented politically. He/she cannot dispose of a shared social and political group consciousness (they cannot represent themselves, they must be represented) and so the Other is susceptible to the ruling ideas of unenlightened, undemocratic, and tyrannical leaders. These dictators must therefore be overthrown in the name of civilization articulated as a Western project of modernity. The collapse of representation in the two senses of *Vertretung* (domination in geopolitics) and *Darstellung* (implying exploitation within global capitalism), more than ever damages the position of women. In the international division of labour, women who are subjected to this double regime of erasure become extremely vulnerable.

Women warriors, such as the Bandit Queen and suicide bombers, are inscribed in a complex regime of representation that not only appropriates them at the level of subject-construction (both for nationalist and transnational projects) but also exploits them within the global context of multinational cultural production (they are marketed as iconic figures of oppression or rebellion). The enduring lesson of feminist postcolonial critique is to stay alert on this reproposed collapse, which is colonialist in nature but is subtly and deceptively disguised in general global dynamics. Sadly the new global order underscores again Spivak's epistemological position that the 'subaltern cannot speak'. The political commitment of postcolonial critique in making the position of the marginalized visible is thus made the more important.

This requires a lot of homework. Postcolonial theory's major intervention into cultural critique is to account for the political in the aesthetic system of representation at a global level, something which has been neglected by other fields of studies so far. This can only be achieved the hard way: through deconstructive analysis as illustrated in this chapter, in order to understand the local articulations of power and resistance and to hear the gendered subaltern voice without recurring to preset paradigms of emancipation and progress and without ventriloquizing (speaking for) the Other.

Notes

1   It is hard to give Phoolan Devi's date of birth with accuracy (1957? 1963? 1968?), the most likely being 1963. What we know for sure is her date of death (2001).
2   The category of the subaltern is something Spivak borrows from the Italian political thinker, Antonio Gramsci (1891–1937). He used the term subaltern to refer to 'unorganized groups' of rural peasants in Southern Italy, who had no social and political consciousness as a group and were therefore susceptible to the ruling ideas, culture, and leadership of the state. In postcolonial terms, and in Spivak's inflection, the subaltern is everything that has limited or no access to the range of cultural imperialism and which constitutes a space of difference.
3   After the controversy with Channel Four, Phoolan Devi sold her story many more times. It is clear that it is hard to evaluate the extent to which Devi manipulated the Western media as she has offered them different versions of her story. The same goes for the way in which she keeps being retold in the same format – meaning the emphasis of heroism and victimhood, for the sake of Western's voyeurism and paternalism.

4   Viz. the novel *David's Story* (2002) by the South-African writer Zoë Wicomb. Dulcie is a female member of the ANC guerrilla unit and sacrifices for it both her voice and her sexuality. She is never fully articulated in the novel, but her importance in David's life and to the movement is invaluable. Dulcie's elusiveness is a statement of the elusiveness of the double victim of colonialism and patriarchy. The novel confirms Spivak's argument that representation at times wholly inadequately articulates the non-dominant voice, such as the women involved in the movement.

Questions for further research

1   Try and form an image of the part played by white women in the colonies, by studying Chapters 5 and 6. Describe your impressions and emphasize the way in which patriarchal relations and racist superiority are related to each other in the colonial setting. Consider also the influence this relation has on the roles assigned to women. Involve in your reading the notion that the beginning of modernity and feminism date from the same time period and consider the fact of differences between town and country. Alternatively, you can answer these questions by analyzing novels that address the power relations between the colonies (*Out of Africa, A Passage to India, Indochine, Heat and Dust, Chocolat, Autremer, Nowhere in Africa*, etc.).

2   What are the possible relations between colonizers and colonized women? In answering this question, address the insights on gender and 'race'/ethnicity from postcolonial studies. If you wish, you can use work by, among others, Laura Ann Stoler, Clancy-Smith, Frances Gouda, Elisabeth Locher-Scholten, Anne McClintock, and Sandra Ponzanesi. Consider the way in which the practices of different European powers differed from one another.

3   Search the Web for examples of the portrayal of colonized women in Western media (literature, paintings, photography, postcards, travel accounts, diaries, films, songs, letters, and documents and papers). Regarding Spivak, do you think it is possible to retrieve the position and voice of colonized women?

4   Is it always the case that Orientalism determines the representation of the Other? Describe, explain, and analyze typical 'orientalist' aspects in travel brochures or advertising campaigns.

5   What are the alternative images construed by postcolonial women in order to resist dominant representations? Give some examples of the differences between postcolonial feminism and feminism in general.

6   To what extent do you believe that colonial dividing lines still determine the world order, for instance in the discourse on the 'clash of civilizations'? Would you say that colonialism is at the heart of globalization? What then are the differences between these two phenomena?

The arena of sexuality: The *tomboy* and *queer* studies

7

renée c. hoogland

*7.1 Tomboy Shane from the
TV series* The L-Word.

> It's bad enough to be a girl, any-way. When I like boy's games, and work, and
> manners. I can't get over my disappointment in not being a boy . . .
>
> (Louisa M. Alcott, *Little Women,* 1868)

With these memorable words, Jo March, one of the four *Little Women* in the eponymous novel with which Louisa M. Alcott established her reputation as a writer, sets the tone for a series of novels and stories that centrally revolve around the figure of the 'tomboy'. The term tomboy refers to a boyish girl who would rather wear trousers than skirts, who is more interested in climbing trees and building huts than in embroidery or dolls, and who generally prefers the company of boys to that of girls. In the nineteenth century, such a boyish girl still largely evoked innocent connotations. Indeed, it is precisely because of her unruly behaviour that the rebellious figure of Jo March has become a treasured role model for generations of young female readers, both inside and outside the United States. The main source of Jo's attraction is her resistance to the constraints imposed on members of her sex by prevailing gender conventions. She has big feet and large hands, dresses sloppily, and loves to use slang. Rather than sitting at home drinking tea with her sisters, she wants to go out into the world and become a soldier. Few readers of what would become the 'most popular girls' story in American literature' (Mott, 1947: 102), focused their affections on any of the other 'little women' in Alcott's all time bestseller: 'Most readers who love *Little Women*, love Jo March' (Stimpson, 1990: 967).

Jo March is a fundamentally contradictory character: she is not merely charmingly mischievous, but also quite sadistic and occasionally mean; she is not just a cute and tough little girl, but literally identifies with masculinity; she is not just a transitional figure, balancing on the brink between childhood and adult femininity, but also prototypical of what later would become the stereotypical lesbian. As a nineteenth-century literary configuration, the tomboy's ex-centricity would, in the first place, appear to derive from her non-conformist gender behaviour. As rebellious object of love and desire for predominantly female readers, however, the figure can be seen not merely to undermine the ostensibly stable gender categories of male and female, but also, through her explicit male identification and her all but incestuous relationship with her mother, to transgress the boundaries of normative sexual behaviour. As such, the figure of the tomboy has always presented a decidedly 'queer dilemma'. Or, as Karin Quimby puts it: 'If we understand *queer* to mean what undermines or exceeds the fantasy of stable identity categories of gender and sexuality, then the tomboy may well be seen . . . as paradigmatic' for sexual and gender ambiguity in Western (literary) culture generally (Quimby, 2003: 1).

Taking Quimby's suggestion as a starting point, this chapter will focus on two central issues. On the one hand, I will explore the literary significance of the figure of the tomboy, especially in the guise in which she would subsequently appear, that is, as the female adolescent. The tomboy will function here as a particular representation of the woman warrior, as a cultural configuration that not only speaks to the imagination, but that also, precisely *as* a literary construction, offers possibilities for alternative, empowering processes of subjectivation in actual, social reality. On the other hand, I will argue that only a sexually sensitive – or indeed queer – critical perspective allows us to recognize the profoundly radical potential of the literary tomboy or, more generally, of the cultural inscription of female adolescence. Using the tomboy as a specific representation of the figure of the woman warrior, I hope to suggest and demarcate a queer critical perspective from a merely gender-sensitive approach.

Queer

Let me begin, however, by briefly explaining the term 'queer', and commenting on the way it has, since the 1990s, conjoined with the word 'theory', evolved into a critical perspective spreading across a wide range of scholarly disciplines. In the traditional sense of 'strange' or 'unusual', the term 'queer' was first used in the sixteenth century, to describe someone with an unusual lifestyle or eccentric behaviour. In the course of the nineteenth century, 'queer' began to acquire largely sexual connotations, being mainly used in a derogatory or pejorative sense. Throughout the twentieth century, 'queer' was, and for some people today, continues to be a term with exclusively negative and offensive connotations. However, in the course of the last few decades, 'queer' has simultaneously grown into an umbrella term to designate a wide range of sexually 'deviant' – that is to say, non-heteronormative – modes of being and behaviour. In this context, 'queer' does not so much serve to insult or offend, but rather functions as a term of self-determination, not only to suggest, but also deliberately to appropriate a non-normative sexual/gender position. It is in the latter sense, as a term of pride claimed by sexual 'deviants' themselves, a term of alternative self-identification, that 'queer' has come to play a significant role in critical theorizing.

The phrase 'queer theory' is usually attributed to Italian-American theorist Teresa de Lauretis (1991). De Lauretis introduced the idea of 'queer theory' at a conference on lesbian and gay studies in 1990, in order to call into question and to problematize all forms of gender and sexual categorization. Such categories, she argued, should not be considered in and of themselves, or only on their own terms, but rather be thought in relation to other aspects of identity, such as class or 'race'/ethnicity. Queer theorists, then, do not simply accept 'homosexual', 'lesbian', 'heterosexual', or 'bisexual' as fixed categories – or identities – but instead explore the genealogies and shifting meanings of any such terms of personal and collective identification. They investigate, for instance, the different contexts in which terms such as homosexual and hetero-sexual emerge at different moments in history, and try to assess their shifting meanings and equally divergent effects. Or they may examine the various interests that historically have been – and indeed still are – at stake in the representation of gender and sexuality as 'natural' categories, and in the classification of people in terms of gender and sexuality as such. Queer theorists are, in other words, not so much concerned with defining and establishing sexual and gendered identities, but rather focus on the question of how such seemingly 'natural' categories come into being, and on the ways in which they function in specific cultural contexts: What does it mean to identify as homosexual or as heterosexual at a given sociohistorical moment? How are the experiences of an African-American lesbian in twenty-first century downtown Detroit different from those of a white homosexual in a nineteenth-century European suburb? What goes into the making of a man, and how does a woman become a woman? How can we explain the existence of 'masculine' women and of 'feminine' men, if biological sex is taken to be a 'natural' given?

Such questions had, of course, been variously explored by both feminist, and lesbian and gay scholars, well before de Lauretis attempted to shift the focus of critical sexuality studies by coining the phrase 'queer theory'. Her attempt to open up what had, by that time, become known as 'lesbian and gay studies', was nonetheless a timely one, for the early 1990s did, in fact, mark a shift in the development of this relatively young discipline. The gradual establishment and growing success of lesbian and gay studies in the (Eurowestern) academy had, inadvertently, also led to a certain immobilization of thought within the field. The insistence on the legitimacy of 'lesbian' and 'gay' identities might have been helpful in the struggle for political and personal liberation in the context of an overwhelmingly heterosexual sociocultural order, but it had also resulted in a relative neglect of the problem of sexual classification as such – whether in conformity with, or in defiance of the heterosexual imperative. Moreover, the all but exclusive focus on sexuality within lesbian and gay studies had obscured the operations of other differences, such as those of 'race'/ethnicity and class, both within the (inter)discipline of sexuality studies itself and within society at large. The major impetus for the shift of focus in lesbian and gay studies, however, came from the gradual establishment, in the course of the 1980s, of poststructuralist and deconstructive thought, according to which any form of identity is a sociocultural and, indeed, largely discursive, construct, rather than a given or a natural fact.

As a result of these developments, a growing number of scholars began to turn to theoretical issues of a much more fundamental nature than had been called for during the days of social struggle and political activism. As suggested before, this shift in interest was partly a response to the gradual acceptance of the phrase 'lesbian and gay studies' itself which, having lost its revolutionary ring, had become somewhat of a limitation to radical, innovative thought. Another aspect that called for a shift in theoretical direction was the relative colour-blindness of gay and lesbian studies, which tended to focus largely on the problems and concerns of gay white men and lesbian women, to the neglect of black homosexuals and lesbians, and of people of colour. A growing awareness of these limitations/blind spots within lesbian and gay studies itself productively converged with the establishment of social constructionism and poststructuralism in the Eurowestern academy generally. Around the time that de Lauretis introduced the phrase 'queer theory' to mark a critical theoretical shift in radical sexuality studies, philosopher Judith Butler – commonly regarded as one of the founders of queer theory – and literary critic Eve Kosofsky-Sedgwick published their respectively seminal studies, *Gender Trouble* (1990) and *The Epistemology of the Closet* (1990). The American journal *differences* devoted several thematic issues to 'queer' topics, and the concept subsequently became the operative analytical tool in countless studies on a wide range of social-cultural phenomena (Doty, 1993; Gever and Breyson, 1993; Ringer, 1994; Brett, *et al.*, 1994).

Since queer theorists are mainly concerned with deconstructing traditional critical models and modes of thought, and with calling into question any form of 'common sense' knowledge or 'natural' meaning, it is very hard to define what the queer project is, or even to map out its parameters (Turner, 2000; Sullivan, 2003). While some queer critics seek to subvert established notions of 'natural (hetero)sexuality' from a predominantly philosophical or theoretical perspective, others try to show the ubiquitous presence of 'queerness' in a social/cultural reality that nonetheless assumes normative heterosexuality as its foundation. Yet others attempt to denaturalize all forms of gender and sexual identity, by analyzing their various permutations as performative processes whose success depends on the enactment of socially imposed, hence historically shifting, and largely unconsciously internalized rules of appropriate behaviour. And yet others celebrate a form of sexual multiplicity or plurality as a means for bringing about socio-political change.

What all queer theorists nonetheless share in common is, on the one hand, a central focus on sexuality as one of the most important organizing principles of both society and individual subjectivity and, on the other, a profound distrust of any form of heteronormative categorization, irrespective of whether it is obtained on social, political, cultural, collective, and/or personal/subjective levels. By disrupting normative chains of thought on gender and sexuality, queer theorists not only seek to produce alternative theoretical models, but also to open up alternative modes of being, and make them equally available to those who do, and to those who do not, consciously identify as queer. With these underlying thoughts in mind, we now return to the literary tomboy as an empowering configuration of subversive, queer desire.

Escape fantasy

The enormous success of Louise M. Alcott's bestseller, immediately after its release and for many decades to come, indicates, first, that leading a traditional woman's life – and especially being confined to home and hearth – was not a particularly attractive prospect in the eyes of many young female readers. The unorthodox figure of Jo March offered them the possibility, at least imaginatively, to escape from established gender conventions, even if the spirit of independence, as represented by this prototypical tomboy, remains restricted to a phase of development that would later come to be known as adolescence. For Jo March, too, eventually succumbs to prevailing gender norms, albeit by marrying the atypical figure of Professor Bhaer, a man who appears to be a role model, a substitute father, and a close friend to her, rather than the proverbial knight in shining armour. In short, Bhaer is far removed from the traditional male figure who, in the bourgeois context of the nineteenth-century novel, served to guarantee the teleological operations of both the romantic plot and of prevailing gender scenarios.

In the collective consciousness of nineteenth-century North America, female rebelliousness had to be confined to the transitional phase between childhood and adulthood. This suggests that the literary figure of the tomboy, in her distinct, yet inexpressible queerness, represented a threat to established gender relations in everyday social reality. The enforced limitations of conventional women's lives, in particular the lives of adult, hence sexually less innocent, white middle-class women, were nonetheless poignantly brought to the fore in contemporary literary texts, especially in a genre that, following Kate Chopin's *The Awakening* (1986), would be designated, 'the novel of awakening'. The female protagonists of such novels and short stories experience a process of growing self-awareness, usually more or less obliquely defined in terms of sexual awakening, after which they can no longer resign themselves to their assigned roles of wives and mothers. Most of these women pay for their unruly behaviour with their own lives: at the end of her 'awakening', Chopin's protagonist Edna Pontellier walks desperately out into the sea, never to return. The elusive main eponymous heroine of Henry James's novella *Daisy Miller* (1986 [1878]) meets with a similar fate. Having, in the earlier parts of the novella, cheerfully danced through the pages as a wayward and defiant example of the 'American girl', her subsequent existence as an adult woman is inevitably doomed: her transgressions against sexual and gender conventions eventually render her victim to the Spanish flu. A stifling marriage, death, or both: these are the most common destinies of unruly adult female characters in nineteenth-century American novels.

Against this backdrop, it may be surprising that the tomboy – as a legitimate configuration of female rebellion, dissidence, and revolt – could exist at all, not merely in the United States, but in Western culture as a whole. A partial explanation for this may be found in the fact that the pre-adult stages of female development were, at the time, considered to be absolutely sexually innocent. In order to carefully preserve this idea – which continued to hold sway up until the early years of the twentieth century – it was necessary for the majority of literary tomboys to be ultimately kept under heterosexual control through the enforced assumption of their appropriate positions within the system of adult gender relations (Rich, 1980). Their surrender to dominant gender regimes usually also signified the end of their literary existence. The tomboy's eventual insertion into the heterosexual order often strikes readers as highly contrived and implausible as, for instance, in the case of Jo March. Numerous surveys indicate great disappointment among readers over their heroine's marriage to Professor Bhaer; an unfortunate course of events that many simply decide to ignore or deny, by disregarding the story's ending and concentrating their attention on the middle parts instead. This suggests that the tomboy's sexual innocence was hardly self-evident and that, more often than not, it had to be – sometimes violently – imposed.

Beyond innocence

Had it, in the nineteenth century, still been possible to conceive of sexuality as an exclusively adult phenomenon and to attribute to children and youngsters an absolute sexual innocence, by the beginning of the twentieth century, this dream had been definitively put to death. There is no general agreement among cultural historians about the precise historical moment at which 'adolescence' began to be recognized as a distinct phase of human development (Dalsimer, 1986: 4). However, its explicitly sexual connotations may be traced to the 'invention of sexuality' *per se* in the nineteenth century (Foucault, 1990), and to the dissemination of the ideas of the Viennese psychiatrist Sigmund Freud (1856–1939) at the beginning of the twentieth century. Especially Freud's assumption of a polymorphous infantile sexuality, in tandem with his suggestion that a (hetero)sexual object choice is by no means the result of a natural course of events, but rather the precarious outcome of a complex process of psychosexual development – a process, moreover, that does not reach its (provisional) completion until the stage of pre-adulthood – have contributed significantly to the subsequent, general acceptance, at least in the Western world, of a notion of adolescence as by far the most important phase in the process of identity formation.

The significance attributed to the adolescent phase issues directly from the fact that the categories of gender and sexuality are neither naturally given nor stable or fixed once and for all. Indeed, as Jacqueline Rose suggests:

> the fact that Freud used a myth to describe how [sexual and gender] ordering is meant to take place (the myth of Oedipus) should alert us to the fictional nature of this process, which is at best precarious, and never complete.
>
> (Rose, 1993: 14)

Since the possibilities for infantile identification and desire – the founding principles of subjectivation – are virtually infinite and ultimately uncontrollable, powerful ideological measures are required to maintain the fiction of a natural (hetero)sexuality, and to ensure normative gender development (Butler, 1990). In this context, the 'invention' of adolescence acquires an important, enabling role.

The explicitly sexual connotations of adolescence within both medical-sexological and in psychoanalytical discourses notwithstanding, the twentieth-century notion of adolescence has primarily operated as a social-discursive 'technology' (de Lauretis, 1987; Foucault, 1988), whose primary function is to ensure the young person's insertion into the dominant gender system. By suggesting a direct connection between body, gender, and (heterosexual) desire, the institutionalized concept of adolescence thus functions as an 'ideological apparatus' (Althusser, 1984), which urges children to take up their social positions as (hetero)sexually gendered subjects. As such, the concept operates as an instrument of constraint.

At the same time, however, adolescence is generally recognized as a period of legitimate rebellion, a necessary phase of emotional and mental confusion, (sexual) experimentation, and irresponsibility. Such instability is, at least in the Western world, the exclusive prerogative of adolescents. Adults – with the possible exception of artists and similarly 'anomalous' subjects – are henceforth expected to conform to the rules of the social order, especially to the founding rules of gendered heterosexuality that maintain the existence of the sociosymbolic order as such. It is not so surprising, therefore, that the period of adolescence in retrospect tends to evoke ambivalent feelings. On the one hand, one's teenage years represent a period of anxiety and sexual confusion, coupled with a devastating sense of non-existence and non-significance; on the other, the period marks a space/time in which the subjective process has not yet been fully reined in by the constraints and demands of a given sociosymbolic order. Because such restrictions tend to impose themselves much more powerfully, and to much more limiting effect, on girls than on boys, the figure of the female adolescent takes up a specific position within Western culture; a position that, with all the contradictions it involves, simultaneously constitutes its radical potential.

Borderline figure

The general terms in which I have thus far described adolescence, that is, as a crucial stage in the process of self-becoming, may suggest that we are dealing with a universal phenomenon that happens to everybody everywhere in the same way and to the same effect. This is definitely not the case. Different cultures define the transitional period between childhood and adulthood in different ways, and thus, rather than a period prompted and marked by distinct stages of physical development, adolescence is a cultural and social phenomenon that has acquired different meanings at different moments in history, as well as cross-culturally. The form of adolescence at the focus of this chapter is clearly an invention of a nineteenth-century white, Western, bourgeois culture, one of whose main interests it was to efficiently impose a distinct social order on distinct segments of its population, preferably through a system of self-regulation. This becomes effectively, and occasionally heartbreakingly, clear from the adolescent quest of one of the best-known twentieth-century North-American incarnations of the nineteenth-century *tomboy*: Frankie Adams, the protagonist of Carson McCullers' novella, *The Member of the Wedding* (1962).

The Member of the Wedding relates the events that take place in the course of slightly more than a week in the life of twelve-year-old Frankie Adams. Frankie – whose mother, we learn, has died in childbirth – spends the long, hot summer days, while her father is out to work, talking to and playing cards with black housekeeper Berenice Sadie Brown, and her six-year-old cousin, John Henry West. Throughout that last week of August in 1944, World War II, which would come to end with the Allied victory a year later, figures ominously in the background. While not directly affecting the course of narrative events, the war provides a specific historical setting that adds to the gloomy atmosphere that permeates the novella. Like most of her other novels and short stories, McCullers (1917–1967) situates the story of Frankie Adams, whose name, in the course of the narrative, changes first into F. Jasmine, and subsequently, into Frances, in a provincial town in the Deep South of the United States. Although most of McCullers' characters can be classified as eccentric, lonely, and dislocated people, who are often depicted in rather grotesque terms, Frankie, and the character of Mick Kelly in *The Heart is a Lonely Hunter* (1940), are the only representations of the female adolescent in the writer's oeuvre.

Up until the 1970s, both male and female adolescent characters in McCullers' work were largely analyzed in putatively gender neutral terms. Such readings, in which the initiation into adulthood tends to be presented as a universal phenomenon, were subsequently called effectively into question by feminist critics. Such critics not only directed their focus to the specificity of the *female* adolescent process, but also foregrounded the significance of the background of Southern culture against which its operations, in McCullers' work, are set. The significance of this particular cultural-geographical location is closely linked up with the ideal of femininity personified by the so-called Southern Belle, the archetypical upper-class young woman, who is both elegant, hospitable, and flirtatious, and at the same time, emphatically chaste, decent in her appearance, and extremely well-mannered. The all-pervasive image of Southern womanhood imposes distinct restrictions on the possibilities for achieving adult femininity for McCullers' tomboy characters. Feminist critics have correctly emphasized the gender-specific and cultural aspects of Frankie's adolescence struggle. Thus, they have opened up possibilities for analyzing, in gender-critical terms, the specificity of strictly defined cultural inscriptions of this 'formative' stage in subjective development.

What such feminist readings have markedly failed to do, however, is critically to interrogate, or even to take into account, the sexual dimensions – as aspects that are just as crucial and, indeed, indissolubly related to those of gender – of the adolescent female figure. In order to do justice to the fundamental sexual ambivalence, or queerness, of the tomboy character, it is therefore necessary not only to adopt a gender-sensitive but also, if not primarily, a sexually sensitive critical perspective. A feminist perspective that is exclusively, or predominantly, focused on gender hence needs to be supplemented with, and in fact modified by, an explicitly queer critical framework.

On the face of it, the protagonist of *The Member of the Wedding* does not depart dramatically from most of McCullers' other adult characters, in that they are all presented as fundamental outsiders, 'loose persons', or deviants – in short, as freaks. The word 'freak' here is not used in its contemporary sense, to describe somebody with an unusual personality or special talent, but rather to suggest its earlier, less politically correct meaning, to define a physically distorted or deformed body. However, the fact that we are dealing with a *female* adolescent gives Frankie's freakishness particular significance. As Rosi Braidotti has argued, women's bodies, being 'capable of defeating the notion of fixed *bodily form*', for example, during pregnancy, have traditionally been regarded as 'morphologically dubious' (Braidotti, 1994: 80). Frankie, moreover, additionally finds herself hovering on the boundary between childhood and adulthood and, because of her male identifications and desires, in a sort of liminal state between masculinity and femininity. Being positioned in between everything, as a borderline figure that fundamentally calls into question any form of stable identity, the twentieth-century tomboy therewith acquires revolutionary significance. The body of the female adolescent, as a configuration of both gender *and* sexual ambivalence, represents a space/time of unlimited becoming, of infinite possibilities of being. As such, she operates as a source of attraction and, at the same time, as a potentially undermining force, 'challenging the very notion of discrete (feminine) identity' (Gleeson-White, 2003: 12). At once a site of resistance and a site of monstrous becoming, her significance resonates far beyond the bounds of established age categories.

Freak

In the first part of the novella, the threatening implications of her sense of non-belonging dominate Frankie's consciousness. Her masculine appearance and her equally unfeminine pursuits – she sports a close crew-cut, usually walks around in a BVD-undershirt, shorts, and sneakers, loves throwing knives, and dreams of joining the army – have, up until now, been fully socially acceptable. At the age of twelve, however, she is expected to begin the transformation from tomboy into Southern Lady. This typical 'point of no return' painfully instils itself upon our heroine when her father, at the beginning of the summer, jocularly remarks that the 'great big long-legged twelve-year-old blunderbuss' she has become can no longer 'sleep with her old Papa'

(McCullers 1962 [1946]: 32; hereafter *MW*). Suddenly being banished from the 'innocent' realm of childhood, Frankie ends up with a 'queer tightness in her chest' that lasts all summer and that forces her to reflect upon 'who she was and what she was going to be in the world' (*MW*: 32). Her dreams – of travelling all over the world, to South America, Hollywood, or New York City, of flying aeroplanes, and of becoming the most famous radio reporter of all times – in no way correspond with the prescribed rules of Southern womanhood. Because she fails to conform to prevailing gender conventions and persists in her disruptive tomboy identity, she is excluded from everyone and everything. Her main source of grief during this endless hot summer is, hence the fact that she appears to be unfit to be a member of anything. Not being a boy, she cannot become a marine and join the war, the Red Cross will not take her blood because she is too young, and the older girls, the 'club-members' who, until this summer, had allowed her to hang on 'like a younger member of their crowd' (*MW*: 17), now scorn her company, and walk by her window at night, 'dressed in clean, fresh dresses' (*MW*: 113).

Frankie's anxious thoughts about her dislocation in the world, about her non-membership, and her fear of eternal exclusion, persistently return her to her own freakishness, and especially to the uncontrollability of her body. As suggested above, the body of the female adolescent functions in heteropatriarchal culture as a primary site of the struggle over the meanings of femininity and heterosexuality. Whereas pubescent boys are encouraged to explore their bodies and develop their physical abilities, and expected to grow into tall and strong men, girls are implicitly and, more often explicitly, given to understand that they should keep the excessive operations of their unruly flesh firmly in check. It is no coincidence, therefore, that Frankie's liminal position is consistently described in terms of 'tightness' and constriction which, at a certain moment, forces her to reflect that 'it was better to be in a jail where you could bang the walls than in a jail you could not see' (*MW*: 184). However, her body refuses to play by rules and, in its relentless growth, appears to insist on breaking free from the straitjacket of traditional femininity, leaving Frankie helpless and afraid:

> She stood before the mirror and she was afraid. It was the summer of fear for Frankie, and there was one fear that could be figured in arithmetic with paper and a pencil at the table. This August she was twelve and five-sixths years old. She was five feet and three-quarter inches tall, and she wore a number seven shoe. In the past year she had grown four inches, or at least that was what she judged. Already the hateful little summer children hollered to her: 'Is it cold up there?' And the comments of grown people made Frankie shrivel on her heels. If she reached her height on her eighteenth birthday, she had five and one-sixth growing years ahead of her. Therefore, according to mathematics and unless she could somehow stop herself, she would grow to be over nine feet tall. And what would be a lady who is over nine feet tall? She would be a Freak.
>
> (*MW*: 25)

Whereas it at first seems as if Frankie is merely trapped in the sweltering heat of the kitchen, and in the small provincial town from which she longs to escape, it swiftly becomes clear that her unspeakable fears this summer are directly linked to her (in)ability to meet the strict terms of heterosexual femininity. That femininity and heterosexuality are indissolubly interrelated is confirmed when Berenice urges Frankie 'to begin thinking about a beau . . . a nice little white beau', and to this purpose, 'to change from being so rough and greedy and big', and to 'fix [her]self up nice in [her] dresses . . . and speak sweetly and act sly' (*MW*: 98). And although Frankie does not care at all about the heterosexual role that Berenice tries to impose on her – 'I don't want any beau. What would I do with one?' – her lack of interest in adult (hetero)-sexuality does in no way diminish her fear of her own startling and unmanageable body nor, indeed, her growing sense of disconnection from the world, a world 'fast and loose and turning faster and looser and bigger than it had been before' (*MW*: 46).

That Frankie's fear primarily revolves around her own incomprehensible self is poignantly reflected in her anxious identification with the Freaks she has seen at the 'Chattahoochee Exposition' when it came to visit her hometown last October. From among the assorted inhabitants of 'The House of Freaks' – The Giant, The Midget, The Wild Nigger, The Pin Head, The Alligator Boy, and The Half Man-Half Woman – it had been the latter in particular who had evoked her fear and fascination. But she 'was afraid of all the Freaks', for it had:

> seemed to her that they had looked at her in a secret way and tried to connect their eyes with hers, as though to say: we know you. She was afraid of their long Freak eyes. And all the year she had remembered them, until this day.
>
> (*MW*: 27)

Afraid that she might be a freak herself, Frankie seeks refuge in the domestic safety of the kitchen. The only people she feels somehow connected to this summer are Berenice and John Henry, but because of the respective ways in which these figures are also fundamentally 'other' to her – in terms of age, race, and gender – her kitchen companions are not particularly helpful in trying to find a recognizable sociocultural position. Feeling trapped in this unusual triangular relationship, she must try to escape from herself. Listing all the things that she longs to do – 'to leave this town'; '[to be] going somewhere for good'; 'to have a hundred dollars, and just light out and never to see this town again', her ultimate desire is '[to be] somebody except me' (*MW*: 12). This wish enables her to develop a fantasy that should put an end to all her troubles: she dreams of becoming a 'member' of her brother Jarvis' and his fiancée Janice Evans' wedding. Her belief in this dream, as well as the pressing need to escape from the stifling and paralyzing heat of the kitchen, eventually force Frankie actually to attempt to meet the requirements of ideal Southern womanhood.

Failed membership

In the novella's second, middle section, we meet Frankie in a new guise, and under her newly chosen name, F. Jasmine. Convinced that her brother and his fiancée are 'the we of me' (*MW*: 52), she envisages a new future for herself, far away from the sweltering Southern heat. She pictures herself, after the wedding – an event taking place in the attractively cool city Winter Hill – entering a world with Jarvis and Janice, a world in which she will have her place, a world in which she can be someone. The fact that F. Jasmine suddenly feels 'included' in the world and 'connected' to everyone and everything she sees, now that she has become a 'member' of a completely fictitious trinity (*MW:* 59), underlines the constructed, and hence imaginary, nature of the sex/gender system, to which one must nonetheless submit oneself in order to acquire a recognizable social position. F. Jasmine's somewhat naive attempts to play by the rules of traditional sexual and gender relations not only point up the artificial nature of heteronormative gender roles but, more importantly, also make painfully clear that there is a price to be paid, especially for girls, if one wants to be 'known and recognized' (*MW:* 73) as a socioculturally viable subject (Wittig, 1992).

To prepare for the wedding, the first thing for F. Jasmine to do is to scrub herself clean, and thus to erase the marks of boyishness from her body. Berenice admonishes her to '[g]et clean for a change. Scrub your elbows and fix yourself nice. You will do very well' (*MW:* 28). Squeezed into her 'pink organdie dress', and wearing her 'patent leather shoes', F. Jasmine sets out into town to buy a new dress. The artificiality and strangeness of her feminine trappings dawns on her when she tries 'automatically to lift the Mexican hat that she had worn all summer until that day': finding nothing, her 'gesture wither[s] and her hand fe[e]l[s] shamed' (*MW:* 72). The idea that she is now a member of something, that she is finally 'included,' even if only in her imagination, nonetheless puts a temporary end to her fears. F. Jasmine is no longer afraid when she thinks about the world. The world no longer is 'fast and loose and turning, faster and looser and bigger than ever it had been before' (*MW:* 46). The more people in town she tells about the forthcoming wedding, and about her envisaged place in it, the stronger her 'wedding frame of mind' (*MW:* 89) becomes, and the more connected she feels, no longer alone.

Her intense 'need to be known for her true self and recognized' (*MW:* 74) forces F. Jasmine to assume the tokens of heterosexual femininity without, however, grasping their immediate significance nor their potential implications. How contrived and complex the rules for the proper performance of a self-evident, and putatively natural, femininity actually are, emerges when Berenice later points out that F. Jasmine's choice for a wedding dress is not quite appropriate. In her 'orange satin evening dress', silver slippers and with a silver ribbon in her hair, she looks, Berenice dryly observes, like a 'human Christmas tree in August' (*MW:* 107). F. Jasmine thus fails miserably in her attempts to meet the terms of Southern womanhood. Indeed, she almost renders traditional femininity into a caricature. This does not prevent her, however, with her tomboyishness being provisionally stripped off, from making herself unwittingly available for the heterosexual plot underlying the binary gender system. Her glorious day in town, the day before the wedding, the day on which her 'need to be recognized for her true self was for the time being satisfied' (*MW:* 76), ends with her being sexually assaulted by a drunken soldier in a cheap hotel room. F. Jasmine barely escapes from this most common female 'fate' by knocking the red-haired aggressor out with a water jug.

In the third and final part of *The Member of the Wedding*, the protagonist reappears under her new name Frances. The section opens with a flashback, in which the disastrous unravelling of Frankie's/F. Jasmine's wedding fantasy comes glaringly to light. Her memories of the entire wedding day have turned into a nightmare for Frances, since 'all that came about occurred in a world beyond her power'. Despite her desperate pleas – 'Take me! Take me!' – her brother and his bride had driven off, away from her, into their newly shared lives, while Frances had been forced to ride back home on the bus with her father, Berenice, and John Henry. Inconsolable in her helpless disappointment – '[she] wanted the whole world to die' (*MW:* 168) – Frances forges a new plan to escape from her frustrating and constricting life: 'The wedding had not included her, but she would still go out into the world' (*MW* 175). But her attempt to run away equally fails: the police find her before she has even left town, and she is once again delivered at her father's doorstep.

In the few remaining pages, the story is swiftly wrapped up, with great narrative distance. Frances finds a new girlfriend, but is also getting ready to move with her father to another city. Berenice decides to get married just once more – to her fifth husband. John Henry tragically dies of meningitis. This speedy, almost hasty, narrative conclusion suggests that it is not the narrative events themselves, but rather the struggles and inner conflicts of the protagonist that form the central focus of *The Member of the Wedding*. On the one hand, Frankie is eager to be somebody, and to belong – to anyone or anything – and thus, to be accepted as a member. On the other hand, however, she refuses to acknowledge the limitations inherent in traditional processes of gendered and sexualized becoming. As the materialization of such contradictory needs and desires, and as the embodiment of all the possibilities suggested by her 'unfinished' condition, the borderline figure of the female adolescent can be argued to be intrinsically subversive.

Imaginary space

Neither child nor adult, endowed with ambivalent gender attributes, fluctuating between boyishness and girlishness, and with no fixed place in the world, the figure of the tomboy represents 'possibilities of being' (Gleeson-White, 2003: 31), suggesting a productive potential of endless transformation. Being unfinished, the (female) adolescent often suffers from the anxieties produced by her own undefinability, and from the pain inflicted by a world in which the boundaries between genders, between age categories, and between what is normal and what is abnormal, are carefully drawn and strictly maintained. The price to be paid for such 'abnormality' is either social exclusion, or being branded as a freak. As a literary configuration, the female adolescent can be interpreted as an open-ended formation, an ambivalent time/space, at once attractive and disconcerting. Julia Kristeva describes the 'mythic figure' of the literary adolescent as 'less an age category than an open psychic structure' (Kristeva, 1990: 8), a figure who maintains a 'right to the imaginary' that is lost to adults, but that may be regained 'as a reader or spectator of novels, films, paintings . . . or as artist' (ibid.: 11).

Under the protective cover of linguistic or symbolic ordering, the reader's/ spectator's imaginary investment in the adolescent, Kristeva goes on to suggest, 'initiates a psychic reordering of the individual' (ibid.: 8) and thus allows for a rewriting of the story of our selves.

The configuration of the female adolescent does not merely function as an 'open psychic structure' that opens up possibilities for the 'genuine inscription of unconscious [psychic] contents within language' (ibid.: 9) and, as such, a potential escape route from the straightjacket of psychically deeply inscribed gender rules. It is above all in her queerness, because of her fundamentally sexual indefiniteness and infiniteness, that the erotically overdetermined time/space of the literary adolescent constitutes a revolutionary configuration. Since, at the most profound levels of subjectivation, the boundaries between identification and desire cannot be clearly drawn, the tomboy's unstructured sexuality does not allow for a split between normative and deviant forms of sexual desire. Only a queer perspective enables us to bring the radical sexual potential of this particular woman warrior to the surface.

As the representation of an infinite, queer, yet creative process of becoming, unrestricted by social-sexual regulation, the configuration of the female adolescent can be regarded as a transformational force, as the embodiment of a radical potential, which generates possibilities for new and alternative modes of self/becoming, in interaction with one another. As such, the significance of this borderline figure extends well beyond the age categories it simultaneously inscribes. The female adolescent subject is a genuine woman warrior, because she represents a challenge to any form of normative identity, to any presumably fixed and stable mode of gendered and sexualized being. What we, as readers, are confronted with, is the fundamental indeterminacy of the subjective process as such, so that, in our encounters with (female) adolescents, we are forced to acknowledge the open-endedness of all forms of adult subjectivity, including our own. But more than anything else, the literary tomboy confronts us with the infiniteness, as well as the uncontrollability, of our own desires, sexual and otherwise. In her irreducible queerness, in her liminal state between childhood and adulthood, and between masculinity and femininity, the female adolescent is a virtual threshold figure and, as such, radically subversive. At once attractive and disturbing, she represents the possibility of infinite change and ongoing transformation, of becoming rather than being. The indeterminacy of her 'lines of flight' defines her promise as well as her inexorability.

Questions for further research

1   What is the common fate of rebellious women in nineteenth- and twentieth-century Western literature? Why do you think this is?

2   Why could the figure of the tomboy still be seen as an 'innocent' role model in the nineteenth century, but no longer in the twentieth century? Illustrate your answer by giving several examples of twentieth-century tomboys.

3   On what grounds can the figure of the tomboy be regarded as a representative 'queer dilemma'? Incorporate a definition of the term 'queer' in your answer, and explain the relationship between gender studies and queer studies.

4   What is the most important difference between queer studies and lesbian/gay studies? Try to find out if there are universities in your country that offer queer studies and/or lesbian and gay studies programs.

5   Why does the protagonist's name in Carson McCullers' *The Member of the Wedding* change in each of the novella's constituting parts?

6   Why is it, especially from a queer perspective, important to read the figure of the tomboy primarily as a cultural configuration, and not as an embodied human being? Compare, in this respect, Chapters 7 and 11.

Disciplines

PART
II

Madonna's crucifixion and the woman's body in feminist theology

Anne-Marie Korte

8.1 Pop star Madonna's crucifixion scene from Confessions on a Dance Floor.

In the summer of 2006 Madonna, America's greatest female pop star ever, once again managed to upset many people all over the world with a provocative performance. This time it involved her staging a crucifixion scene for the *Confessions on a Dance Floor* tour, a show she performed in the United States as well as in a number of European countries. In this show Madonna, suspended on a huge shining silver cross and wearing a thorn crown, sang one of her already famous songs called 'Live to Tell', orchestrated for the occasion with an organ-laden, 'churchly' sound. At the end of this song, when Madonna stepped down from the cross and kneeled on stage in a gesture of prayer, pictures of African AIDS orphans and texts from the New Testament were projected onto a big screen behind her:

> For I was hungry and you gave me food, I was thirsty and you gave me drink, a stranger and you welcomed me, naked and you clothed me, ill and you cared for me, in prison and you visited me.

These are Jesus' words from the Gospel of Matthew (25, 35–36); and these sayings refer to the Christian summons to love God as well as one's neighbour, in particular the one who is helpless or in pain. 'Whatever you did for one of these least ones, you did for me' (Matt., 25, 40), was the message that shone in large letters over Madonna's head.

This crucifixion performance was denounced, reviled, and qualified as pompous and melodramatic.[1] Madonna was not only accused of megalomania and bad taste, but her act was also denounced as blasphemous and sacrilegious. She was fiercely criticized by religious organizations in the United States, but later met similar reactions in Europe too. In Rome, the Catholic, Muslim, and Jewish leaders united to condemn her decision to stage her crucifixion scene when performing – on a Sunday – in the Italian capital, a stone's throw away from Vatican City. Roman Catholic Church leaders, in particular, declared her act was disrespectful, provocative, and a publicity stunt in bad taste: 'Being raised on a cross with a crown of thorns like a modern Christ is absurd. Doing it in the cradle of Christianity comes close to blasphemy.' The Vatican cardinal Ersilio Tonini called Madonna's crucifixion scene an 'act of public hostility' towards the Roman Catholic Church. But other Christian churches too emitted negative verdicts. The Russian Orthodox leaders judged Madonna's act to be blasphemous and the female Lutheran bishop of Hanover, Margot Kässmann – the first woman ever to hold this ecclesiastical position in Germany – declared that 'to put oneself in the place of Jesus is an extraordinary manifestation of an inflated ego'.

In almost all countries where Madonna's *Confessions* tour was scheduled, actions were initiated by Christian organizations to stop performances of the show, or at least prohibit the crucifixion part. In Italy, the Vatican tried to stop the show and in the Netherlands a Christian political party tried to prevent Madonna from staging the crucifixion scene by appealing to the Dutch minister of justice, Piet Hein Donner. Although Donner empathized with the concerns of the *Staatkundig Gereformeerde Partij* (SGP) – the Protestant Reformed Party – he held that only a court could take action against the show. He considered Madonna's performance to be a reprehensible way of attracting attention at the expense of the deepest feelings of many people. But Donner warned that the fact that feelings had been hurt did not imply that the act could be classified as intentional blasphemy in the legal sense. The youth wing of the SGP announced they would file a lawsuit against Madonna for blasphemy following the Amsterdam shows. 'The SGP youth wing regrets that the freedom of expression is declared to be so sacred that insulting the Son of God is part of that freedom', it said in a statement. But also more violent actions were undertaken. In the Netherlands, a pastor of the Dutch Reformed Church announced a bomb threat – a hoax, as it turned out. Six bombs would explode in the Amsterdam football stadium at the moment that Madonna would perform her crucifixion scene.

What is less well-known and discussed in the media, is that Madonna's crucifixion act was also highly appreciated and admired. Pictures and clips of this scene were shared on the Internet, and comments on websites and weblogs showed that Madonna's performance in this act was considered to be impressive, moving, and inspiring, especially with the young. But at the same time the authenticity and sincerity of this crucifixion scene, and of Madonna's motives, were the subject of heated debate on the Internet. Madonna herself explained that the message of her crucifixion scene was concerned with the ongoing importance of fighting AIDS and taking care of the millions of AIDS orphans in Africa; a message which is, according to her, fully in the spirit of the teachings of Jesus. She stated that the act she performed is not unlike that of a person wearing a cross or 'taking up the cross' as mentioned in the Bible. She did not consider her performance to be anti-Christian, nor sacrilegious or blasphemous. 'It is my plea to the audience to encourage mankind to help one another', she said. 'I believe in my heart that if Jesus were alive today He would be doing the same thing.' The fact that Madonna, in the wake of her *Confessions* tour, adopted an AIDS orphan from Mali – who turned out to be not a full orphan – was taken both to prove and disprove the authenticity of her performance. Apparently, the crucifixion scene intensified the debate on the exemplariness and credibility of Madonna as pop icon.

Actually there are many people who believe that Madonna's personal identification with the crucifixion of Jesus Christ in this show is indeed rather questionable, if not completely unacceptable. The question I want to raise here is whether the fact that Madonna is a *female* artist and pop icon who identifies herself with the central Christian symbol of the crucifixion, contributed to the controversy – the reactions of both aversion and admiration – surrounding her crucifixion act. What exactly is the role of gender aspects, both in the act and in the controversy that arose from it? In order to answer this question, I will analyze Madonna's crucifixion scene from the perspective of gender studies in theology and religious studies. I will also compare Madonna's crucifixion act with other visualizations of female crucifixion and with contested works of art that address the idea of a female Christ.

Gender and religion in Madonna's crucifixion scene

Although Madonna has been the object of feminist studies and discussions for more than fifteen years, the debate whether her presence, performances, and personality cult support or rather undermine contemporary feminist agendas has not come to an end yet.[2] However, the aim of this chapter is not to find out whether Madonna 'fits' any feminist programme or theory – or vice versa. The fact that Madonna, as a female celebrity, performer, and pop icon, is able to unsettle standing feminist reflections and debates is far more interesting. Her deliberate effort to strive after this unsettling effect is even more intriguing. She states:

> I present my view on life in my work. The provocation slaps you in the face and makes you take notice, and the ambiguity makes you say, well, is it that, or is it that. You are forced to have a discourse about it in your mind.
>
> (Arrington, 1991: 58)

I consider Madonna to be first of all an extraordinarily successful business woman and second, a passionate artist with a comprehensive and interesting, though highly controversial oeuvre. The fact that she constantly and deliberately shocks and provokes in order to attract attention I take to be part and parcel of her profession as artist and performer. Or, to put it more eloquently:

> Madonna is more than a witness of the epoch, she is an active reflection of it, she is an iconoclast, and her aesthetics do not give a damn about 'good taste'. She seizes the trends of the moment with vampire-like gluttony, recycles them in her very own way, and then throws them in the face of the establishment.
>
> (Martine Trittoleno, *Vogue* (1993) in Guilbert, 2002: 148)

It is obvious that religion plays a major role in Madonna's statements and provocations. As was stated by Georges-Claude Guilbert, a French literary critic who wrote a book on Madonna as postmodern myth:

> Madonna, star, queen and divinity, but also sometimes scapegoat, is a privileged source of scandal and mythology. [. . .] Goddess and priestess of her own cult, she upsets the adepts of the more traditional cults: Christians, Muslims and Jews.
>
> (Guilbert, 2002: 160)

Madonna's crucifixion scene in the *Confessions* tour could be seen as one more instance of her well-known trademark of staging religious texts, images, symbols, and gestures in combination with hyper-sensualized and stylized gender roles, erotics, and sexuality. Being raised in the United States in an observant Roman Catholic working-class family of Italian immigrants, Madonna is familiar with Roman Catholic rituals and morals, although she maintains a firm critical distance. Together, familiarity and critique form the playground of many of her songs and clips. Her admired and despised video clips *Like a Virgin* and *Like a Prayer* are telling cases in point.

The crucifixion scene in the *Confessions* tour partly consists of religious themes and symbols that Madonna had used in earlier works, in particular the cross and the crucifix. But a closer look reveals that the crucifixion scene differs substantially from Madonna's previous controversial songs and performances. Before, Madonna had worn and handled crucifixes in ways that were perceived as sacrilegious. The Roman Catholic habit of wearing a small crucifix was challenged by Madonna who sported grotesquely enlarged crucifixes while scarcely or provocatively dressed. What was novel in the *Confessions* tour was that now she directly associated herself with the crucifixion of Christ in staging herself in the role of the one who was crucified. Although this identification already had quite a history in popular music, it was the first time in her own career that Madonna overtly and personally identified with Christ on the cross.

At first sight, gender aspects do not appear to play an important part in denouncing this scene. The objections and comments cited above do not explicitly address Madonna's womanhood and are, actually, rather general in character. Madonna mocks the Christian symbols and misuses them to attract attention, she shows disrespect for Christians and for religion in general, and she openly defies Christian churches and organizations. The reproach that she 'puts her self in the place of Jesus' is a very general objection too and is related to the respect and distance towards divine persons that the faithful should observe. But it is hard to fail to notice that the person in question here is *Madonna*, whose name, artistic history, and public reputation are all connected to consciously-styled and embodied female images and models. As will become clear, the association with the female body is a factor of major importance in the controversy surrounding the crucifixion scene.

In order to arrive at a more systematic analysis of the aspects of gender and the body that are involved in this controversy, it is necessary to relate Madonna's crucifixion scene to other contested art works that equally are thought to bring female corporeality (too) close up to the sacred symbols of established religious traditions. First, the main questions and the frame of reference applied in this analysis will be introduced.

'Iconoclash' between sacred symbols and the female body

Several recent cases of alleged blasphemy in Western countries have remarkable common traits in their contested imagery:[3] they connect live, almost palpable female bodies to the central sacred symbols of religious traditions, as for instance the sacred text of the Koran or the crucifixion of Jesus Christ. Notorious examples are, apart from Madonna's crucifixion scene, the short film *Submission – Part One* by Ayaan Hirsi Ali and Theo van Gogh (2004), and controversial works of art and performances by female artists, such as Renee Cox and Alma López, with the artists themselves appearing as Jesus Christ or the Virgin Mary (1999–2002).[4]

The works of art concerned are created by female artists and performers who state that they wish to contribute to the emancipation of women and ethnic minorities. To this end, they confront and in certain ways re-enact the religious traditions they were raised in. Their work purposefully joins emancipatory issues to the religious imagery of respective faith traditions. They focus in particular on the representation and staging of human bodies (including their own), that draw out the most sensitive aspects – nakedness, delicacy, sensuousness, vulnerability, wounds, torture, etc. According to them, this is the material or medium by which they envision their most hurtful as well as their most hopeful and joyous experiences.

Why do precisely these 'religiously embodied' works of art so easily fall prey to the accusation of blasphemy, and why do these accusations attract so much media attention? The issue at stake is far more complicated than the provocative character of combining sex and religion that many assume to be at the heart of the matter in these cases. The more fundamental issue that needs to be confronted concerns the role and meaning of gendered corporeality in the religious imagination of the three great monotheistic religions, Judaism, Christianity, and Islam. As ground-breaking feminist theologians such as Carol Christ, Rosemary Radford Ruether (1983), Judith Plaskow (1992), and Rachel Adler (1998) have shown, these religious traditions share a common heritage: in Western history and culture, female and non-white corporeality is perceived and valued at the far end of the transcendent, lofty holiness of the one God such as professed in the Jewish, Christian, and Muslim faith traditions.[5] Where in these great monotheistic religions God is seen as transcendent, sovereign, male, and not bound to material existence, women are conceived to be totally 'other' than this God. In particular, female corporeality is seen as the opposite of divine essence.[6] To connect female corporeality closely to the established symbols of divine presence and reality thus easily entails the risk of denunciations of blasphemy or sacrilege.

In addition, the Western understanding of acts of blasphemy and sacrilege contributes to the conviction that female corporeality should not be connected to the sacred images and symbols of the great monotheistic religions. In Judaism, Christianity, and Islam, the judgement of blasphemy is founded upon the understanding that core religious symbols are transcendent or God-given. According to these religions, it is no coincidence, for instance, that the symbols that refer to God are exclusively masculine, because this is how they are revealed. These symbols are therefore considered as confined and closed in actual form, content, and meaning. Affecting or transforming the form and content of one of these central symbols, for instance the Christian symbol of crucifixion, even with the aim to explore and elucidate its meaning, is almost immediately seen as an offensive act towards the origin and 'procurer' of this symbol, the transcendent God. Therefore the offensive acts of blasphemy (words and images) and sacrilege (gestures and acts) are taken to be very serious transgressions from the perspective of the faithful.

With more detachment and from a broader cultural-philosophical perspective, the accusations of blasphemy and sacrilege can also be considered as core disputes about religious identity and meaning in multicultural and multi-religious societies. They can be studied as examples of what is actually experienced, claimed, and disqualified as 'sacred'. In multicultural and multi-religious societies, clashes between different understandings of what is thought to be sacred cannot be avoided. Cultural philosopher Bruno Latour coined the term 'iconoclash' to address these situations, a neologism that combines the aspects of clashing and of iconoclasm. Iconoclash describes the unsettled – and unsettling – clash between different scientific, religious, or artistic worldviews such as engendered or embodied by an object, image, or situation. These iconoclashes characteristically create ambiguity and hesitation of interpretation, because they counter images with other images and combine aspects of image-breaking with those of image-making (Latour, 2002: 12). In an iconoclash, images combat each other without providing clarity about what exactly is at stake. The idea of an iconoclash takes into account the manifestation and actual collisions of different scientific, religious, and artistic worldviews and is therefore an excellent concept for approaching and evaluating gender aspects in contemporary accusations of blasphemy and sacrilege.

Let us return to Madonna's crucifixion scene. It follows from the above that it is, actually, the image of *female crucifixion* that determines the controversy of this scene. The image of female crucifixion enacts an iconoclash: the density of meaning of the Christian cross and the crucifixion of Jesus as the 'Son of God' collides with the problematic status of femaleness, corporeality, and sexuality in Western religious and secular imagination. Still, although the representation of female crucifixion is highly likely to cause an 'iconoclash' within Western culture, it does not follow that this image has always been experienced as blasphemous or sacrilegious, or should be experienced as such. The question of the reason why accusations of blasphemy arise – and when – is highly complex and depends on many factors. In this chapter, one such factor is discussed. I will argue that the controversy of female crucifixion is related to the actual and contemporary gender context and gender representation. In order to grasp the particular characteristics of Madonna's crucifixion scene, an exploration of some other examples of visualizing female crucifixion in Western culture is required to create a comparative context.

Late-medieval images of female crucifixion

Until the late twentieth century, the visual exposure of female crucifixion in the context of public worship and publicly exposed art was very unusual. Although Christian memory still recalls female saints and martyrs who were crucified in the first centuries AD, representations of these women did not involve their being suspended on the cross. Rather, the cross was included as one of their attributes. Interestingly, in some exceptional periods or specific contexts of European (and also Latin-American) culture, images of female crucifixion did and do appear, attracting huge attention. These depictions have in common that they appear in times and social contexts that are characterized by changing and disputed gender relations, by an increasing and more visible participation of women in churches and society, and by a fierce public debate on the nature and role of women. Caroline Walker Bynum and Margaret Miles are feminist historians of Christianity who show that in these contexts religious images and theological concepts are deployed with greater gender sensitivity. Both masculinity and femininity are emphasized, contrasted, and explored to a greater extent; and the physical as well as cultural aspects of both genders are more elaborate in art and literature (Walker Bynum, 1987, 1991; Miles, 1989). Margaret Miles argues that the first collective shift of women moving from the private to the public sphere during the European Renaissance caused female nakedness to become the focus of a newly explicit public and controversial figuration in the arts as well as in religious imagery. In this period we also find an iconographic tradition of a female crucifixion that is related to the very popular devotion of a female crucified saint, which from the fourteenth to the sixteenth century existed all over Europe.[7] The visual remnants of this cult can be found in late Medieval manuscript illustrations and paintings and in devotional sculptures that in some cases still can be seen in monasteries and churches, as for instance in St Stephen's Church in Nijmegen, the Netherlands.

This female saint was known as Saint Uncumber (or 'Sinte Ontkommer' in Dutch). According to legend, she was a noble Christian virgin who was crucified because of her refusal to denounce the Christian faith. There are several versions of her story. In most cases she is a princess, the daughter of a heathen king of Portugal. This princess was promised to the king of Sicily, also a heathen, but as she was a Christian she wanted to live a virgin life and so she refused to marry him. In answer to her prayers, she received the growth of a beard which evidently made her unsuitable for marriage. Her enraged father ordered her to be crucified, and this scene, the crucifixion of a well-dressed, crowned, and bearded woman, has become the best known depiction of St Uncumber.

She was venerated on a large scale in the High Middle Ages in Northern and Middle Europe. Her name had many local variations, but all names point towards her capacity to free people from their pains and sorrows. She was also very popular in the Netherlands, where probably both her name of Wilgefortis (meaning *virgo fortis* or 'strong virgin') and Uncumber came into being in the fifteenth century. From the late sixteenth century onwards, after Reformation and Contra-Reformation repressed the mediating role of saints and other intercessors, the cult of St Uncumber was combated and militantly suppressed by the church authorities. Most of her paintings and sculptures were destroyed.

A longstanding explanation for these extraordinary visualizations of a female crucifixion argues that they are based on a misunderstanding. The images of the crucified saint do not refer to a woman at all, but to Jesus Christ, who is depicted in the majestic style of eastern Christianity, where Christ on the cross is portrayed in the role of a king and high priest, and thus fully and richly dressed. From the twelfth century onwards this image of the crucified Christ in royal robes was venerated in Western Christianity alongside the Gothic depiction of the almost naked suffering Christ. The adoration of the so-called 'robed Christ' existed in particular in connection to the famous sculpture of the *Volto Santo* (Holy Face) or *Sante Croce* (Holy Cross) in the Cathedral of Lucca in Tuscany, which became a famous place of pilgrimage from the thirteenth century onwards. According to the 'misunderstanding' thesis, the many copies of this image that over the centuries were created and spread ceased to be interpreted as images of Christ with the symbols of sacred kingship and royal priesthood. Rather, the particular details of this image, such as the precious robe, the ornaments, the crown, and the shoes, contributed to the growing idea that the statue was, in fact, that of a woman rather than of Christ.

But far more interesting than the 'misunderstanding' thesis is the question of why and how the figure of a crucified female saint could become so important and accepted, that even an established and popular image of the crucified Christ could be taken to be representative of her. A shift of interpretation like this is not unthinkable if placed in the context of the cultural and religious transition towards a more earthly understanding of, and a more personal devotion to Christ and the saints in the later Middle Ages. In this context, the triumphal nature of the earlier crucifixes that signified Christ's victory over death increasingly gave way to a more sombre vision on human nature and existence. This changed the religious interpretation of Christ's passion and death considerably. The preferred image of Christ became centred on the scene of suffering, bleeding, and dying on the cross. This rendered Him more human and more connected to ordinary human existence. As Caroline Walker Bynum has shown, this implied that in the later Middle Ages, women could identify themselves more directly with the suffering Christ and, vice versa, that Christ could be perceived as being closer to women, in particular in the human aspects of suffering, bleeding, and dying to further new, eternal life (Walker Bynum, 1987; 1991). So, in this unique and very temporal situation of changing gender relations and a less gender exclusive understanding of the passion of Christ, female crucifixion could be imagined, depicted, and even cherished without becoming blasphemous or sacrilegious.

Late twentieth-century controversial Christa sculptures and paintings

A second example of visualization of female crucifixion consists of late twentieth-century *Christa* sculptures and paintings, notably the bronze sculpture *Christa* by the American Edwina Sandys (1974), the bronze sculpture *Crucified Woman* by the Canadian Almuth Lutkenhaus-Lackey (1976), and the three-dimensional panel *Bosnian Christa* by the British Margaret Argyle (1993).[8] These *Christas* are works of art made in the context of women's political, cultural, and religious emancipation in Western countries. They were not made as or intended to be religious works of art in the sense of objects of devotion or meditation, or objects to be placed and handled in religious settings. They reflect, according to their makers, an individual creative reworking of the central sacred symbol of Christianity, the crucifixion of Jesus Christ.

One of these artists, Margaret Argyle, sees this female Christ as a symbol that addresses the situation of Bosnian women during the ethnical cleansings and civil war in former Yugoslavia in the early 1990s: 'A Christa, which would speak about the obscenity of rape clearly and graphically.' The suffering woman on the cross created by Argyle reawakened, in her eyes, the symbolic meaning of the cross of Jesus Christ and of the faith in God who is in the world and is present wherever anyone suffers. Her panel refers to the specific suffering of women during war but at the same time it suggests the idea of the Christian cross guarding a vulva and prohibiting the violation of women's bodies.

These *Christas* all gave rise to similar reactions of indignation, which I will illustrate here by considering the example of Sandys' *Christa*. This sculpture was the first of the three works of art that was publicly exposed. But it only became perceived and disputed as controversial when, ten years after its creation, it was exhibited in a Christian ecclesiastical and liturgical setting. In 1984 it was placed near the main altar in the Episcopal Cathedral of St John the Divine in New York City, during Holy Week, when the passion, death, and resurrection of Jesus are commemorated. The display of the sculpture in this context evoked very emotional stances pro and contra, fired by church leaders and publicists on both sides of the debate. The opponents declared that the sculpture, by showing a naked suffering woman on the cross, was 'symbolically reprehensible' and 'theologically and historically indefensible', while the defending party argued that the sculpture revealed in a confronting way the inclusiveness and depth of the theological meaning of God's incarnation in Jesus Christ. After eleven days, the sculpture had to be removed from the Cathedral due to ongoing protests. Six months later, the sculpture was displayed in the Memorial Chapel of Stanford University in California, causing similarly mixed reactions.

There are two remarkable aspects about the response to the *Christas*. First, the three works of art only became contested when they were put in ecclesiastical and liturgical settings. They were not disputed while displayed in other public spaces such as museums or galleries. Only in these religious settings, when the *Christas* entered the sacred space of collective Christian remembrance and imagination, they became forms of iconoclash. Second, these contested works of art proved to be capable of bringing about theological debate on the meaning of one of the central tenets of the Christian faith: God becoming human and participating fully in humanity's existence and suffering. By suggesting similarity and comparability between the suffering of women and the crucifixion of Jesus Christ, the *Christas* more or less deliberately put a gender-critical strain on the familiar meanings of this symbol. This strain can be interpreted as a threat of erasure and destruction, but also as an invitation to reconsider and re-appropriate the meaning of this central symbol of Christianity. In these cases, both reactions occurred. The three works of art were considered blasphemous for the fact that they alter the sex of God and associate Jesus Christ with the naked body and sexuality of women, but they were also experienced as revelatory, by women as well as by men, by lay people as well as by church leaders, for connecting God and God's incarnation in Jesus Christ to the suffering of women. For the female Christ refutes the idea that only a male person can symbolize and 'bear' human suffering, and brings the actual but often neglected suffering of women ineluctably into view.

One of the reasons why these works of art did not only bring about shock and aversion, but also generated incentives to theological debate and reflection, lies in the particular gender aspects of these visualizations of female crucifixion. The *Christas* clearly show the naked body of a woman, but this body is in all cases very restrained and tenuously stylized in the characteristic pose of crucifixion. The difference between these thin female bodies and that of the suffering Christ on the cross is minimal. Pictured this way, the crucified female body has a great figural likeness to the suffering body of Christ, and in this fusion of images the naked crucified bodies of women seem to transcend their primarily sexual connotation. The sacred, solemn, and non-sexual associations summoned by the suffering body of Christ can counter or absorb the ambivalent reactions that are commonly evoked by the exposure of the naked bodies of women. This specific constellation of images has supported the acceptance of these *Christas* and generated the rise of the *Christa* as a theme in works of art all over the world in the past two decades.

However, this growing acceptance of the *Christas* still is a very uncommon and unique outcome of the clash between the central sacred symbol of Christianity and female corporeality. A discussion of two other controversial works of art by contemporary female artists may illustrate the exceptional status of the *Christas*. In these cases, as we shall see, the clash between the central sacred symbols of Christianity and the naked female body is insurmountable.

Contemporary feminist works of art figuring the artist as Jesus or Mary

Yo mama's last supper by Renee Cox (1999) and *Our Lady (of Guadalupe)* by Alma López (2001) were created more recently than the *Christas*.[9] Both are works of art by female American artists who have a Catholic and non-white background and who in their works of art address the issues of gender and racial equality. The works considered here are part of a series of photo-collages in which the artists themselves appear as Jesus Christ or the Virgin Mary. These artists do not stage crucifixion scenes, but use scenes from the Christian sacred narrative and imagination that are almost as central, such as the Last Supper, the Pieta, and, of great importance in the Roman Catholic iconography of Latin America, the appearance of Mary as Our Lady of Guadalupe (Mexico).

Yo mama's Last Supper by Renee Cox was exhibited from February to April 2001 in the Brooklyn Museum of Art in New York. Cox, an African American artist of Jamaican descent, specializes in photographic art and lives and works in New York City. Raised as a Roman Catholic in the United States, she has created a number of works in which she reworks classic Christian themes in the light of the struggle for gender and racial equality, often using herself as a model. *Yo mama's Last Supper* is a five-panel work consisting of a photographed *Last Supper* that refers to Da Vinci's famous homonymous work and features famous black artists as the apostles. Cox herself appears fully naked as Jesus Christ in the centre of the panel. She explains that she wanted to challenge the fact that both women and people of colour are cancelled in the visual representation as well as the power structure of the Christian churches, the Roman Catholic Church in particular.

The panel was first exposed at the 1999 Biennale in Venice, Italy, where it was displayed in a Roman Catholic Church in Venice, without drawing much attention. The controversy arose when it was exposed together with other works by Cox in the Brooklyn Museum's survey of work by black photographers (*Committed to the Image: Contemporary Black Photographers*) in the spring of 2001. The museum had a recent history of accusations of blasphemy: two years earlier the New York City mayor, Rudolph Giuliani, had tried to cancel a substantial part of the funding for this museum because of Chris Ofili's controversial painting of 'The Holy Virgin Mary', which was said to contain elephant dung.

This time Mayor Giuliani again accused the museum of 'anti-Catholicism' with regard to the display of Cox's *Last Supper*. The controversy rose high, because local officials of the Roman Catholic Church and the national Catholic League for Religious and Civil Rights joined forces in condemning the work, while Renee Cox defended her work very eloquently in interviews in journals and on television. As a result of this conflict, Mayor Giuliani established a commission to set decency standards for museums that received city funding.

At about the same time, in the spring of 2001, the Chicano artist Alma López exposed her *Our Lady* in the International Museum of Folk Art in Santa Fe, New Mexico, at an exhibition titled *CyberArte: Tradition Meets Technology*. López, a Roman Catholic born in Mexico, grew up in Los Angeles and became an artist and storyteller who works in paint, photography, and video. Like Cox, she addresses women's and ethnical issues in her work, as well as lesbian themes. *Our Lady* is a computerized photo-collage of the Virgin of Guadalupe, acknowledging and re-appropriating the Virgin's history as a symbol of liberty and equality for Mexican and Chicano Christians.

López copied the classic devotional picturing of Our Lady of Guadalupe and changed the Virgin into a contemporary Chicana-in-bikini after her own likeness. She replaced the male angel at the feet of Our Lady by a bare-breasted woman, thereby also hinting at her lesbian identity. Again, local Roman Catholic officials and the national Catholic League together organized a protest campaign against this 'repulsive, insulting and even sacrilegious' work of art. They demanded the immediate removal of the work from the museum and the resignation of the museum directors concerned. Local governors became involved and threatened to cancel the museum's funding. The museum officials stood firm, they defended the display of *Our Lady*, and organized a public debate on the controversy, but in the end they had to shorten the run of the whole exposition.

So, both these works of art were exhibited in museums of major American cities in the recent past and became targets in the so-called 'culture wars' of the Religious Right in the United States against 'offensive' and 'blasphemous' art that is sponsored by governmental money. The protests against exposition came from well-organized groups of Roman Catholics who did not demand the removal of these works of art from a sacred or liturgical space, but from a public museum financed by governmental funding. The offences reported by these groups concerned their identity as Roman Catholics in general rather than their personal beliefs or their central faith tenets. They accused the public museums of anti-Catholicism and disrespect for religion, thereby showing that their concerns were directly related to identity politics and the position of Roman Catholics and other Christians in a contemporary multicultural and multi-religious society.

It is most interesting that these rather general accusations and concerns of anti-Catholicism and disrespect for religious beliefs were linked to works of art that relate Jesus Christ or the Virgin Mary to a non-white female corporeality – a connection that was perceived as inappropriate or even perverse by those who felt offended. Although in these situations other works of art from this exposition could easily have been picked out for the same kind of general accusations, apparently the issue of female sexuality was considered to be the outstanding provocation.

At closer inspection, however, it becomes clear that it is not only the aspect of female nudity that makes these works of art controversial. In these cases and differently from the *Christas,* the naked female body is not a suffering, abstract, and Christ-like body, but the vital body of a coloured woman in the likeness of the artist. The distinguishable personal presence of the female artists in these sacred scenes is as problematic as their nudity. The fact that there was no reconciliation in these cases and that the complete expositions in these public museums were cancelled, indicates that the offensiveness of these works of arts could not be overcome or wiped out.

Madonna's cross: Gender representation in Madonna's crucifixion scene

I will now return to the case of Madonna's crucifixion scene and evaluate its controversy in the light of the cases I have analyzed above. First, I want to point to the fact that this scene introduces a new gender element in Madonna's use of religious imagery. In her earlier songs, clips, and performances, Madonna made abundant use of *female* religious imagery, in the sense that she played with the female characters and roles from the Christian faith tradition, in particular from the rich symbolic repertory of Roman Catholicism. Sinful and holy female persons, Eve and Mary, the temptress and the chaste maiden, the whore and the virgin: Madonna has appropriated all these contrasting female models over and again. As the feminist theologian Grietje Dresen argues, Madonna has to be permanently in utmost control of the functioning as well as the appearance of her own body in order to play this ambitious game that figures an astonishing number of impeccably reproduced religious and cultural female stereotypes. Madonna, according to Dresen, seems to have incorporated very well her Roman Catholic education in which the beauty, purity, and self-control of the 'immaculate' Virgin Mary is presented to girls as the standard of perfection (Dresen, 1998).

In the crucifixion scene of 2006, Madonna for the first time embodies a *male* religious character, who at the same time is the most outstanding, sacred, and meaningful male person in Christianity. At first sight, when looking at the crucifixion scene as actually performed on stage, there appears to be a striking resemblance with the representation of the female body in the medieval imagination of female crucifixion. Madonna, surprisingly, resigns from her usual provocations while taking on the role of the crucified Christ: she does not take off her clothes in this scene, nor is she provocatively dressed. Rather, she shows herself on the cross in a very modest, androgynous style, fully dressed with a blouse, trousers, and boots – only the beard is missing. The modesty and serenity Madonna displays resemble the gender bending and gender ambiguity of the medieval devotional paintings of St Uncumber. These paintings, as we have seen, address the redemptive significance of female crucifixion and the gender inclusiveness of divine incarnation in Jesus Christ, not overtly or provocatively, but in a rather subtle and ambiguous way.

When, in looking at Madonna's crucifixion scene her openly stated intentions with this act are taken account of, the conclusion might be that the staging of her act resembles still more the restrained feminist criticism of the makers of the *Christas*. Like them, Madonna aims at critically appropriating the symbol of crucifixion as a protest against injustice, violence, and suffering, in particular the suffering caused by AIDS that often remains unnoticed or tends to be forgotten. Like the *Christa* artists, Madonna fuses the symbol of the suffering Christ with the figure of a not-too-corporeal woman to put a gender-critical strain on the familiar meanings of this symbol. And like these artists, Madonna restages the crucifixion scene with references to contemporary situations of suffering and injustice. In Madonna's crucifixion act, the abandoned mourning women – Jesus' mother and His female friends – below and behind the cross of classical Christian iconography, are replaced by (the faces of) abandoned mournful children, the orphans and victims of AIDS.

It is possible, considering Madonna's staging of the crucifixion scene and in view of her intentions, to interpret this performance theologically as a contemporary, inclusive representation of Jesus' suffering. In doing so we may value her act as a contribution to feminist theology and liberation theology, as was suggested by some theologians (Häger, 1997; Thienen, 2007). However, although the *Christas* indeed evoked a theological impetus like that, it is doubtful whether Madonna's act could ever bring about a similar effect. In the case of Madonna, provocation dominates the scene: her objective is to advance the iconoclash itself, not to contribute to its effacement.

Moreover, Madonna's interest in religion has never been theologically focused: it consists of a combination of distrust towards institutional religion and an eclectic individual form of spirituality. Her motive for using rosaries, crosses, and religious images in her work is, in her own words:

'to take these iconographic symbols that are held away from everybody in glass cases and say, here is another way of looking at it [. . .]. The idea is to bring it down to a level that everyone can relate to it.

(Arrington, 1991: 58)

This postmodern idea that religious symbols are there 'to relate to' and 'to give meaning to' is also practised by Madonna in her own oeuvre. This becomes clear when we take a closer look at the content and the connotations of *Live to Tell*, the song that forms the musical and textual core of her crucifixion scene.

Live to Tell already had a long and burdened history in her own work. The song was originally composed for the movie *At Close Range* (1986) featuring Madonna's former husband, Sean Penn. Madonna did not act in this movie, and she only contributed with *Live to Tell,* the song that closes this film. Both the movie and the song address a very painful father-son relationship from the son's perspective. He tries to resist his unreliable and malicious father and to keep his faith in 'the beauty, goodness and truth within' as a way of surviving. In the end, the son refrains from acting out his rage against the father and does not turn to murder and violence. The song expresses the mixed feelings of fear, deception, loyalty, and compassion entertained by the son with respect to his father.

The second time this song occurred in Madonna's work was in her filmic self portrait *Truth or Dare*, launched in Europe as *In Bed with Madonna*. In this documentary film, Madonna included a life-performance of *Live to Tell* which she sang on stage, leaning on a kneeling bench. Scenes of this performance are alternated with views of Madonna stating a declaration to the press in which she opposed the Pope's condemnation of her show for reasons of blasphemy. One may guess that the painful father-son relation the song addresses is here transposed to Madonna's relation with her churchly father, the Pope.

So *Live to Tell* was already a song charged with several layers of meaning, and with personal conflicts over religious issues, before Madonna took it up again and arranged it in the form of the crucifixion scene in the *Confessions* show. The painful, ambivalent, and inescapable father-child relation, seen from the perspective of the child, seems to be the continuing theme in all these cases. This might be the reason why younger people, in particular, report to feel appealed to and moved by this song. But this state of affairs also indicates how Madonna 'relates', to use her own words, to the symbol of crucifixion: she connects this to the rather universal existential theme of the painful father-child relation. Her stance is that of the child who rebels against the fathers and priests and 'all the men who made the rules while I was growing up' (Arrington, 1991: 56). Thus Madonna's crucifixion scene is mostly informed by personal motives and a postmodern play with religious symbols.

Finally, Madonna's staging of the crucifixion scene resembles most closely those works where the female artists/photographers explicitly pose *themselves* as Jesus or Mary, such as Renee Cox and Alma López. The *presentia realis*, the real, ineluctable presence of women of flesh and blood in these works of art, intensifies the iconoclash between sacred symbol and female corporeality. In the case of Madonna, the idea of identifying the artist with the character she plays may seem unjustified, in light of the many personae Madonna assumes in her performances and her artistic strategy of continuous self-transformation. However, unlike the photographer Cindy Sherman, whose case is discussed elsewhere in this book, Madonna-the-artist does not disappear behind her creations. She rather manifests herself by and in these acts. The creation of scenes and images in which she herself, Madonna, attracts all attention, has become her trademark. Even if in her crucifixion scene there is no exposure of her body in a provocative, sensualized, or eroticized form, *Madonna* still is there. Madonna can be characterized as the prototype as well as the master of the female sexualized icon, who turns herself into a female idol. This image constantly interferes with the perception and the appraisal of her crucifixion scene. We, her audience, are relentlessly exposed to Madonna as pop star and celebrity and associate her, whether we like it or not, with the provocative, sensualized, and eroticized exhibition of her female body. This means that Madonna's crucifixion scene is not likely to lose its controversy due to its exemplary status of an iconoclash between sacred symbol and female corporeality.

Notes

1 Media reactions to Madonna's performance, as described and quoted in this paragraph, have been gathered from national and international newspapers and the Internet during the period June to December 2006.

2   For feminist and queer analyses of Madonna's person and works, see among others, Schwichtenberg (1993), Grigat (1995), Dresen (1998), Bosma and Pisters (2000), Guilbert (2002), and Fouz-Hernandez and Jarman-Ivens (2004).

3   Several recent cases of alleged blasphemy in Western counties have remarkably common traits in their contested imagery. For the background and meaning of contemporary reproaches of blasphemy and sacrilege, see among others, Lawton (1993), Levy (1993), Häger (1997), Fisher and Ramsay (2000), and Plate (2006).

4   Pictures of the works of art that are discussed in this chapter can in most cases easily be found on the Internet; see also the publications of Friesen (2001), Heartley (2004), and Clague (2005).

5   In Western history and culture, female and non-white corporeality is perceived and valued at the far end of the transcendent, lofty holiness of the one God, such as professed in the Jewish, Christian, and Muslim faith traditions. Islamic feminist theologians, such as Amina Wadud (1999), Asma Barlas (2002), and Kecia Ali (2006), have addressed this tension regarding Koran and Hadith.

6   Pioneering and challenging studies on this theme have been written by feminist theologians and philosophers Mary Daly (1973), Naomi Goldenberg (1979), Luce Irigaray (1987), Melissa Raphael (1996), and Barbara Newman (2003).

7   The discussion in this paragraph is based on art historian Ilse L. Friesen´s monograph *The Female Crucifix: Images of St Wilgefortis Since the Middle Ages* (2001).

8   For an excellent feminist-theological discussion of these works of art, see Julie Clague (2005).

9   For an interesting analysis of these works from the perspective of feminist art criticism, see Eleanor Heartley (2004).

Questions for further research

1   Until the twentieth century, women were not admitted to theology or religious studies. Women who became known for their religious writings had different opinions about this exclusion. Teresa of Ávila (Spain, 1515–1582) believed that theology was something for men as women could receive divine instructions directly and without mediation, whereas the protestant learned lady Anna Maria van Schurman (the Netherlands, 1607–1678) argued that women had the same mental capacities as men and should therefore be allowed to explore and understand divine matters. Try and reconstruct the position of these women and their arguments in light of their respective writings, historical context, and biography. The difference between theology and mysticism should provide focus to your argument. The aspects of thinking difference and thinking equality may further help to illustrate your argument.

2   Do you think that the positions of Schurman or Teresa of Ávila are still relevant today? Why?

3   Mary Daly is the founding mother of feminist theology and a true iconoclast. In her book *Beyond God the Father* she famously stated that 'If God is male, then the male is God'. She argued for abstract, genderless concepts and images of God in order to prevent the sanctioning of power structures by religion. Carol Christ countered in 'Why Women Need the Goddess' (1978 [1987]) that women had on the contrary an interest in a religious language that referred to the body, life-world, and suppressed history of women. Reconstruct the argumentation in these texts and compare the position of these two scholars in referring also to their concepts of feminism and religion.

4   Do you think that the discussion of Question 3 is relevant to the other areas of culture, such as discussed in this book?

5   Read Luce Irigaray's essay on 'Divine women' that argues in favour of the necessity of female divine images, necessary for women as identification points because otherwise they are mere negation or absence. Discuss the meaning of the Christa images from the perspective of Irigaray's argument and involve the views of the artists in your discussion, as well as this chapter and the article by Clague, 'Divine transgressions: the female Christ-form in art'.

6   Read the article by Bruno Latour of iconoclash and try and define other contemporary examples of iconoclash where religion and gender are concerned.

The rising of Mary Magdalene in feminist art history

9

Ann-Sophie Lehmann

This chapter's woman warrior is Mary Magdalene, one of the best-known and indubitably most exciting female figures in the New Testament. She is traditionally represented as the repentant prostitute, but recently this image experienced a radical metamorphosis. In the past decades, her active and intellectual role in salvation history was highlighted as a result of historical, theological, and feminist research, and the conventional identification of Mary Magdalene as a prostitute was abandoned. The adjustments in the field of scholarship have had enormous consequences for the way she is currently perceived and represented in popular culture. In the wake of the unequalled success of *The Da Vinci Code*, Dan Brown's novel (2003), she is celebrated as the most important apostle, Jesus' equal partner, and indeed the long suppressed but re-emerged female 'other' of Christianity. Rather than the embodiment of sin and repentance, she is now the epitome of courage, leadership, loyalty, and strength (Burstein and Keijzer, 2006).

The new Mary Magdalene is the outcome of a process that is often presented as a spectacular revelation: behind the biblical figure, who in the early Middle Ages was purposefully branded a whore by the patriarchal Church Fathers intent on marginalizing her role, looms an apparently truthful historical figure. However, although the active, quasi-historical woman may be a more balanced and certainly a more realistic version, in the end she is a construct, just like the passive eroticized saint. Both are the result of kaleidoscopic alterations, the product of an intricate network of signification constituted by the disparate strands of biblical narration, myth formation and historical facts, theological dogmas and interpretations, academic theories and fashionable desires. Moreover, the ruling image depends on the interests and power relations in different historical periods. If, in the past, Church Fathers had an interest in the concept of a passive sinner, then a vigorous female saint is the preferred type in the twenty-first century.

Those fluctuating interpretations have found their way in a host of concrete representations in the visual arts. The earliest depictions of Mary Magdalene date back to the early Middle Ages and today she continues to inspire a variety of fascinating and very different artworks. A feminist perspective is not necessarily required for the art historical analysis of these works. Stylistic features may guide a discussion of representations of Mary Magdalene through the ages (what does a typical baroque Magdalene look like?), or her compositional function in the artwork may form the object of study (why is Mary Magdalene kneeling down in crucifixion scenes, whereas the Virgin Mary is standing upright?). However, without a gender sensitive perspective, the answers to these questions will lack in depth and remain purely descriptive. A satisfactory analysis will have to consider how the stereotype of the fair penitent determine the lascivious nudes of the Baroque and investigate the connection between kneeling down and a particular image of femininity.

This chapter is the fruit of such an analysis. The visual story of Mary Magdalene told here serves to present various methods of interpretation in art history. Because the representations of Mary Magdalene are very diverse, she is eminently suitable for an exposition of the way interpretations of art are affected by a feminist perspective. At the same time, the analysis of Magdalene images provides the contours for outlining a historiography of the arts, including methods and theories, from a feminist perspective.

Since the earliest interventions from a feminist point of view, roughly three approaches can be distinguished in retrospect:

1 Rediscovery of female artists from the past and critical judgement of the situation for contemporary female artists (1970s)
2 Critical visual analysis of representations of women in the visual arts (1980s)
3 As a result of these phases, development of interpretative models based on psycho-analytical, semiotic, and poststructuralist theories (1990s).

Naturally, the three approaches share a number of features and are not clearly demarcated from one another. To a greater or lesser extent, each approach will be illustrated in this chapter, which moves on two planes: the core narrative about the heroine and the frame-tale about the way in which art history changed due to the impact of feminist issues.

Kneeling or squatting: Mary Magdalene's position in art

The Mary Magdalene never existed. Not, in any case, as a single coherent historical personage. Mary Magdalene is an amalgam of different women who surface at key moments in the New Testament's four gospels. Sometimes they are named Mary, but in a number of instances they are nameless. Their major common denominator is their conversion from sinner to main female disciple. Mary of Magdala was never called a prostitute in the Bible. The different Mary figures were related to each other in early Christianity and between the fifth and seventh centuries they were amalgamated into one personage. Only then was she labelled prostitute (Jansen, 1999). Given this history, Mary Magdalene could be described using the metaphor of a fan which, when opened, displays a range of historical, biblical, and apocryphal elements; but when closed, only displays a single woman (Kunstschrift, 2005; Apostolus-Cappadonna, 2006a).

In the visual arts, this woman acquires a homogenous appearance. She is young, beautiful, with her hair usually blonde and often flowing freely. She has a prominent presence at the vital scenes of the Passion: the crucifixion, burial, lament, and resurrection of Christ. Apart from the Virgin Mary, this Mary Magdalene is incontestably the most popular woman in the New Testament. The visual range of her depiction is much wider, however, than that of the Madonna. Her patched genesis, 'sinful' past, her influential existence, according to early Medieval legend, after the death of Jesus and her eventual death in old age as a hermit, all contribute to a more pliable and thrilling image. Both pliability and thrill (often eroticized) have challenged artists to create wide-ranging variants of Mary Magdalene: spectacularly naked or clothed in the finest garments on the other; with modest or strikingly expressive gestures; and in a remarkable quantity of postures. In terms of iconography, the depictions can be subdivided into roughly three groups: Magdalene in representations of the biblical narrative; as patron saint (to be recognized by her attribute, the jar of ointment); and as hermit in the wilderness.

To begin with, a number of Mary Magdalene depictions will be observed here by means of a classic art historical method, visual analysis. Such an analysis is primarily work-immanent, which implies that only the object proper will be considered, independent from contextual information about the artist, commissioner, the artwork's original place, or the comparison with other works of art in the same period. Nonetheless, visual analysis can be an important step towards feminist interpretation, because the representation is approached as a construction. A formal analysis shows that the positioning of certain objects in space, the colours chosen, the distribution of light and shadows in a painting, etc. are no objective givens, but are carefully selected with the intent to create a certain effect. The deconstruction of visual effects forms the first step in the critical analysis of the representation of women in the visual arts.

Many of the representations of Mary Magdalene, which are directly based on the biblical text, share a remarkable characteristic. Magdalene almost always occupies a position in the bottom half of the painting. Although converted into a genuine disciple of Jesus and no longer a 'fallen' woman, it appears that in being portrayed she is literally incapable of getting up from the ground and the viewer will have to look down in order to see her. The low position can be related to the scene in which she makes her first appearance in the Bible, which is also the origin of her attribute, the jar of ointment. All four gospels mention a woman anointing Jesus with precious oil in Simon's house. She pours this oil over His head in Matthew (26: 6–13) and Mark (14: 2–9); washes His feet with her tears, rubs them dry with her hair, and then anoints them in Luke (7); and anoints first His feet and then dries them (with her hair) in John (12: 1–8). The latter is the only one to identify this woman as Mary, sister of Martha and Lazarus. Those present at the scene criticize the thoughtless waste of precious oil, but Jesus understands this caring deed as an act of love and moreover as symbolically anticipating the anointment of His own dead body.

A Dutch fifteenth-century painting by Albrecht Bouts depicts the scene from the gospel of Luke in a particularly detailed fashion (Figure 9.1). In order for her tears to reach the feet of Jesus, Mary Magdalene is crouched under the table and holds her head

9.1 *Albrecht Bouts'* Mary Magdalene washes the feet of Christ in Simon's House *(after 1440)*.

very low, close to the floor. The interplay of the realistic depiction of tears, feet, hair, and head thus form the intriguing focal point of the painting. The painting encompasses two positions: on the one hand, Bouts depicts the Christian virtue of humility, but because this virtue is embodied by a woman, the biblical stance that woman is inferior to man is likewise illustrated. It would have been more advantageous for Mary Magdalene's position if she had been portrayed as anointing Jesus' head (as described in Matthew and Mark) rather than His feet. However, to my knowledge, this variant never made it to art, probably because it would have involved a superior position for the Magdalene, who in anointing Jesus' head would have towered above Him and the other men sitting at Simon's table. In other words, her superior position was textually allowed, but it was unthinkable to depict and hence manifest this superiority pictorially.

The decision to place Mary Magdalene at Jesus' feet returns in other iconographies. In representations of the crucifixion, for example, the Virgin Mary is traditionally standing to the left of the Cross and John the Evangelist to the right. The Magdalene, however, often clothed in red and with loose hair, is kneeling at His feet. This is her place both in Italy as well as north of the Alps. In the *Descent from the Cross* by the Italian Renaissance painter Rosso Fiorentino, other biblical figures are present too, but an impressive triad of grief is formed by Mary, Mary Magdalene, and John in the lower half of the composition (Figure 9.2). Interestingly, none of the three conveys the emotion of grief on their faces – Mary has fainted and her eyes are closed, John covers his face in dejection, and Magdalene averts her face from the viewer – but in their

9.2 *Rosso Fiorentino's* Descent from the Cross *(1521).*

9.3 Detail of Mathias
Grünewald's Isenheim Altarpiece
(between 1512–1516).

gestures and movements. The postures of John and Mary are conventional depictions of sorrow, but this is not the case with Mary Magdalene. Here, the artist has, it seems, experimented with posture and has in the depiction of a disorientated, crouching, pleading figure achieved a visual climax of grief.

A no less spectacular retable in Germany, roughly dating back to the same period, the so-called *Isenheim Altarpiece*, similarly makes Mary Magdalene the primary emotional protagonist. The painter Mathias Grünewald has positioned her again at Jesus' feet, her head is bent backwards and her hands are raised in an imploring gesture (Figure 9.3). In an allusion to her alleged sinful past, the Magdalene is often robed in expensive garments. In Grünewald's painting, the extravert expression of grief is emphasized even more by the beautiful folds of her veil and the lavishly flowing blonde hair (another allusion to prostitution). In both paintings, Mary Magdalene forms the nodal point for femininely coded elements – garment, hair, posture, and gesture – thus embodying emotions that cannot be expressed by the other figures in such immediate fashion. The mother and the male apostle remain subdued and restrained, whereas the beautiful young woman shows her feelings with abandon. Such a distribution appeals to the viewer, who in taking in the work of art can identify with several representations of sorrow.

Apart from symbolizing humility and primary emotions, Magdalene's position close to Jesus' feet also implies proximity. She is often touching Christ. She washes His feet and rubs them dry, she anoints His head and later His body. In this respect her attribute, the jar of ointment, is also a sign of intimacy. Subsequent to His burial and finding the empty grave on Easter Sunday, however, there is a reversal in this bodily contact, the well-known '*noli me tangere*' (don't touch me). Spotting Jesus, Mary Magdalene at first does not recognize Him, but when she does and wishes to touch Him, He stops her (Apostolus-Cappadona, 2006b; Baert, 2006). This encounter has inspired many representations in art. Again, Magdalene finds herself to be enacting a spatial submissiveness to Christ. It is worth noting, however, that the impression of rejection implicit in the 'don't touch me' message, together with Christ's gesture of keeping her at bay and the kneeling, imploring posture of Mary Magdalene, do not agree with the closing passages of this biblical episode. Mary Magdalene is not only the first to witness Jesus resurrected, but He also tells her to notify the other apostles of His resurrection – a sign of great trust in her authority, because Jesus obviously thinks that the others will believe this improbable message. Such a positive reading of the *noli me tangere* argues for re-interpreting visual representations that at first sight appear to express rejection (Baert, *et al.*, 2006; 2008).

In summary, visual analysis shows that in placing her close to the floor or ground, Mary Magdalene becomes the vehicle for portraying humility, emotionality, and intimacy. Although these qualities traditionally carry female connotations, it is possible for both female and male viewers to identify with the Magdalene and thus experience a proximity to Jesus. The representation of gender specific qualities therefore is not necessarily connected to gender specific perception, as will also become apparent in the analysis of a naked Mary Magdalene below.

It has also become clear that there is a predilection to depict certain moments (rather than others) in the visual arts: not the anointment of His head but the washing of His feet; not the joyful message to the disciples but the *noli me tangere*. The concentration on a determinate iconography subsequently constitutes a dominant visual tradition that, in reality, only represents part of the story. This is typical for the history of art. It is the reason why knowledge of the historical context and textual sources – the scripture in the case of Mary Magdalene – forms a prerequisite if the interpretation of visual analysis is to carry any weight. In general, this means that feminist analysis should not be restricted to the interpretation of representations and that artworks should not be deployed for illustrating a theory. Because they are material artefacts with a specific history, interpretations have to acknowledge a work's context and its historical and geopolitical gender relations.

The reclining nude, or 'Do women have to be naked to get into the museum?'

Apart from the work-immanent and comparative visual analysis of artworks and their embedding in historical contexts (what do we see and why?) it is important to examine the aesthetic, social, and cultural effects of artworks in detail. This yields a different set of questions, such as: What is the effect of an artwork on the viewer, why, and to what extent is this effect intended? Who are or were the artists and what audiences do they address? These questions are crucial in the critical investigation of both the representation of women and the situation of female artists throughout the ages.

They become especially acute indeed when the genre of the female nude is considered. Representing a long tradition in the visual arts, the nude literally embodies the art historical tradition of the West, ranging from the classical *Venus Pudica* to Picasso's *Demoiselles d'Avignon* and including such famous pictures as Botticelli's *The Birth of Venus*, Titian's *Venus of Urbino*, Rubens' *Het Pelsken* (Portrait of Hélène Fourment), and Manet's *Olympia*. The blatantly erotic nature of these paintings has long been neglected in art historical research because it was felt that 'true' art should be clearly demarcated from other genres such as pornography. Critical analysis of the erotic only became possible in the late 1960s, when eroticism was acknowledged as an attribute of art. Early feminist research in the 1970s stressed the object-like character of the female body in art: naked women, it was argued, are depicted by male artists and, primarily, for male viewers. In traditional art history, the erotic effect was ascribed to the woman in the picture ('she is looking at us provocatively'), but the feminist perspective highlighted the hidden motives of image makers and recipients ('the artist *gave* her a provocative look'). Early feminist research also argued that the representation of women displayed as passive objects for a voyeuristic (male) gaze is not merely sexist as such, but has an impact on the perception of real-life women and their bodies as well (Berger, 1972; Duncan, 1973; Pollock, 1996).

In search of alternative images, female artists created an idiosyncratic 'feminine' formal language for representing the body – *The Dinner Party* (1974–1979) by the American artist Judy Chicago is the most well-known example – or they would appropriate and rework existing representations, for instance by painting male models in similar poses as the famous female nudes mentioned above. It turned out that both these strategies had certain limitations. The artificial creation of a 'true feminine style' is no different in the way it functions, in the end, from such condescending notions about art by women as typically 'elegant', 'sentimental', or 'amateurish'. Both suppose a direct link between gender (of the artist) and aesthetic hallmarks (of art) and that art made by women, therefore, can be distinguished by a number of essential aesthetic features. The strategy of appropriation on the other hand rejected such essentialist ideas, because in modifying iconic nudes, the visual cliché of the naked, passive woman is criticised. Nonetheless, this strategy entails a dependency on the originals that continue to loom in view – albeit in modified form (Parker and Pollock 1981: 129–130). This approach was therefore rather short-lived, as artists began to explore the representation of the (female) naked body in other ways, for example in performance art, photography, and video (see Zarzycka in this book).

In response to the changes in artistic practices, art historical research in the 1990s was focused on a more balanced theoretical concept, modifying the strict dualism of observing – masculine, active – and being observed – feminine, passive (Nead, 1993). It was argued that images as such are not repressive, but that they are discursively employed in order to determine power relations. In other words, a representation of a naked woman is not sexist in itself, because it is possible for the represented object to discard the victim's role and take up a subject position (for example, when the woman in the image is looking back at the viewer) and because female viewers too can observe the (female or male) nude with pleasure or excitement (McDonald, 2001). There is also a less restricted view on the body, as it turns out that feminist image critique is applicable to other, male, and non-Western bodies, too (see 'The Body' in Pollock, 1996). In the visual arts, therefore, it appears that the initial critique on representations of the female body as by definition sexualized has become a thing of the past. However, it is a different matter for the image in popular culture. Here, the question of whether dominant forms of representing female bodies can affect real bodies is still acute: does the perfect beauty of models in fashion magazines achieved through digital enhancement encourage cosmetic surgery to model the real body upon the represented one? Is the sexual behaviour of teenagers affected by extreme stereotypes presented in video clips? To tackle these questions within the academic domain, early feminist criticism of visual representation of women can be very useful indeed.

The history of the feminist view on the female nude body becomes palpable in the figure of Mary Magdalene, because in her most popular appearance she, too, is naked. It was argued above that the preferred positioning of Mary Magdalene in the visual arts was close to the ground. Low, both symbolically and literally, despite the fact that her authority is acknowledged in the Bible, where she is not just kneeling or squatting, but walks upright and delivers important messages. When Mary Magdalene is shown naked, she is even closer to the ground: only covered by her hair, she represents her sins in the wilderness. Interestingly enough, this iconography variant, which reached its zenith in the Italian Baroque, is only marginally related to the biblical Magdalene. Two legends meet in this trope. The legend telling the life of Mary Magdalene after the death of Jesus is fused with the story of a different saint, the so-called Mary of Egypt.

Mary of Egypt allegedly was a prostitute in Alexandria, sometime after Christ. She joined a group of pilgrims, but an invisible force kept her from entering the temple in Jerusalem. On seeing an icon of the Virgin Mary, she became aware of her sins, after which her entry was permitted. After her conversion, she retired into the wilderness to do penance. Forty-seven years later she was found by a monk – naked and with only her hair covering her body. She died after he administered to her the Holy Communion and a lion came to dig her grave.

There are clear parallels in this story to the *vita* of Saint Serome, which turns Mary of Egypt into the prototype of the female hermit. The legend of Mary Magdalene on the other hand, was noted down in the thirteenth century by Jacopo da Voragine, who compiled a collection of hagiographies into his *Legenda Aurea* (The Golden Legend). According to da Voragine, Mary Magdalene went to France after the death of Jesus, where she converted the French people to Christianity and subsequently retired to live as a recluse in a cave in the vicinity of Aix-en-Provence. When she was dying, angels carried her naked body covered with her hair to the church of Aix, where she received communion, died, and was buried. In accord with this story, some mediaeval images of Mary Magdalene often depict her sprouting tiny hairs all over her body, but in the course of the sixteenth century, a new motive is introduced that has no counterpart in textual sources. Painting transforms the old, naked, and hairy woman of the *Legenda Aurea* into a young and sexy saint with luscious locks rather emphasising than covering her nakedness. Here, the prostitute is superimposed onto the elderly hermit.

The body hairs of the Magdalene-as-hermit can be read as symbols of purity and return to the original state of innocence, as religious equivalent to the noble savage. During the course of time, however, the hair was transformed into an erotically charged symbol of temptation (Baert, 2002: 17–20). A paradox is the result: the story of the female hermit, which refers to religious contemplation and repentance, is suddenly charged with eroticism and the resulting ambiguity made the subject highly attractive to painters. However, the naked Magdalenes were quickly unmasked as attempts to legitimize eroticism with biblical iconography. An example of critical judgement already occurs in the late eighteenth century, in the German philosopher Wilhelm August Schlegel's *Gemäldebetrachtungen* (Schlegel, 1996 [1799]). This unconventional guide-book describes two men and a woman perambulating through the Museum of Fine Arts in Dresden. Together, they study the paintings in the collection and offer the reader learned, artistic, moral, and sometimes ironical commentary. Arriving in the Italian wing, Louise, Reinhold, and Waller are struck by the quantity of Mary Magdalenes. The naked saint is portrayed no less than five times. The men amply discuss the ambivalent presentation of the matter. They wonder, for example, whether Magdalene is really reading the book before her eyes – or rather preoccupied with the arrangements of her scant drapery? Casting winks, they ask whether Magdalene's ostentatious pleasure in penitence is not a form of vanity because she enjoys being looked at so much. At the peak of these chauvinist musings, Louise intervenes, remarking that her male co-viewers are resorting to frivolity too easily in discussing the 'fair penitent'.

Here, the philosopher Schlegel manifests himself at various levels as the critical observer of gender stereotypes. In pointing out the ambiguity in representations of Mary Magdalene, he allocates the critical voice to a woman who actively looks at art in a museum. To little effect because until far into the nineteenth century, eroticized Magdalenes remained all the rage, all the way to slightly pornographic versions that explored the sadomasochistic tensions between eroticism and penitence. Schlegel's Louise merely supplements the viewing attitude of her male friends with a marginal note, but still this marks the beginning of a critique on the voyeuristic gaze.

If Louise had lived two hundred years later, she might have been an activist in a gorilla suit. In 1989, the Guerrilla Girls, an artists' collective (www.guerrillagirls.com) presented an artwork that confronted the number of female nudes in the Metropolitan Museum of Art in New York with the number of female painters represented in the Museum's collection (Figure 9.4). The *Grande Odalisque* by the nineteenth-century

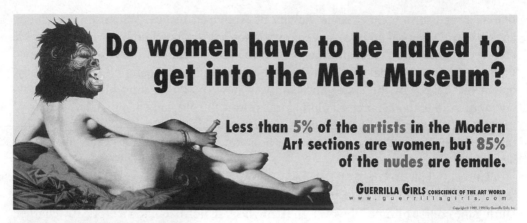

9.4 (above)
Poster by the Guerrilla
Girls (1989).

9.5 (left)
Donatello's Maria
Magdalene (ca 1457).

painter Jean Auguste Dominique Ingres, is displayed on the billboard poster – the collective's medium for bringing their message across, in analogy to commercial strategies – yet not without an important modification: the Odalisque fashions the head of a gorilla, the trademark of the Guerilla Girls. Next to the picture, astonishing statistics are spelled out in giant letters: 'Less [sic] than 5% of the artists in the Modern Art sections are women, but 85% of the nudes are female.'

As we have seen, Mary Magdalene, too, appears to figure mainly in the nude in the museum. The idea that a 'good' Magdalene should be repentant, but most of all young and sexy, is well illustrated by the almost physical disgust apparent in Jacob Burckhardt's rejection of a work where these criteria were not met (Kaegi, 1947–1982, III: 35). Burckhardt, the most eminent art critic of the nineteenth century, judged that the fifteenth-century wooden statue of the famous Italian sculptor Donatello looked like a 'decrepit whore' (Figure 9.5). However, much more in accord with her hagiography, Donatello shows an *old* rather than a young female hermit. The paradoxical appearance of the sexy penitent has dominated representations of the Magdalene in the visual arts up until today. Even contemporary variations on the theme by women artists are in fact critical comments on the visual exploitation of Mary Magdalene and represent her physical and mental abuse (Baert, 2002: 66–71).

Have the visual arts then produced no representations of Mary Magdalene that show her influential and active role? Are there no traces of a positive image of Mary Magdalene, the active and intellectual woman, currently celebrated in academic research and popular culture?

Magdalene rises and sits down to think: Reclaiming female agency

Donatello's Magdalene for one is standing almost upright, but the statue forms an exception. Paintings of Mary Magdalene with both feet on the ground are almost exclusively restricted to representations of her as a patron saint. Fine examples in which the artists concentrated on the rich garments and flowing hair described earlier as important attributes of the saint are for instance the *Magdalena* by Carlo Crivelli (Amsterdam, the Rijksmuseum) or the stately Mary Magdalene in Hugo van der Goes's *Portinari altar-piece* (Florence, Uffizzi). These serene women seem far removed from the naked Magdalenes in the wilderness. However, lifted from the biblical context and without the sense of action that their standing position might have implied, they do not constitute a visual counterweight either.

In the Jacopo da Voragine's vita, Mary Magdalene is described as an extremely active woman with great cogency. After going ashore in France and before her retreat into the wilderness, she preached and not only converted the king and queen of France to Christianity, but the entire population of France as well. While the lives of the majority of female saints are characterized by the passive endurance of atrocious torture, Mary Magdalene travels, preaches, performs miracles, and writes sermons. Apart from the legend, there exists some historical evidence to her crucial role, an apocryphal gospel ascribed to Magdalene (*The Gospel*, 2002; Boer, 2005). This text and the role women played in spreading the Christian faith have recently gained a lot of attention in academic research. In numerous theological and historical studies, some speculative, others based on new historical and archaeological insights, the traditional ideas about women in early Christianity are being revised (e.g. Schaberg, 2002; King, 2003).

The main protagonist of Dan Brown's novel *The Da Vinci Code* – Robert Langdon, Harvard Professor in Christian iconology – draws on this research in unfolding his theory of the 'holy bloodline', which presents Jesus and Mary Magdalene, ancestors of a family with descendants in the here and now, protected by a secret religious brotherhood. At the narrative level, the hypothetical relationship between Jesus and Mary Magdalene is mirrored by the dynamism between Robert Langdon and Sophie Neveu, the French cryptographer, who saves and assists Langdon and turns out to be one of the last offspring of the holy bloodline. The thriller thus presents a craftily construed pseudo-historical plot that popularizes feminist research in branding Mary Magdalene the female element in Christian tradition. Brown turns to the visual arts to illustrate his plot, when he lets Robert Langdon unmask Leonardo da Vinci's *Mona Lisa* and his *The Last Supper* as a covert tribute to the 'sacred feminine'.

Having escaped at last the cliché of the chaste whore, popular culture now burdens Mary Magdalene with a new stereotype. It is attractive to imagine her as Christ's female alter ego, but the relationship remains a romantic construction. Still, the hype around *The Da Vinci Code* resulted in an increased interest in Mary Magdalene and may have led to a larger acceptation of the active role of women in Christianity beyond academic circles.

The alleged tribute to Magdalene in Leonardo de Vinci's *The Last Supper* however is entirely fictitious and in reality there are only few representations that attest to Mary Magdalene's possibly active role in disseminating Christianity. There are, for example, illustrations of her *vita* in the mediaeval retable by the anonymous Master of the Magdalene legend, who shows her preaching like an apostle, and a preaching Magdalene is also depicted in the twelfth-century psalter (a personal prayer book) of Christina of Markyate (these and other examples in Baert, 2002: 11–13).

While these examples are hardly known, there exists within the visual convention a mode of representation that is not primarily focused on Magdalene's (naked) body or various subdued positions at the feet of Jesus. It can be found in a number of famous paintings, which seem to foreground her actions while sticking to familiar visual elements. Action here takes on the form of reflection; and the various postures we have come across in works of art (standing, squatting, kneeling, and lying down) acquire balance in a new compositional arrangement: Mary Magdalene is sitting inside a room, thinking or reading. Paintings of an introverted Magdalene belong to the type of the so-called *Andachtsbilder* – meditational images inviting the viewer to contemplate faith by imitating Mary Magdalene's contemplation. The allusions to a sinful past, penitence and conversion are still present in these paintings, for instance in the bared shoulders or a skull, but she is not simply put at the disposal of the viewer's gaze, as the reclining naked saint was.

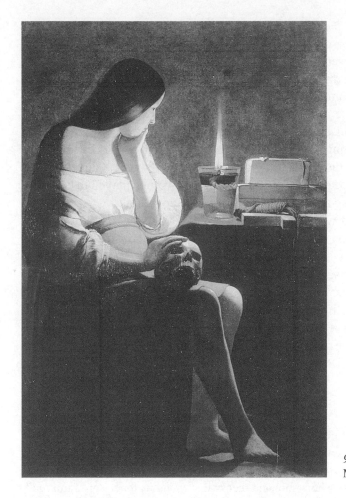

9.6 Georges de la Tour's Maria Magdalene *(1625–1630).*

Examples are the reading Magdalene painted by Piero di Cosimo (1490s Galleria Nazionale d'Arte Antica, Rome); or Georges de la Tour's celebrated *Madeleine de la Nuit* of which he painted three versions in the early seventeenth century (Figure 9.6). The viewer can admire the accomplishment of the artists who did not opt for the ambiguous depiction of provocative penitence, but decided instead to create the less sensational image of contemplation with an impressive display of the luminous effect of candlelight on hair, skin, metal, and glass. Apart from their compelling artistic force, these paintings form the best match to the idea discussed in the beginning of this chapter, of Mary Magdalene as a 'fan fully spread', displaying all her diverse appearances. The moment of a woman reading peacefully is so convincingly depicted, that she acquires a past and a history: the woman has not always been sitting quietly like that, like the nude Magdalenes seem to be frozen in their reclined position or the patron saints, eternally presenting the jar of ointment. This Magdalene has sat down after a long day, to rest and think. About a book perhaps, a conversation, a new sermon. As viewers we can think along with her and the emotional identification offered by Magdalene at the feet of Jesus has made way for the opportunity of intellectual identification.

Reading Magdalene-representations in this way is, of course, a present-day projection. But in historical terms, taking into account recent research on the active role of women in early Christianity, the sitting Magdalene lost in thought is perhaps the most real figure of all those discussed here. Further research on the function of these Magdalene representations might provide evidence for this thesis.

My interpretation of the sitting Magdalene as an active woman at rest does not only take account of research on the historical Magdalene, but also of a recent development in feminist art history, where research into the historical role women played in creating, selling, criticizing, or sponsoring art has regained in focus. Now, however, the issue is not women's absence in the art world (famously addressed in 1971, for example, by Linda Nochlin in her essay 'Why have there been no Great Women Artists?') or their secondary, victimized position in art works (Nochlin, 1971). Rather, feminist art history now is guided by the assumption that women have always had an active part in art history as artists, collectors, patrons, and commissioners and that research should make women's agency in art visible again. Such is argued by Norma Broude and Mary Garrard in *Reclaiming Female Agency: Feminist Art History after Post Modernism* (Broude and Garrard, 2005). The allusion in the subtitle serves to stress the importance of a politically aware art history moving beyond interpretational models of psychoanalysis and semiotics to convince a broad audience of the important role of women in art:

> the critical emphasis of recent decades on the cultural impasse of women has created, we believe, a distorted picture of female participation in culture, one that portrays women as paralyzed within and by an abstract system of social relationships and representational construct. The current feminist scholarship and theory that found its touchstones in Freud, Lacan, and Saussure, in systems of psychology and linguistics grounded in masculinist principles, has in effect, if not by intention, reified existing power structures, often producing an elaborate justification of the status quo. More generally, art historians working in the gender studies mode, deferential to postmodern scepticism about the modernist heroizing of individual artists, have focused less and less on the work and agency of individual women artists, shying away from the idea of a feminist expression grounded in women's real life experience.
>
> (Broude and Garrard, 2005: 2)

The call to explore history and theory in search of real women and their influence on the history of art should not, of course, be misinterpreted as a legitimization of heroine-worship or mythification. Rather, it holds an invitation to ink in the grey areas of the map by means of historical research. If a methodological turn can be signalized in feminist art history, then such notions as the canon or the individual (artist), which were rejected by postmodernism, can be put to good use again. Simply discarding the canon as a mere masculine construct has been rather futile given the fact that this theoretical gesture changes little about the dependency of female artists on the economic pragmatics of a canon (i.e. whose art is being bought and for how much money, which work finds its way into museums, etc.). Instead of discarding the canon, it is much more effective to create historical and theoretical awareness of the ways artists are excluded from it. Securing the position of women in art history requires well-founded historical and interdisciplinary research. Detailed monographic research forms a part of this task, just as big survey exhibitions aimed at calling attention to the work of female artists of the past (van der Stighelen and Weston, 1999).

Epilogue: Mary Magdalene at *The Dinner Party*

One important aspect remains under-exposed in this art-historical narrative of Mary Magdalene: the role of female artists (Chadwick, 1990). Apart from the contemporary works by Marlene Dumas and Kiki Smith, not many women artists seem to have been inspired by the Magdalene. Perhaps because the dominant visual tradition of the eroticized sinner called for criticism but beyond that was simply not very inspiring. However, Mary Magdalene is represented, be it only in writing, in what probably is the best-known feminist artwork, *The Dinner Party*, by Judy Chicago (www. judychicago.com).

As mentioned above, Linda Nochlin famously raised the issue of the absence of women artists in 1971. Eight years later, Judy Chicago caused a stir inside and outside feminist art history with her art project *The Dinner Party*, which consists of a huge triangular table, the setting for 999 imaginatively present historical and mythological women for a celebratory dinner party. The names of all these women are embroidered on richly decorated tablecloths. Thirty-three places are laid for women such as Emily Dickinson and Giorgia O'Keeffe, metaphorically represented by their personalized ceramic plates. *The Dinner Party* represented a giant leap in recovering lost ground at all levels of art production: Chicago worked with a female collective to undermine the myth of the solitary male genius; she employed materials and techniques with traditionally female connotations; and she used a figurative style as a statement directed at the dominating styles of the time such as abstract expressionism and minimalism. In search of a genuinely female artistic language, Chicago turned to organic forms and the ceramic plates explicitly resemble vaginas: Emily Dickinson's plate is a vagina adorned with Victorian lace and Giorgia O'Keeffe's depicts a vaginal flower. Chicago was fiercely criticized by feminist critics and researchers for literally reducing women to their sexual organs, but still *The Dinner Party* had an enormous artistic and political impact and the controversy surrounding the work can teach us a lot about the motives, contradictions and challenges of feminist art history (Jones, 1996).

Mary Magdalene is one of the 999 women present at Chicago's *Dinner Party*, yet without a plate of her own. Thirty years have elapsed and perhaps with the renewed art historical interest in female agency, the time has come for a new, conceptual

Dinner Party, to be put together by countless researchers and artists and with an unlimited number of guests, with a new 'plate' for everyone and naturally for Mary Magdalene, too.

Questions for further research

1 How are women represented in art? Make use of this chapter and an art historical survey work in outlining your argument.

2 Did women have access to art education? Were they allowed to join art academies? What can be learned from studies on the practice of in- and exclusion in this respect?

3 Where did women make their art? Did they have studios, could they buy artistic supplies? What can be learned from studies on the practice of inclusion and exclusion in this respect?

4 What was/is the range of subjects female artists present and what subjects were considered suitable and not suitable (still life, flowers, interiors, portraits, often of other women, children, or relatives because models were out of reach)? What does it mean when a female artist does/did not conform to that norm?

5 Which genres were available to women, which were not? Did women work mostly in the applied arts or in fine art? In what way is, or was, art by women characterized?

6 What media did women artists use, and which are seen as 'typically' feminine or 'typically' masculine (oil-paint, marble, bronze versus pastel, aquarelle, embroidery, patchwork, and ceramics)? Is it possible for a medium to have a gender connotation? What about new media?

7 Search the Internet and try and assess the influence of women in the art world today. Where do they work as artists, critics, collectors, museum directors, or directors of other cultural institutions?

Cindy Sherman confronting feminism and (fashion) photography

10

Marta Zarzycka

10.1 Cindy Sherman's Untitled #122.

There is something hypnotic about the woman in the photograph; it is impossible to stop looking at her. She wears a platinum blonde wig and a dark shoulder-padded overcoat. Long, very untidy hair covers her face, so that we do not see her facial expression. Only one blood-shot eye is partially visible, but she does not look directly at the spectator; rather, she is just staring into the void. Her arms are by her side, her fists tightly clenched, her shoulders hunched. The whole silhouette emanates unreleased tension and rage, as if ready to burst at any moment. The woman looks as if she is about to attack either her potential aggressor or herself. Although her figure does not fill the frame completely, she remains the only theme of the composition. The background details, except for a shadow cast by the woman, are kept to a minimum. The woman's dark coat and her shadow form a powerful contrast with her almost white, overexposed hair and the white wall behind her. Although the moment is charged with tension, the viewer is left in the dark about the story that is being told here. The photograph provides no real answers.

The photograph is *Untitled #122* (colour photograph 89.5 x 54 cm, edition of 18, Collection of the Eli Broad Family Foundation, Santa Monica), made in 1983 by Cindy Sherman, an American photographer. The female figure is modelled by the artist herself. She is in a fight; however, it is unclear who she is fighting. And this is exactly what the artist intended.

This chapter looks at that particular photograph while presenting Sherman as the artist who is undeniably crucial to feminist art criticism. The reflection on this work concerns the reception of Sherman's art by art critics, the kind of debates it has been placed in, and the continuing relevance of her work to feminist theory today. How has Sherman's photograph from her *Fashion Series* been received? Does it comply with the dominating notion of femininity in Western society? In this approach, Sherman and the character of *Untitled #122* are presented *as* warriors, in order to demonstrate how a gender sensitive analysis can embrace the fluctuating nature of artistic practice. What has changed since the time it was made and how has that change informed our perception of the photograph?

(Non)self-portrait

To tackle these questions, the relation between Sherman the artist and the different personages she re-enacts will have to be reviewed first. Who would be the ultimate woman warrior in that photograph: Sherman-the-artist or the character she plays? Certainly, Sherman *is* the artist who has persistently been using her body on almost every photograph she makes. They both have the same body at their disposal: the body they use for fighting, either by making fists or by triggering the camera's shutter. However, it is hard to hold on to a stable notion of the artist in the hundreds of distinct personae she assumes. The range of Sherman's artistic self-transformation is astonishing. Using wigs, makeup, dresses, props, background, and lightning, she acts any age, personality, body type, mood, and narrative. Sherman's face becomes a prop, as unstable as the series of identities represented in her photographs. As an actress, director, stylist, and camera woman all in one, she turns herself into the image that she herself directs. Throughout her artistic career, Sherman has reconstructed various characters; the artist and the role merged into a whole with different levels of ease and comfort. Dressing up, Sherman sometimes reveals the structure of that masquerade by showing herself holding the shutter-release cord.

Sherman said in an interview:

I don't do self-portraits, always try to get as far away from myself as possible in the photographs. It could be, though, that it's precisely by doing so that I create a self-portrait, doing these totally crazy things with these characters.

(Bronfen, 2002: 413)

As is often recalled in feminist texts, Sherman, when she moved to New York after graduating from art school in Buffalo, was scared by the city. Dressing up was the way to overcome her shyness. For months she would stay in; she would dress up but would not leave the apartment. Working as a receptionist, she would sometimes come to work in a nurse uniform or dressed as a secretary from the 1950s. Still, these biographical details do not sufficiently explain the whole context of her art. Art always converges with other art.

The classical genre of the self-portrait usually shows an artist in a staged pose, in an attempt to communicate the 'essence' of the artist's personality. However, Sherman's photographs are very stereotypical, almost-but-not-quite-recognizable pictures, with a wide number of possible readings. They testify to the fact that the self-portrait has become a problematic genre in the twentieth century. No longer seen as the sign of the artist's authority and unity, it has lost its exemplary status. Although Sherman's self-portraits could be inscribed in the long tradition of women's self-portraits, where women artists perform the act of looking and not only of being-looked-at, she actually performs self-transformation. She presents the self as a number of shifting identities rather than as a unified whole. That is why the kind of feminist theory that works at deconstructing the notion of a stable, coherent identity and stresses the fluidity of the subject, has embraced Sherman's art (Krauss, 1993; Braidotti, 2002).

While in art history the figure of a woman traditionally constitutes a framework for exploring femininity, femininity here is deconstructed by way of presenting media images and cultural clichés. In using her own body, Sherman (re)creates over-familiar archetypes of the film starlet, fashion model, housewife, or career woman. She uses herself as a blank canvas and never refers to her individual features. All those changes make her body – the signifier of the artist's presence – disappear. In her photograph of Cindy Sherman, Annie Leibovitz emphasized this erasure by placing the artist among other women who were identically dressed and all had their hair slicked back in the same way (Leibovitz, 2006). Among all the non-descriptive faces, it is very hard to distinguish the artist. She could be anyone.

That self-effacement is disquieting and troubling; it signifies the loss of self rather than its actual presence. Nevertheless, we cannot fail to notice that the materiality of the body restricts the artist and prevents her from being totally detached from her image. Being white, she only explores white femininity. Being a woman, she almost always presents female figures. Sherman occasionally escapes those restrictions by using artificial parts, masks, or mannequins, but still her photographs prove that we almost never experience ourselves out of our bodies. We are always basically able to distinguish ourselves from others by setting physical boundaries. Even if, when looking at our image in the mirror, we sometimes experience the feeling of distance and detachment, we still are the subject of this image. To constitute ourselves as embodied subjects through technologies of representation, we need the body. The body in Sherman's case performs the function of a screen that does not only reflect the artist, but also the network she is immersed in.

Feminism's (un)personal favourite

Sherman in her art refers to various fields where representations of sexual difference, often harmful to women, pertain: Hollywood films, Western art history, pornography, fashion industry, mass media, and entertainment. Her earliest series, *Film Stills*, has been widely discussed and has been considered as the most artistically and commercially successful to this day. *Film Stills* (1977) show the artist in a series of clichéd roles from the 1940s and 1950s low-budget melodramas and *film noirs*: seductress, femme fatale, working girl, housewife, murder victim. Vaguely alluding to certain films (e.g. those by Hitchcock), although difficult to pin down, they offer viewers an unlimited number of readings.

The female body in the later *Disaster Series* (1986) is manipulated and shattered by the voyeuristic gaze. It can no longer bear any pretence to wholeness and integrity: Sherman here abandons her own body and recedes into the plastic prosthesis, dolls, and masks, or becomes a mere reflection in various objects. This series is marked as a symbol of a pathological, disintegrating identity and is situated by art historians in a visual, parallel to the horrifying etches of Francisco Goya (Cruz, 1997). Another series, *Sex Pictures* (1992), also uses dolls. It evokes the instrumentality and absence of sexual taboos in pornographic and advertising practices. There is no escaping the body's dramatic reality: its disintegration, fragmentation, artificiality, and displacement.

In her *Art History* series (1989), Sherman alludes to famous paintings by great masters, such as Raphael or Caravaggio, by re-enacting the female nude. The female body, the favourite theme in Western art history and almost a symbol of it, here becomes the scene of the interplay between seductive surface and rotting insides. The recent *Clown Series* (2003) might be seen as the synthesis of all of her art, considering that all impersonations of feminine stereotypes in Sherman's photographs often verge on the clownish, absurd, and grotesque. Although a clown usually is culturally genderless, the clowns in Sherman's photographs are sometimes very explicitly gendered beneath the heavy white make-up that disguises their faces: clothing, accessories, and props such as artificial breasts make them immediately identifiable as male or female.

For over thirty years now, Sherman's work has been observed through the lens of its relevance to postmodern theory and the concomitant new aesthetic of irony, self-reference, masquerade, hybridization, and multiplicity. Her work embraces the main concepts of postmodernity, such as the gaze (Mulvey, 1975), the abject (Krauss, 1993), the real (Foster, 1996), authorship (Crimp, 1980), and pastiche (Solomon-Godeau, 1991). As a consequence, Sherman has been established as one of the key artists working on the female self and embodiment. The body in her art is conceptualized as a vehicle for passions, emotions, and desires, as the site of sexuality or of disease and death in reference to the massive AIDS awareness in the 1980s and 1990s, and finally, as the space marked as other (Cruz, 1997). As Sherman's work has always been produced in and around embodiment and the feminine subject, it necessarily relates to a feminist problematic of the subject. The major critical writing on Sherman consists of a corpus of explicitly feminist texts on difference, gender, and sexuality.

It is difficult to interpret her work, since the artist does not offer any explicit commentary. A title may provide some indication of the content of an artwork, but by leaving all her works untitled and just numbering them (most of the series' titles are made up by critics), Sherman disclaims any ownership of the meaning of her work and refuses to disclose personal motives. In interviews, she claims that the public and critics are free to interpret her pictures as they wish; her work is like an empty vessel, ready to receive any meaning. It is the artist's intention that the personages she creates have a life of their own. Her silence is protected by critics, who express themselves in tentative terms: 'I would like to think of Sherman in dialogue with . . .' or 'I imagine her reflecting on . . .' (Krauss, 1993). The absence of crystallized meaning continues.

Thus, Sherman's art remains fully open to different approaches and interpretations. But there is one common conclusion: women in the patriarchal order are alienated from their own bodies and their sexuality. Just as it is useful for feminist purposes, Sherman's art can be considered as re-enacting the long history of female oppression. It has been speculated that Sherman's enormous commercial success is based not on the artist's irony and detachment, but on the voyeuristic pleasure in looking at images of women. Presented as passive and preyed upon, her characters are threatened by the media-produced male gaze. Sherman's female subjects can be related to psychiatric disorders such as borderline cases, depression, eating disorders, and so on. She portrays dead, sick, unconscious, crazy, and pathological women who are caught in the dramatic moments of collapse or madness; women who are half-animals, mannequins, and hybrids surrounded by dirt, rubbish, chaos, vomit, emptiness, and darkness. In looking at her personages, they are stripped of any form of integrity as a subject. Sherman's photographs (particularly after *Film Stills*) reveal 'a monstrous otherness behind the cosmetic façade' (Mulvey, 1996: 70). They form a postmodern critique on the dominant ways of representing female form in art as deviant, deficient, and problematically figured.

Nevertheless, I want to argue that while Sherman shows her women characters in the network of standing power relations, her work simultaneously questions those relations. This is why her recognition among feminist art critics is justified. The lack of contamination with a 'real', 'correct' meaning and of fixed ways of interpreting, provide a new route for applying various concepts. Any form of disrupting the patriarchal codes of presenting women as passive, victimized, eroticized, and voiceless constitutes a form of resistance. Those codes are re-examined and twisted; their structure is exposed. It is that process that allows one to see Sherman as a contemporary version of a de-mythologized warrior. Without this critical dimension, as one of Sherman's critics noted, she 'might just as well be Helmut Newton' (Solomon-Godeau, 1991: 57).

Fighting fashion

The mention of Helmut Newton, one of the world's most famous fashion photographers, is not coincidental. The photograph opening this chapter is taken from Sherman's *Fashion Series*, which started in 1983. This series has received somewhat less critical attention than *Film Stills*, but it is a wonderful example of the circulation of images of women in both art and popular culture. Sherman, wearing clothes by Jean-Paul Gaultier and Comme des Garçons, quotes extensively from fashion photography in this series. The photographs are an exaggerated, comical parody of glamorous and stylish high fashion shots. Some are rather silly or flirtatious, but several others are more sinister as gradually Sherman begins to present herself as extremely upset and distraught, and possibly abused or assaulted.

What started as a simple superimposition of 'ugly person versus fashionable clothes' (artist's notes, in Cruz, 1997: 118–119), ended as a revelation of the dark, pathological self, covered in designer outfits. Although one might expect torn or soiled garments, it is not the clothes that indicate violence or a fight in *Untitled #122*. It is obvious that the clothes are made by fashion designers and part of the high fashion world that usually radiates the image of success. Rather, it is the female body and its gestures that signify crisis. The dark suit does not seem to speak the same language as the body: the two are not coherently related.

Fashion photography is a particular target in discussions on the construction of femininity and gendered representations. The fashion industry relies on the heightened sexuality of the image. Fashion is the primal space where, to use Berger's words, 'men look at women. Women watch themselves being looked at' (Berger, 1972: 47). The increasing fragmentation of the body in recent commercial photography causes the female body to be more and more commodified and packaged. In fashion photos, garments represent socially and culturally determined codes and conventions for dealing with sexuality. To use fashion for envisioning and assuring a good life is to employ a system of cultural discourses on the self: social relations, representation, imagery, consumption, and mechanisms of inclusion. Fashion disciplines the body and subjects it to the reign of signs while promising a better, upgraded life – a process that is described as 'imprisonment-through-liberation' (Winkel, 2006: 57).

From nineteenth-century corsets, via heroin chic in the 1990s, up to contemporary pre-pubescent models, fashion has remained recalcitrant to feminist theory. In addition to the critique on fashion for materialism, classism, conformity, and manipulation, the main argument against fashion from feminist quarters concerns the association between fashionable gear and the eroticized female body, which constitutes a passive object for the male gaze (Thompson and Haytko, 1997). In the fashion shoot, as traditionally understood, an eroticized, sexually alluring female body is represented in a seductive pose. Subjected to a fixed catalogue of gestures, it is turned into a commodity; it is an image that sells. Even while a woman's corporeal presence is contained in the visual image, her identity usually is not. The fashion magazine displays the body, reshaped to appear as a perfect body and carefully staged to induce consumption. Fashion is therefore a form of compulsory masquerade, a play with identity induced by societal pressure; it is a socially acceptable and secure way to distinguish oneself from the other, while at the same time it ensures social adaptation and imitation. Clothes accentuate what they conceal and make negotiable what first is made noticeably invisible (Wright, 1992).

The concept of fashion can be approached from psychoanalytic theory. The suggestion is that picturing the body is fundamental to the construction of a gendered identity, with fashion allowing the possibility of displacing the feelings about the body onto dress. Fashion thus is connected to fetish, the masculine perversion which consists in deriving sexual gratification from generally inanimate objects with feminine connotations, such as fur or velvet. Such an object substitutes the mother's missing penis and commemorates the scene where the little boy sees the mother's genitals and is at once horrified and in disavowal (Wright, 1992). Fashion is a coded system of assemblage and separation, an artificial montage of bits and pieces that cuts up the body into partial objects, such as feet, legs, hands, hair, buttocks, and breasts.

For a long time, *Fashion Series* was read as a reversal of what is commonly seen as the representation of the desirable female body in fashion photography. *Fashion Series* formed an antithesis to glamorous advertisements in the glossy fashion magazines from the 1980s. Any pleasurable exhibitionism is obstructed by the disturbing ugliness and visible flaws in the appearance of the woman in *Untitled #122* and other characters from the series, with their dripping makeup, blemished skin, and traces of blood on their fingertips. There are no perfect bodies here. What had started as the artist working in commission with a clear commercial purpose, resulted in a powerful and quite disturbing commentary on the entire concept of the fashion industry, which sells fantasy identities to women. Introducing the notion of the imperfect but perfectly dressed body, Sherman undermines the cultural idea that fashion should be viewed as a multiplicity of practices that permit individuals to attain happiness, purity, and a sense of belonging. Instead, she shows that fashion violently enforces the conformity of a standard, prescribed look of attractiveness and sexual seductiveness. It is a cultural procedure for manufacturing insatiable desire. The discourse tackled by Sherman constitutes the opposite of a good life.

However, the changing aesthetics of fashion photography have made Sherman's rebellious reversal much less obvious. Since the 1990s, fashion photography has developed a preference for an uneasy mixture of repulsion, beauty, and disgust, where the sexy and the uncanny, luxury and poverty, vulgarity and sublimation are blended. These are exactly the aspects for which Sherman's work was appreciated. Recent fashion photography is not sterile, slick, and seamless, but in fact very similar to Sherman's aesthetics from the *Fashion Series* van (Winkel, 2006). Particularly the more alternative or less mainstream magazines, such as *I-D*, *Wallpaper* or *Another Magazine*, exhibit disturbing, ugly, and often anxiety-provoking female bodies. In the art/fashion magazine *Blend* (no 4, issue 23, 2007), the series of photographs titled *Simply Cindy* contain direct references to Sherman's *Studio Portraits* from 2000. Fashion photography is the medium that appropriates the most diverse formats and genres: *film noir*, docudrama, body art, street theatre, soft porn, neo-realism, drag show, and slapstick (Winkel, 2006). In current fashion photography, the distinction between pastiche, homage, and persiflage are hardly noticeable. The fashion shoot is often determined by the joint effort of photographer and stylist to re-enact the narrative and stylization of *Blue Velvet*, baroque paintings, or Surrealist collage. Bruce Weber's photographs for Calvin Klein, for example, manifest the influence of work by Leni Riefenstahl, the German film director who collaborated with Hitler (Wells, 2004).

By quoting or travestying art, the fashion image pretends to stand aloof from the commercial context of advertising, since most fashion spreads are commissioned by magazines, not directly by the manufacturers of clothes. It supplies the magazine with an open structure that advertisers easily fit into. Although it employs various artistic discourses, fashion photography remains a form of studio photography: pure, clinical, to-the-point. It differs significantly from snapshot-like photography of intimate relationships and day-to-day life (e.g. by Nan Goldin), which is characterized by fake amateurish mistakes (out-of-kilter framing, blur, uneven flashlight, discolorations) and intentionally signals the intimacy between photographer and subject. Fashion photography is blatantly concerned with the constructed photograph. It also relates to the exotic, dramatic, glamorous, and different. The impact of recent technologies on fashion photography has been enormous, just as on other areas of art, design, and media. New techniques of software application facilitate changing the constructions of reality. An image that was once made with an optical lens now exists as an electronic file, which makes fashion more provisional, hybrid, mutable, and more *perfect* than the fixed images of analogous photography. In that light, Sherman's images resemble the most cutting-edge fashion productions, where clothes are mere attributes in the story or mood created by images.

In view of recent changes in fashion photography and its aesthetic, the readings of Cindy Sherman's work presented above are not the only possible ones. The troubled body about to fight (back) in *Untitled #122* has been appropriated by the fashion industry as the desirable body that seduces viewers and makes them buy consumer goods. Perhaps Sherman's caricature of fashion photography is in fact imitated by the object of caricature. Sherman's work may have influenced fashion photography, in marking a shift from unemotional and elegant models of the 1980s to the narrative, mysterious scenes in the 1990s campaigns by Prada or Alberta Ferretti. Quite a few of Sherman's contemporary artist colleagues present fashion as a violent tool of female oppression. The Dutch fashion photographer Erwin Olaf shows, in his *Fashion Victims* series (2000), the beautiful, toned bodies of models whose heads are covered by shopping bags with designer logos. Similar work was done by Inez van Lamsweerde, significantly active both in the field of art and fashion, in her *Thank you Thighmaster* series (1993). Pictures that look as of they were taken from high fashion magazines are digitally mutilated, cut, and abused. The models are so beautiful that they seem unreal and esoteric; their flawless, unblemished skin forms a shocking contrast with the bloody cuts.

Is it still possible to talk about the split between Sherman's work and the kind of contemporary fashion photography that strikes a balance between irony and fetishism? What about the revolutionary nature of Sherman's *Fashion Series*, considering that fashion has increasingly become engaged with art (and art with fashion)?

Fighting art?

Given its absolute and tiresome omnipresence in our contemporary world, photography both fulfils the traditional role of the art of painting and acts like a window on the world (Warner, 2002). The present status of fashion photography addresses the interdependent relation between art and mass culture. The traditional division between art on the one hand (confrontational, critical, independent) and mass culture on the other (conformant, stereotypical, capitalistic) is challenged. In fact, photography in general is situated both in the gallery system and beyond it, thus gnawing at a capitalist, bourgeois art tradition by toning down the aura of the sacred, authentic, and original art object. Since the 1960s, photography has been centrally implicated in the expansion of mass media . . . just think of fashion shoots, album covers, or photo-journalism. The horrific images of war atrocities seen by the public all over the world are mediated through photography and television. Pop artists, such as Andy Warhol or Richard Hamilton, made photographical comments on lifestyle and consumerism.

Since the 1980s, photography has been the dominant mode of visual production in the museum and gallery world, as well as among collectors and artists. Painting and other genres in the visual arts have acquired a more marginal position. Nowadays, the canon of 'master' photographers has vastly expanded; prices for photographic art are skyrocketing; and photography is prominent in private and corporate collections. Creating the illusion of immediacy and of being directly in touch with the world, photography is perfectly suited to the speed, impatience, and lack of time that determines the life of the contemporary citizen.

Violence is often taken to be a characteristic trait of photography. From the start, photography has made connections with the sick, pathological, colonized, exotic, or eroticized body; as is exemplified by the photographs of hysterical female patients that were circulated in nineteenth-century Paris (Bronfen, 1998). The camera functions as an instrument of appropriation, possession, and objectification. Sontag (2001) saw photography as a way of violating, objectifying, and even killing people: 'Just as the camera is a sublimation of the gun, to photograph someone is a sublimated murder' (Sontag, 2001: 14–15).

The violence of a photograph is not derived from its content, but from its 'filling the sight by force' (Barthes, 1981: 91), that is, catching someone in the frame of a picture. The terminology of photography is connected to the lethal language of a murderer whose weapon becomes the camera. Barthes (1981) noted that one simple click embraces the life/death paradigm, since one speaks of 'aiming' the camera and 'shooting' the image. The sexual economy of looking at a photograph (not just erotic or pornographic ones) represents the heterosexual male gaze. Psychoanalytic terms, such as scopophilia (the pleasure in looking), voyeurism, and fetish are theoretically structured around a male viewer and his pleasures/traumas. These terms are indeed very relevant to the medium. So one might wonder to what extent the medium of photography can become the discursive field where women fight for recognition. In answering that question, it is important to realize that the feminist analysis of photography is not a supplement to other discursive studies on photography theory, but constitutes an epistemological shift to the effect that patriarchal power structures are deconstructed (Solomon-Godeau, 1991).

Although the history of photography-as-art tends to be presented as a history of 'great' or master photographers and although this history is contextualized through the exposure in galleries, museums, and artists publications, it is noticeable that photography is a particularly welcoming medium for women artists – far more accessible than painting or sculpture. To name but a few well-known women photographers: Dorothea Lange, Immogen Cunningham, Jo Spence, Lorna Simpson, Barbara Kruger, Sophie Calle, Hellen van Meene, Rineke Dijkstra, Celine van Balen, or Sarah Lucas. Apparently, this new medium was not burdened with the notion of the genius that is usually connected to the white male in the history of Western art (think of painting, sculpture, or architecture). The momentary act of taking a photograph questions the idea of the immanent, unique artwork that is created in the intimacy of a rented studio, with time unlimited, by an artist who is not bothered by household chores. Women artists now had the opportunity to enter the artistic field more easily. Photography evokes the aspect of reproduction, an infinite regress of copies of copies. The presence of the photograph both emphasizes and evokes the absence of the original (Crimp, 1980). Jean Baudrillard called such an absence the *simulacrum*: the photograph has no referent in the world beyond it and is understood or critiqued in terms of its own internal aesthetic organization.

The term 'photography', in other words, refers to a wide range of objects and practices: daguerreotypes, 35-millimetre prints, Polaroids, snapshots, and pixels. It appears in discourses that include optics, journalism, fashion, documentary, erotica, and criminal investigation. Accordingly, two fields converge in *Untitled #122*: art photography (through its context) and fashion photography (through its content).

Looking at *Untitled #122*, one sees Sherman as an example of the woman artist who deploys the specificity of the medium for her own purposes. The photograph is like a series of images of various bodies rather than of one specific, identified body, as in a strip of negatives. The lack of ownership or identity is also apparent in Sherman's refusal to call her work self-portraits. She forsakes total control over her artistic self-image. She stresses the fluid character of the photographic image and its possible circulation within the domain of fashion and of artistic production and relates it to many layers of visual culture. Sherman uses the 'openness' of the medium to circulate concepts and ideas about women in contemporary culture.

Conclusion

Sherman's art is a journey through the image of a female body in various stages of dressing, disguise, and artificiality. She relinquishes ownership of the body and refuses to mediate meaning. Thus, Sherman uses the medium of photography as a strategy for revealing the fluidity of cultural constructions designated as feminine. What kind of gendered subjectivity can we imagine in the face of these insistently overlapping representations, these disintegrating genres? In her art, the artist moves from the dreams of a young American girl enchanted with Hollywood movies, via the exploration of various psychological states and images of violence, to the disturbing portrayals of sick, dysfunctional bodies, threatened by a sense of death and decay. Sherman's women are situated in the process between cliché and revelation. They are unable to fit any category permanently. In the constant confrontation of anguish, fear, seductiveness, and role-playing, there is a multiplicity of subjects, narratives, and personages engaged in the discourse of the feminine.

Untitled #122 is strong in its violence and affect, in positioning the woman in the picture on the plane of aggressor and a victim. Very clearly staged, *Untitled #122* is dynamic and powerful. Although it is believed that any sort of artistry or aesthetic manipulation diminishes the audience's belief in the sincerity of a photograph (Sontag, 2003), *Untitled #122* moves us in the determination of both woman and artist.

This chapter forms a demonstration of the way the changing concepts of art and photography can contribute to furthering feminist theory. Sherman's *Fashion Series* and its reception illustrate some of the contemporary tensions between fashion and art photography. While considered as 'gallery art' before, art photography now is less easily slotted because its codes are very similar to those of the fashion image. The current fashion image, on the other hand, often plays with the conventions and images of art tradition. What is true for Sherman's work also applies to fashion photography: pastiche and parody, caricature, quotations, derivations, and plagiarism are impossible to distinguish from one another. The fact that many of Sherman's photographs have equivalents in fashion and lifestyle magazines, that her treatment and recycling of stereotypes and clichés does not structurally differ from the very way fashion photographers work, may be confusing to a viewer. However, a gender sensitive analysis helps to position this photograph in a certain cultural context. The binaries and hierarchies of disciplines are no longer relevant; it is rather the crossovers of spaces and discourses informing each other that make Sherman's art still fascinating to watch and a source of inspiration for feminist analysis.

What does *Untitled #122* tell us about gender issues and what critical questions does it raise? Feminists see Sherman's art as a critique and deconstruction of patriarchy, capitalism, and consumerism. It is a representation of the decentred self. It is not the 'truth' or 'essence' of femininity that is of particular importance to those photographs; it is rather the changing politics of inclusion/exclusion that govern representations. Critical response to them involved the main frames of postmodern art theory: the specificity of the medium, the negotiations between art and popular culture, the position of gender in representational strategies and institutional critique. However, with the change of those concepts, the reading of Sherman's art undergoes a number of shifts. Valid feminist art criticism today needs to acknowledge those shifts. The warrior quality in Sherman's art is the critical circulation of meaning. This awareness forms, in a certain sense, the most important subtext of her work. The woman warrior, at the same time threatening and caught in the networks of popular culture, vitally resists patriarchal representational strategies.

Questions for further research

1   What are the opportunities offered by photography to women? Search the Internet or your library for interviews with famous photographers and involve these in your answer.

2   What is the most recurrent image of the female body in Western media?

3   Buy or borrow a recent magazine (such as *Wallpaper*) with a great deal of fashion photographs. How are the men and women depicted? Are there any examples of intertextuality? Does the fashion photographer make use of other forms of visual art? Do these other forms of visual arts strengthen or weaken the male/female image?

4   How do the concepts of author, genius, or tradition relate to female creativity?

5   What do you think is the definition of a female self-portrait? Please give some examples in illustrating your answer and refer to the traditions of thinking equality and thinking difference in answering this question.

6   Do you think there is a difference between work by male and female photographers? Can you name some of these differences?

Peter Pan's gender and feminist theatre studies

Maaike Bleeker

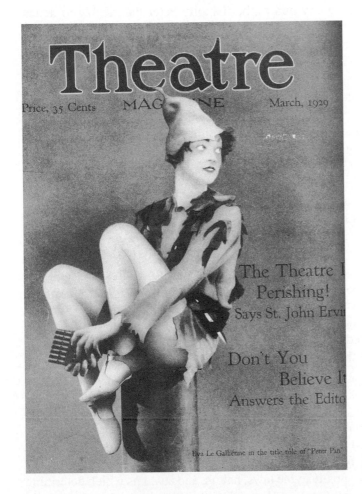

11.1 Eva Le Galienne's Peter Pan.

In 1904, *Peter Pan, or The Boy Who Would Not Grow Up* by James Barrie, had its premiere in the Duke of York's Theatre in London. This play tells the story of Wendy, John, and Michael Darling who, one evening when their parents are out, are visited by a strange boy by the name of Peter Pan. Together with the fairy Tinker Bell, he is looking for his shadow which he lost during an earlier visit. Peter Pan finds his shadow in a drawer in a nursery cupboard and tries to stick it on again, without much success. Luckily he is helped by Wendy, who sews the defiant shadow onto Peter with a needle and thread. Peter teaches Wendy and her brother to fly and takes them with him to Neverland, a fairyland beyond the stars, inhabited by mermaids, Red Indians, and pirates. Peter Pan lives there in a cave under the ground with the Lost Boys, a group of boys who, like him, do not want to grow up. This is the very mystery of Peter Pan: his successful refusal to become an adult. He remains eternally young in a world where the only adults are fairytale figures and, together with the Lost Boys and the Darling children, in that fairyland he experiences all sorts of adventures, until Wendy decides that it is time to go back home because their mother might be worried about them. On the way home, they are kidnapped by pirates, but happily Peter Pan is able to defeat Captain Hook, so that they can return home safely. The Lost Boys are also able to find themselves a place in the real world once again. However, Peter Pan returns to Neverland, still determined never to become an adult.

From the first performance, *Peter Pan* was an enormous success, in particular in Great Britain and the United States, where the play quickly assumed a permanent place in the repertoire as a Christmas pantomime. The story of the play was later brought out by the author as a novel, has been filmed a number of times (among others, the famous Disney cartoon in 1953), and has been produced as an equally popular musical. In the course of time, a number of figures from the story have come to lead their own lives in amusement park attractions (Michael Jackson's private amusement park is even called *Neverland*) and in films such as *Hook* (Steven Spielberg, 1991), the Disney cartoon *Return to Neverland* (2002), and *Tinker Bell* (Disney, 2008).

Peter Pan has developed into a seemingly autonomous figure in the collective unconscious; a mythical figure who turns up now and then to take children to his magical world. Barrie himself actively contributed to the mystification concerning the origins of the story. In his introduction to the published edition of the play, he suggests that he did not invent Peter Pan, but rather that Peter Pan had made himself known to him and a group of child friends.[1] It is as if Peter Pan also exists beyond the realms of the play and has always existed, as part of a world which only children have access to, access which they lose when they grow up and forget how to fly.

Peter Pan does not want to grow up. That is why he has fled to this fantasy world populated by fairytale figures, a world in which time has no hold and where he therefore does not grow any older. The only reason he sometimes returns to the ordinary human world is to listen to fairytales told by the Darling children's mother. This could already be regarded as an indication for how the fantasy world of Neverland – although it is emphatically presented in the piece (and in the myth concerning the origins of the piece) as being opposite to the laws, habits, and customs which determine what reality is – ultimately has its roots in reality, and is the product of it, as a fantasized way out. Within this world, Peter Pan is the exception, which confirms rather than denies the rule. More than this, it is precisely through the way in which he manifests himself as being an exception, that the piece presents these rules as a matter of course. Because, although Peter Pan may have successfully withdrawn from the world of adults, his refusal to subject himself to the laws of that world is not a criticism of the role patterns which structure this reality. His refusal is primarily linked to the roles which he does and does not want to play within these patterns.

In the first place, in *Peter Pan*, not wanting to grow up means not wanting to become a man and in the context of the piece this refusal is presented as being very understandable. There is not a single adult man in the story who can be taken seriously. The Darling children's father is an idiot who spends his days carrying out inferior work at an office and who cannot even tackle the dog at home. With his long curls, frivolous clothes, and crying fits when everything threatens to go wrong, neither can Captain Hook be considered as a real man, nor the other pirates. The only adult character presented who can be taken seriously, is mother. She is admired and much-liked by everyone. And yet she is also not what Peter Pan wants to be. Such identification would be inconceivable within the universe of this piece.

It is not just the Peter Pan character who does not cast any doubts on traditional role patterns; these patterns are not queried anywhere in the entire piece. And regarding the voluntary or involuntary subjection to them, a striking asymmetry can be said to exist. Whereas the piece concerns the way in which we as viewers are able to identify with Peter Pan's refusal to grow up and become a man – and following on from this, the resistance of the Lost Boys, Captain Hook, and the pirates to the rules and habits in the world of grown-ups – Wendy's acceptation of her role as a woman and mother is simultaneously depicted as completely self-evident. At the beginning of the piece, when one of her brothers proposes playing mummies and daddies, Wendy accepts the role of mother without a murmur and she follows all his instructions about carrying out this role without protest. When she first meets Peter Pan, she immediately steps into the role of the little woman, who has to help him, the silly boy, with sewing on the shadow. She knows exactly how it should be done. As a matter of course, she then takes on the role as his potential lover, which places her in a position of jealousy for Tinker Bell. Meanwhile, Peter Pan is oblivious to all of this. He wants to remain a child forever, who not only listens to fairytales, but also experiences these fairytales in reality. For him, Wendy is not a potential lover, but the promise of a mother who can tell fairytales and yet is not an adult. Wendy is a mother whom he can take to Neverland. She has not even arrived there yet and he already calls out to the Lost Boys: 'Great news, boys. I have brought at last a mother for us all' (Barrie, 1995: 112).

Peter Pan is a play which, despite all the criticism of the world of adults, confirms conventional gender patterns in such an extreme manner that it is almost painful viewing for an early twenty-first century audience. In particular, the highly simplified Disney cartoon version, in which Wendy, Tinker Bell, and the Indian princess Tiger Lily are depicted as three little coquettish women who, as a matter of course, immediately take on the role of rivals for Peter's love, sends shivers down your spine. The original piece by Barrie is more complex and reads much more as the struggle to which Disney offers a one-dimensional answer. This not only lies in the many scenes which have been left out of the Disney version, but to a great extent also has to do with the fact of it being a play staged for the *theatre*. The original *Peter Pan* acts out a doubling of role playing, pretence, and a fact/fiction confusion which simply do not occur in the cartoon film. The theatre itself already creates a situation for playing roles, where actors take on the role of characters and where the spatial here and now which we look at as an audience, can be a different world with different rules for the duration of the performance. This doubling is crucial for the way in which the piece plays with the viewer, which makes the piece fascinating as an example, on the one hand, of the many ways in which gender plays a role in theatrical practice and, on the other, of gender itself as theatre.

The play *Peter Pan* is absolutely full of playing with role patterns. The context of Neverland, where everything is about playing and the inhabitants are children, sets the framework for a series of situations in which mutual relationships are shaped by playing out well-known roles and exploring their implications. This child's play, which for a great part also takes place in a fantasy world, enables the patterns to be depicted in an often grotesque manner – the fairy Tinker Bell, immediately jealous the moment Wendy appears on stage, without any scruples gets one of the Lost Boys to shoot her rival out of the sky with a bow and arrow. But what is presented as child's play often has very real consequences – Wendy is really in danger of dying – and as such can be interpreted as a commentary on the utmost serious character of role play in daily life. Once again, however, it is not a case of questioning here, but much more a demonstration of the way in which these role patterns and the behaviour associated with them produce reality. This piece thus provides an example of Judith Butler's observations about gender as performance before the terms even existed.

In *Gender Trouble* (1990) and *Bodies that Matter* (1993), Butler talks about gender and performance in daily life, not in the theatre. She proposes that what appears to be male or female in daily life is the effect of a culturally specific performance. In performances, bodies appear male or female. To a great extent this gender performance occurs unconsciously through the repetition of time-worn patterns and as a result of culturally negotiated desires and behaviour. In *Peter Pan*, the behaviour of the characters appears to be a demonstration of such time-worn patterns. At the same time, we are naturally dealing with a play in which actors are very consciously performing theatre. It is precisely because of this layering that this play is an interesting example of how gender is a performance and how this performance is given meaning in relation to a culturally specific viewer. What makes *Peter Pan* particularly interesting is the relation between the visualization of gender and the presuppositions in the gaze of the viewer, and what this relation reveals about what in psychoanalytical terms is referred to as the gaze. This will be further considered in this text on the basis of a noteworthy aspect of *Peter Pan*'s performance history: the fact that, since the very first performance, the role of Peter Pan has more or less always been played by a woman.

Cross-casting: Tradition and history

Peter Pan is not the only role with a tradition of *cross-casting*. In Shakespeare's time, for example, it was considered improper for women to appear on stage and therefore all the women's roles were played by young boys. Shakespeare's plays consist of all sorts of allusions to the ambiguity of this situation, which are often even further redoubled by stories in which these female characters dress up and pass off as men. This ambiguity often has erotic overtones and there is a play on what in more contemporary terms is referred to as *queering* the dominant heterosexual perspective. In other cases, cross-casting is coupled with criticism or commentary, as for example in the case of Cinderella's ugly stepsisters, where the tradition of these female characters being played by men confirms that they cannot be taken seriously as women. As far as this is concerned, *Peter Pan* is an exceptional case because it does not concern eroticism or commentary.

'Why is Peter Pan a woman?' asks Majorie Garber (1992) in her essay 'Fear of Flying or Why is Peter Pan a Woman?' She cites Roger Lancelyn Green who, looking back at the first fifty years of *Peter Pan*, states that 'Peter Pan is the ultimate ambition of all actresses just as Hamlet is of all actors' (Garber, 1992: 165). Once again this is a case of a curious asymmetry, because after all, both Peter Pan and Hamlet are male as far as gender is concerned. Yet Hamlet is the ultimate ambition for actors, whereas Peter Pan is the ultimate ambition for actresses – at least, if we are to believe Roger Lancelyn Green. The role of Hamlet has, for that matter, been played by women, among whom are some of the greatest actresses of their time, such as Sarah Bernard. Yet you would not usually consider Hamlet to be the ultimate ambition of every actress. On the other hand, the role of Peter Pan has been played by actors, but this concerns a few exceptions. Garber cites the example of the Royal Shakespeare Company who opted for a man in the leading role in 1982. This was an attempt to do justice to the tragic qualities of the piece 'elevating it from the ghetto of children's theatre' (quoted in Garber, 1992: 165). About which Garber (1992) subtly remarks: 'Like *Hamlet*, *Peter Pan* could be a national masterpiece of tragic drama; all it needed was the RSC and a star with a phallus. It was a matter of putting the "Peter" back in *Peter Pan*.'

Eva Le Galienne, an actress who played both Hamlet as well as Peter Pan, commented in relation to her performance as Hamlet (in 1936):

> If one thinks of Hamlet as a man in his thirties, the idea of a woman attempting to play the part is of course ridiculous. But Hamlet's whole psychology has always seemed to me that of a youth rather than of a mature man . . . It is possible for an actress at the height of her powers to give the impression of being a boy, while having at her command all the craft, range, force and subtlety which such great roles require. This has always been true of Rostand's L'Aiglon, which, with a few insignificant exceptions, has always been played by women; also De Musset's Lorenzaccio, and – in a very different mood – Barrie's Peter Pan.
>
> (Le Galienne, 1983: 51)

Hamlet played by a woman can be believable if you interpret the role in a specific manner: not as an adult man, but as a boy, according to Le Galienne. Just as in the Royal Shakespeare Company's decision to cast a man as Peter Pan, the choice of a woman as Hamlet is linked to a specific interpretation of the role. A major difference naturally still remains between the two situations: in the case of Peter Pan, the casting is an exception in accordance with the gender of the role, whereas in the case of Hamlet, it is the cross-casting that is the very exception. Peter Pan played by a woman represents a situation which, to cite Peggy Phelan (1993), appears as *unmarked*. The choice remains imperceptible as a choice and instead appears as self-evident. It is this self-evidence which enables the choice to be made. In contrast, Hamlet played by a woman is a clear example of a *marked* decision: a manifestation which is perceptible as an exception to the imperceptible norm. In this light the situation in the case of *Peter Pan* is not comparable to that of *Hamlet,* but precisely the opposite. *Peter Pan* represents the highly exceptional situation whereby cross-casting manifests itself as unmarked.

Why cross-casting? Ambitions and opportunities

Lancelyn Green states that Peter Pan is every actress' ultimate ambition. In this, he not only concludes that Peter Pan is played by women, his conclusion moreover assumes that this is also their ambition. Le Galienne does not talk explicitly about ambition, but her observation would also seem to suggest this. As if Hamlet and Peter Pan not only enabled actresses to demonstrate their capacity of convincingly playing the role of a boy, but more than this: the role offered them the opportunity *per se* of demonstrating their capabilities in a way where women's roles offered few opportunities. Le Galienne is referring to a situation of limited provision of roles for women to excel. This was also the case for the roles which women could perform outside the theatre in those days. Their roles in the theatre were a reflection of the opportunities they had outside it. As far as this is concerned, it could be regarded as typical that actresses had to pretend to be boys in order to excel.

The various traditions of cross-dressing and cross-casting, and the role that these phenomena played within the history of the western theatre, are the subject of Lesley Ferris' *Crossing the Stage. Controversies on Cross-Dressing* (1993). In her introduction she quotes from Le Galienne, but also from Erika Munk who formulates herself a little more critically in relation to cross-casting Hamlet. Munk indicates how such a choice in casting not only assumes a specific interpretation of *Hamlet*, but that this interpretation of *Hamlet* in turn implies a fairly negative image of women:

> Hamlet stereotyped as a waffling neurotic prone to violent fits, is considered proper for women to enact, unlike Lear, Henry V, Caesar, Coriolanus, or Falstaff. . . Basically, such casting comes from producers' gimmickry and actresses' frustration, from the fact that most playwrights and most big roles are male; as long as men aren't clamoring to play Mother Courage or Juliet or Amanda Wingfield, Hamlet as a woman re-emphasizes the universalist pretensions of maleness, the specific limitations of femaleness, in our culture.
>
> (Munk quoted in Ferris, 1993: 3)

In short, the opportunities afforded to women such as Le Galienne and the way in which they were afforded them ultimately confirms the limits of the cultural imagination instead of stretching these limits or questioning them. The individual actress is perhaps afforded an opportunity, but in a way that, considered from a gender sensitive perspective, ultimately produces a negative effect when it concerns the sort of image of woman which is confirmed by it.

The implications of the way in which men and women's roles take shape within the repertoire of our cultural canon is the subject of much criticism from a feminist perspective. Critics indicate how these roles not only form a reflection of a problematic *status quo*, which is also constantly repeated and reaffirmed when these pieces are performed. Many women's roles in the Western repertoire reflect a patriarchal world order and a corresponding patriarchal world image. They are pieces in which roles are imposed on women that make them appear in ways that meet the desires, values, and assumptions which belong to a traditional Western heterosexual male perspective.

Just as Peter Pan imposes the role of mother on Wendy so that the fantasy world in Neverland satisfies his desires, so are women depicted in drama in roles in which their appearance confirms the desires, values, and assumptions of the average male viewer. It is from this perspective that the appearance and behaviour of these women are to a certain extent self-evident. At the same time, by constantly reappearing as the object of male desire, these women confirm the assumed normality of the sort of femininity that they represent. For example, take Wendy: by self-evidently depicting her as happy to be adopting the role of mother, this confirms that this is normal and even desirable. After all, the story is constructed in such a way that this behaviour is not only demanded and expected of Wendy; the story suggests that this option really makes Wendy happy and that it is her own desires – and not those of the viewer – which she is fulfilling with her choice.

In more critical stagings, cross-casting is often used as a strategy for critique. By having women playing men's roles or vice versa, the self-evident relationship between specific roles and the men and women who play these roles is undermined and questioned and, following on from this, also the construction of the role itself. Contrary to what Le Galienne describes, this does not concern the question of how and why women are able to depict a male character believably, but the assumptions which are implied in what can appear as self-evident and what cannot. Which perspective do these plays offer about what is male and what is female, and whose perspective is this? What sort of viewer are these plays geared towards in the way they represent men and women, and in which way are the viewer's opinions and desires either or not confirmed? This perspective is also what Marjorie Garber's analysis of cross-casting Peter Pan is about, and in her analysis she demonstrates how this tradition is a confirmation of the sort of assumptions which are also implied by the perspective that psychoanalysis offers about the formation of sexual identity.

Why is Peter Pan a woman?

In a situation where there is a lack of roles for women in which they can excel in all their capabilities, it is conceivable – although not necessarily acceptable or unproblematic – that women opt for male roles and even aspire to these roles. However, this does not yet provide an explanation as to why it is possible that they are able to play these roles convincingly, why they are afforded the opportunity of doing this, and why they are afforded the opportunity of playing these specific roles. The fact that actresses want to play the roles of Peter Pan or Hamlet, because these roles could offer them the opportunity of demonstrating their capabilities in a way other roles do not, does not yet explain why it is precisely in these roles that they are afforded the opportunity, why producers prefer to opt for this, or why the audience accepts and values this choice. Producers' decisions and audience appreciation are naturally often linked, certainly in more commercially set-up productions, such as is the case in the large-scale stagings of *Peter Pan*. For that matter, women have more often aspired to roles which are traditionally played by men, both on and off the stage. Yet ambition alone does not explain why and how they have succeeded in playing certain roles and not playing others, and why they have been greatly successful with them or, contrariwise, have failed.

It is striking that in the case of Peter Pan the choice has more or less consistently been for a woman right from the very beginning. This also makes *Peter Pan* very different from *Hamlet*. A possible explanation advanced for this is of a very practical nature. Casting a young boy as Peter Pan would cause problems in view of the fact that in those days (when *Peter Pan* had its premiere) it was forbidden for children to appear on stage night after night. For this reason quite a few of the Lost Boys were also initially played by women or they were, along with the Darling brothers, played in turn by different casts. In this situation, what is normally a restriction for women in interpreting Hamlet and other men's roles works to their advantage. Women are used precisely because, in the prime of their acting careers, they can convincingly pass themselves off as young men. Adult men cannot do this and casting real children is not practical due to the law and, moreover, certainly in the case of the leading role, unfeasible due to the lack of acting experience for making it a success.

This explanation provides an answer to some questions, but once again, the most important one is left unanswered. Just as the aspirations of actresses and the lack of women's roles help us to understand why actresses would *want* to play Peter Pan, this explanation helps us to understand why it is *handy* to allow a woman to play the role. But this still does not provide an answer to why it is *possible*: Why can an adult woman look convincing, to an audience, as a young boy who refuses to grow up? Why is this not considered to provide a specific interpretation of the role or to constitute a kind of commentary on it? What is it about Peter Pan that he can look like an adult woman or, vice versa, what causes an adult woman to look like a young boy who does not want to grow up? Why is this believable and apparently so unproblematic that it has been regarded as suitable for children for more than a century? Whose perspective is this?

'Why is Peter Pan a woman?' asks Majorie Garber, and her answer is: because a woman will never become a man. According to her, the tradition of a woman playing Peter Pan is a symptom of a fundamental asymmetry in the cultural perspective in which gender is given form. The same asymmetry can also be found in the psycho-analytical perspective about sexual identity. According to Freud (1961), sexual identity starts taking shape at the moment when boys and girls become conscious of the difference between their bodies. This discovery marks the beginning of what Freud refers to as the castration complex. The boy, who sees that the part of the body which is so important to him is missing in the girl, experiences her as castrated, as if something has been taken away from her. He is overcome by the fear that this could also happen to him. Moreover, he experiences all sorts of fantasies about what could have happened to the girl. The girl becomes conscious of her castrated self, or her lack, and thus of her inferior position.

Feminist critics have pointed out that within this psychoanalytical discourse there can actually be no talk of a difference between men and women, but only men and non-men. The origins of becoming conscious of sexual identity do not lie in the differences between the sexes, but in becoming aware of the presence or the absence of one single sex-specific factor. Moreover, this account presupposes a sex-specific viewer. Because when viewed from a woman's body, there is no lack and the man's body just has an extra component (a 'prop', in the words of Garber). The lack of this part of the body can only assume the dramatic significance of castration or inferiority in a cultural situation in which men have a privileged position. In short, castration, lack and/or inferiority are not 'discovered' by the girl at the moment she becomes aware of difference, but constitute a culturally specific explanation of a physical difference, an explanation which children are taught.

For Freud, the discovery of difference marks the beginning of a development which he describes in terms of two processes: the above-mentioned castration complex and the Oedipus complex. The Oedipus complex takes its name from a well-known story from Ancient Greece about Oedipus who, without being aware of the situation, murders his father and marries his mother. In Freud's theory, this story signifies the longing that small boys would develop for taking over the position of their fathers. The growing insight into the position of the father as the one who bears power and is the mother's lover deprives the child of his feeling of omnipotence and his position as the object of the mother's undivided attention. Because of this, castration is a threat on the symbolic level.

Psychoanalysis: Possibilities and limitations

Peter Pan offers plenty of possibilities for Freudian interpretations and they have appeared in abundance. A boy who does not want to grow up and a girl who wants to become his lover, but is forced into becoming his mother, provide plenty of food for thought. And what about a small boy who enters into conflict with Captain Hook, first 'unmanning' him by chopping off his hand and finally defeating him to save his 'mother' Wendy? Captain Hook's hook is his 'synecdoche': it is what defines him and where his name is derived from. The hook is also the ever-present identifying sign of what he lacks and represents his castration. Peter Pan fed Hook's chopped-off hand to a crocodile which, having acquired the taste, has since that time lain in waiting to consume the rest. The crocodile can be seen as a visualization of the Captain's deepest fears.

Here it is interesting to note how the crocodile is given form in the Disney film, such that it conjures up associations with what is referred to in art history as a *vagina dentata*, a vagina with teeth, an image that fuses a fascination for the female sexual organ with the deeply rooted fear of it – who knows what will happen if you stick it in? The crocodile in the Disney film is constantly lurking to swallow up Hook whole in the pink depths of her jaws that are bordered with rows of sharp teeth. In relation to this, the 'dance' that Hook carries out in the Disney film in his attempts to escape the crocodile is also interesting. With all his strength he attempts to push the jaws of the crocodile apart with his legs, while without further ado, the crocodile in the meantime snaps in the direction of his crotch and pulls down his trousers.

Peter Pan, regarded from a Freudian perspective, contains the promise that it may be possible to escape the castration complex. That it may be possible to withdraw from the power of the father and marry your mother, and to do all of this without becoming an adult. *Peter Pan* embodies the promise of an escape from the laws which determine existence. But it is an escape which, such as clarified above, takes shape along the lines of exactly the same laws and in doing so confirms those laws instead of denying them. It is within this cultural perspective of which both Barrie and Freud are exponents – Barrie wrote *Peter Pan* at more or less the same time as when Freud published his ideas about sexual identity – that Garber explains the phenomenon that Peter Pan is a woman. And it is precisely that which marks the limitation of this perspective.

What is special about Garber's analysis is that her explanation about why Peter Pan is a woman does not use psychoanalysis to explain Peter Pan, but that she arrives at an explanation of this phenomenon from the *limitation* of the psychoanalytical perspective. She points to structural similarities between the story told in the *Peter Pan* play and the Freudian story about the formation of sexual identity, and how those similarities create an understanding for what becomes perceptible or remains imperceptible within this perspective. In this way she provides a critique of the way in which gender is presented in this play, as well as of the limitations of psychoanalytical theories as far as gender is concerned, and of the way in which psychoanalysis is employed to read *Peter Pan* as, for example, a reflection of the complicated psyche of the author Barrie, or as the ego ideal of the character of Wendy.

In the first case, possible connections are pointed out between the author's personal life history and the construction of the imaginary world in *Peter Pan*. That imaginary world is understood to be the product of psychological processes which can be explained with the help of psychoanalysis. The assumptions of psychoanalysis thus remain beyond consideration and, moreover, the question is what precisely is learned from such an analysis: does such an analysis tell you anything about the play, or is the analysis of the play actually a means to find something out about the author?

In the second case, psychoanalysis is set free on one of the characters and used to explain the behaviour of this character as if it were a real person. Peter Pan can do what Wendy as a Victorian girl may not: experience adventures, fight with pirates, and smoke the peace pipe with the Red Indians. In this regard, casting a woman as Peter Pan can be explained by the fact that the piece depicts Wendy's rite of passage to adulthood, a development in which she first identifies with Peter Pan – literally recognizes herself in him – but in the course of time, she learns to let go of this mistaken ideal to finally accept her correct role.[2]

However, such a reading does not consider the fact that in Barrie's play Wendy does not try and be like Peter, but rather takes on the role of his lover. Her problem is not her own role, but his refusal to play the role that she wishes him to play, namely that of her husband. However much we may not be in agreement with the role Wendy performs, certainly from a contemporary standpoint, the piece does not indicate that she may have any difficulties with it. Moreover, this explanation does not consider how this play *works* in the theatre. In other words, before an audience. Casting a woman as Peter Pan has to look convincing, not for Wendy, but for the audience. For that audience Peter Pan has to be convincing as the boy who does not want to grow up, who is eternally young, and who does not understand anything about Wendy's advances, or those of Tinker Bell or Tiger Lily. Just as Captain Hook is pursued by a crocodile who had once eaten his hand and now has her eyes on the rest, so is Peter Pan pursued by three women who would dearly love to make a man of him – their man – whereas meanwhile Peter Pan appears to be oblivious to what they want. The casting confirms that this is a hopeless enterprise: this Peter Pan is never going to grow up and become a man.

Story and audience

In her reading based on the parallel between the psychoanalytical perspective and *Peter Pan*, Garber points to the connection between the story told and the viewer to which it relates. A viewer with specific desires, fears, and assumptions about what is believable, acceptable, and desirable. This connection is essential in the theatre, but regarding this point, the theatre can also offer a model for the way in which the credibility of performances and gender performances outside the theatre should be understood from the relation between that performance and a viewer, whether the performance or gender performance is now consciously directed towards that person – and the gaze of that person has thus been calculated as it were – or not.

The *Peter Pan* play was written with the audience in mind. The stage directions consist of all sorts of humorous comments in which the reader is constantly reminded that this is a play. The construction of the piece can also be regarded as a comment about how theatre organizes the relationship between the audience and the imaginary world. The play starts in a nursery which, according to the stage directions, looks like one that the children in the original audience would recognize. Here the audience becomes acquainted with a number of children just like themselves and subsequently a fairytale figure appears who takes these children – and the children in the audience who are invited to identify with these children – to a fantasy world. The fantasy world can only be reached if you believe in it, just as the theatre also requires you to temporarily suspend your disbelief and go along with it. At an important moment in the plot, this question is also asked explicitly. When Tinker Bell is in danger of dying, the Peter Pan character addresses the audience directly with the question: 'Do you believe in Fairies?' He asks the children in the audience to confirm their belief in fairies at the top of their voices, because it is only that belief which can save Tinker Bell.

This moment is surely an example of 'dramatic license', as referred to by Davis (2005). The rules of the dramatic illusion are deliberately undermined, but in such a way that the audience is required to actually confirm the dramatic illusion. *Peter Pan* subverts the division between the imaginary world and the audience and in this way undermines the suggestion that this world exists autonomously, independently of the audience. At the same time, the audience is thus asked to confirm their belief in this world and its existence. In this, according to Davis, *Peter Pan* (or actually the author Barrie, naturally) presents the audience with a choice which goes beyond the context of this play. She thinks that this moment in *Peter Pan* can be read as an invitation to the audience to express recognition for the existing fairies, gypsies, and others whose existence in the margins of what is recognized as reality is threatened by advancing rationalization and industrialization. With this interpretation of Peter Pan's question, she points to the relationship between what we are prepared to accept as true in the theatre and outside of it. Naturally, the imaginary world in the theatre is not the same as the world outside, but in both cases, the same assumptions, desires, and fears play a role in our judgement of what we accept as believable and what we do not.

However, you may wonder, the audience has already concurred with quite a lot before Peter Pan comes up with his explicit question. Does the explicit answer to his question about fairies not imply the much more radical and encompassing acceptation of a whole system of assumptions, values, and norms which remain unspoken? Because the question here about belief is in relation to fairies, and following from this fantasy world of Peter Pan as different from reality, is it not indeed the status of the 'normal' world which is affirmed as self-evident, and with this, the belief in the self-evidence of the assumptions which determine what reality is?

Woman warrior?

'Why is Peter Pan a woman?' Majorie Garber asks herself and her explanation makes it clear that the phenomenon of Peter Pan is a symptom of the cultural perspective on reality and who can play a role in it. But would this also make Peter Pan a *woman warrior*? For that matter, is it not so that being a woman remains to a great degree imperceptible, in the case of Peter Pan? As far as this is concerned, Peter Pan is a symptom in many respects, a symptom of the practical limitations which women have been faced with for a long time (and to a lesser extent, are still faced with), a symptom too of the limitations of the gaze with which their performance (on and off stage) is perceived, and finally a symptom of the way in which perception and reality are linked.

Peter Pan is pre-eminently a figure from the theatre. The complexity of this figure only manifests itself in the theatre, in other words, in a performance of the piece. For that matter, it is only then that the implications of casting a role come into play. The theatre is the place where Peter Pan simultaneously is and is not a woman. As a figure of the theatre, Peter Pan thus undermines the categories which lie at the basis of what sort of reality will take place. Peter Pan is theatrical in the sense described by Barbara Freedman in her *Staging the Gaze: Postmodernism, Psychoanalysis and Shakespearean Comedy*. Freedman asks herself what we actually mean when we say that someone is theatrical and she writes: '[is] theatricality more concerned with the act of showing than with the inherent quality of what, in fact, is shown? Or is theatricality precisely the challenge to try to separate the two?' (Freedman, 1991: 51).

Peter Pan embodies the impossibility of making this distinction and at the same time he is an example of how the ambiguity and equivocality of what actually can be seen remains unperceived within a cultural-historical specific gaze. Peter Pan is an example of how a univocal distinction between, for example, man and woman is produced and reproduced within that gaze and how this signifies a reduction of ambiguity to univocality. This reduction strips Peter Pan of his/her ambiguous character.

Peter Pan is thus a woman warrior despite himself/herself, a woman warrior who indicates the necessity of making us conscious of what guides our gaze and what appears as male or female through this. This is not only a consequence of how people behave or are depicted, but also of how we look at them. Peter Pan is a historical example of the way in which viewers can be blind to the equivocality of what can be seen through their own gaze. As woman warrior, Peter Pan indicates the necessity for opening up to such ambiguity and equivocality, for accepting and embracing the theatrical, not only in Peter Pan's case on stage, but also with off-stage gender performances.

A proposal by Susan Foster (1998), for making a distinction between performance and choreography as far as gender is concerned, is helpful in this regard. Foster observes that, in Butler's approach, the emphasis lies on the verbal dimension of gender as performance and how gender is shaped as a product of repetition. In *Bodies that Matter*, Butler's only example of a non-verbal text is the film *Paris is Burning*. In her analysis of this text, Butler describes the various roles which are carried out at drag balls by cross-dressed performers. Through their subversive behaviour, these performers literally demonstrate gender as performance and thus confirm Butler's argument that gender is the effect of performance.

However, in the case of *Paris is Burning*, the significance of these performances does not only lie in the way in which they reproduce or undermine the norm, but also to an important extent in the complex relationship between the individual performer and the pattern of conventions which are performed by him/her. After all, the subversive power of drag can be found in the discrepancy between the conventions and the physique of the performer who confirms these conventions. Foster therefore proposes making a distinction between, on the one hand, gender as a cultural historical specific choreography of behaviour and means of expression and, on the other, gender as the performance of an individual who carries out these patterns consciously or unconsciously, and consciously or unconsciously varies them and gives them a personal twist.

The relation between gender as performance and gender as choreography is not that of static system to dynamic user, because both are constantly in transformation and the choreography of gender partially changes through the transformations that it undergoes in the performance. Think, for example, about the choreography of a dance such as the waltz or the tango: there is a choreography which the dancers learn and constantly perform time and again, and yet dancers each have their own style, so even a faithful performance of the choreography will be an individual interpretation. Moreover, the choreography changes during the course of time. The way in which we waltz today is not the same as our ancestors did a hundred years ago, even if continuity in the choreography can be said to exist. The changes in the choreography of the waltz reflect changes in manners, musical preferences, and other outlooks and habits.

When we look at *Peter Pan* once again, the distinction proposed by Foster can be helpful in making a distinction between gender as a choreography which is implied in Peter Pan's role – a choreography which is a reflection of a constellation of conscious and unconscious conventions in relation to male or boyish behaviour as is prescribed by the role – and gender as the effect of the performance of the actress who carries out the role of Peter Pan – an actress who, in her performance, relates to the choreography as it is implied in the role.

The role of Peter Pan contains a perspective on gender – a perspective which is expressed in the proposed choreography for the role – whereas the actress' performance contains a perspective on the role. The role is viewed from and embodied in the cultural historical moment of the performance, including its accompanying conscious and unconscious presuppositions about what is believable, attractive, and interesting and what is not. The distinction between choreography and performance can thereby help to focus the attention on the complex combined play of perspectives and behaviour that negotiates the way in which *Peter Pan* can be played and viewed.

Notes

1 Barrie's own introduction to the text of the play *Peter Pan* is entitled 'To the Five: A Dedication'. In this text he asks himself whether he can indeed dedicate *Peter Pan* to the five children indicated in the title because he has absolutely no memory of writing *Peter Pan* (in contrast to his other plays) and he also does not have the original manuscript. Is the piece by him? He dedicates the piece to the five because of 'that laughter of yours in which Peter came into being long before he was caught and written down' (Barrie, 1995: 77). In the 'Introduction' to *Peter Pan and Other Plays*, Peter Hollindale refers to a number of other examples of mystification surrounding the authorship and history of origins. The history of origins of the play and Barrie's relationship with the five children is the subject of much speculation and was also the reason for the fictional film *Finding Neverland* (2004).

2 What is interesting in relation to this is the film *Peter Pan* (Hogan, 2003), in which much more of the original play is used than in the Disney cartoon film and also a number of new scenes have been added. The additions are to a great extent concerned with Wendy's role. In a totally new opening sequence, Wendy's difficulty with her role as Victorian girl and her struggle with growing up are central. She is torn between what her parents want to see and wanting to join the pirates. It would seem that the filmmakers have done their best to make the story more acceptable and convincing for a contemporary viewer and that in this, it is primarily the role of Wendy which is regarded as an obstacle. The result is not entirely satisfying *gender-wise*, but invites some interesting speculations. It is not only the changes in Wendy's role, but also, in relation to this, the fact that in this film the role of Peter Pan is played by a young actor and not by an actress is striking. Are Peter Pan's attempts to place Wendy in the role of a virginal mother a means of eliminating her as a competitor? Initially Wendy is at least as tough, if not tougher than Peter Pan. It is noteworthy that in this film heterosexual tension between Peter Pan and Wendy can actually be said to exist and quite ironically so in the casting. Its presence

has an effect comparable to its absence in cross-casting, in relation to the way in which Wendy is pushed into the 'correct' gender direction by the story. Here it is not Wendy who, as a matter of course, wants to turn Peter Pan into her husband, but rather Peter Pan who, through the way in which he plays with Wendy's burgeoning feelings, introduces heterosexual love and eroticism in her life and through this, puts her in a state of confusion concerning the role she sees set aside for herself. It is as if she, through her induced burgeoning sexuality, is seduced into accepting the traditional gender role which goes with it.

Questions for further research

1   On the basis of annual reports (which can be downloaded from the Internet), find out what the man-woman ratio is in various drama schools (acting, directing, writing, designing, etc.).

2   Which roles do women fulfil in different aspects of theatrical practice and where can women be found in managerial positions? In which sector are most women found? What does this say about current gender relations?

3   Which women theatre makers are mentioned for which works in theatre history textbooks?

4   What are famous roles for women and what sort of roles are they?

5   Find out from newspapers/magazines which actresses have recently won prizes and for what.

6   Which woman's role could be played convincingly by a man and why?

Lara Croft, *Kill Bill*, and the battle for theory in feminist film studies

12

Anneke Smelik

12.1 Uma Thurman as Beatrix Kiddo in Kill Bill.

An eye stares at us in extreme close-up. The camera zooms out and we see Lara Croft hanging upside-down on a rope. Somersaulting, she jumps onto the ground of what mostly looks like the ruins of an Egyptian temple. Silence. We see beams of sunlight shining between the pillars and grave tombs. Dust dances in the sun. Lara looks warily around. Then the stone next to her violently splits open and the fight begins. For minutes, Lara runs, jumps, and dives in an incredible feat of acrobatics. Pillars topple over, tombs burst open. She draws pistols and shoots and shoots and shoots. Her opponent, a robot, appears to be defeated. The camera slides along Lara's magnificently-formed body and zooms in on her breasts, her legs, and her bottom. She falls to the ground and, lying down, fires all her bullets at the robot. Then she grabs his 'arms' and pushes the rotating discs into his 'head'. She jumps up onto him, hacking him to pieces. Lara disappears from the monitor on the robot, while the screen turns black. Lara pants and grins triumphantly. She has won.

The first *Tomb Raider* film (2001) opens with this breath-taking action scene, featuring Lara Croft (Angelina Jolie) as the 'girl that kicks ass'. What is she fighting for? No idea, I can't remember after the film has ended. It is typical for the Hollywood movie that the conflict is actually of minor importance. It concerns a struggle between good and bad, where it is established in advance that the good, and thus the Hollywood hero or heroine, will win. As a true 'warrior' Lara goes to battle, but for what or why is of no concern. Lara is super strong, invincibly strong. But also stunningly beautiful, unbelievably beautiful. This combination has characterized film heroines since the 1990s.

The action hero in Hollywood was traditionally a man. In the 1980s, the female action heroine emerged, fighting and swearing like a man (Tasker, 1993). At the end of the 1990s, the action heroine once again became as erotically attractive as the early female stars. Lara Croft is exemplary of this ambivalent woman's image: eroticized as a woman and masculinized as action heroine. The action film is a violent genre and the woman warrior therefore fights in the midst of a battlefield of torn-out eyes, hacked-off limbs, spouting fountains of blood, and innumerable dead bodies. In this chapter, I will trace how the image of woman as the 'warrior' has come about and how it can be interpreted with the help of feminist film theory. For this purpose, I discuss two women warriors: Lara Croft from the *Tomb Raider* films and Beatrix Kiddo from the *Kill Bill* films.

Although the films were made in the same period, at the beginning of the twenty-first century, and more or less belong to the same action genre, they nevertheless represent two different tendencies in contemporary visual culture. Where Lara Croft can still be analyzed with the help of classic feminist film theory, this is not the case for Beatrix Kiddo. Art and popular culture sometimes stride ahead of academia. New cultural practices require new theoretical concepts. This can be demonstrated on the basis of these two 'warriors', each of whom embody a different gender performance. In this chapter, I will discuss what has by now become classic feminist film theory (for a detailed summary, see Smelik, 2007). With the help of the two action heroines, it will become clear whether this body of theory can still be used or needs to be adapted.

Looking and being looked at: The voyeuristic gaze

Feminist film theory developed in the early 1970s under the influence of the women's movement. That process ran parallel with the emergence of structuralism within the humanities, through the influence of Marxism, semiotics, and psychoanalysis.

It was the period when film studies started to become established in academia. From the post-structuralist and structuralist perspective, it was not so much the content that mattered (what is the meaning of this film, television series, or video clip?), but how meaning was *acquired*. It is a given that film should not be regarded as a *reflection* of meaning given in advance, but as a *construction* of meaning. In recent years, a shift has taken place to paying attention to the sensory and affective *experience* of watching films.

From the early outset of film theory, questions such as class, gender, and ethnicity have been central in this new subject area. Within film studies, and more generally within visual studies, it is still customary to pay attention to these social and ideological issues. The feminist analysis of 'the gaze' is generally accepted in cultural studies. In other words, feminist theory has been an important factor in film studies ever since it came into existence.

Film studies has interpreted the fascination for film with the help of psychoanalysis. The absorbing effect of film – in the cinema you are all ears and eyes – can psycho-analytically be explained as a primary identification with camera and projection (Metz, 1982). Moreover, the fascination for film is linked to sexuality. According to Freud (1905), eroticism begins with looking: *scopophilia*. Touching and the sexual act follow on from the desiring gaze. Film theorists were quick to propose that the medium of film is in fact based on scopophilia: in the darkness of the cinema, the viewer is a voyeur who can unlimitedly look at the silver screen. Watching films has thus always had something of the erotic, in contrast to the theatre where voyeurism is disrupted because the actors can look back. The television and the computer do not have the same voyeuristic setup as film either, because in the living room the lights are on, people are talking, the screen is much smaller, and there are all sorts of distractions.

Laura Mulvey (1989 [1974]) advanced the idea that active and passive aspects of scopophilia, the urge to look, are shared among the sexes. In his well-known book *Ways of Seeing*, John Berger had already proposed that in Western culture, from painting to advertising, 'men act and women appear' (1972: 47) or rather: men look and women are looked at. Mulvey's analysis is based on the classic Hollywood film, the commercial black and white films in the years between 1930 and 1960. According to Mulvey, in the Hollywood film (but the principle also applies to European films) this works as follows. The male character looks at a woman and the camera films what the man sees (a so-called 'point of view shot'). Because the camera looks along with the male character, the viewer is invited or rather forced to adopt a male position. The spectator in the cinema thus looks through the eyes of the male character at the woman. It is a case of a threefold 'male' gaze: camera, character, and spectator. In addition, the woman's body is 'cut up' by editing and framing; the image of the woman's body is thus fragmented in a two-dimensional space.

In Mulvey's analysis, it is important that the cinematic apparatus, such as the camera work, the framing, the editing, and the music objectify the woman's body and turn it into a passive spectacle for the voyeuristic gaze: to-be-looked-at-ness. One can find classic examples of this kind of voyeurism in classics such as *Gilda* (1946, with Rita Hayworth), *The Postman Always Rings Twice* (1946, with Lana Turner), *Written on the Wind* (1956, with Lauren Bacall), and *Psycho* (1960, with Janet Leigh), but also in more recent films such as *Sliver* (1993, with Sharon Stone) and *True Lies* (1994, with Jamie Lee Curtis; incidentally, Janet Leigh's daughter).

Mulvey continues her analysis by considering the notion of the castration complex. The voyeuristic gaze at the woman's body is unsettling for the man because it is different; in Freud's words 'castrated' (Freud, 1931). At an unconscious level, the man is reminded of the threat of 'castration' because the female body is not complete. In Freud's words, the female body is inferior and in Lacan's view, she is the bearer of a lack. As twenty-first century feminists, we can neutralize these deeply misogynist interpretations, by shifting the rather anatomical notion of a castrated female body to a more symbolical reading where the female body signifies difference in a culture of men. In most cultures, it is the case that the woman-as-other, namely other than the man, gives meaning to sexual difference. In that more neutral reading, the woman constantly reminds the man of her otherness, without our having to translate this in the loaded terms of castration and lack.

In cultural products, in this case films, the male fear of the female body has to be averted. According to Mulvey, this happens in two ways. The first is through sadism: the woman's body has to be controlled and inserted into the social order. Sadism usually is given form in the narrative structure. The erotic gaze is often followed by violence, such as rape or even murder. It is no coincidence that in the classic Hollywood film, more often than not, it is the femme fatale who is killed, as in *Double Indemnity* (1944, with Barbara Stanwick). In the 1990s, the sexually active woman still dies, as in *Fatal Attraction* (1987, with Glenn Close) and *Thelma and Louise* (1991, with Susan Sarandon and Geena Davis). *Basic Instinct* (1992) is perhaps one of the first films where the femme fatale (Sharon Stone) is allowed to live on at the end, followed by *The Last Seduction* (1994, with Linda Fiorentino).

According to Mulvey, the second way of averting male fear is through fetishism, a strategy of disavowal (Freud, 1927). The female star is turned into an ideal beauty, a fetish, whose flawless perfection turns any attention away from her difference, her otherness. The camera endlessly lingers on the spectacle of female beauty, allowing the male spectator to disavow her physical 'lack'. At such moments of 'spectacularization', the film's story is temporarily brought to a halt, and all the cinematic means are geared to fetishizing the female body: glamorous make-up and costume, lighting, framing, and music. All Hollywood female film stars are fetishized, but the most classical examples are Marlene Dietrich and Marilyn Monroe. A contemporary example is Angelina Jolie.

Mulvey's feminist analysis dates from the 1970s, but has been of great importance for insights into visual culture to this very day. Her influential article is one of the most quoted in film studies. Due to feminist film critique, the image of the passive woman in cinema has been deconstructed in recent decades, because Hollywood wants to reach out to an important segment of the market. A more active role for actresses is more often available and women are able to play the leading part, even active and violent ones, in many different genres of action movies, such as horror (Neve Campbell in *Scream*, 1996), science fiction (Angela Bassett in *Strange Days*, 1995), adventure films

(Angelina Jolie in *Tomb Raider*, 2001 and 2003), the revenge films (Uma Thurman in *Kill Bill*, 2003 and 2004), and as a soldier in the action film (Demi Moore in *GI Jane*, 1997).

The analysis of the gaze does not only pertain to gender, but also to ethnicity. Dyer (1997) demonstrates that the Hollywood system is geared towards the white star, for example in the lighting schemes or in the dominant position that they adopt in the narrative. Both Hall (1997) and Nederveen Pieterse (1992) provide an extensive historical analysis of the way in which coloured and black people have been depicted in Western culture. It was often a case of stark stereotyping, such as the fetishist exoticism of black women in European films, or the image of the black man as sexually threatening in American films (Gaines, 1988). 'Another' ethnicity in films is nearly always linked to sexuality (Young, 1996). Although currently in European films, inter-ethnic relationships can also end positively, such happy endings are still rare in the American film (Smelik, 2003). The most recent example is *Monster's Ball* (2001) for which Halle Berry, as the first black woman, was awarded an Oscar for best actress in a leading role.

The voyeuristic look in today's visual culture

Although classic voyeurism occurs less frequently in today's cinema, the voyeuristic gaze is still prominent in advertising, fashion photography, and the video clips. Video clips and fashion shows are nearly always constructed around fetishized women's bodies and the sexualized play of looking and being looked at. A number of trends can be discerned. First, voyeurism is less directed through the male gaze, which means that the spectator does not look along with a male character, but rather with a 'neutral' camera. At the same time, it seems that the visual spectacle of to-be-looked-at-ness has increased in recent decades. Representations of the female body are increasingly more naked and erotic. This can be referred to as a certain *pornofication* in today's visual culture (Levy, 2006).

Second, certain subcultures are strongly zeroing in on voyeurism, in particularly rap and hip-hop video clips with 'pimp' and 'ho' stereotypes. On the one hand, this can be read positively for its visualization of the black body as erotic and attractive, but on the other hand, this macho culture can be criticized for its sexist view of women.

Third, the phenomenon of the voyeuristic gaze has been extended to the male body that is objectified in films, advertising, fashion, and soaps (Hall, 1997). Since the 1990s, the male body has been fragmented, objectified, and eroticized (Simpson, 1993). This was at first an influence from the gay movement, but now the male image has been made more heterosexual in the figure of the metrosexual. The spectacle of an often nude and wet Daniel Craig in the latest James Bond film testifies to this recent development.

Fourth, the body has changed dramatically in recent decades due to the fitness culture: male and female stars are not only expected to be beautiful, but they also have to be super thin and super fit. The fuller figures of Marilyn Monroe, Jane Russell, and

Ava Gardner have been replaced by the streamlined bodies of Gwyneth Paltrow, Nicole Kidman, and Keira Knightley. In Hollywood, older actresses also have to meet the norm of 'thin is in'; in *Alien Resurrection* (1997), Sigourney Weaver has arms of steel. Skinny and muscular models and actresses are the new image of women in the twenty-first century.

Sometimes this new body form provides anachronistic images. When Angelina Bassett plays the role of Tina Turner in *What's Love Got To Do With It* (1993), she sings a rock'n'roll song in a sleeveless 1960s dress. Her muscular arms are out of character and the viewer realizes at once how the body has changed in a couple of decades. As Svendsen (2006) argues, a 'natural' body does not exist, because the human body is just as much subject to fashion as the clothes that cover it. For today's film or pop star, plump arms are taboo and sculptured biceps are a must. We can even argue that women's bodies have been flattened out, with the exclusion of the breasts which, with the help of silicon or digital manipulation, are unnaturally large and are unnaturally high up on the body. Breasts should never fall prey to the force of gravity. Arms, legs, bottoms, and tummies should no longer be round or soft, but just as hard and muscular as in a male body.

Contemporary culture expects both women and men to discipline their body (Foucault, 1977), which sometimes leads to dangerous combinations of diets, starvation, laxatives, colon irrigations, and 'fitness bulimia'. We can say that the voyeuristic gaze has been internalized in impossible norms for a thin and yet strong and well-formed body. Even after pregnancies, actresses have to prove that within the shortest amount of time they will once again fit into size 8. Although a film such as *The Devil Wears Prada* (2006) mocks this predilection for perfectionism by, for example, labelling a woman with size 10 as 'fat', nobody shirks from this norm in the story. However, there are some signs of rebellious reaction against this trend of always being younger and thinner. The cosmetic brand Dove launched an advertising campaign in 2005 with 'ordinary' women with round forms and in 2006, for older models. Actresses such as Kate Winslett, Scarlett Johansson, and Jennifer Lopez present their female forms as healthy. The modelling world has proposed a minimum weight to prevent extreme cases of anorexia.

To summarize, we can say that at the beginning of the twenty-first century, classic voyeurism has changed, because the spectator does not look from the perspective of a dominant male gaze. This means that the gaze of the camera has become more neutral, allowing both the male and the female viewer to enjoy the erotic spectacle of either sex. In addition, the fetishization of both the female and the male body has strongly increased in an eroticized body culture. The voyeuristic gaze has then shifted to a more equal representation of gender, which takes place at the level of looking (the gaze), as well as the level of being looked at (the object), in which activity and passivity are shared among both sexes.

Take for example *Tomb Raider*. Lara Croft plays an active role and holds her ground as far as fighting and violence are concerned. Her body functions as an erotic spectacle for the viewer (m/f) without being mediated through the eyes of a male character (Kennedy, 2002; Mikula, 2004). Angelina Jolie may well have gorgeous breasts, but her body is also hard and muscular. Her fitness and her 'phallic' weapons turn her into an invincible warrior. Moreover, she is not available as an erotic object for the male characters in the narrative. She is even quite lonely and does not maintain any sexual relations.

We can extend this analysis to Jolie's partner, Brad Pitt. Since the eroticization of his backside in *Thelma and Louise* (1991), he is an example of the contemporary hero who functions as an object of the female gaze. His body has also become considerably well-built in the course of time; compare his early physique with his well developed torso in *Troy* (2004). In *Mr and Mrs Smith* (2005), Jolie and Pitt are represented on equal terms with regard to activity and passivity, to looking and being looked at. On the one hand, they are a perfect match for each other in fighting skills, although Jolie is the better contract killer because she has killed dozens more people than Pitt has. On the other hand, the camera exploits their reputation as the most beautiful man and most beautiful woman by eroticizing their bodies on the screen.

Looking and being looked at: The narcissistic gaze

Where film studies took the notion of scopophilia from Freud, it was primarily Lacan's theory of the mirror stage that was adapted to clarify processes of identification. Film theorists such as Metz (1982), Baudry (1992), and Mulvey (1989), used Lacan's concept of the mirror stage to explain the complexities of cinematic spectatorship. In this perspective, there is a primary identification of the spectator with the cinematic apparatus, and a secondary identification with the hero. The film thus functions as a mirror in which the spectator recognizes his or her ideal 'I' (ego).

Lacan (1977) postulates the mirror stage as one of the early moments of ego formation of the subject. This narcissistic process takes place when the baby is six to eighteen months old, preceding language in a phase that Lacan termed the Imaginary. He suggests that the child learns to recognize itself in the mirror and develops the first inklings of self-consciousness by identifying with the specular image. The mirror image is always an idealization, because the child projects an ideal image of himself or herself, thus constructing an 'Ideal-I' (Lacan, 1977: 2). While the child still has little control over its own fragmented body, it sees itself reflected as an autonomous entity in the mirror. This ideal self-image leads the child to a 'jubilant' (ibid.: 2) recognition of itself; the first awareness of the ego in its idealized form. The mirror stage is thus a narcissistic gaze directed at the self, while the voyeuristic gaze is directed at the other.

It is crucial for Lacan that the first formation of the I is based on an image, that is the reflection in the mirror, and hence on a source outside of itself. Thus the formation of the I is, from the very start, based on an alienation from itself. The identification of the self with the mirror image is thus a 'mis'-recognition (*méconnaissance*, ibid.: 6) or, in other words, an illusion. The child identifies with its own image as an-other, that is, as a better self than he or she will ever hope to be in the future. According to the ever pessimistic Lacan, this is a tragedy for mankind: we construct our own identity on the basis of an ideal image to which we will forever aspire. In his eyes, we are therefore always existentially deprived; our ego is basically a gaping lack that will never be fulfilled.

As the mirror is a visual *topos* in paintings, films, video clips, advertisements, and fashion photography, it is easy to recognize the Lacanian mirror stage. In visual culture, the mirror functions as a moment of narcissistic (self-)reflection for the character or model. In the classic Hollywood film, it often indicates the weakness or even mental illness of the female character (Doane, 1987). Today's visual culture depicts narcissism even more often than before, but now it rather points to the character's power and independence. The fact that Lara Croft does not enter into any relationships underlines her narcissistic autonomy. In addition to an active role in the story, narcissism enables the female star to be in charge of her to-be-looked-at-ness. In this respect, Lara Croft fits the trend of contemporary representations of female (and also male) beauty of film or pop stars that serve a narcissistic rather than voyeuristic gaze; think of Madonna, for example.

The concept of the mirror phase also applies to the spectator. By identifying with the powerful, attractive hero, the spectator relives the identification with an ego ideal. The screen or image then functions as a mirror. For Mulvey and other feminist film theorists, the problem with classic Hollywood films was that the female spectator could only positively identify with the male hero as an ideal image, because identification with the objectified heroine was marginal or masochistic (Doane, 1987). The search and even demand for the visual and narrative pleasure for the female spectator has long dominated feminist film theory (Bergstrom and Doane, 1989). Many critics have also explored the possibilities of a specific black (hooks, 1992; Grayson, 1995; Hall, 1997) and lesbian spectatorship (Gever and Breyson, 1993; Smelik, 1998b; Dyer, 2003; Aaron, 2004).

With the arrival of powerful heroines in the 1970s, negative identification mostly disappeared. Lara Croft may serve again as an example here. The female spectator can identify with the ideal image of a woman who has power and agency, but who is also beautiful and attractive without losing her independence. Film stars such as Angelina Jolie, but also pop stars and models, offer us ideal images for identification. Fan culture is to a great extent based on narcissistic identification (Stacey, 1994).

There are some drawbacks here. In a culture that celebrates youth, fitness, and beauty by presenting perfect models in digitally manipulated images, the ideal image is becoming increasingly unattainable. Identification through the narcissistic gaze then corresponds with the internalization of the voyeuristic gaze, as discussed above. This results in an extensive culture of disciplining the body (Foucault, 1977) with, for example, diets, fitness, and products from the beauty industry. This is problematic in so far as it concerns a self-imposed ideal that is derived from the visual culture that surrounds us everywhere: on television, in cinemas, in glossies, fashion shows, and on billboards. Few people can recognize themselves in the ideal image of contemporary visual culture and many become dissatisfied with their own image. This may lead to frustration and sometimes to drastic measures such as cosmetic surgery, or to illnesses such as anorexia and bulimia. In these cases, the narcissistic gaze fails in the mirror of pop culture, because identification leads to dissatisfaction with oneself instead of strengthening one's self-image.

Oedipus

So far I have emphasized the complex play of looks that regulate identification and desire in films, because it is characteristic of visual media. Voyeurism arises from the desire to *have* someone and narcissism from the desire to *be* someone. Another psychoanalytical concept that has played a major role in film studies (just as in literary studies) is the Oedipus complex (Freud, 1900; 1925; 1931). Because of the emphasis on the oedipal element as a structural element of the cinematic story, psychoanalysis is less suitable as an analytical framework for television and the computer. Those media are less characterized by narrative, and more by spectacle, fragmentation, and inter-activity.

Hollywood movies abound with oedipal motifs. The conventional film story has the following structure: good wins over bad, son wins over father, hero gets girl, the dangerous woman or ('even worse') the homosexual is punished or killed, and the symbolic order is restored (Kuhn, 1999). I will not repeat this obvious analysis of such film narratives. The interesting point here is that structuralist film theorists have primarily interpreted the Oedipus complex as a structuring device for the narrative. The oedipal structure thus would pertain to any classic Hollywood film, for example, in the rivalry between men in westerns, or the father and son struggle in adventure films such as *Indiana Jones*.

We have already seen that Lara Croft does not engage in sexual relationships with men, but the oedipal motif is foregrounded in *Tomb Raider*. Lara has a complex relationship with her father, whose approval she is constantly seeking until reconcili-ation finally takes place. The cinematic relationship between father and daughter is doubled up in 'reality', because Jolie has a much publicized complex relation to her father in real life, the actor Jon Voight, who plays the role of Lara's father in the film.

The structuralist analysis of the Oedipus complex dominated film theory for some time and also influenced feminist analysis. For example, Teresa de Lauretis (1984) claims that a story always has an oedipal structure because the narrative is inevitably driven by the oedipal desire of the male hero. Just as Mulvey proposed that sadism needs a story, de Lauretis argued that a story cannot do without sadism. Could any Hollywood movie, or European film for that matter, escape oedipal ideology? Apparently not. Melodrama was the only Hollywood genre that addressed a female audience, but the vicissitudes of the oedipal plot made it into a true tearjerker for women: staging tyran-nical mothers, a suffocating mother-and-daughter relationship, the unhappy and forever unfulfilled housewife, and unattainable or treacherous men. However, more marginal genres, such as horror and science fiction, did break with the oedipal pattern by flagrantly depicting the uncanny or the abject (Creed, 2005), but they hardly made for more positive representations of femininity.

Because female characters in cinema are always defined as the object of male desire, the question of female desire becomes an important one. This can be understood as a reformulation of the Freudian question: 'Was will das Weib?'. Silverman (1988) and de Lauretis (1994) have tried to theorize alternative forms of female desire, but they remain within the orthodox framework of psychoanalysis. According to Mulvey and others, the exploration of female desire and subjectivity was only possible within an experimental aesthetic that radically breaks with the oedipal plot. In the 1970s, female filmmakers such as Chantal Akerman, Marguérite Duras, Ulrike Ottinger, Helke Sander, and also Laura Mulvey herself produced avant-garde films (Kaplan, 1983; Kuhn, 1994). But the avant-garde is notoriously inaccessible for the general public. In *And the Mirror Cracked* (Smelik, 1998a), I therefore tried to stretch the limits of psychoanalysis by reading mainstream women's films. The question was how female directors expressed female subjectivity and desire within more or less conventional narrative structures. This can be done, for example, by systematically giving the narrative and visual point of view to the female character. She thus acquires an active role within the narrative and dominates the look of the camera, allowing for narcissistic identification while blocking a voyeuristic gaze. Another way of shaping female subjectivity is by representing an inner life on the screen in dreams, fantasies, or hallucinations.

Recently, the domain of cinema is broadened to 'visual culture' (Carson and Pajaczkowska, 2001; Sturken and Cartwright, 2001; Jones, 2003). In addition to film and television, this field also consists of new media, such as the Internet and computer games. The academic interest in these media requires a different theoretical framework. These developments have led to new theoretical trends in media studies that attempt to go beyond Marxism, semiotics, and psychoanalysis.

The sword fighting Nemesis

The question is whether semiotics and psychoanalysis today can still provide a fruitful or innovative framework for interpreting contemporary visual culture. Postmodern culture and digital technology have produced new forms of cinematic aesthetics that break with the classic structures of representation and narration (Stam, 2000). The postmodern film foregrounds spectacle, sensation, and affect at the expense of a tight plot and round characters (Kramer, 1998). Narrative fragmentation in contemporary films can be regarded as a radical break with the oedipal plot. A good example is *Kill Bill* 1 and 2 by Quentin Tarantino (2003; 2004).

Kill Bill is a typical action film, hybridized with many violent genres such as the spaghetti western, the Japanese samurai, yakuza and anime, the Chinese kung fu, the American blaxploitation, the gangster film, and 'rape revenge' film. The latter is a horror genre for an audience of young men, in which a female warrior, the 'Final Girl' who survives the horror at the beginning of the movie, takes revenge on her rapists for the full length of the film, often in gruesome ways (Clover, 1992). In the two *Kill Bill* films, this act of revenge takes nearly five hours.

Uma Thurman plays the main female character: Beatrix Kiddo alias The Bride alias Black Mamba alias Arlene Machiavelli alias Mummy. She is a warrior who was once part of the 'Deadly Viper Assassination Squad', a group of merciless warriors from the underworld under the leadership of a certain Bill. When Beatrix becomes pregnant she tries to escape from this life by settling in an ordinary job and marriage, but Bill finds her and orders the Squad to kill all those present in the church during a rehearsal for the wedding. Bill personally shoots the highly pregnant Beatrix in the head. But, as fits a real heroine, she survives this murder attempt and wakes up after four years in a coma, with a bullet in her head and no baby in her belly. Turning into an angel of revenge, she traces and kills the three women and two men that made up the Squad, and incidentally, single-handedly massacres with her sword entire gangs, such as the 'Crazy 88' in Tokyo. Finally, she confronts her ex-lover and father of her daughter, Bill (David Carradine). The child was born in the hospital during her comatose state and kidnapped by Bill. The full story can only be understood at the end of the two long films, because the chronology is fragmented and the narrative constantly jumps in time, thwarting any attempt to stitch the story together. Even the name of the heroine is only disclosed at the very end.

Kill Bill is a typical product of the globalized film industry, being recorded in studios in Beijing. The films are inspired by the Japanese cult classics *Lady Snowblood: Blizzard from the Netherworld* (1973) and *Lady Snowblood: Love Song of Vengeance* (1974), which also feature a merciless heroine undertaking a bloody journey of revenge with her flashing sword. Another source of inspiration is the funky blaxploitation genre with the 'Queen of Blaxploitation' Pam Grier in the main role. As a James Bond-like figure, she adopts the role of Cleopatra Jones in the film of the same name (1973), fighting the drugs mafia as a special agent. In *Coffy* (1973), she plays a nurse who takes revenge for her younger sister's drug addiction. In the blaxploitation genre, the awakening Black movement meets the cheerful spirit of the 1960s in a hippy mix of violence, sex, and humour. Tarantino pays an impressive tribute to Pam Grier in *Jackie Brown* (1997), where she plays an intricate trick on both the gangsters and the police and escapes with the money. Grier plays the role with a certain panache and cool eroticism, thus creating a female icon that is seldom seen in Hollywood: a dignified and attractive 'older', black woman. The sources of inspiration for *Kill Bill* thus show that the figure of the female warrior has its predecessors in film history.

There is a world of difference between Beatrix Kiddo and Lara Croft. The latter is transferred from a game to a film and therefore remains a rather one-dimensional character (Walden, 2004). In contrast, Kiddo is a highly complex character with a whole range of emotions. She excels in courage, power, and perseverance, always saving herself from the most awkward situations. She wins impossible fights (on her own against eighty-eight men) and literally steps out of a grave where she was buried alive. A striking difference with Lara is that Kiddo's body is never eroticized. The camera does not glide along the contours of her body, nor to any of the other female warriors in the film. Of course, we see that Uma Thurman has a slim and fit body that meets the contemporary norms for the blond beauty. But she is never an object of the voyeuristic gaze like Lara. Rather than fetishizing her body, the film fetishizes her 'Hattori Hanzo' sword. We do not see her eyes reflected in the mirror, but in the glimmering steel of her sword. While *Kill Bill* avoids a voyeuristic gaze, the narcissistic gaze is mediated through the weapon and becomes part of her revenge.

Despite the absence of eroticism, *Kill Bill* is nevertheless a very physical film. It is, after all, a continual fight full of blood, sweat, and tears. The film relishes in showing vulnerable flesh that is cut, beaten, or slashed. But we also see how Kiddo time and again emerges victorious from the battle. She may be smeared with the blood of her victims and she may be wounded and shaking with exhaustion, but she wins every fight, one after another. With valiant courage, she constantly wrestles to find a way through her fears and despair.

From a feminist point of view, the special emphasis on motherhood is most striking in *Kill Bill*. Motherhood is generally not popular in the commercial Hollywood film. Being a mother is just not sexy or glamorous – at least not in Hollywood terms. Mothers do feature in the genre of melodrama, and in the TV variant, the soap, where motherhood is usually a source of suffering and problems. Kiddo's pregnancy and the loss of her child is an important motivation for her nemesis. It is only much later that she learns that her daughter is still alive, a knowledge that renews her fighting spirit.

The first fight in *Kill Bill* takes place between Kiddo and Vernita Green (Vivica Fox). In the middle of the intense fight, Vernita's four-year-old daughter comes home. The two women stop the blade fight immediately, concealing the knives behind their backs. Panting and bloody, with torn clothes in a smashed-up living room, they talk in soft tones to the girl who stares at them in amazement. Once the girl has gone upstairs, the women chat on and Kiddo says: 'Don't worry. I won't kill you in front of your child.' But when Vernita suddenly fires a bullet at her, Kiddo kills her instantly with the knife. While Kiddo wipes the blood off her knife and face, she apologizes to the daughter for having killed her mother.

This strange mixture of mercilessness for the enemy and tenderness for the child is characteristic of the fighting women in *Kill Bill*. When Kiddo carries out a pregnancy test during an assignment to kill a certain Lisa Wong in another city, Lisa shoots her way into the hotel room. While the women hold each other at gunpoint, Kiddo shows the strip and tells Lisa that she is pregnant. The other woman retreats slowly and yells out 'congratulations' as she runs away. It is the only fight which does not result in death. The film also visually emphasizes Kiddo's pregnancy in the flashbacks.

When Kiddo, at the end of her long quest for revenge, forces her entry into Bill's house to kill him, he holds their four-year-old daughter in front of him while he gently talks about 'Mummy' who has now finally come to meet the child. It is the first time in the film that Kiddo cries. For nearly five hours we have watched a strong, cruel, and violent 'warrior' who yields to nothing or no one in her furious desire for revenge. We regularly share the pain for what has happened to her, but we have never ever seen her cry. Together Bill and Kiddo put the child to bed and talk about their feud (it is only now that the viewer gains insight into the complex story). The spectator is almost lulled into believing there may be a reconciliation, but during a short fight, Kiddo kills Bill with the 'Five Point Palm Exploding Heart Technique' that she has learned from her Chinese master. The spectator knows this is quite special, because this Pai-Mei 'hates whites, loathes Americans and despises women'. Even Bill was not allowed to learn this deadly technique. It is thus an honour that Kiddo can carry out her ultimate revenge in this way.

Affect

Psychoanalytical concepts such as voyeurism, narcissism, and the oedipal narrative structure are little help in analyzing *Kill Bill*, or more in general, for insights into the complexity and paradoxes for contemporary visual culture. There are various sources for new inspiration within film studies, such as the concepts 'performativity' and 'intermediality' from theatre studies, or ludology from new media theory, but in this chapter I will consider the Deleuzian body of thought, because this has offered the most resistance to Freudian and Lacanian psychoanalysis.

The work of the philosopher Gilles Deleuze and the psychoanalyst Félix Guattari (1977; 1988) has only recently been received within film studies (Rodowick, 2001). With its psychoanalytical orientation, film studies was unable to take stock of their pioneering ideas. Deleuze and Guattari propose a non-verbal and anti-oedipal model to break away from the semiotic preoccupation with meaning, representation, and interpretation (Colebrook, 2002). In recent years, film theory has therefore witnessed a shift to an exploration of rhythm, energy, emotion, fragmentation, and rhizomatic connections (Flaxman, 2000). This perspective allows different questions to be addressed: rather than asking 'what does it mean?' the question becomes 'what does a film do?' (Kennedy, 2000).

The importance of such questions is immediately clear in relation to *Kill Bill*. The chronology of the story is fragmented to such an extent that an oedipal structure cannot be detected, whereas the oedipal plot dominated *Tomb Raider*. For an analysis of *Kill Bill*, it may be more productive to explore the rhizomatic connections between past and present, between people, cultures, and genres. The film is a ballet of violence in which rhythm and energy are more important than meaning and signification. This choreography of revenge, however, gives much room to emotion, whereas in *Tomb Raider* the action completely overrides emotional depth. Kiddo is driven by a motherly desire to protect her child and to raise it in a 'normal' environment. Her motherhood is the source of affect in the *Kill Bill* films.

O'Sullivan (2006) argues that in order to understand the power of contemporary visual culture, we need to address the aesthetic experience that defines art, but which was left out of the analysis in semiotics and psychoanalysis. This experience can be understood in physical terms, as 'haptic' (Marks, 2000), or in emotional terms, as an affective event (Hemmings, 2005b). Such a perspective enables the film theorist to place the analysis beyond questions of narrative and representation. The semiotic and psychoanalytical frameworks have long inspired film studies, but they threaten to keep it imprisoned in contexts which do not help in understanding contemporary visual culture. The focus on the sensory and emotional experience of the audiovisual medium of cinema also brings the analysis beyond the purely textual and visual that dominated film theory in past decades.

This is necessary because contemporary visual culture is changing. Perhaps it is more productive to analyze video clips in terms of rhythm, energy, and affect, rather than search for their meaning. Cinema is also changing as a consequence of digital technology and cultural influences. Developments in recent films could be described as a movement from sensation to affect. If postmodern cinema can be characterized by sensational pastiche and performance (for example, *Kika*, *Moulin Rouge*, *Lola Rennt*, *Huit femmes*, *Chungking Express*, *Pulp Fiction*), then the contemporary (post-postmodern?) film can be regarded as an aestheticism of affect, with abundant attention to small signs of humanity in a world full of violence (for example, *Todo sobre mi madre*, *Volver*, *21 Grams*, *Babel*, *Kill Bill*, *Eternal Sunshine of the Spotless Mind*, *2046*, *Le temps qui reste*, *Caché*, *Marie-Antoinette*). Sometimes this development takes place within the work of one and the same filmmaker, such as Tarantino, Almódovar, Ozon, or Kar-wai Wong. Now that films represent affect in new aesthetic forms, often in a choreography of violence, a careful analysis is needed of the way in which subjectivity and identity are reconfigured and remediated.

Within psychoanalytical theory, at any rate such as it has been processed and applied in film studies, subjectivity and identity are often linked to a negative view on desire, love, and happiness. Deleuze and Guattari resist the classic idea of desire as repressed or as a lack. Instead of looking for the repressive forms of an oedipal structure, the film theorist can explore how a film embodies multiple forms of desire. In the best case, this touches upon the moment of affirmation in cinema. Deleuze and Guattari refer to this affirmative process as 'becoming' (*devenir*). That is the moment of resistance, of change, of escaping from an identity that imprisons us. We thus return once again to the revolutionary attitude which started film studies in the 1960s, but hopefully with a new passion that opens up to the moment of 'becoming', in which the spectator can establish a different, that is, affective, relation to the film (Kennedy, 2000).

This can be illustrated with the last scene of *Kill Bill*, where the affective power of motherhood is shown in a moving way. After Bill's death, the scene switches to a hotel room. The camera films the little daughter who lies on the bed watching television. A crane shot takes the camera to the bathroom. In a strangely framed shot from above through the ceiling the spectator sees Beatrix Kiddo lying on the floor between the washbasin and the WC totally overcome with emotion, crying and laughing at the same time, while she quietly calls out 'thank you, thank you, thank you'. Kiddo's emotional release is really touching. The film demonstrates her long process of becoming a warrior, her years of training, and her months of revenge. But in the last scene she has become a mother. *Kill Bill* thus represents a complex form of female empowerment, which consists of her becoming a warrior as well as a mother. In the very last image of the film, Beatrix Kiddo radiantly embraces her daughter: for the first time in ages she is happy.

Questions for further research

1   In 2009, fewer than 10 per cent of film directors are women. Compare the situation in your country to Hollywood and consider questions such as: How many women are enrolled in film schools? Which careers are available for women in the film industry? What are their earnings? In which genres are women active as producers, directors, and actresses? Which genres attract more women in the audience? Compare the ages of successful actors and actresses. Give reasons why cinema is a field that is relatively difficult for women to access or to be successful in. You may want to replace the medium of film with television; then take the various channels, broadcasters, and TV companies into consideration in your comparison.

2   Is the action heroine an example of successful emancipation or not? Provide theoretical arguments in support of your answer. You may want to compare cinema to the genre of video clips, for example, *Smack My Bitch Up* by The Prodigy. Or to television soaps such as *Desperate Housewives*.

3   Images of nude or half-nude women appear in visual culture all the time. Discuss in small groups whether this is liberating or oppressive. How does this relate to the image of nude or half-nude men? Look for examples of nude men and women in various media (film, TV-soap, video clip, advertisements, etc.) and carefully analyze the voyeuristic and narcissistic play of looks. Now return to the original question: has your opinion about the liberating or oppressive nature of the images changed?

4   Choose a film with a female leading character with whom you strongly identify. With the help of the concepts discussed in this chapter, analyze how the identification is constructed and how it works. Do the same for a film with a male leading character. Does your viewing experience differ; and if so, how?

5   In contemporary visual culture (cinema, television, video clips, fashion, advertising, etc.) look for images of the female body that deviate from the current Western ideal of beauty. In other words, look for women's bodies that are *not* white, slender, young, taut, or fit. Note everything that attracts your attention, for example, quantity (how many of such images do you find); digital manipulation; interference with the body; visual design and aesthetics; context. What seems to be the greatest taboo? Black? Fat? Old? Look for examples where the image is clearly manipulated – for example, Naomi Campbell with blue or green contact lenses; black women with dyed blond hair; digital manipulation to make plump women look thinner (e.g. Kate Winslett on the cover of *Quote*), or to make older women look younger (which is the case for every Hollywood star of forty years and above). Look for counter examples. Present your data in a PowerPoint presentation and discuss them. You may also want to do the same for images of the male body.

6   Make a short film with an alternative image of a woman (or of a man) and put this on YouTube.

Hacking Barbie in gendered computer culture

13

Marianne van den Boomen

13.1 Vintage Barbie #3 (1960), reproduced with kind permission from Annigje de Jonge

She came into the world in 1959, seemingly out of the blue. Barbie, an eleven-and-a-half-inch tall doll for girls, but radically different from the usual dolls for children: she had the looks and shape of a mature woman. And how! Torpedo boobs, an incredibly thin waist, long legs, and a confident, almost arrogant facial expression. She could be twenty- or thirty-something, but was, anyway, a woman of the world, with her fashionable hairstyle and heavy eye make-up. Not to mention her clothes: summer dresses, jumpsuits, party outfits, nurses' uniforms, and business suits. Apparently, Barbie had money and several jobs to go with it, ranging from a fashion model to a CEO. She seemed to be a woman who had everything. Well, not everything. She did not have nipples or a navel, let alone genitals or hair other than on her head. She did not have parents or a husband. Okay, she did have a kind of a boyfriend, Ken, a lethargic male doll, who did not even have real hair. But he was more an accessory than part of her life, as any girl who ever played with Barbie dolls knows.

An adult doll, almost real. Imagine what a revelation, yes revolution, this must have been in the minds of little girls in the early 1960s. Suddenly there was a doll you need not nurture or take care of by changing diapers and cuddling around. Barbie was not a doll to practise your assumed future role of being a mother, but a doll you could project any imaginable occupation and identity on. The introduction of Barbie marked the coming of age of a new generation of girls and women. Raised with Barbie dolls, they came armed with other role models. 'Girls can be anything', came to be the new message.

Can Barbie be considered as a heroine of women's lib? Frankly, most feminists do not think so. Indeed, girls could be anything, but Barbie's implicit extra message was: 'Yeah – as long as they wear the right clothes, have the right body, and buy the right products.' Feminists condemned her as a gender-dichotomizing commodity marketed for the stereotypical white heterosexual girl, an icon of the 'cultural plastic' that women's bodies have become in a technological age (Toffoletti, 2007). Barbie's caricatural femininity, her abundant consumerism, and her weird blend of tits, ass, and anorexia constitute everything feminism abhors. However, as M.G. Lord (1994) states in *Forever Barbie: The Unauthorized Biography of a Real Doll,* everyone projects her own perspective and fantasies on Barbie. Feminists may also highlight her importance as an economically independent role model or they may point at practices of counter-hegemonic Barbie appropriation in gay and transvestite circles. Barbie collectors and artists, instead of blindly complying with the ideals of femininity Barbie is supposed to represent, negotiate and transform ascribed meanings (Spigel, 1994; Rand, 1995; Strohmeyer, 1997). Barbie seems to lend herself particularly well to such appropriation, and to a variety of self-identifications and types of gendered behaviour.

From a feminist perspective, therefore, Barbie is at least an ambivalent figure who embodies a rigid gender dichotomy as well as a broad range of 'femininities'. We may need exactly this ambivalence to think through the shifting and clashing configurations of femininity of the last fifty years. Barbie, as the plastic and virtual embodiment of these shifts, may teach us something about gender constructions and diversifications. In this chapter, I take up Barbie as an ambivalent women warrior on the battlefield of work and play and connect this to the development of computer technology and new media culture. Entering this field, from Barbie's perspective, enables us to transcend and reconsider the sweeping generalizations about women and technology and reconsider the social-cultural history of computer culture from a gender sensitive approach.

In this context, Barbie can be considered as what Sherry Turkle (1995) has dubbed an 'object-to-think-with'. While all objects can of course be thought about, an object-to-think-with is more closely connected to the way we think and frame the world around us. An object-to-think-with can be defined as an object, however mundane or trivial, which cannot only be deployed as an instrumental *tool* (or toy, for that matter), but can also function as a reflective *mirror,* invoking questions regarding the human subject and its condition. Turkle has been studying computers as objects-to-think-with (Turkle, 1984; 1995), conceiving them as 'postmodern machines' which reflect and reinforce post-structuralist notions of decentred subjects and fragmented identities. She has pointed out how computers, and especially the Internet, provide people with 'the chance to express multiple and often unexplored aspects of the self, to play with their identity, and try out new ones' (Turkle, 1996: 12). Turkle's notions about identity play have often, and all too easily, been reduced to 'on the Internet you can be anything you want'. Such a shortcut does not do justice to her work, neither to the complexities of Internet dynamics and its interwovenness with daily life roles and identities. Yet, here we have a first connection between computers and Barbie. As objects-to-think-with, they both seem to suggest 'you can be or do anything'; both seem to provide a projection screen for enacting different subjectivities. In the following sections, I will explore whether this is as uncomplicated as suggested. After a brief historical survey of Barbie and dolls in general, I will address the implications of Barbie's messages about work and play, especially in relation to computer work and play.

Nipples and bumps

Barbie can be considered to be the most potent icon of American hegemonic popular culture in the late twentieth century. Such an icon can be studied in several ways: historical, economical, and sociological. In the context of the history of children and their toys, Barbie is significant in light of the rise of a huge toy industry from the moment plastic became malleable and the emergence of the child as a consumer and market target. Such a history would also include the topic of mediatized branding and advertising, as Mattel, Barbie's manufacturer, was one of the first companies that used television commercials, children's panels, and psychological research as marketing instruments. Tracing Barbie's history as a manufactured object would expose her roots as the German Lilli doll, originally a comic figure in *Bild Zeitung,* sold in the 1950s as a semi-pornographic gag gift for men. Barbie's history would be sparkled with hilarious sex and gender details, such as the heated debates in Mattel's board room about the proper size of Ken's 'bumps' (Lord, 1994: 49), or the shocking nipples the first Barbie-prototypes appeared to have had (ibid.: 33). However, such an exhaustive genealogy would go beyond the scope of this chapter. Yet, some historical background is needed. It should be noted that Barbie was by no means the first doll in history modelled after an adult. Such dolls were the standard until the early nineteenth century, just as children were seen as small adults, not as a social and psychological category in their own right. Baby dolls made their entry in history when children were no longer regarded as small adults but as immature beings, to be educated and socialized into adults.

Media-ecologist Neil Postman (1982) connects the emergence of childhood as a separate life sphere and development stage to the advent of printing press culture.

Teaching children to read and write meant that a social boundary between adults and children was constituted, a gap between those who knew and those who had to learn. In his rather culture-pessimistic study *The Disappearance of Childhood*, Postman argues that this boundary is perverted with the arrival of television, which he takes to have destroyed the original enchantment of childhood. Due to televised media culture, adults have become more childish and children, with all the secrets of adulthood now revealed to them in prime time, have become more adult. Postman suggests in his conclusion that maybe the advent of computers, which call for a general computer literacy, would re-establish childhood as a separate youth culture (Postman 1982: 149). Apparently, Postman envisioned computer literacy as something which had to be formally transferred from adults to children, just like print literacy, which would thus re-install a proper hierarchical generational divide between adults and youth. However, computer literacy has turned out to develop differently; children do not acquire computer skills primarily under the supervision of adults. As 'digital natives' they learn bottom-up by playing, surfing, and tinkering around, in contrast to the education-oriented adult 'digital immigrants' (Rushkoff, 1997; Prensky, 2001).

True as this may be, such quasi-general approaches ignore that children do not just get socialized into adults, but are also, in the process, gendered into two mutually exclusive gender categories. This starts with the assignment of appropriate clothing and toys – dresses and dolls for girls; trousers and trains for boys – and this gender dichotomy is extended into youth media culture and finally into adult work. In that sense, gendered toys are social barometers, reflecting and projecting social expectations: baby dolls prepare girls for future motherhood and care; trains and cars prepare boys for movement and construction.

The quiet revolution in work and play

What are the implications for patterns of gendering when baby dolls are transformed into mature dolls? To what extent did the message 'girls can be anything' come across? Indeed, since the 1950s, the figures in Western societies show a general increase in the number of women entering education, college, and paid labour. The women's labour force participation rate increased in the US from 34 per cent in 1950 to 52 per cent by 1980 and to 59 per cent in 2007. European countries roughly reveal the same pattern (Kutscher, 1993; Tijdens, 2006). Goldin (2006) specifically points at what she calls the 'quiet revolution' in the mid-1970s, a social-psychological revolution regarding women's mental 'horizon, identity, and decisions', which resulted in women planning their education with an eye on their future in the work force. Is it a coincidence that this was also the first generation of women who had grown up with Barbie dolls? Barbie's promise to little girls, that there are more options available than becoming a mother and housewife, seemed to have fallen on fertile soil.

Yet, when taking a closer look at these shifts, we see women being overwhelmingly over-represented in sectors such as child care, healthcare, administration, and retail, while in construction, science, technology, and informatics, they are highly under-represented. Especially in informatics and computer engineering, the numbers are alarmingly low. Women make up 56 per cent of the total US workforce, yet they occupy only 27 per cent of ICT related jobs (NCWIT, 2007). In Europe the figures are different, ranging from high – 50 per cent female ICT workers in Italy and Spain – to extremely low – Belgium 16 per cent, Germany 14 per cent, and the Netherlands 11 per cent (Luijt, 2003; Collet, 2005). All in all, the picture is one of gender segregation: typical women's work is still predominantly about care and relations, working with people, and men's work is still predominantly about construction and technology, working with things. Moreover, women's work is consistently paid less than men's work, and is under-represented or absent higher up in the hierarchies of any employment sector.

Was it Barbie's fault? Her estimated eighty professions included being a flight attendant, rock star, police officer, presidential candidate, veterinarian, nurse, astronaut, and aerobics instructor. She did have business suits right from the beginning, and Mattel eventually also issued a doctor's and a pilot's uniform to her initial nurse and stewardess outfits, but today Barbie's represented activities consist mainly of shopping, house cleaning, and caring for her young siblings (Pearson and Mullins, 1999). Yet, in the early 1960s, Barbie was conceived and marketed as a single career girl who did not do rough housework. And who was definitely *not* into motherhood, as Lord (1994) stipulates. After Mattel had issued wedding clothes for Barbie and Ken, children clamoured for Barbie to have a baby. Though Mattel usually responded to market demands, Ruth Handler, Barbie's 'founding mother' at Mattel, refused. Never would Barbie's physique, life, and freedom be compromised by having babies. Eventually she came up with 'Barbie Baby-Sits,' including accessories such as a baby, bottles, and self-help books with titles like *How to Get a Raise* and *How to Travel* (Lord, 1994: 50). Apparently, it was not enough. Girls did get Barbie's message about work but somehow the gender segregation in play – 'dolls for girls, trains for boys' – was metaphorically extended into adult professional life.

What did Barbie actually teach girls about play? Mattel kept on issuing new packages of scenes and dolls (kitchens, post offices, camping sites, Rapunzel, Twiggy, television stars, etc.), providing a perpetual stream of opportunities for identifications. Yet, the rules of play were always the same: you were to identify with Barbie. Projecting yourself on Barbie, you could *be* that actress, that school teacher, or even that striptease dancer. No matter how broad the range of roles, Barbie play always involves dressing up and role play (or rather role buy, though some girls did bravely engage in sewing tiny unmanageable Barbie clothes). Though role play is in itself a rich and variable activity, by which creative, social, managerial, and other skills can be acquired (Copier, 2007; Klaver, 2008), one might query the meaning of role play when this is enacted solely by identification with an object which has no other functionalities than enabling this identification.

Compare this to classic toys for boys: the trains, cars, and guns. While these toys enable role playing too, they also embody other things: speed, movement, manipulation, mechanics, and causality. Here, role play does not occur by means of identification with the toys. You do not identify with a train or gun; you imagine yourself being in charge of these objects. You use and manipulate these things as an extension of your role – driver, cop, good guy, bad guy – within the game setting. The toys are objects to be handled, not so much objects-to-think-with, mirrors of subjectivity. Moreover, these toys are an assemblage of separable parts, constituting a machinery, a system, which can be explored, decomposed, and sometimes rearranged. That is quite different from Barbie's pseudo-organic coherency. While also composed of movable parts, she is clearly not meant to be decomposed. Taking Barbie as an object, and role play *with* her (not being her), say, as a surgeon, vivisectionist, or slasher killer, is completely outside the advocated repertoire of Barbie role play. Though probably all girls tried to take a Barbie apart at least once, they soon found out this was inappropriate and irreversible.

No wonder girls stop playing at a certain age. They leave their dolls behind when they go to college and to work, ready to become their own Barbie. As Rousseau already stated in *Emile*:

> The doll is the girl's special plaything; this shows her instinctive bent towards her life's work. [. . .] she sees her doll, she cannot see herself; she cannot do anything for herself, she has neither the training, nor the talent, nor the strength; as yet she herself is nothing; she is engrossed in her doll and all her coquetry is devoted to it. This will not always be so; in due time she will become her own doll.
>
> (Rousseau, 1762: 421–422)

Hence, in due time, playing time is over, for girls – but not for boys. Their specific toys, manners of play, and acquired skills can be easily extended into college and work, into the adult world, which turns out to have a proper place for such play: in construction, technology, and, most of all: computing.

Hacking trains and computers

The same year Barbie started to mobilize a new generation of girls, a boy's toy marked the beginning of another new generation. In 1959, the Massachusetts Institute of Technology (MIT), 'the repository of the very brightest of those weird high school kids with owl-like glasses and underdeveloped pectorals' (Levy, 1984: 18), housed the Tech Model Railroad Club, a student's hobby club. MIT provided a permanent clubroom, which was filled with a huge train layout including a town, industrial areas, and, of course, lots of trains and tracks. Underneath this layout there was a massive mix of wires, relays, and switches constantly modified, improved, or screwed up by the railroad boys. As Steven Levy writes in *Hackers! Heroes of the Computer Revolution* (1984), here the first computer hackers came into being. A 'hack' used to be MIT slang for an elaborate college prank, but the Railroad Club used the word to describe any puzzle-solving project undertaken with wild pleasure in mere involvement. The club members took pride in any hack on the railroad system, but also on other systems: computers, locks, phones, Chinese menus, or the shortest subway route past all stations on one ticket. Every systematic puzzle could be hacked, opened up, and appropriated.

Hacking is thus basically an epistemological and playful attitude sustained by direct action, aimed at opening black boxes. To hack is to appropriate technology, by solving riddles, tinkering around, and creating your own tools.

At that time, MIT owned a computer, a giant punch card reading machine, which was heavily guarded and only accessible by system operators. When the Railroad Club managed to get hold of a smaller test computer, this was a revelation, yes a revolution: a computer you could lay your hands on and watch while it executed your program. You could feed it with punched paper tape, and you could modify your program. Eventually, the trains were left behind; the hackers had found a new toy. This was the dawn of the famous Artificial Intelligence Lab at MIT.

The hackers adhered to what Levy (1984) calls 'the hacker ethic'; a set of principles, silently agreed on. Most important was the 'hands-on' principle: access to computers – and anything which might teach you something about the way the world works – should be unlimited. The imperative was to share what you got with others, to make it accessible and public. As such, hacking may even be considered a political movement. During the roaring sixties, when other students were protesting against the Vietnam War and demanding rights for blacks, women, students, and gays, these pale nerds constituted an underground movement; a movement which eventually had an equally powerful impact on the shaping of society as did the other revolutions.

Several, subsequent generations can be distinguished in hacker culture. While the 1960s, MIT generation was about open access to institutional machines, the second generation, organized in home-brew computer clubs, constructed hardware, that is, the computers themselves. In 1975, Stephen Wozniak and Steve Jobs assembled in their garage the first prototypes of devices small and cheap enough to use at home. Steve Jobs finally built his Apple enterprise on these first models, and soon other companies, such as IBM, followed and developed what came to be known as personal computers. The third hacker generation, of the 1980s, focused on the development and distribution of application programs, especially games. It was the time of the early basement and kitchen-table companies in Silicon Valley, which eventually transformed software development and systems engineering into an established and powerful industry. During the 1980s and early 1990s, the personal computer found its way into offices, factories, and homes. Especially when, from the mid-1990s, Internet access became widely available, which was enforced by a fourth hacker generation aiming at Internet 'access for all' (Van den Boomen, 1993), computing and tinkering with computers was no longer confined to nerdy hacker subcultures. The computer and the Internet became mainstream and were used by ordinary people, whether for work or for pleasure.

Barbie culture and hacker culture

It would be clear that a historiography framed as the 'heroes of the computer revolution' takes the absence of women in computer clubs for granted, implicitly or explicitly assuming a lack of interest. A gender sensitive approach reveals that such a gender dichotomy is not so much empirically grounded, but rather constructed by the very way the history is told. After all, women have been working with computers from the moment these machines made their entry in history, long before the MIT hackers did so. In fact, the very first computer hacker was Lady Lovelace who, in the 1830s, wrote programmed instructions for Charles Babbage's analytical machine. And when the first electronic computers were built during World War II, the programmers again were women, the so-called Eniac girls. The very term 'computer' itself originally referred to women working as professional calculators, performing endless mathematical calculations by hand (Hayles, 2005).

In Levy's account of the history of computing, the names of more than a hundred boys and men pass along. A handful of women are also mentioned by name, but only Roberta Williams, who designed the first visual adventure game and ran a kitchen-table company in Silicon Valley, comes near the qualification of hacker, in a chapter with the telling title: 'The wizard and the princess' (the wizard being her husband). To be sure, Levy did address the issue of the absence of heroines in hacker culture:

> The sad fact was that there never was a star-quality female hacker. No one knows why. There were women *programmers* and some of them were good, but none seemed to take hacking as a holy calling [. . .] the substantial cultural bias against women getting into serious computing does not explain the utter lack of female hackers.
>
> (ibid.: 84)

Levy does not connect this 'cultural bias' to the gendered material practices around the tools and toys he described. Would it have been imaginable to have a Barbie Clubhouse next to the Railroad Room at MIT? No way. Barbie's non-hackability seems to preclude any playful extension into college culture.

What had happened to the historical association between women and computing? It has been argued that the history of the computer is marked by a frame shift: from supportive tool towards a framing in terms of high technology and management, and therefore masculinity (Oldenziel, 1999). Yet, such a shift could barely explain why the participation of women in ICT jobs and education has been steadily declining, especially since the mid-1980s (Taylor, 2002; NCWIT, 2007), while other techno-sciences, such as physics, chemistry, and engineering have been affected by Barbie's quiet revolution: during the same time span, these fields show a general (though slow) increase of female participation in the work force. This is remarkable, considering that during the very same period the computer became popularized throughout society as a multi-purpose tool-toy in one, matching the hands-on principles of hacker culture. How could a general increase of women's participation in work and education combined with the popularization of computing yield a *decrease* in computer jobs? Does this imply that Barbie culture and hacker culture are deeply antagonistic?

This question is also raised in Douglas Coupland's novel *Microserfs* (1995), which reads like an account of a fourth generation of hackers who are immersed in early corporate Internet culture. The novel also incorporates female computer nerds. Yet, the issue of women hackers puzzles the main character, who suspects Barbie has something to do with it:

I asked Dusty if she grew up with Barbie dolls and she said, 'No, but indeed I rilly, *rilly* lusted after them in my heart. Hippie parents, you know. *Rill* crunchy. [. . .] **sigh**. So instead I played with numbers and equations. Some trade-off.' [The boy continues his Barbie quest:] I asked Karla if she grew up with Barbie dolls and she said (not looking up from her keyboard), 'This is so embarrassing, but not only did I play with Barbies, but I played with them until an embarrassingly late age – ninth grade. [. . .] But before you think I'm a lost cause, you should know that I gave my Barbie admirable pursuits – I took apart my brother's Hot Wheels and made Barbie Toyota Assembly Plant, giving Barbie white overalls, a clipboard, and I provided jobs for many otherwise unemployed Americans.'

(Coupland, 1995: 242–243)

Such literary evidence at least testifies to female hackers' existence, and appears to argue that Barbie-play does not necessarily keep girls from tinkering with computers, by showing that the combination of Barbie play and computing may involve more diversified gendered behaviours. Still, ICT work and daily computing are predominantly represented and experienced in a binary frame of toys versus tools, echoing play-oriented hacker culture versus work-oriented Barbie culture. Various researchers agree that boys and men are more likely to play games, to program or tinker with programs, and to see the computer as a playful recreational toy; girls and women, on the other hand, tend to view the computer as a tool, a means to accomplish tasks (Ogletree and Williams, 1990; Culley, 1993; Kelan, 2007).

Barbie, as a limited toy-to-play-with, may have contributed to such a division by imposing a split between toys and tools. Admittedly, Mattel did undertake serious efforts to extend the Barbie brand into a hybrid tool-toy. Not by creating a Hacker Barbie, but by producing Barbie computers, Barbie cell phones, and Barbie MP3 players. These full-fledged devices all came in the typical Barbie design; the computer (1999) was silver with pink and purple floral accents, and had a flower-bedecked mouse and digital camera; the BarbieGirl MP3 device (2008) looks like a flat Barbie doll, and can be 're-decorated in a mass of different outfits as well as shoes, purses, and hairstyles' (Mattel, 2008). Again, such tool-toy Barbies are marked by ambivalence. On the one hand, they represent the plain commodification of gender stereotypes and a non-serious lock-in to pink girls-only technologies, but on the other hand, it may be that such Barbiefied technologies engender more diversified and extensible notions of both femininity and hacking. After all, why should tinkering with outfits and shoes not count as hacking?

Barbie hacking

Meanwhile, Barbie herself turned out to be not completely hacker-proof. As a toy she was gradually endowed with some technological enhancements which turned her into a cyborg. Talking Barbies have been issued since 1968, at first with a mini-gramophone player inside which enabled her to utter sentences such as 'Let's go shopping!' This was succeeded in 1992 by the Teen Talk Barbie, which came with an implanted chip which did the same trick more sophisticatedly: it was programmed to say 4 out of 270 possible phrases. One of these phrases was 'Math class is tough!', leading to harsh criticism by feminist groups. Mattel eventually withdrew the sentence and offered a return service to anyone with a Barbie denouncing math. Still, Barbie's repertoire remained obsessed with clothing and shopping, with sentences such as 'Do we ever have enough clothes?' and 'Let's plan our dream wedding!' As if to complete the caricatural gender picture, Mattel's competitor Hasbro sold Talking Duke GI Joe, a doll for boys, which howled sentences like: 'Attack!', and 'Dead men tell no lies!'

In 1993, the so-called Barbie Liberation Organisation decided it was enough. The group bought allegedly three hundred Talking Dukes and Talking Barbies, painstakingly swapped their voice boxes and put the manipulated dolls back on the shop shelves. Now Barbie roared for vengeance, and GI Joe cooed about shopping. The hacked dolls came with a leaflet urging buyers who did agree with the group's anti-sexist, anti-violent agenda to inform news media in the area. The action received a broad press and Internet coverage, including reports of boys and girls who were really happy with their funny unconventional dolls.

So, Barbie could be hacked, after all. It looked a perfect techno-political hack, not only showing and sharing how it was done – including technical do-it-yourself manuals on the Internet – but also making a firm statement about the absurd gender messages inscribed into children's toys. However, none of the shops allegedly attacked could find any manipulated Barbies or GI Joes on their shelves, although some hacked dolls had been shown to reporters. While the BLO described itself in the *New York Times* as a 'loose network of artists, parents, feminists and anti-war advocates' (Firestone, 1993), the action was probably a media prank, enacted by ®TMark, a collective of performance artists. One of their other famous political-cultural interventions was the so-called Toy-war in 2000, an online shareholders game mobilizing an army of 'Toy-soldiers' into the domain-name battle of etoy.com, their art site, against etoys.com, owned by the giant Internet toy retailer eToys Inc. Such a deliberate blend of tools and toys, activism, art, pranks, and hacks has been dubbed 'culture jamming' (Dery, 1993) and can be seen as a typical form of Internet activism which evolved during the 1990s. Barbie was there, in the front line. The BLO action inspired several spin-offs, such as the Barbie Disinformation Organisation, which pasted stickers such as 'Barbie Lesbian Barber Shop' on boxes of Barbie's Stylin' Salon, including instructions on how to give Barbie a 'Dyke Haircut'. And, of course, on the Internet there are numerous Barbie hacks in the same culture jamming tradition: AIDS Barbie ('nice girls don't use condoms'), Terminator Barbie, Teen Pregnancy Barbie, Homeless Barbie, even a Hacker Barbie, and lots of SM and otherwise blasphemous Barbies.

Games for girls and boys

No matter what playful Internet culture did to subvert her image, in the 1990s, the officially marketed Barbies predominantly represented middle-class sweetness and shallow-brained desires for shopping and fashion. Surprisingly, it was Mattel itself that finally succeeded in swaying Barbie play into the heart of computer culture, while strictly adhering to the pink Barbie frame. In the winter of 1996, the company issued a computer game called *Barbie Fashion Designer*. It was an immediate hit. It sold half a million copies in its first two months, that Christmas outstripping blockbusters such as *Doom* and *Quake*, and finally shipped almost two million copies, probably all to girls. This was remarkable, since gaming was at that time considered a typical boy thing, with only a poor 15 per cent of girl gamers; a negligible market share for the growing game industry, which focused safely on top-selling games in the realm of action, speed, and combat. Female protagonists were usually absent from these genres, unless as a passive princess waiting to be rescued. Roberta Williams (the 'Princess' in Levy's hacker history) was one of the first who incorporated female protagonists in her games, and other companies followed, after they had seen that it did not turn off men and boys. While *Tomb Raider*'s protagonist Lara Croft – a cross-over between Barbie and Indiana Jones – mainly attracted boys and men, *Barbie Fashion Designer* proved that another strategy of Barbiefying could persuade more girls into gaming.

The secret of BFD's success was not the Barbie brand as such; Mattel had also issued the games *Barbie Storytelling* and *Barbie Rapunzel* (where Rapunzel had to rescue the prince), which did not sell particularly well. Was it in the game itself? BFD in fact just enabled girls to design and create clothes for their physical Barbie dolls: you could select styles and patterns, print the result on paper-backed fabric, and finally sew the outfits together. It had none of the features of top-selling games: no violence, no speed, no competition, no levels, and no adversaries. Sunrahmanyam and Greenfield (1998) argue that these features account for the game's appeal to girls, but they also wonder whether BFD is a 'genuine' computer game at all, for the same reasons: lack of action and predefined goals; lack of obstacles to overcome; and no immersion in a virtual fantasy world. Indeed, BFD is an extension of playing with physical Barbie dolls, more a tool than a game. But it may be that we have to reconsider the very definition of games and action if we want games to be gender inclusive. According to empirical research, girls seek different kinds of complexity and action in games: character development and cooperation rather than violence and competition, familiar real life settings rather than fantasy worlds (Cooper, *et al.*, 1990; Kafai, 1996).

Gradually, the game industry began to realize that girls do play computer games and feminists realized that computer games provide an easy lead-in to computer literacy and ICT jobs (Loftus and Loftus, 1983; Greenfield and Cocking, 1996). This yielded to a 'girls game movement', a 'highly unstable alliance between feminist activists (who want to change the "gendering" of digital technology) and industry leaders (who want to create a girls' market for their games)' (Cassell and Jenkins, 1998: 4). Such alliances between the culture industry and counter movements are not unfamiliar in the field of new media, for example, in fan culture and open source software development (Jenkins, 2006; Schäfer, 2008), but in the context of girls' games it is a tightrope to be walked.

The anthology *From Barbie to Mortal Kombat: Gender and Computer Games* (1998) assembles the debates and perspectives on this tightrope. Barbie as a main actor in the title is no coincidence: she is a pivotal icon of girls' play, while *Mortal Kombat*

– a violent computer game – stands for boys' play. Such a binary opposition between masculine and feminine is of course a social-cultural construct, conceived of differently in different cultures, historical periods, and contexts. The issue is whether girls should be encouraged to beat boys, or that a girls-only place should be created? The first scenario implies that girls change and ignore their different cultural interests; the second adheres to a stereotypical Barbiefied frame and confines girls to a separate world. Yet, we should be careful in dismissing traditional girls' interests. Much feminist scholarship has been dedicated to reclaiming and revaluating the disdained areas of 'women's stuff' (gossip, quilting, romance novels, soap operas), revealing instead the unacknowledged cultural and moral politics of these practices, including subversive uses and readings. And this may well hold for Barbie play and Barbie gaming too. Meanwhile, both scenarios assume games to be 'boy's own', and both may result in the disparaging of girls' interests, which are certainly more diversified than either *Mortal Kombat* or Barbie. A third scenario, also probed by the girls' game movement, consists of transforming game genres towards 'gender neutrality'. As the editors wrote in 1998:

> With time we expect that, by pushing at both sides of the spectrum of what games for girls might look like, a gender neutral space may open up, a space that allows multiple definitions of both girlhood and boyhood, and multiple types of interaction with computer games of all sorts.
>
> (Cassell and Jenkins, 1998: 36)

Ten years later, the book was updated. In *Beyond Barbie and Mortal Kombat,* the editors note 'how little has changed, how much has changed, and how much needs to be done if more meaningful changes are going to occur' (Cassell and Jenkins, 2008). Gone is the optimism about the ability of female-run start-up companies to transform the game market; they were either bought up (mostly by Mattel), or just went out of business after the dot-com bubble burst. Game stores nowadays do not have a pink corner, there are not many girls' games – but there are millions of girl gamers, now accounting for 30 to 40 per cent of computer gamers. Online role playing games, such as *World of Warcraft* and *Second Life*, have proved successful in attracting female gamers. Most of all, the offline 'real life simulation' game *The Sims* attracts girls and women – more than half of its players are female. *The Sims* 'shares many of the traits of the girls' game movement without calling attention to them as such' (Jenkins, 2001). Particularly interesting is that *The Sims* thrives on a dedicated fan community, which creates and distributes user-generated content in the form of so-called 'mods' (modifications) and 'cheats' (work arounds) for the re-appropriation of characters, environments, and rule sets. Finally, girls seem to be overtly hacking their dolls, toys, and tools. But there is also bad news. During the last ten years there has been no growth in the number of women working in the game industry, and the total number of women in computer science and jobs had continued to decrease. Girls may be playing and tinkering around more with computers, but this is not converted into computer job participation.

Meanwhile, Mattel struck again with a pink offensive. In April 2007, the company launched the *BarbieGirls* platform, 'a hybrid online-offline play experience that blends a fashion-forward, doll-inspired music player with the first virtual world designed exclusively for girls' (Palmeri, 2007). This Barbie world looks like a pink, cartoon-like cross-over between *The Sims* and *Second Life*: girls can create a personalized virtual character, design their own rooms, shop with B Bucks (virtual money), play games, watch videos, and have real-time chats with other girls. It was an immediate hit, attracting three million users in its first two months, reaching now (September 2008) fourteen million *BarbieGirls*, 85 per cent of which are 8- to 15-year-old girls. Mattel claims this is the 'fastest growing virtual world in history', and this may well be true: *Second Life* took three years to get to one million users, and has now reached fifteen million; whereas *World of Warcraft* now counts ten million users.

While fourteen million *BarbieGirls* still is peanuts, compared to the one hundred million copies sold of *The Sims*, the message is clear: pink, Barbiefied formatting is still alive and kicking and in urgent need for further research; for example, into the ways girls play nowadays. Though Barbiegirls.com is a highly protected, moderated, and predictable world, on several Internet forums, little girls can be found rushing in, screaming for cheats and codes to un-lock special features for their *BarbieGirls*. Maybe, in due time, they will create them themselves. Maybe, in due time, they will become their own Hacking Barbies.

In any case, Barbie, as an object-to-think-with in the triangle of work, play, and computing, continues to be a potent yet highly ambivalent figure. Having developed from a 1960s role model into a cyborged connection between dolls, devices, and virtual worlds, she has taken firm residence in computer culture. Though she is as yet confined to the domain of gossip, fashion, and shopping, this at least indicates that Barbie play can be extended, taken out of her box, into virtual and real worlds. Girls' toys and play modes could surely benefit from such extensions towards participatory Internet culture. And maybe she can be extended even further, brought into college and adult working life, proving Barbie culture is not necessarily incompatible with hacker culture.

Questions for further research

1   Check industrial (www.theesa.com) and academic (www.digra.org) resources in order to find current data about the share of girls and women as players of computer games. Figure out differences between countries, and between different game types (online/offline, genres, consoles). Do you find significant gender and age differences related to different types of game play?

2   Check demographic and ethnographic surveys (www.pewinternet.org) regarding PC use and Internet use: do men and women enact different activities and pursuits? Can you find indications of a toys versus tools pattern?

3   Check out YouTube or other Internet sites for more examples of culture-jamming appropriations of Barbie. What is the main target of their critique or parody?

4   Compare the characteristics of Barbiegirls.com with those of *Second Life* and/or *The Sims*. What similarities, and what differences can be found? Do you consider Barbiegirls.com a participatory culture (Jenkins, 2006)? Explain why, or why not. What does this imply for the feminist potential of Barbiegirls.com?

5   Could you think of another contemporary or historical object-to-think-with which functions both as a tool, and as a mirror of subjectivity and identity? What kind of gender constructions are invoked by this object-to-think-with?

6   In the field of computer game studies, several analytical frames of the concept of 'game' circulate, each foregrounding different aspects, such as narrative, ludology, or magic circle. Which frames or definitions are able to give an account of *Barbie Fashion Designer* as a computer game? If you consider none of the existing frames appropriate, could you come up with your own proposal for a non-biased, gender inclusive, and gender sensitive definition of 'computer game'?

Gender, history, and the politics of Florence Nightingale

Geertje Mak and Berteke Waaldijk

14

14.1 Florence Nightingale.

One of the best-known women in world history is a nurse, Florence Nightingale (1820–1910). The uncontested heroine of Britain's national history, she is known throughout the world as the reputed 'Lady with the Lamp'. She is particularly known as the woman who, for the first time in history and practically on her own, made sure that the sick and wounded among common soldiers received decent care. Foot soldiers were rotting away and dying like flies in the military hospitals of the Crimean War, the war where France and Britain fought the Russians on Turkish territory between 1854 and 1856. Infectious diseases represented a much greater cause of death than actual battle wounds. With the help of a small brigade of nurses, Florence Nightingale managed to bring some relief in this living hell. She ensured the heavily soiled hospital was thoroughly cleaned, brought in clean sheets and fresh clothes, and personally surveyed the arrival and distribution of medical supplies and other stock. Her personal care for the soldiers and the letters she wrote to relatives in the case of a death immortalized her with the British people. She was no sweet lady, however. She was struggling against a rigid military administration and made use of well placed connections in the Ministry of War to achieve her ends. Deft at spin, she made sure the press reported favourably about her activities abroad during her stay in the Crimea. As a consequence, she was hailed as a national heroine upon her return from war.

Before her rise to fame, however, Florence Nightingale had to fight a long and hard battle with her very well-to-do upper-class family. Since her youth, she had felt a calling to do something important with her life and help the impoverished classes; and she had put her stakes on becoming a nurse. For someone from her background this was unheard of at the time. She might as well have expressed the wish to become a servant (Strachey, 1986 [1918]), a telling comparison as it goes. Nurses were recruited from the lower classes and had a reputation, among the upper classes, of uncouth manners and coarse language; they were also suspected of taking to drink. Nightingale was excellently educated and knew several modern languages, apart from Latin and Greek. She was well travelled (her name alludes to the city of her birth), well-off, and very well-connected. In short, she was well equipped to become an excellent wife and appeared to be all set to take up her rightful position as a lady in the upper classes. However, this was a destiny the young Florence Nightingale bitterly rejected, as appears for example from *Cassandra*, a piece of writing that was one of her first and most pronounced feminist texts (Showalter, 1981).

In the end, she managed to get what she wanted by shaping her desire for work as a religious calling. When she was about thirty, she trained as a nurse in Germany – well camouflaged by her mother as a visit to a Spa accompanied by her sister – after which she acquired the position of head nurse in a home for impoverished upper-class women. When the gruesome reports on the Crimean situation filtered through to England and the Minister of War appealed to her to travel to Scutari in the Crimea with a group of nurses, she immediately grabbed her chance.

She became seriously ill in the war and would never fully recover. At home and often bedridden, she passionately continued her vocation and worked hard to achieve her ideals. Again she used her connections in the government and the press to pull strings in order to enforce countless reforms in hygiene and popular health in the army, in British society, and in the colonies. Moreover, she founded a school for training nurses which would become the model throughout the whole world. A career in nursing gradually became a respectable profession and an important possibility for women in diverse classes to earn an honourable living and become emancipated.

One might say that as a 'woman warrior', Nightingale was fighting her battle on two different fronts. The front of nursing care and proper hygienic conditions for the large impoverished masses; and the front of emancipation for middle- and upper-class women who were looking for legitimate employment. She was one of the very few women to gain a slot in traditional historiography with one kind of struggle, whereas with the other she became a heroine in the women's movement. Of course, it is interesting that a nineteenth-century woman was able to acquire such fame. However, a gender sensitive analysis does not just consider someone's gender in isolation, but is also concerned with the question of how the forces that shaped a heroine are gendered too. Therefore, the next sections focus on the ways historiography, citizenship, and the public/private division are affected by gender. Such an investigation, which serves to exemplify a historical gender sensitive analysis, will place Nightingale's struggle in a much wider context.

History, the nation, and women: Similarities and differences

Beyond the memory of men and women, people have narrated history. The stories of the past, whether written down or orally delivered, confirm the identities of individuals, families and lovers, communities and institutions. In the beginning, these stories had a mythical or religious nature. They would explain, for example, the divine creation of human beings. Factual matters intermingled with the fantastic, the possible, or the desired. Hence, historiography was first and foremost regarded as a form of art with its own proper muse, Clio, a situation that held sway until the late eighteenth century. The early fifteenth-century *Book of the City of Ladies* by Christine de Pizan, provides a fine example of this art. Referring to myths, histories, religious contemplations, and anecdotes, Christine de Pizan presents a motley range of stories about the origin of female qualities (De Pizan, 1984 [1405]).

However, from the early nineteenth century onwards, a new kind of historiography arose in Europe. The past became the subject of academic study and historians examined this past in analogy to natural scientists who studied nature. The idea was to retrieve the truth about the past with rational and objective means, which meant that the blurred boundary of fact and fiction had to be clearly demarcated. Professional historiographers sought academic tuition and distinguished themselves from novelists, chroniclers, and storytellers (Grever, 1994).

This development was concomitant to political developments at the time. Following the Napoleonic wars (1805–1815), new political entities emerged throughout Europe, so-called nation-states. The legitimacy of the large European empires of old (Austria, Russia, the Ottoman Empire) governing various populations was questioned ever more. The unity of kingdoms or empires was determined by the monarch's sovereignty, whereas the unity of nation-states was determined by the people or the nation. The new nation-states justified their new-found unity by turning the people into the true heroes of national histories.

Professional historians stated that it was possible to render the national past with objective and scientific means. The people of the nation-state were depicted as a self-evident entity whose shared past went back a long time. For the Netherlands, for example, this meant that the idea of a unified Dutch people, whose origin receded beyond the memory of men and women, was fortified by stories of a tiny nation's brave struggle against the mighty Spaniards and the 'embarrassment of riches' in the Golden Age – for example, with seafaring and trading with 'the East', and artists such as Rembrandt or the poet/playwright Joost van den Vondel. Such histories were of crucial importance in evoking a sense of community, of identifying with the nation. Of course, there was more to such nation building than establishing a shared past. Elements such as a flag, national feast days and commemoration days, a fixed language and grammar, a literary tradition, a national anthem and monuments dedicated to national heroes or commemorating the fallen, all contribute to the 'invented traditions' of the nation (Hobsbawm and Ranger, 1983). This has also been analyzed as creating a so-called 'imagined community', a very strong emotional identification with the essentially abstract idea of a nation-state. With most Europeans, the idea of a national identity gradually became ever more natural during the course of the nineteenth century, as is testified, for example, by the deeply felt and almost involuntary emotions welling up when compatriots win a gold medal at the Olympics. It even goes much deeper than that: the feeling that one belongs to a nation-state makes millions of men ready to sacrifice themselves for their motherland when asked to do so (Anderson, 1983).

Two clearly gender specific consequences resulted from the shifts in the manner of dealing with the national past. Historiography became the business of men, both in the figure of the historian and in subject matter. The new demands of scholarly investigation meant that historiography became the prerogative of men, as women were not admitted to universities until the end of the nineteenth century. Women with a propensity for history therefore had to remain content with the status of 'amateur' (Smith, 1998). For the object of historiography, these shifts in dealing with the past meant that historiography was supposed to be concerned with the past of a national entity. By definition, this meant an orientation on political and military events. The occasional eminent philosopher or major artist might adorn the proud past of a nation, but as Jane Austen dryly commented in one of her novels (and that such a comment is made in novels rather than in historical writing should not be a surprise), history was mostly about 'quarrels of popes and kings, with wars or pestilences in every page' and has 'hardly any women at all' (Austen, 1856). By definition, indeed, women are absent from such histories, apart from some particular queens of days gone by, who had acquired their position through heredity (Mak, 2007).

The idea was that women had made no contribution to such histories. Yet, they could still symbolize the nation. At a symbolical level, the nation-state was often represented as a woman; think of the Dutch Maiden, Marianne for France, or Mother England. The nation-state might be pictured as a mother who had nurtured her children – the people – and therefore should be protected against attacks. The nation-as-woman metaphor likewise emerges in war rhetoric where the conquered land is represented in terms of 'rape'. Yet, the active protection, defence, and reverence of this female gendered nation-state were reserved for men. They served in the army to protect her and defend her honour (Mosse, 1985; Yuval Davis, 1997; Blom, et al., 2000).

Nightingale's highly special position should be appreciated in this context of a history characterized by battles, religions, generals, politicians, and other great men. She was one of the first women to acquire, on her own merit, a place in the gallery of honours of British national history. Perhaps only Jeanne d'Arc took precedence in terms of historical fame and renown. Even today Florence Nightingale is one of the very few women who figures in textbooks on pre-twentieth-century European history, and the other women are almost exclusively present due to their dynastic position.

In the meantime, there have been many changes in the field of historiography. From a socialist perspective, working-class people became a focus of interest. This led to social-economic history, an increasingly important branch of historiography in the twentieth century. Then there was growing attention for the history of art and culture, which widened the field of research for historians too. In the 1970s, feminists began to voice critique on the scant presence of women in historiography, which led to women's history or gender history, a specialism that addressed different historio-graphical areas. The attention for the history of colonialism and imperialism made it clear that racism and economic exploitation surpassed national borders: the nation was not an autonomous, clearly demarcated entity at all, but on the contrary thoroughly shaped by its relation to the colonies it depended on. All these innovations contributed to toning down the role of the nation-state in historiography.

Nevertheless, the discussion on the national past keeps occupying a central position in historiography. Regardless of the critical points in that discussion, its agenda is often still determined by the history of a country and its citizens. In recent years, history has again been used in many European countries to cement national communities. In the Netherlands, for example, a government-installed committee of learned men and women launched a much debated canon of fifty 'windows' (specified areas) on Dutch national history only recently, in 2006. Similar discussions took place in France (Grever, 2007). Governments and historians in other countries too are looking for national histories. The history of women and gender in such national canons is by no means self-evident. When historians depart from the notion of the political unity of a nation-state, women are present in such histories only from the moment they become emancipated as citizens of that nation-state, in other words, when their position is *equal* to that of male citizens (Mak, 2007).

The first examples of feminist critique and suggestions for alternatives were mostly oriented on the absence of important women in (national) historiography. The start of a worldwide women's movement dates back to 1860. This so-called 'first wave' of feminism inspired female historians – who often lacked academic qualifications – to search the past for the presence of women. They were keen on finding proof of their feeling that historiographers had perhaps been a little blind to the feats of women, in the attempt at shaping a national past. With a little effort it was not too difficult to find some women whose contributions to the national past could be matched to those of men (Grever, 1994). In the Netherlands, for example, amateur historians and novelists told stories about women resisting Spanish rule in the Eighty Years' War (1568–1648). They considered these women as the living proof that women could perform just like men if circumstances allowed them. In the US, to take another example, Mary Beard wrote *America through Women's Eyes* (1933) on women's role in history. In these texts, women of the past became the exemplary precursors in the struggle for emancipation and citizenship. Florence Nightingale too was such an icon in British histories and even the Dutch feminist and historian Johanna Naber had three publications on this 'pioneer' (Naber, 1909).

In the early phases of the second feminist wave (1965–1990), female historians undertook a renewed attempt at this search for female precursors or women who deserved a place in the gallery of honours. At present, a lot of gender historical research is still concerned with retrieving women from the past who had been, in the historical sense, undeservedly forgotten. Florence Nightingale is made a little less unique by this research, because other well positioned women, such as Josephine Butler or Aletta Jacobs, similarly pined for an objective in life and fought for education, freedom, and a profession.

Yet such attempts at adjusting the inequality in historiography led to some foreseeable problems. Could the imbalance in historical accounts really be completely ascribed to the prejudice of male historians regarding the feats of women? Was it not just the case that fewer women than men had accomplished feats that merited a mention in historical records? And, granting the limitations in education and otherwise, should it not be acknowledged that Florence Nightingale was indeed the exception to the rule? The approach of 'adding' women to national histories in the end did not yield much for a gender sensitive historiography, because the women lost and found are, like Nightingale, the exception to the rule. Their presence in even the most traditional history books did not change much about the way these books were set up – they continued to be 'blind' to the significance of gender.

So what actually qualifies as a historical feat? What are the (implicit) *criteria* in deciding what is historically important? Perhaps women contributed to history in a completely different way. And so the idea arose that gender historians should stop the hunt for women who met those masculine criteria, because the norms for historical importance should be queried as such. This question entailed a wholly new vision on historiography, a novel idea about the relative notion of historical value. What signified a milestone for men did not necessarily constitute such an interesting development for women. One of the first criticisms that reflected this angle was voiced by Joan Kelly in her famous essay 'Did women have a Renaissance?' (1984). This line of thought held that women's history should not aspire to include as many women as possible in national historiography, but that instead new – female – criteria should be developed for the 'historical'.

This process caused a shift in attention towards the way in which selection of what was thought to be historically interesting was related to the position men and women took up in the story of the past. Women's historians were inspired by developments in other women's studies disciplines and began to address the question of binary opposition. They wondered whether historiography was also affected by this division, in which the world is split into domains that implicitly have either masculine or feminine connotations. In this approach to historiography, unspoken norms are exposed and subverted in the conscious decision to investigate the history of 'other' – suppressed or excluded – themes and domains. The social rather than the political takes up central position; the history of reproduction rather than of production; the private sphere of sexuality, marriage, and education rather than the public life; the history of the body rather than the history of ideas; the history of folklore rather than of organized religion; of witchcraft rather than of science; the experiences of colonized peoples rather than colonial politics; popular culture rather than high culture; the violated woman rather than the unknown soldier; and the history of nursing care rather than the history of warfare. Such historical research foregrounds certain allegedly feminine domains at the expense of affairs with masculine connotations, such as politics and warfare. *Equality* is no longer the objective of scholarship as women's *difference* to men is acknowledged. This perspective has yielded groundbreaking results.

However, the problem with such an approach is in the implicit suggestion that dominant and marginal domains are mutually exclusive or even contrary to one another. Women are relegated to a kind of historical ghetto of difference and otherness. Many historians believe that this is an unfortunate effect and gender historians therefore attempt to *deconstruct* binarity. They show that certain ostentatiously mutually exclusive terrains actually presuppose and define one another (Scott, 1988) and that gender is a category that can be used for deconstructing binary opposition. Such a gender sensitive approach examines how societies in the past were in a broad sense suffused with gendered oppositions, and what this meant to men and women's potential (and lack of it). It is an approach that offers possibilities for the analysis of any past society. Women turn out to be interesting objects of research because they appear to be balancing on the fault line of these alleged oppositions. Perceived from this perspective, the story of Florence Nightingale changes again. The remainder of this chapter will take the case of Florence Nightingale's historical significance and give a demonstration of such an approach.

Martyrdom and citizenship

> Lord, I ask you the grace not to die in my bed, but that of shedding my blood as you did for me.
>
> (Florence Nightingale in McDonald, 2001: 60)

To sacrifice oneself for a big cause – rather than just dying in bed – that is what the young Florence Nightingale had in mind. According to Lynn MacDonald, her biographer, she found her opportunity in the Crimean War. There, her wishes, which appear to have been inspired by Christianity – the Passion of Christ – could be fulfilled. The suffering, impoverished masses of the Crimea appeared to her indeed as the face of Christ (MacDonald, 2001: 60, 64–5). Yet her sayings also plainly refer to another dominant discourse of her era, the one on citizenship. The meaning of this concept in the nineteenth century needs to be clarified in order to understand the significance of Nightingale's allusion.

The nascent European nation-states of the nineteenth century were no longer based on the sovereignty of monarchs or dukes, but on the idea of a sovereign people. The same people were appealed to in defending the nation and at once *all* men were potential heroes because they were prepared to sacrifice themselves for the nation. In earlier times, only a few noblemen endowed with courage, masculinity, and a self-sacrificing spirit could aspire to this status, as wars were fought with mercenary armies. In concrete terms, this meant that from the start of the nineteenth century, a form of general conscription for all male citizens was established in most European nations. This development was less linear and abrupt in Britain, where the distinction between honourable officers on the one hand and soldiers who were seen as the scum of the nation on the other hand, was prolonged much longer. However, from the second half of the nineteenth century, heroism was gradually more democratized with the institution of volunteer corps (Rose, 2007: 171–5). Throughout Europe, the willingness to sacrifice oneself for the motherland by means of the army was becoming the unconditional prerequisite for citizenship in the nation – an unattainable condition for women. Women from all layers of the population were excluded from political citizenship. They did not have the right to vote and could not be elected in national or local representation. They were even barred from taking part in governmental advisory committees (Kelly, 1984).

Yet, women were not completely excluded from the discourse on the nation. They were also expected to make an effort for their country. It is striking, though, that the rich variety of radical new ideas on the position of women, stemming from the Enlightenment, appears to have evaporated. At the time of the early Enlightenment, the principal equality of men and women was publicly propagated in various ways. The French Revolution, for example, inspired women such as Olympe de Gouges in France and Mary Wollstonecraft in England to claim equal rights in composing the *Declaration of the Rights of Woman and the Citizen* (Gouges) or a *Vindication of the Rights of Women* (Wollstonecraft) as a counterpart to the revolutionary *Declaration of the Rights of Man* (Scott, 1989; Caine and Sluga, 2000; Stuurman, 2004; Israel, 2006). However, in that very same revolution, all attempts to ameliorate the political position of women were crushed and women's organizations were even prohibited. The introduction of the Napoleonic Code in large parts of Europe meant, moreover, that the new marriage laws involved unprecedented restrictions for women in their freedom to act and power to control. No appeal was made on women as political citizens. Their contribution to the nation consisted of the self-sacrifice involved in motherhood, exhorting their soldier husbands and sons, and mourning those who fell for their country. Their nationalism, in short, took shape in the private sphere and could not lead to possible claims on political citizenship.

In other words, both men and women were expected to identify with the nation and to be prepared for immense sacrifices. But only men who might become martyrs on the battlefield – and at first only taxpaying men – were rewarded with political citizenship. What remained for women was the duty to be a good mother and to care for the family – the 'nursery of the nation' (Blom, *et al.*, 2000; Caine and Sluga, 2000).

14.2 Extract from a letter written by Florence Nightingale.

In nineteenth-century depictions of heroic moments on the battlefield, classic masculinity appears to be a far cry from home. At first sight, the images of men who emit the last breath while reclining backwards in the arms of fellow soldiers do not appear to refer to courage and heroism. However, at closer inspection they call to mind particular paintings depicting the Descent from the Cross of Christ, where the dead body of Jesus is removed from the cross and lamented by Mary and his disciples. The nineteenth-century paintings of battlefield scenes thus nicely encapsulate nationalism, Christian symbolism, and masculinity (Von Erffa and Staley, 1986: 58). This returns us to Florence Nightingale. In petitioning God to be spared a simple death in her bed and to offer her blood for a noble cause, as Jesus had done, she was perfectly in step with the contemporary discourse on the heroic sacrifice of the courageous soldier. Without explicitly saying so, she had a shot at being fully acknowledged as a citizen of her country.

Unlike some of her female precursors, she did not literally aspire to become a soldier. There is, of course, the famous example of Joan of Arc, but there were also many cases of women joining the battlefield dressed up as men in the *Ancien Régime* (the period before the French Revolution) and during the revolutionary wars. And especially in France these women were venerated as national heroes for a long time. Only late in the nineteenth century did the thought arise that these women might be somewhat 'deviant' with respect to their sex. Or, if these women were described in laudatory terms, it was pointed out that such behaviour was inconceivable 'at present' and that women were better advised to quench their thirst for serving the nation by joining the ambulance corps – in other words, to behave like Florence Nightingale (Mak, 1997).

In rushing to the front with a brigade of female nurses following suit, then, Nightingale identified with the fate of soldiers. The fact that she was deeply concerned with the *common* soldier impressed the British nation deeply, if only because it became apparent that the soldier who supposedly was a vital figure to the nation had in fact been scandalously neglected by the army. Her sacrifice occurred precisely at the cutting edge of masculine war heroism and feminine care. This created the unique position she has taken up in historiography right up to the present day: a woman who is both a national hero and martyr.

Yet the kind of work she performed – tending to the sick and wounded, ensuring the hospital was cleaned, and supervising hygienic measures – was not at all novel in history. In fact, the awful neglect of the common soldier is directly related to yet another history: that of the gradual expulsion of all women from the army. During the *Ancien Régime*, for example, women formed a large part of the armies: as washerwomen, sutlers (merchant women), lovers, wives, and prostitutes. These women looked after crucial aspects of warfare: provisions, hygiene, and nursing care. These essential logistic contributions are hardly acknowledged in the majority of military historiographies. Gradually these women disappeared from the scene in the early nineteenth century, when the army became more and more an exclusively masculine domain (Hacker, 1981). As happened in other professions as well, the process of institutionalizing and professionalizing warfare entailed the exclusion of women and 'side' affairs commonly associated with women. In reality, Florence Nightingale reclaimed and re-invented a position which women had long before. Thus she smartly joined the masculine discourse on professionalism, by claiming professionalism for nursing too – to be carried out by women.

Private sphere and public sphere

> For Florence Nightingale, every moment spent in a drawing room was a lost opportunity to do God's work, every diversion from the appointed task betrayed those who had already given their lives for the cause.
>
> (Poovey, 1991: xxviii)

Today, many historians see the struggle of women in the nineteenth century against suffocating Victorian morals, which expected women to be like 'angels in the house' as one of the founding structures for the contemporary women's movement. Women such as Florence Nightingale are therefore considered as feminists *avant la lettre*: strong women who actively opposed the exclusion of women from public life. They may not have fought for the right to vote for women, but they certainly paved the way for women who wanted to enter the public sphere and take up professions.

As mentioned above, the downside to this narrative is that it reduces gender history to the history of women who conquer male privileges in the public sphere. With this, the opposition between public (the areas of politics, army, science) and private (family, sexuality, love) appears to be absolute and to stand firmly and unalterable. Yet, it is one of the aims of gender history to *historicize* that opposition – track the changes in the course of time – in order to deconstruct it.

Gender historians have been pointing out that the gender specific distinction and opposition between private life and public sphere is not of all times, but is typical indeed for Western societies in the nineteenth and twentieth century. This had to do with the rise and growth of industrial capitalism. The division between production (in the factory) and consumption (in the family) condemned many women to an existence of housewife and mother. In an agrarian society, women had an important task in many different economical activities, but now it had become their job to raise their sons as socially adapted employees, citizens, and soldiers. They were to be like angels in the house: loving and caring and of impeccable sexual behaviour. They were not supposed to be exposed to the dangers of public life. Rather, it was proper for them to be weak and feel the necessity for shelter and respect that the private sphere proffered.

Many women lived a different kind of life in practice, but the ideology that women should be homebound had an enormous impact. Working-class women, who had no other choice but to work in factories, increasingly felt it was immoral to have paid work. Other women overtly referred to this ideology when defending their interests. There is an example in the case of Sojourner Truth, a woman born as a slave in the United States, who campaigned as an abolitionist around 1850. Her speech 'Ain't I a Woman?' famously describes her past life as a slave, with the hard physical labour at the plantation and the thirteen children she had, most of whom were sold off to slavery. With the rhetorical charge that *she* too was a woman, she sharply voiced a critique of the ideology that naturally protected white women, but refused the same protection where women in slavery were concerned.

It was not just the private sphere which acquired a new dimension. The male coded domains of politics and the state were similarly subjected to change. A proper assessment of the life and work of Florence Nightingale must not be limited to her gender alone and the expectations and restrictions this entailed. Gender related opportunities in the changing society that was her field of operation are therefore also considered in this chapter. There are three types of historical change in the second half of the nineteenth century that merit our attention:

- First, the growth in state regulated welfare of citizens supplied Nightingale with unprecedented opportunities for realizing her ideals.

- Second, she benefited from the new fields of activity entailed by the offshoots of contemporary imperialism.
- Third, the rise of modern mass media had an impact on political styles.

During the course of the nineteenth and twentieth centuries, the national governments in Europe took more and more responsibility for social welfare. Via poor relief, education, and public facilities such as waterworks and sewerage, national governments increasingly penetrated the lives of citizens. Historians interpret this as the shift from the so-called 'nightwatch' state, a state form mainly oriented on warranting internal and external security, to the welfare state where the authorities were responsible for various aspects of citizen welfare. In the twentieth century, social legislation and proper healthcare were generally implemented and everyone was entitled to a pension or a form of health benefit. Before, only the rich could count on these types of security. Historians usually ascribe this historical shift merely to the rise of organized labour movements, which would have enforced social legislation. However, this kind of explanation is blind to gender. Gender historians have demonstrated that women played an important part in the historical shift from nightwatch state to welfare state.

Social problems, such as neglected children, youth prostitution, alcohol abuse, and work shyness, were mostly stigmatized as the failure of motherly care in the nineteenth century. This doctrine implied that women supposedly 'knew' about the significance of proper domestic relations, which meant, according to Denise Riley (1988), that women could manifest themselves as the experts where social problems were concerned. So the right to speak out was derived from the fact that women had always been supposed to know about proper care for children and the sick. As a result, they acquired an authoritative public voice in areas which, until then, had been defined as private. Through an appeal to the social sciences, they also managed to add the weight of professionalism to such innate aptitude. Florence Nightingale can be seen as the embodiment of this strategy. Thus, she managed to acquire public fame by doing what many people associated with the task of women in the private sphere, nursing the sick. She took the radical step of deciding to refuse to do this kind of work quietly in the shelter of the domestic sphere. She went out into the open, she moved into public space. Behind the scenes, she managed to exercise much influence on government policy. Two royal committees for investigating healthcare in the army and in India, respectively, were instigated at her intercession. She personally selected the members for these committees, formulated queries and analyzed the data herself (MacDonald, 2001: 31–39). She insisted on the necessity of proper training facilities (establishing a school for nurses herself) and of improving hospitals and state healthcare for the sick. She was the author of an infinite row of articles, letters, brochures, and instructions, all dedicated to detailing the art and science of hospital nursing. Nursing the sick was converted into a theme for public debate.

This was not about individual care – she abhorred the stereotype of bedside nursing geared to establishing a bond between patient and nurse. Rather, she took the systematic view. She argued for social reform, such as a system of public healthcare for curing and nursing the sick who could not afford medical care; nurse training facilities; or the use of statistics in healthcare. She did not only advocate free healthcare, but also argued for professional norms which respected the civilian state of those under care, rather than treating these patients like beggars. With such norms and ideals, Nightingale was one of the pioneers of the modern welfare state, where care is no longer a favour bestowed upon individuals, but an undeniable right for the entire population (MacDonald and Vallée, 2006).

Thus, a gender sensitive analysis shows the impact (upper-class and) middle-class women such as Nightingale had on formulating new ideas about the national government tasks. They championed the right to work and asserted a public voice in discussing social problems. In the perception of these women, the state was not only a father who ruled the nation, protected it against enemies, and punished its citizens. The state increasingly became a nurturing mother who looked after her subjects and procured social security.

Florence Nightingale was active in a period of unprecedented colonial expansion for the British Empire. It was not just that new territories were added to the British Crown (the scramble for Africa); colonial rule was also intensified in previously colonized territories. Both developments were accompanied by a great deal of military violence. It is notable, in this respect, that the Crimean War, which became Nightingale's platform, was a colonial war too, as the stake for Britain was about retaining influence in the Ottoman Empire. This war then provided Nightingale with the opportunity to draw the attention of the public at large to the miserable state of care for the sick and wounded. In her youth, she had witnessed the scandalous neglect of the sick in British poor houses, but this area was deemed unfit for young upper-middle-class women and so she could not do anything about it. It was inconceivable for a woman of her class to go and work in the poor house and relieve the allegedly self-incurred fate of the poor. However, the colonial war against Russia was a different matter altogether. Here you had soldiers defending British interests abroad and so the government was held accountable for their fate. What is more, the army was supported by the entire nation. After her breakthrough in the struggle for good nursing care for soldiers, she had acquired a platform for advocating proper care for the sick and poor on British territory.

Most colonial powers had as yet to develop an eye for public healthcare in the metropolis, while paradoxically the task of colonial authorities abroad was defined in much broader terms. As the Western countries believed that political power implicitly entailed that civilization was brought to the new territories, the difference between civilized and uncivilized was defined in terms of Western behavioural norms in the private sphere. Thus, they claimed to protect the women and children of the colonized people against supposedly 'primitive' customs and traditions. Ann Stoler, a historian who integrates gender in her research of the history of colonialism, maintains that the notion that it was up to the authorities to teach people to live hygienically and according to bourgeois family values was tried out in the colonies first (Stoler, 1995). This created the space for female input in colonial policy: Florence Nightingale wrote extensively on colonial rule and public health and hygiene in India, venting her opinions and bombarding colonial civil servants with advice and ideas about the lay-out of hospitals. She was probably the first British woman to be *publicly* involved with colonial policy.

Her public stance also testifies to the fact that there was more to British imperialism than mere rifle power.

Finally, Nightingale, the woman warrior, can be located in a context of a changing political style. By the end of the nineteenth century, liberal democrats were in the ascendant in ever more European countries. In Britain, the male population as a whole gradually became more involved in local authorities and national government; daily newspapers and the illustrated press began to cater for the new mass of voters. Until then, politicians were expected to discuss politics rationally and in a dignified, detached manner. However, with the rise of mass media and political mass movements at the end of the nineteenth century, new, rather more emotionally oriented, political styles were developed (Armstrong, 1987; Schwegman, 2001). Public opinion became a matter to reckon with for politicians and this opinion was no longer fostered exclusively by members of their own social class.

The Crimean War was the first war to be covered by photo journalists. The British home front was shocked by stories of unbearable sufferings endured by soldiers at the front. Press photographs brought personal experiences to the public domain. Nightingale was quick to seize the opportunities of the popular press. She had good connections in the press and all her actions and lobby work were sustained by newspaper articles, letters to the editor or – just as effectively – the threat thereof. Thus, she capitalized on the emotional reactions to her support of the common soldier in the popular press.

Yet Nightingale was more than just the 'Lady with the Lamp', who introduced emotions (such as pity or outrage) into the public debate. She also consciously deployed rational and scientific arguments in her struggle for better nursing. Effortlessly, she juggled personal experience and statistical analysis in her writings (MacDonald, 2004). Until then, emotions were a public subject in so far as they were mediated by fiction, often written by women who occasionally used male pen names (Armstrong, 1987). Nightingale clearly opted for a different course. The approximate eight thousand pages of her collected works contain only one work of fiction, *Cassandra*. She felt that a factual approach was better suited to the subject of nursing: social sciences and statistics were indispensable for developing and designing good, efficient nursing. She invented the pie chart and was an honorary member of the British Statistical Society. She clearly did not only take advantage of the tendency of a new kind of politics that was more emotionally driven, but contributed to the development of another innovation as well: the rise of statistics and social sciences as a manner of publicly discussing social problems.

Conclusion

This chapter on gender history has centred on Florence Nightingale. It has become clear that a gender sensitive approach argues that she can no longer exclusively be seen in terms of the lone warrior, one of the very few women to make it into the historical canon. That would involve the unquestioning application of criteria for what is or is not historically relevant, in which case only a woman whose accomplishments are *equal* to famous men can be properly laurelled. Gender historians wished to escape this snare and looked into those areas which had conventionally been excluded from historiography: household tasks, care, nursing, sexuality, and the like. However, in emphasizing only *difference*, Nightingale would be depicted as a sort of super nurse, as if there were a female universe completely set apart from the rest of history. That was the reason why the *norms* for what is and is not historically important became the subject of a critical gender perspective. First, it was shown how Nightingale related to discourses on citizenship and the nation and how she sought to join these discourses. By subsequently *deconstructing* the public/private opposition – and usually historians achieve that feat by *historicizing* this opposition – it was possible to argue that Nightingale was able to make use of important political transformations in the later nineteenth century and also contributed to them.

Can we say that a gender sensitive analysis in historiography is always concerned with the case of an actual woman or a concrete group of women (e.g. nurses, servants, or prostitutes)? The answer is no for two reasons. First, such investigations can also involve men and the gender connotations of their lives, their potential (or lack of it) and their ideals. The instrument of gender remains a prerequisite for such research. Second, and this becomes the closing statement for this chapter, it is important to realize that gender connotations occur everywhere. Nearly every social, cultural, and political distinction is coloured by associations with masculinity and femininity. Gender historians therefore relate gender to conceptual pairs which, at first sight, appear to have little to do with gender, such as nature/culture, sacred/profane, or high/low culture. It is therefore important to observe in which ways other categories such as ethnicity and class are mutually affected by gender. This is illustrated in this chapter through the use of many different types of gender sensitive analysis which are not limited to the history of a single individual, but rather concern several key concepts in history. Just think: citizenship, the nation-state, the army, class, state interference, social sciences, colonialism, and political style were all passed in review. They always turned out to be both essentially entangled with gender and subject to historical changes. This is how gender history puts the challenge to historiography. A reliable political, military, social, or cultural history cannot afford to do without gender.

Questions for further research

1   When and where were women allowed to be assigned to combat units in the army? What was the legitimization for that decision?

2   The women from the past were marked out by first- and second-wave feminists as precursors; who were they? What kinds of arguments were given for their selection? Are these women still seen as heroines in the twenty-first century?

3   What were the attributes ascribed to women that formed an argument for a greater female public voice? Look for concrete examples and quotations on the Internet or in the library, accounting for cross-national differences.

4   What was the relation between masculinity and citizenship in the nineteenth century? Was class or ethnicity important in this respect? Look for concrete examples and quotations on the Internet or in the library, accounting for cross-national differences.

5   What kind of opportunities did the 'civilization mission' of colonial powers involve for women? Distinguish women in the colony from women in the metropolis and account for ethnicity. Take an example from a novel or an encyclopaedia in answering this question for a specific colony.

6   The changing role of the state and the authorities can be described in terms and metaphors with either masculine or feminine connotations. Argue this by referring to concrete examples in one of the following domains: social welfare, security, migration, healthcare, education, and tuition.

Hélène Swarth and the construction of masculinity in literary criticism

15

Maaike Meijer

15.1 Hélène Swarth.

The poet Hélène Swarth was born in Amsterdam on 25 October 1859. She was the youngest of seven children. When she was six years old, the family moved to Brussels, where Hélène received private tuition. Four years later, however, her mother's intense homesickness caused the family to move back to Amsterdam. Hélène experienced this return as an irreparable break with the happy days of childhood. From that moment the child was imbued with a sense of sadness from which she would never recover, even though only a year later her parents decided to return to Brussels once more. She was sent to a boarding school, where she was poorly educated, as was customary with girls. Nevertheless, she managed to master the French language fluently and even began to write poetry in French. When she was nineteen, she had composed her first book of poems, *Fleurs du rêve*, which was published in Paris (1879). Two years after this publication she had a new book, *Printanières*, which another two years later was followed by *Fleurs mortes*.

From the start she manifested the astonishing productivity that she maintained until her death at the age of 81. Her poems were romantic and sad from the beginning. At seventeen, she lost the brother she had been very fond of, a sensitive boy and her dearest friend. This loss caused the second trauma of her life and many poems were dedicated to him. She appeared to pick up when she fell in love with Max Waller, a young man of her own choosing – at the time the custom of being married off still held sway – but his parents forbade him to marry the protestant Swarth. Hélène kept hoping for Max,

15.2 *Example of poetry written by Hélène Swarth.*

who was a poet too, until his death ten years later. At twenty-five, she settled in the town of Mechelen in Belgium. From then on, she wrote in Dutch. A little less than ten years later she was married to Frits Lapidoth, a Dutch author. Theirs was not a happy marriage and after fifteen years she divorced him. She lost her first and only child. Yet all these sad life events did not detain her from an immense literary productivity.

She was staggeringly famous as a poet and writer, both in Belgium and in the Netherlands, the heroine of Dutch literature at the time. Her fame lasted until about 1910. It is likely that her early recognition as a French poet contributed to her status. When she began to compose her poems in Dutch – at the instigation of her literary mentor, Pol de Mont – and had her work published in the periodical *De Nieuwe Gids* (*The New Guide*, a platform for modern and innovative authors at the time), her foreign standing added metropolitan glamour to her work. Academic studies of her early work in French appeared in another prestigious periodical, *De Gids*, in 1992. No less than nineteen poems by Swarth were included in J.N. van Hall's anthology of contemporary poetry, *Dichters van dezen tijd* ('Poets of our time'), a collection published in 1894 (a seventh reprint appeared in 1910). To give an indication of her standing at the time: the eminent poet Willem Kloos had to be content with only eight poems in the collection, Albert Verweij with only seven, and such renowned poets as Herman Gorter and Frederik van Eeden were represented with even fewer poems (van Hall, 1894). As from 1910, her esteem began to shrink little by little and by the time of her death in 1941, it had completely evaporated. She certainly is not the only woman writer to have attracted large audiences and much adoration in her own time, only to sink into oblivion later. Sometimes it seems as if unbridled success really constitutes a ticket to oblivion; and this seems to be true for female authors, more than for male.

Swarth wrote lots of very sound and fine poems. Her technique was fabulous. Despite her impressive productivity and eminent standing in the literary life of her day and age, however, today's readers are not particularly attracted to the romantic subject matter of her poetry, manifest in the emphasis on the theme of love in her work and more particularly in her melancholy and tendency to dwell on the agony of love. Yet, there is much reason to appreciate her work when it is situated in the context of her era. For example, her writing on the erotic was exceptionally candid and paved the way for other women poets who, until then, had been condemned to the subjects of religion, nature, and sugary romanticism. She also wrote a number of compelling poems that voice a critical view on love. The following poem is an example.

Like a savage

Like a savage who presents
The crooked, cruel white man
With treasures of his blooming isle
And calls him lord and master;
For a handful of glass beads
Barters solid gold,
Gladly, slings the worthless necklace

Around his unfettered neck;
Licks the dust of the stranger's feet,
On his own neck plants it,
Meekly kisses the selfsame hand that
White may drip of blood;
    Woe! So did I – off'ring treasures
Of my lonely blooming isle,
Solid gold and precious pearls,
All – for a handful of glass:
Smoothly polished, large and round,
Pretty beads, red and blue,
Loosely threaded, airily,
On elastic string.
In fact I fancied, in my naivety
To have made a good exchange,
Nature's simple child I was
On my unspoilt isle!
Jubilantly I knelt down
Kissed the open hand
Meekly took his foot and placed it
On my proud, unfettered neck.

He – the lord of my small isle,
Me – piling treasures,
Solid gold and precious pearls,
At my master's feet –
    And the brittle gaudy necklace
Breaks, the glass beads
Roll in the sand – the elastic string
    Is flung in my face.

Oh, I'll get a new choker,
Even prettier perhaps,
Now surely I know its true worth
And – my treasures, they are lost.
    (Swarth, 1973: 16–17, trans. AF)

The structure of what is communicated in this text is as follows. Like a 'savage' who is allured by the sly stranger's worthless beads, so I too was deceived by you. The first sentence introduces a long comparison that leaves no room for doubt about how much the 'savage' is tricked by the 'crooked, cruel' white man, the colonial master. The speaker of the poem identifies with the 'savage' and portrays his naivety and innocence in very extreme images, as in 'Jubilantly I knelt down' (one kneels down to a divinity, if at all) and in 'Meekly [I] took his foot and placed it / On my proud unfettered neck.' Self-elected submission, in other words.

The 'precious pearls' offered by the native contain an allusion to the expression of 'casting pearls before swine', with the white man playing the part of the swine. Everything that pertains to the 'savage' – unfettered freedom, treasures, pride, what is pure and real ('solid gold and precious pearls'), credulity – is opposed, during the course of the poem, to what the white man hands out in return – freedom enslaved, worthless junk, falsehood, vain promises, and violence. When, on top of it all, the string of beads breaks and the elastic cord rebounds in her face, tears almost well up in our eyes at this poignant image. The choker mentioned at the close of the poem has the obvious connotations of suffocation and repression and contains a visual allusion to a dog's collar – in selecting this word, here, for necklace, the view on colonialism as a dehumanizing form of subjection is underscored once again.

The metaphor of natural man/woman who is deceived and enslaved does not only give a clear indication of what Swarth thought about the colonial adventure. Her indignation is reminiscent of Multaltuli (1820–1887), the Dutch author of the novel *Max Havelaar*, a classic indictment against the Dutch colonial enterprise in the East Indies. However, because the extended metaphor turns out to symbolize a love relationship, Swarth is also telling us that exploitation and enslavement can likewise take place in relationships between men and women. In the way this poem utilizes the analogy between black/native and female, it is like a premature version of John Lennon's feminist song 'Woman is the nigger of the world'.[1] In other words, the Homeric comparison creates an analogy between the subjection of indigenous peoples on the one hand and the subjection of women on the other. In that respect, the poem is in line with the topics of first-wave feminism. It gives an acute image of the downside of romantic love and the disillusion of marriage for women, who remained without power to control, were trapped in their own house, and completely financially dependent – in the early twentieth century a woman's assets would all fall to her husband once they were married.

Thus it appears that Swarth is very progressive, both in her anti-colonial views and in her feminist outlook on the heterosexual bond. Yet there is a certain ambiguity in this progressive perspective. The savage's role in his/her own enslavement is significant and borders on the masochistic. The white man's cruelty is pictured in general terms, whereas the grotesque submission on the part of the natural man is detailed in such actions as kneeling down and licking the dust of his master's feet or kissing his open hand, willingly planting one foot on his (her) own neck, calling him lord and master, and so on. Thus, a rather facile good versus evil opposition is created that belongs to the tropes of melodrama with, in this poem, the savage embodying innocence in distress. In comparison to the Dutch author Multatuli, who allotted a much more central position to the greed for power on the part of colonizers and displayed an acute sense of the way the colonial system worked and how it invited the native's complicity, Swarth's literary indictment is somewhat gross. There is a certain gratification in flaunting self-torment and in deploying the thick-brushed contrast between perpetrator and victim, aspects which form Swarth's trademark. She is very good at this. She wrote many other poems which begin with a Homeric comparison and endlessly forestall the thunderclap of unveiling the metaphor's tenor. Her unsurpassed poem, *The Doll*, for example (analyzed in the *NRC*, a quality paper, by the famous Dutch poet and anthologist Gerrit Komrij in 1998), raises huge levels of tension.

As said, the value of Swarth should be appreciated against the backdrop of her time. She is very apt at using the immensely popular conventions of melodrama – imported from France – as is testified by a number of poems, which also explains why these poems have not really stood the test of time in comparison to more temperate parts of her oeuvre. She would rank prominently in a history of literature which would truly reflect the history of literary taste – one that would not be based on the selection of historical texts which really suit our present-day preferences.[2]

The discourse of literary criticism

The remainder of this chapter discusses not so much Swarth's work, but her heroine status in the eyes of others. The focus is especially on studying both the making and breaking (in the long run) of her reputation in literary critical discourse. How was this heroine decapitated? The method used for addressing these questions is discourse analysis, with gender as an important analytical tool. Looking critically at the language used for understanding and evaluating women authors is an important component of feminist cultural research. For a long time, the genre of literary criticism was the exclusive domain of men and even today it continues to be dominated by men. Yet, it was also the sole source of information for women's writing – apart from the texts themselves, insofar as these were not destroyed and mutilated, as for example in the case of Sappho, or rewritten and made 'decent', as in the case of Emily Dickinson.

Pioneering research on the way work by female authors has been represented by male authors, reviewers, and literary scholars was carried out by Mary Ellmann, Elaine Showalter, and Joanna Russ (Showalter, 1972; Ellmann, 1979 [1968]; Russ, 1984). A pattern was laid bare: women authors have been briefly glorified and subsequently reviled; they have been trivialized, more than once they have been expelled from serious literature and relegated to such special niches as the 'sentimental novel' or 'ladies' novel';[3] and often they have been undeservedly forgotten, unpublished, or underrated (Meijer, 1988). Some of these vicissitudes befell men as well and their fate too can occasionally be explained by the particular gender constellation that held sway at the time. Gender does not just regulate the relationships between men and women, but men's mutual relations with one another as well.

The point of departure for the analysis of male critical discourse in this chapter is that the discursive process constructs gender for both the object and the subject in this discourse. Male enunciations about female poets should therefore be read in light of the question of male benefit, of what is in it for them. What kind of self-image is built with these statements? How can we explain the striking intergenerational imitation which occasionally hallmarks the discourse on women poets? Why do men repeat each other's sayings? The reception of Hélène Swarth's work certainly yields answers to these questions. This chapter defends the notion that male discourse on female poets does not produce ideas on femininity alone. It also, particularly, produces ideas about men. The paradoxical function of male writing about women is that it has the potential to create – stealthily, indirectly, but very effectively – a normative masculinity. Sometimes this is very overt indeed. Consider, for example, what is written by Willem Bilderdijk in the introduction to a book jointly written with his wife Katharina:

> What my spouse contributed to this collection appears from the characteristics of these pieces. Here, the gentle and dear heart will be recognized that is the hallmark of woman, who is formed only to be the joy of her husband and has no other desires.
>
> (Schenkeveld-van der Dussen, 1997: 777)

A bit further on, Bilderdijk describes himself as a great strong tree, whereas his wife is but a sweet little twig sprouting from his own side, again, 'wholly claimless'. As is testified by intensive historical research carried out by Schenkeveld, *et al.* (1997) and Streng (1997), woman is often the weaker vessel, the lesser poet in the discourse of many a critic and fellow poet. This discourse functions as a drawn-out male self-congratulation. It implies a culturally sanctioned projection on women, which meanwhile entails the constant illusion of superior masculinity. For too long feminist critics were exclusively focused on the construction of femininity, but we should have known better since Virginia Woolf's *A Room of One's Own* (1929). There are also some interesting psycho-analytical aspects to such male projections on women, which are addressed below.

Kloos about Swarth

Without exception, Swarth's work was very well received by her male colleagues. The Dutch poet and critic Willem Kloos had a major part in this positive reception. Kloos met Swarth in Brussels when she was twenty-five, with her fame in Belgium already established as the author of three volumes of French poetry. He briefly fell in love with her. There is some dispute among his biographers and Dutch studies scholars about the nature of this short-lived passion – was it love, admiration, or friendship perhaps? At any rate it is clear that Kloos felt he had met a great fellow poet. He sent her four sonnets, especially dedicated to her; Swarth responded with four sonnets that further developed his themes (van Eeten, 1961; Kralt, 1986). If he felt at all erotically attracted to her, then this was unrequited. Swarth was probably still suffering from the loss of Max Waller, but she and Kloos did become friends. It was at his instigation that she began to write poems for the prominent periodical *De Nieuwe Gids*. From then on, she was ranged with the *Tachtigers* (Movement of (Eighteen-) Eighty), the literary avant-garde of that moment, consisting of romantic and individualist poets who were all publishing shortly after 1880. Some interesting phrases were used by the leaders of this movement in characterizing their new fellow poet. Lodewijk van Deyssel reviewed her first poetry book in Dutch – *Eenzame bloemen* (Lonely flowers, 1884) – and is pleased to note that Swarth introduces a new, open, and explicit love lyricism in Dutch literature: 'And that in the Netherlands this is done by a woman who gives herself so truthfully to the people – this is very special [. . .]' (in Reitsma, 1985–1986: 60). Willem Kloos writes somewhat more exaltedly, that Hélène Swarth is:

> the singing Heart in our literature, which gives itself to the world, naked in glorious beauty and goodness, fair in its breathing, bleeding humanity, as an offering on the altar of the Muse.
>
> (Kloos, 1898)

The metaphor of the 'singing Heart' is significant. 'Singing' is a gender neutral topos for writing lyrical verse, but 'Heart' has clear female gender connotations. It refers to the deeply rooted gendered division of human qualities: he has the head, she the heart.[4] Likewise, the expression of 'giving herself' – as the poetic activity of Swarth is qualified both by van Deyssel and Kloos – can be seen as a gendered metaphor. To give oneself to the people or the world can be interpreted as a form of being completely open about oneself. Indeed, women were sooner and more generally thought to write autobiographically, to speak from experience, as it were.[5] However, 'giving oneself' implies a form of sacrifice too, a loss of self which is (and was) associated with femininity rather than with masculinity in the cultural imagination.

Masculinity evokes a contrary set of associations, such as command and control, self-possession, the capacity or need to observe the boundaries between self and other. The only man who ever gave Himself completely to the world was Jesus Christ. The heart 'that gives itself to the world, naked in glorious beauty and goodness, fair in its breathing, bleeding humanity' in the Kloos quotation above clearly alludes to Christ, as Christ too is often represented in terms of nakedness, glory, the good and beautiful, blood, and the humane. Thus, the image of Christ who sacrifices Himself – a move that implicitly represents poetry as a form of religious sacrament – is fused with the image of the beautiful, alluring woman who offers herself in all her naked beauty. In this blend, sacred poetry is evidently made feminine.

Willem Kloos here advances Hélène Swarth – unintentionally, probably, because this is really a battle for attention between two dominant discourses – not just as a poet, but through his specific phrasing as a *female* poet in particular. Is it conceivable that he would have used these words for describing a male poet, that he would have said *he* 'is the singing Heart of our literature, that gives itself to the world, naked in glorious beauty and goodness, fair in its breathing, bleeding humanity, as an offering on the altar of the Muse?' That is highly unlikely indeed, because it does not agree with the dominant discourse on masculinity, or with the implied discourse on the male poet.

In two essays, Kloos compares Swarth to a Pythia-like prophetess who is being stared at by great gatherings of people:

> This is no longer a human voice speaking, this is the supreme lament of a seer, who loud and calmly and with majestic gestures unveils before the amazed crowd the great visions of her soul pledged to the divine.
>
> (Kloos, 1887)

Elsewhere, he evokes a similar image of Swarth being admired by a crowd. She was still living in Mechelen:

> She should keep away from The Netherlands and continue to sing on, always to sing, so that the people in those narrow-minded regions will learn to see, arising before their eyes, her elevated looming figure that is like a faraway, strange Creature who generously disperses the flow of lament over teeming heads, her rhythms of jubilation, dreaming and picturing, seated like a divinity in her heaven at the horizon. I do realize that I'm merely crafting fantasies, that Miss Swarth is just a human girl who lives in a Belgian town and has great sorrow – but what the matter? I have always loved to embellish my life with my own imaginings [. . .]

(Kloos, 1898)

First, he turns her into a divine creature, a Goddess – comparable to the way the woman who is loved by two men is seen as a goddess in the famous Bizet opera *Les pêcheurs de perles*: as the crowd reverently and dramatically sinks to its knees, the two male rivals burst out in song: 'Oui c'est elle, c'est la déesse/plus charmante et plus belle [. . .] et la foule est en genoux' (Yes it is her, it is the goddess, ever more charming and beautiful [. . .] and the crowd is kneeling down).[6] The image of the admired Goddess is also comparable to the vision of the Goddess/Muse in Jacques Perk's poem *Sanctissima Virgo*. However, after magnifying Swarth to divine proportions, he subsequently cuts her down to size again: in truth she is just an ordinary sad girl. It seems strange and contradictory, this curious magnification and subsequent reduction. Both the praise and the disdain are somewhat over the top. Yet it can be understood when we look at the beginning of Kloos' essay. Here, the view is spelled out that the lyrical poet perceives everything, all the time, through the lens of his own powerful poetic imagination. The poet always sees a higher reality behind ordinary reality. In this passage, Swarth is used like a guinea pig for putting this view into practice. Kloos is actually giving a demonstration of the power of his imagination: he is capable of raising Swarth to a divine level, of giving her the classic appearance of a Muse. But then the essay is not really about Swarth the poet at all. It is about Kloos himself. He, not she, is the hero of this history. In other words, the passage should be taken to prove Kloos' own lyrical capacities and give evidence of his power to perceive the ephemeral through the lens of his own powerful imagination. The fellow poetess is mere raw material for the visionary poet and provides the stuff that his Muse is made of. It is hard to find a more cynical example of a procedure which erases female creativity in order to replace it with male creativity as a source for art. The text by Kloos is extremely ambivalent in appreciating Swarth – it is in fact a monument of egocentrism.

Swarth was often called 'The Dutch Nightingale'. The epithet 'nightingale' appears to be exclusively reserved for female poets. Giza Ritschl, a Dutch poet originally from Hungary, who more or less wrote in the same period, was known in her literary life as 'the Hungarian Nightingale'. The nightingale evokes the image of a sweet wild warbling bird and this image is definitely gendered. Willem Kloos never acquired the tag of the 'Amsterdam Nightingale'. The nightingale is associated with smallness, loveliness, and gracefulness and it contains a hidden allusion to the cage in which a singing bird might be kept. In other words, it would be inappropriate as a metaphor for the male poet. These discursive strategies ensure that gender is ever again imported into the literary field, where it creates a symbolical dividing line between male and female poets, between men and women. The language of literary criticism is a worthy object of study when it comes to the role it has in producing gendered values in the literary field. Consider also the strong language used by groups of emerging male poets when they present themselves in manifestoes and polemics, stressing while they are at it that they are *male* innovators, so that in the long run masculinity and innovation mutually define each other (Showalter, 1987).

Willem Kloos' ambivalent praise of Swarth was often repeated, not only by all literary historians, but also by a number of people who 'rediscovered' her work. The poet, J.C. Bloem made an attempt at rehabilitating Swarth in 1952, with a selection of her work entitled – with a nod at Kloos – *Het zingende hart* (The Singing Heart). He displays a mixture of admiration and disqualification in his introduction, which is reminiscent of Kloos. Hans Roest is wholeheartedly positive in his compilation of her work, *Een mist van tranen* (A Mist of Tears, 1973). Neither a critic nor an author, but just a personal friend of Swarth and a great admirer of her poetry, Roest had no part in the Dutch literary world. This explains perhaps his open-minded attitude. In other words, there is no need for him to guard literature's masculinity, because he has no position to defend in that domain. A third attempt to include her in the canon again – and yet another half-hearted effort it was – was undertaken in the 1980s by the Dutch author and critic Jeroen Brouwers. The iteration of the same ambivalent appreciations is quite interesting, as they are a tribute both to Kloos and to Swarth. The series of repeats manifests an intergenerational literary exchange between men; with the younger heroes building their own heroic status on the foundation of the elder heroes' heroic acts; and with the woman as the object of exchange. This leaves little room for any heroic status for the woman writer, as will be argued in a detailed discussion of Jeroen Brouwer's writings on Hélène Swarth.

Brouwers on Swarth

Jeroen Brouwers has devoted two entire books to Hélène Swarth (and a brief survey article in 1986). The first is a biographical study, ostentatiously restricted to the time of her marriage to Lapidoth: *Hélène Swarth: Haar huwelijk met Frits Lapidoth 1894–1910* (Brouwers, 1985). The second book, *De schemerlamp van Hélène Swarth* (Hélène Swarth in the Twilight, 1987), pretends to offer an analysis of her fame and subsequent fall into oblivion. Ambivalence characterizes both books. What is strange about the biography is its focus on her marriage to Lapidoth – a mere fifteen years in a life that spanned eighty-one years. Lapidoth was not half as important as Swarth. No doubt, being married to her, he had an impact on her life and work, but that does not justify the position he is allocated in the title of the book, as if he is an equally worthy subject for this study. As it turns out, the title is not very accurate because Brouwers describes Swarth's life and work before her marriage to Lapidoth too, as well as afterwards. Brouwers justified his decision by his professed reluctance to duplicate an earlier biography by Herman Liebaers (1964), which was about her early life in Belgium. One can have sympathy for Brouwer's considerateness, but still it has to be said that Swarth lived outside Belgium, in the Netherlands, for more than fifty years. In other words, there was no cause to reduce Swarth's life to the period of matrimony.

Perhaps there was another reason, both unconscious and trivial, for presenting his subject in this manner. Somehow it was inconceivable for Brouwers that Swarth could stand on her own feet. A woman needs a man. In the conventions of literary and biographical discourse, this is a deeply entrenched idea: search for the man in the life of great woman writers and demonstrate his indispensability. Joanna Russ delivers countless examples from the literary discourse in English for the nineteenth and twentieth centuries, where husbands, male tutors, or brothers acquire undue weight in the lives of writing women (Russ, 1984).

Brouwers states that it is his aim to rescue Swarth from the total oblivion which had become her fate at the time of writing. He recalls her impressive productivity. By the time she was sixty, at least twenty-five individual poetry books had appeared in print, apart from several collections, works in prose, and a number of excellent translations of French authors. The last five voluminous poetry books are kept in the *Letterkundig Museum* (Museum for Dutch Literature) in the Hague, because after 1921 no publisher felt that any profit could be made with these works. She died in 1941, so in fact she kept writing for another twenty years, even though her work went unpublished. Such enormous productivity meant, according to Brouwers, that part of her work was repetitive and of diminished quality. Nevertheless, he highly esteems a substantial part of her oeuvre: Swarth should be ranked in the Pantheon of canonized Tachtiger authors, in the company of Kloos, Perk, Verwey, or Van Eeden.

Indeed she belongs to the literary heroes of the *fin de siècle*, which is the reason why it is so interesting to consider Brouwers' attempt to draw her back into the canon. Nowadays, this is usually the job of feminist scholars, so if men too begin to devote themselves to re-establishing forgotten women artists, this would point at a welcome diminution of gender prejudice. Alas, however, Brouwers does not represent a reliable standard for the feminist project of rediscovering forgotten literary heroines. First of all, he neglects to support his claim for reconsidering Swarth with any serious attention to her work. He quotes the occasional poem but does not take any pains to demonstrate and argue its qualities. He hardly seems to care about what these poems actually try to say. A graver defect is in the way he writes about her person and character. She is the object of disparaging remarks and ridicule, as in the following:

> Till her death at the age of eighty-one, Hélène Swarth remained naive and unworldly like a toddler. Politics? War? Concepts of 'good' and 'bad' that were especially important at the time of the [German] occupation? Oh yes, it was there somehow, but vaguely, at a distance, unrealistic as it were, – not unlike the 'big bad wolf' in the mind of a child.
>
> (Brouwers, 1987: 6)

She was extremely vain, according to Brouwers, and her whole world was centred around the question of who had or had not written a favourable review about her latest book. She naively believed in ghosts and was addicted (still according to Brouwers) to spiritual séances. She only had one subject: love lost. The tiniest affairs of the heart were magnified to mythical proportions. Most of her verse was devoted to the doldrums of being abandoned and betrayed. Brouwers feels for Lapidoth, her husband (who later divorced her):

> That Lapidoth must have been an admirable man, really. He was married to the greatest poetess writing in Dutch of his era, but this was an unfortunate fate, really. She was an impossible, nagging woman, who evoked pity and got in her own way and made herself lonely and was afraid of life.
>
> 'I have seen so very little of the world! And would have enjoyed it so much!' (Towards the end of her life to Jeanne Kloos, not dated). She and enjoying, with her Swarthy mood?
>
> (Brouwers, 1985: 9)

Lapidoth is consistently depicted as an interesting, generous, and happy man. He forms a contrast to his wife in every respect, who continually manifests herself as an old fusspot who wallows in self pity. Brouwers directs his arrows especially at her melancholia. Her persistent depression is treated with scorn. He pursues her with a barrage of devastating character assessments. And so Brouwers' biography becomes a showcase for his own – rather than Swarth's, which would have been more fitting – stylistic qualities. On every page he calls attention to himself: look at me, my biting wit, my cynicism! Kloos, as we recall, performed a similar feat by drawing attention to his own heroic state as a poet rather than to Swarth as a literary heroine; while he suggested that he admired her, this admiration was in fact self-directed.

There is a lot of gossip and *petite histoire* in Brouwer's book. But there is no analysis at all of her poems and no effort is made to contextualize her work and her life. All right, she may have been politically naive, but this had everything to do with the lack of proper education which had affected every girl of her generation. Swarth was no exception, but at least she had the good sense to deeply mourn her lack of a decent education (Reitsma, 1985–1986: 60). In the late nineteenth century, feminists began to protest against deficient education for girls, but this was too late for Swarth, whose education had also suffered from the restless moves of her family.

As an author, Swarth limited herself to the subjects of nature, religion, and most of all of unrequited or thwarted love. This was related to the given that women poets were trapped in the conventions of what were thought to be suitable subjects for women. The pithiness of those conventions have to be appreciated for a good sense of the way Swarth explored and broadened the limits of those conventions – she tested and challenged them by being unusually explicit about passionate feelings. As if, at a subconscious level, she may have decided that if feelings were indeed the domain of women, she would fully explore these in all extremities. However, Brouwers treats Swarth solely as a detached individual. Her development, choice of subject matter, and literary style, are not located in any context or history; he does not read her life and work against the backdrop of historical gender relations. She had no part in creating those historical restrictions, but in cutting her loose from this context, he ridicules her for these limitations, which is very unfair. It is also politically and intellectually naive and to a certain extent it could be argued that Brouwers manifests the same naivety that he believes to discern in Swarth. The same is true for his decision to present Swarth within the limiting frame of her marriage to Lapidoth. He attacks her for her never-ending grief for this lost love – he keeps wondering why this woman was not capable of liberating herself from the restrictions of marriage – but he too imprisons her in the matrimonial perspective for far too long.

Jeroen Brouwers is a very melancholic person too and has frequently written, in fiction and autobiography, about the grave depressions he suffers from. Why then so little compassion with Swarth's fundamental lack of joy in life? His cruel scorn at her melancholy can only be interpreted as a way of distancing himself from a problem he has and recognizes in her. Perhaps he felt attracted to Swarth because the two are so alike: depressive, suffering from the incapacity to live happily, wallowing masochistic-ally in suffering. Swarth yielded to the temptation of every melancholic person: if I can't be happy, I'll create joy in sadness. However, Brouwers rejects this common ground. She is far from being an equal, a soul mate, someone the biographer can understand at an unspoken level. He lacks the courage – in Swarth, he persecutes himself.

The strangest thing is that there is so little discussion of Swarth's work in his books. He does not even include a list of her works. He neglects her work because he does not want to know her – he is keeping her at bay and therefore presents her as this silly creature, slightly daft. But his gaze is cold and without empathy. Perhaps he projects his own incapacity for life on Swarth, in an attempt to liberate himself from that burden. In that case, gender difference functions as a dissociating strategy. Brouwers, the Male, coldly observes the female Other, who is just too depressed to live.[7] This might explain his ambivalence with respect to Swarth. She resembles him – that is why he wants her back in the canon – but she should continue to be different from him – that is why he obstructs her reception in the literary pantheon and appears to want to close that road for ever.

The critical discourse on Swarth is strikingly repetitive. There is, for example, another essay on the depressions of Swarth by Anton van Duinkerken, with the same condescending tone which characterizes Brouwers' appraisal (van Duinkerken, 1965). This essay was deeply admired by Brouwers. He feels more connected, in terms of loyalty, to van Duinkerken than to Swarth, and therefore van Duinkerken is echoed, repeated. This is how Swarth becomes the object of exchange between the two men. Via her, masculinity is built or restored. Male bonding occurs regularly in the critical discourse on women poets and this is an aspect of the literary discourse which merits more attentiveness and study.[8]

Gender effects of literary discourse

The discourse of literature has certain effects on the way men and women, or masculinity and femininity, are understood and experienced. Discourse is taken in the broad Foucauldian sense to imply the whole of spoken and written utterances, behaviour, and its material embedding. The effect of gender is that we become men and women because we wear the clothes, because we move and speak to others, and articulate our desires which are available in the cultural repertoire. Femininity and masculinity are not only acquired in the relatively brief period of socialization in our early years. Gender is acquired in a complex process of discursive massaging that will go on until we emit our last breath. The same process of never-ending massage ensures that gender is not only constituted at an individual level, but at the collective level too. The literary discourse is one of the 'machines' that keeps gender in place as system and structure: individually, socially, institutionally, and symbolically (Meijer, 1997).

This chapter shows that the discourse of literary criticism does not just affect women writers. It creates men too, and symbolical masculine power, and the often hidden gendered literary values that relegate women to 'their place'. Male critics and writers appear to be rather dependent on this discourse for maintaining their masculinity. And so, masculinity turns out to be a fragile and uncertain identity, one which needs constant maintenance.

Notes

1   Using this analogy is not unproblematic. Often, this metaphor implies that the black is male – and the woman white – which in effect means that black women are made invisible. Here, the sex of the 'savage' is not made explicit.
2   Two Dutch studies scholars, Ton Anbeek (1988) and Jacqueline Bel (1993), argue precisely for a literary historical reconstruction of bygone passions and fashions. Thus, a valid historical picture would emerge of what was read and appreciated in the past. Literary history as it is now is like a fashion museum where only the clothes we like to wear today are put on display (Anbeek, 1988); an ahistorical projection of present-day tastes on the past. A good study of melodrama and the sources for its popularity is offered by Peter Brooks (1976). See also Meijer (2006), for the current revival of melodramatic conventions.
3   For the 'ladies' novel', see van Boven (1992). For the 'sentimental novel', see Tompkins (1985a: 81–105; 1985b). See also Meijer (1993) and van Boven (2000).
4   At about the same time – in 1889 – the influential gynaecologist Mendes de Leon applied this idea to the modern Dutch hospital. The medical director – male – was, in his perception, the *head* of the hospital; the head nurse – female – or woman physician, its *heart* (Bosch, 1994: 173). Literary discourses are always connected to extra-literary, social discourses.
5   As appears from contemporary reviews of her work, most critics took her work to be self-evidently autobiographical. The so-called 'autobiographical fallacy' has hit women worse than men, up to the present. Conrad Busken Huet (n.d.) permits himself to observe that Swarth's great belief in romantic love surely meant that her future fiancé would have a good time with her. Male writers often designate Swarth with the term 'girl' or 'child'. Kloos, for example, writes to his writer friend Frederik van Eeden in 1998 about 'that poor child, who whiles away her time in Mechelen and just keeps singing, and has been doing so for six years now, without getting what she wants, a husband *or* a big name' (quoted in Brouwers, 1986). The complete texts of a number of important critiques on her work are online in the DBNL (Digital Library for Dutch literature). Apart from the piece by Busken Huet, there are also Kloos, (1887); van Deyssel (1979a; 1979b); and van Deyssel, *et al.*, (1889). The DBNL also stocks two articles on Swarth: Brouwers (1986) and Poelstra (2000).
6   It is not unlikely that Kloos had this intertext in mind. Bizet's opera dates from 1863, but only hit success in 1886, shortly before Kloos wrote his essay in Swarth. The image of the divine Muse is a widespread cultural image, dating from antiquity and cherished in the *fin de siècle* – it was immensely popular with the Tachtigers.

7   This interpretation is indebted to Silverman's psycho-analytical analysis of the projections of male fear on women in Hollywood movies (Silverman, 1988, esp. Chapter 1).
8   Meijer (1998) attempts to explain the repeated praise for the seventeenth-century sister poets Anna Roemers Visscher and Maria Tesselschade. Their place in literary history appears to be at least partly ensured by their being embedded in a series of self-perpetuating male praise. First, they were glorified by contemporaries. Subsequently, they were discussed by a range of historiographers who often began by verbally repeating what contemporaries had said about these women, which frequently left little room for their own evaluation of the work of these poets. It is likely that such an appeal on male authority serves to legitimize the presence of women in the canon. If Vondel, Bredero, Cats, and Huygens thought well about the sisters, then transhistorical intermasculine solidarity prohibits them from thinking otherwise. Male praise for fellow males does not figure so prominently or repeatedly in work by later authors and historiographers, because the presence of men in the canon does not require legitimization. Men are approached much sooner as subjects who are to be taken seriously for what they are.

Questions for further research

1   Is it possible to describe literary criticism in terms of the Foucauldian 'discourse' concept? Describe how the method of discourse analysis might work for literary criticism.

2   Does literary criticism use different standards or approaches for work by male or female authors? In investigating this question, select a female author, assemble and map the critical reception of this author, and study this reception using discourse analysis as your method.

3   What do the analyses of a literary work and of a work of criticism have in common? Can it be argued that both forms of analysis are in fact a type of representation?

4   Are there any parallels in the restrictions that, in the past, were forced upon female painters or sculptors, poets, composers, musicians, scholars, and scientists? What can be learned from those parallels?

Food for thought

PART

III

Dympna and the figuration
of the woman warrior

16

Rosi Braidotti

16.1 Statuette of Dympna.

Here were the young women of the highest intelligence, and the most daring and ingenious of them, coming out of the chiaroscuro of a thousand years, blinking at the sun and wild with desire to try their wings. I believe that some of them put on the armour and the halo of St Joan of Arc, who was herself an emancipated virgin, and became like white-hot angels.

(Karen Blixen, 2002)

For many years I have kept on my writing desk the statuette of a holy woman warrior. Clad in a wrap-around cloak, looking intently into infinity through slightly downcast eyes, she cuts a rather sad but awe-inspiring figure. She is resting her left hand on a mighty down-turned sword, while holding up a book in her right. I choose to believe it is just any book, though it shows clear signs of being the book of books – the holy scripture of the Christian faith. This statuette is very special as it was given to me by someone I love and lost. We bought it during a day trip to Antwerp and when I first got it, I did not know who she was. Not many people know about Dympna.

Dympna, or Dymphna, was the daughter of a pagan Irish chieftain and a beautiful devoted Christian woman who died when Dympna was still very young. Her father searched the world for a suitable substitute for his lovely wife, but failed to find one. As his daughter grew up into a charming young woman, her striking resemblance to her dead mother aroused an incestuous passion in her father. Dympna resisted his advances and fled with her confessor, Saint Gerebernus, on a ship heading for Antwerp. They settled in the wilds of present-day Gheel, in what was then a small oratory dedicated to Saint Martin, where they lived as hermits and ascetics. However, Dympna's father pursued her to Belgium, found her and her companions and killed them all. He struck off her head with his own sword and left her maimed body to rot in the forest. Such were the ways of incestuous passions in the year AD 650.

This chain of events struck the popular imagination and the local people started the cult of the virgin martyr. Lunatics and epileptics reported being cured at her grave and the crowds of pilgrims were such that, by the thirteenth century, a shrine was erected to her memory. Her body was, and still is, preserved in a silver reliquary in the church. Ever since then, she has been regarded as the patroness of the mentally ill and of those – mostly women – who are driven insane by male violence, rape, and violation. According to the official register of saints by the Catholic Church, Dympna is the patroness of many other causes as well: incest victims; orphans; rape victims; sleepwalkers; epileptics; and the mentally ill as well as mental healthcarers. She protects the weak and the insane with her mighty courage and enormous wisdom, respectively symbolized by her sword and the book.

Even today, Gheel, a town near Antwerp, less than one hour south of the Dutch border, is famous for its thirteenth-century hospital and colony of lunatics, which pioneered the method of organizing mental healthcare on a family and community base. Neighbours, citizens, and, in the olden days, peasants would care for the harmless insane, who in turn undertook unpaid employment in the families and communities. It was a humane and compassionate way of dealing with what were vulgarly known as mad people, so many of them women, at a time when they were treated with contempt and hostility. This is also known as the 'Gheel method' of community care. Dympna's life casts a century-old shadow over them.

Marina Warner refers to Dympna as an example of a folktale adopted as the life of a saint in her classical study of fairytales (1995). Most people would know about Dympna through another version of her story and by a different name. 'Donkeyskin' ('*peau d'âne*'), a fairytale by Charles Perrault, is the most popular transposition of the key elements of my favourite warrior's story. Donkeyskin is the story of the lovely young princess who flees the dangerous family home and her widowed father's incestuous passion. She disguises herself with an ugly donkey skin to hide her astonishing beauty and survives through hard labour, charity, and obscurity. Then she is discovered by her prince, restored to beauty and honour, and rescued from social marginality, anonymity, and paternal rape. Such has been the way of fairytales since the age of the Enlightenment, when faith in the Christian God was replaced by faith in reasonable human behaviour.

Now what does this heroine's tale tell us about gender issues and what critical questions does it raise?

Analyzing the storyline

Dympna is not just a metaphor for the ills and the oppressive aspects of the condition of women, but a real-life character crossed over into myth and legend. Such characters have an important function in cultural and political theories. I refer to this function as 'figurations' and the method of analysis as 'the politics of location'.

The politics of location is a way of accounting for diversity among women, so as not to restrict gender within the category of 'sexual difference', understood as the binary opposite of the feminine to the masculine subject. As a method, it consists of unveiling the power locations which one inevitably inhabits as the site of one's identity. The practice of accountability for one's embodied and embedded locations is a relational, collective activity of undoing power differentials. A 'location' is not a self-appointed and self-designed subject-position. It is a collectively shared and constructed, jointly occupied social space. A great deal of our locations escape self-scrutiny in that they are so familiar, that one it is not even aware of them. The 'politics of location' consequently refers to a process of consciousness-raising that requires a political awakening (Grewal and Kaplan, 1994) and hence the intervention of others. 'Politics of locations' are cartographies of power, which rest on a form of self-scrutiny, a critical and genealogical self-narrative. They are relational and outside directed. This means that 'embodied' accounts illuminate and transform our knowledge of ourselves and of the world. Thus, black women's texts and experiences make white women see the limitations of their locations, truths, and discourses.

The method of a politics of location is expressed through alternative and often colourful figurations. Figurations of alternative feminist subjectivity, such as the woman warrior/the womanist/the lesbian/the cyborg/the inappropriate(d) other/the nomadic feminist, etc. differ from classical 'metaphors' in calling into play a sense of accountability for one's locations. They express materially embedded cartographies and as such are self-reflexive and materially grounded. Figurations, for instance, the cyborg, are both analytical tools and creative devices. They act as the spotlight for aspects of one's practice which were blind spots before. By extension, figurations generate and express knowledge claims. In relation to our theories of the subject, figurations such as the nomadic, the cyborg, the Black subject, etc., function as conceptual *personae*. This means that they are not mere metaphors, but rather materially embedded and embodied accounts of one's power relations. On the creative level, figurations express also the desire for change, transformation, or alternative relations to the power one inhabits: they are affirmative as well as critical tools.

Accounting for one's location is also a way to conceptualize differences: not in a dialectical framework of mutual opposition of self and other, but rather in quite a different logic of multiple, complex, and nomadic or multi-layered inter-relations. As with all figurations, Dympna is not just one, but rather a compound of many complex and internally contradictory aspects. Not one single 'meaning' can therefore be extracted from her. The field of signification inaugurated by this character is multiple or polysemic and complex in a productive sense. Let us see how many layers of meaning we can detect.

1   *The undutiful daughter syndrome*
Dympna is a rebel who dares to stand up against the will and the law of the father and pays for it with her own life. Considering the incestuous violence of the father's will, Dympna's disobedience takes the form of a fight against injustice and abuse. In this case, disobedience is a virtue, both morally and socially, which needs to be re-appraised and upheld. Like Antigone's resistance in the Sophocles play *Antigone* (and later in Hegel and many other philosophers); or Cordelia's in Shakespeare's *Lear* (Shakespeare, 1990), Nora's in Ibsen's *A Doll's House* (Ibsen, 1992), and the rebellion of many million others, Dympna's rejection of the will of the father – her resounding 'no! to masculine authoritarianism' echoes across time as a cry of pain, certainly, but also an encouragement for women to act, to resist, and to take their lives in their hands. This is the advice Virginia Woolf gives to women who aspire to become writers or creators (Woolf, 1978 [1936, 1938]). Woolf recommends that they kill the dutiful daughter within them, that 'angel in the house' of perfectly docile femininity that is a creative woman's worst enemy. Another eminent British writer, Rebecca West (1913), wittily stated that she was unsure of what a feminist was exactly, but had noticed that she was being called that name every time she refused to be treated like a doormat. In a patriarchal culture that rewards submission, disloyalty and disobedience can be positive and empowering practices for women. Feminism is in some ways the movement of undutiful daughters.

2   *'She asked for it!'*
Dympna is a stunningly beautiful woman. She is young, but old enough to sexually arouse men, her own abusive father to start with, and to be held responsible for the effect she has upon them. A woman's sexuality is perceived, experienced, and represented as a form of provocation in a male-dominated culture that assumes male desire to be the rule and the norm and female passivity the desired effect. Even today, in many cultures, rape victims are accused of having provoked male lust and hence male violence by being 'too sexual'. However, what that margin of excess is all about is never rationally explained. Some legal and religious codes and traditions, both in Western societies and elsewhere, blindly rest on the assumption of the intrinsic guilt of women's sexuality.

Radical feminists, such as Brownmiller (1976) and Dworkin (1976), have challenged this assumption and the way it covers up for masculine violence and privileges. These radical feminists have stressed the structural links between male-dominated institutions and sexual violence against women and other minorities. The legal and political battle to stop violence against women is one of the priorities of the International Women's Movement. It involves global human rights campaigns, monitored by the United Nations system, but also cultural movements such as Eve Ensler's *Vagina Monologues* (2003) and the V-Day Foundation (www.vday.org).

3   *Just a girl*

Dympna is a young virgin, barely out of adolescence, innocent but firm in her principles. She clearly would prefer to stay that way for the time being: she wants to live as a hermit in an ascetic community and explore her spirituality in her own terms and time. Sexual activity is not her priority. Her youth may make her inexperienced, but she is neither a fool nor self-ignorant. This degree of lucidity in a young woman may have been unusual back in AD 650, but is commonplace today. The status of young women and girls, of youth and girlhood, has evolved and changed dramatically in our culture. The principle of women's self-determination, which both the first and the second feminist waves fought so hard for, has granted women the right to time and structure their own life choices at all levels, including that of sexual activity. This is nothing short of a revolutionary change in the decision-making mechanisms of traditional societies, which used to be ruled by the will of the father, that is, of older men.

Age has emerged as a major factor in structuring women's access to social and cultural power. The rule by the elders, the authority of the fathers, of senior citizens – also known as 'gerontocracy' – has come under attack since the 1960s explosion of youth and popular culture. The average age of world leaders – once firmly ensconced in the sixty-plus category – has been brought down considerably. Is there a correlation to be drawn between the advanced status of women and minorities and the loss of power and prestige of the traditional gerontocracies, or rule by the elders?

However, it is also the case that in the third millennium sexual liberation – once the golden rule in feminism – has run its course. Virginity and sexual inactivity, once despised by Western feminists as symbols of the traditional oppression of women, are currently being re-appraised as a possible choice on the part of younger women who can see the limitations of contemporary sexual politics. A clear example of this trend is the French movement *Ni putes, ni soumises* (neither whores nor submitted), where the awareness of generational differences is combined with the insight into ethnicity and race relations (Amara, 2003). A re-appraisal of the second wave's sexual politics is also crucial to third-wave feminism (Henry, 2004), which is also deeply affected by the contemporary digital cultural revolution. Moreover, contemporary media culture is completely in love with youth and it markets inter-generational conflicts among feminists in classical oedipal terms: daughters against mothers, or sexually unattractive older women versus sexually irresistible younger ones. This classical topos is very divisive and requires serious critical analysis.

4 Not of this place

Dympna is a foreigner, a refugee, a political exile who cannot safely return to her homeland and has to rely on the kindness of strangers. She is a victim of a hostile patriarchal state authority: a lust-crazed king who happens to be her own unworthy father. She is persecuted, tortured, and ultimately killed by a political leader whose arbitrary will she resists. Unwilling and unable to go safely amid the citizens of a foreign town, Dympna builds her own camp and community near a church oratory in a forest.

How many illegal immigrants in the EU today are still fleeing from hostile political and national powers and end up finding shelter in church buildings and grounds? Is it not striking to see that ancient feudal privileges – such as the relative independence of church from state or local authorities or, for that matter, the equally powerful medieval charter that grants universities their 'academic freedom' – provide useful sites of resistance against the political power of nation-states and governments for unwanted, illegal, or persecuted migrants? In France, the movement of the *sans papiers* (without [identity] papers) regularly squats and occupies churches and chapels, in a time-honoured tradition.

And yet, precisely because of her foreign status, her deep sense of non-belonging, Dympna brings and holds together different communities of the suffering and the oppressed, her own travelling companions, and the local community to begin with. She connects to the compassionate citizens of the city of Gheel and, through them, to the whole country. Dympna's life story shows that you do not need to belong officially to a country in order to contribute to the well-being and social cohesion of a community. Refugees, migrants, colonial and other subjects, are vital elements of our social nexus and should be seen as a resource, not as a problem. Citizenship is not just a bureaucratic measure.

5 A fighter but not a killer

Dympna is a warrior and a fighter, but in a paradoxical sense. Because she could not save herself from persecution, rape, and murder, she ended up fighting for and protecting others. She expresses a relationship to fighting akin to that of the martial arts: she uses self-defence as a weapon against brutal violence. Her strategic use of force clashes with the militaristic relationship to violence exemplified by her unfortunate father-king. Even today, self-defence is taught to women as a way of preventing rape, physical assault, and abuse.

Dympna's down-turned sword is a symbol of stillness, as well as of mighty force. It represents a sustainable alternative to the over-enthusiastic way in which women, emerging from centuries of obscurity, embrace a Joan of Arc-like form of militant emancipation. As Karen Blixen pointed out in the excerpt quoted above, militarism and militantism are very close to each other, but they need to be kept distinct and apart in order to avoid excesses of violence. Feminism, especially its radical wing, is not immune from its own forms of revolutionary violence, though as a movement it stands firmly on the side of peaceful resistance and non-violence.

The warning against militarism is of the greatest relevance today, because since the publication of the Abu Ghraib photographs showing women who abuse their Iraqi prisoners in a US military prison, the issue of women in the army has become very problematic in our societies. The trademark of a genuine warrior, in the martial arts tradition, is to be able *not* to strike back, but to fight the opponent by other means. How does this non-violent use of force by a woman fighter fit into our contemporary media culture, which is fascinated by images of killers of all kinds and genders, from Angelina Jolie as Lara Croft to Uma Thurman in *Kill Bill*? Can we differentiate between a violent and non-violent use of force? What balance can a feminist theorist hope to strike? Is non-violence negotiable?

6   Before secularism: The spiritual quest

Dympna is a holy figure, a guardian, and caretaker, a symbol of religious faith who is officially listed in the register of the Christian church. She is a brand name for Christian pastoral care, the original Florence Nightingale. Studying the official church register of saints and holy martyrs and looking at what areas of human endeavour and suffering Dympna has been put in charge of – namely: incest victims; loss of parents; rape victims; sleepwalkers; epileptics; and both the mentally ill and mental healthcarers – is in itself an agenda-setting exercise. It allows us to make a deeper analysis of church thinking and institutional practices and also to further our understanding of the secular structures of our societies.

Note that, back in AD 650, when paganism was the dominant ethos, converting to Christianity was a radical gesture that led to persecution. One of the radical aspects of Christianity then was precisely its emphasis on loving and on the principle of 'turning the other cheek', or rejecting the tribal law of 'a tooth for a tooth, an eye for an eye'. Christianity supports a more humane definition and practice of the Law, based on principles of justice and individual rights. Still, feminists in the European tradition have an uneasy relationship to organized Christian religion, which has evolved considerably through time. The bulk of European feminism is justified in claiming to be secular in the structural sense of the term: to be agnostic if not atheist and to descend from the Enlightenment critique of religious dogma and clerical authority. As the secular daughters of the Enlightenment and raised in rational argumentation and detached self-irony, our belief-system is civic, not theistic. In other words, we have only paradoxes to offer, as Joan Scott (1996) so eloquently put it.

However, feminists cannot be simply secular, or be secular in a simple or self-evident sense, because global politics today contains an explicit message about the status of women and gays and about the project of emancipation. It involves moreover an alleged clash of civilizations that is Islam-phobic in character. An automatic and unreflective brand of normative secularism runs the risk of complicity with racism and xenophobia.

7   A myth and character in folklore and fairytales

As the inter-textual variations on the theme of 'Donkeyskin' suggest, the tale of Dympna pertains to a centuries-old stock of representations in popular folklore and fairytales. The continuity among the different variations, as well as the evident gender aspects, has been the object of intense feminist scholarship. Feminist scholarship on issues of representation is extensive, so I shall be brief here. Two points are worth stressing. The first is about the practice of critique of representation: this concerns on the one hand analytical tools of criticism, but on the other it also relies on productive and creative forces. One example of the affirmative value of images and representation is the part played by myth making, the creative imagination, and alternative figurations in political and social movements. Counter-cultures create new myths almost by necessity: Che Guevara is a modern example, as well as cultural icons such as Marilyn Monroe. The second point is related to the current digital revolution: media culture has a tendency to mystify all it touches and thus it engenders a proliferation of images. Visual representation is the key to contemporary power. All-pervasive visual representation in a technologically linked world makes myths out of even utterly meaningless figures such as Paris Hilton, the completely ordinary folks of television reality shows such as *Big Brother*, or the characters in TV series such as *Sex and the City* and *Desperate Housewives*. Because media culture is a myth-making machinery, it shares with classical disciplines the tools of the analysis of representation in textual and literary terms.

8 *What does she know?*

Dympna is not a learned woman herself, but she produces and generates knowledge in others who learn from her life history. They identify with her sad story and love her for the courage of her convictions. What does she know, after all? In religious terms, she conveys some of the main precepts and central messages of Christianity – a saint is a high priestess, even though she was not allowed to be officially ordained. That prohibition has not changed: even today the Catholic Church forbids the ordainment of women and gay people. Feminist theologians are critical of Church orthodoxy and argue for powerful spiritual alternatives, both within Christianity and in other religious denominations (Daly, 1978).

In moral terms, she knows about values and rigour, and in legal terms, Dympna knows about human rights, mental health, and well-being. More importantly, she is the patroness of institutions of scientific and psychiatric research. In the course of time, Dympna ended up as a logo, a patent for the specific 'Gheel method' of dealing with and taking care of the insane, especially of women who are driven mad by male violence. She generates institutional know-how and practice. In Foucauldian terms (Foucault, 1965), she is integrated in a set of institutional practices and regulations that aim at the management of the subject's physical and mental health by discipline and pastoral care. She is no revolutionary in this respect, but is, as a generator of alternative knowledge production, instrumental to the system of mental healthcare. This aspect of her story is in open contradiction with the radicalism of her position in other areas – in relation to paternal authority, for instance, or to the age variable. These contradictions are structural and internal to the characters and social actors involved; thus, they must be endured and analyzed, not hastily or forcefully resolved.

9   An icon, image, or visual representation

As a historical character, a myth, a saint, a brand name, a logo, and a patroness, Dympna enjoys a long and rich history of visual representation. The different mutations of her iconographic status or visual history can be studied and compared not only in history, but also across different genres and different branches of the visual arts: painting, etchings, book illustrations, sculptures, engravings, photos, films, etc. Women artists' practice has also reflected seriously on the analytical tools and frames of visual representation and art criticism (Krueger, 1983).

The very image of warriors wielding both the sword and the Bible has become a classic of colonial history and culture which was criticized by post-colonial thinkers. This returns us again to the problematic issue of women and violence and the pacifist tradition of feminism which I discussed above. In the age of 'Guerrilla Girls', 'Buffy the Vampire Slayers', and other fighting heroines, the visual topos of a woman wielding a sword has acquired dramatically different visual, cultural, and moral connotations. These can be studied historically, textually, and iconographically and analyzed in terms of changing gender roles and gender relations.

Psychoanalytic theory may read the sword as a 'phallic symbol', that is to say a substitute and signifier for masculine authority, which is not reputed to be suitable for women. In some ways, the emancipation of women takes the form of repeating certain aspects of male behaviour insofar as the masculine represents power, visibility, and authority. Unless one is prepared to argue that anything phallic is a dirty word, some amounts of mimesis, or strategic repetition, can be empowering (Braidotti, 1994).

10   A death mask

Dympna is a funeral sculpture, a name on a silver reliquary in the Gheel cathedral, and a death mask that expresses the perennial relationship between female suffering at the hand of male abusers and death. There is a deep and culturally consolidated link between women and death. The ritual and practice of mourning is reserved for women in most societies. The most recent example of this was the vast public mourning of Princess Diana after her tragic car accident, with crowds of mostly women, youth, gays, and people of colour gathering all over the world in public rituals of loss and remembrance, and with leaders of the calibre of Nelson Mandela officiating and bearing witness (Kear and Steinberg, 1999; Braidotti, 2002). Also significant here is the story of Sarah Bartmann, known as 'the Hottentot Venus' in colonial terminology, whose body was finally returned from the museum where it was preserved and given a decent burial in her home grounds in South Africa. Both the terms and the conditions of this symbolic burial stressed the complexities of the issue of death and death rituals and their link to reparation and healing.

Because Dympna is immortal as a mythical figure, however, this bond to death is also connected to the persistence of cultural memory. Honouring the dead and the victims who never had a voice, the nameless multitudes who went down violently and silently, is one of the functions of feminist scholarly research. This research carries out a witness function in speaking up on behalf of others while respecting their specificity and individuality. Writing about the missing is a form of mourning.

Theoretical tools and frameworks of analysis

Now that I have identified a considerable, though not exhaustive, list of research questions and areas of analysis of my leading woman warrior, I can move on to the next stage. This concerns the possible theoretical frames of reference and the methodological tools available for us to do justice to such a complex figuration. It is clear that gender does not refer to one single concept, but rather, as Scott (1986) argued, to a set of relations among a number of coordinates such as ethnicity, race, age, sexuality, and, in our case, disciplinary orientations.

In order to proceed, I first need to extract the key theoretical lines out of this much longer list of topics. What are, then, the main theoretical lines that are invoked by the story of Dympna? What is the state of feminist scholarship in these areas? What theoretical frameworks and schemes of analysis are available to us? What have previous generations of thinkers written about this and are these ideas still relevant today?

1 *The ethical line*

The main ethical question raised by this case study is: How does one process the pain and injustice of oppression, exclusion, and even persecution, without actually perpetuating the same kind of violence? The opposition I drew before, between a militaristic use of violence and a martial but not violent relationship to self-defence, is of great relevance. It also entails a distinction between the individual quest for revenge or compensation on the one hand, and the collective involvement of a community in the pursuit of justice on the other. This collective or group-based resistance to state or government abuse is central to the theory and the practice of Human Rights and the respect of humanistic principles in general.

Feminist theory bears a close connection to this tradition, as is evidenced by a large corpus of scholarship in this area (Jaggar 1983; Nussbaum, 1999). Given the pervasive nature of violence against women and the persistence of marginalization of ethnic and sexual minorities, however, feminists have questioned the meaning and value of the notion of 'Human' implicit in the practice of Human Rights. This approach is anti-humanist (Braidotti, 1991, 2006; Eagleton, 2003) and bears a close link to post-modernist critiques and deconstructions of master codes and discourses in our culture, by paying closer attention to power relations and structural forms of domination (Butler and Scott, 1992).

The opposition between compassion or understanding and revenge or hatred of the other is also important for feminist theory and practice. Peaceful resistance in a Ghandian tradition stands against the model of the guerrilla movement or armed violence. The latter was popular in the political history of revolutionary movements of the nineteenth and twentieth centuries and continues to exercise a degree of intellectual fascination even today. A touch of fanaticism in the Joan of Arc model of women's emancipation ends up defeating its own purpose because it perpetuates and thus imitates the very violence it is attempting to beat. Examples of this over-revolutionary zeal are to be found in some of the great texts of the second feminist wave, such as the *SCUM Manifesto* (1983) drafted by Valerie Solanas. This hard-line feminist group (whose initials stand for: Society for Cutting Up Men) was militantly anti-men. Another radical feminist classic is Ti-Grace Atkinson's *Amazon Odyssey* (1974). Kate Millett strikes a more cautious note (1973) and writes a very critical account of how political movements are destroyed by the use of violence in her autobiographical book *Flying* (1976).

The issue of women's relationship to organized violence, be it military, revolutionary, insurrectional, or instrumental, is of topical interest today, now we live in a state of perpetual warfare. The issue of terrorism and women terrorists needs to be looked at again, in the light of the pacifist ethics of feminism. Case studies are the women terrorists of the 1970s, such as Ulrike Meinhof and the Italian Red Brigades described by Mori (1978) and Farranda (2006), but include contemporary examples of women soldiers in various movements in the world today too: Chechenian war widows, Palestinian freedom fighters, indigenous land rights movements, and, of course, women in the regular armies of the Western world. Feminism and pacifism go hand in hand.

This deep commitment to non-violence has also procured the feminist claim that women generate a special moral dimension as life-bearers and caretakers. This school of thought is already present in some strands of early second-wave radical feminism and is voiced strongly by Adrienne Rich in her classic *Of Woman Born* (1976). It becomes more fully articulated in the 1980s. Known as the ethics of care (Gilligan, 1988), it provides the foundation for strong claims to female subjectivity not only in the moral field, but also in politics (Tronto, 1993), as an antidote to purely legalistic theories of political agency. I shall return to this point in the next section.

The claim of a specific moral dimension to women's experience, which is taken as the result of socialization and not as an innate quality, has also been made by feminist psychoanalysts. In the French post-structuralist or Lacanian tradition, for instance, Julia Kristeva (1980) and Luce Irigaray (1985) argue – each in their own way – for the specificity of feminine approaches to caring for and containing the 'other'. Although the basis for such a claim remains the maternal function, psychoanalytic feminists are not biological or psychic determinists and thus take into account the role that culture and society play in constructing women's relationship to others. The school of psychoanalysis, known as 'object relation theory' (Wright, 1992), is especially keen on stressing the role of material social conditions in shaping the moral consciousness and political agency of women. Nancy Chodorow (1978), for instance, argues forcefully that only an equitable sharing of parental duties between men and women can contribute, not only to genuine emancipation, but also to an increase in moral behaviour in our culture. Feminist ethics is the key to a fairer notion of citizenship and in this sense it is a very transformative practice.

2   Citizenship, migration, and ethnicity

As a foreigner without nationality or fixed abode, Dympna illustrates the problematic relationship of women and migrants to the rights and practices of citizenship in the fullest sense of the term: both as a legal and political practice and in the sense of cultural participation. This has been a central concern of feminist researchers ever since Marie Wollstonecraft challenged Rousseau's Romantic marginalization of women in the eighteenth century (Wollstonecraft, 1982 [1792]). Feminist political theory has travelled the reformist road, rather than the revolutionary one. It produces a reasoned critique of the extent to which male desire shapes the social sphere (Pateman, 1988), causing a structural and systematic exclusion of women (Okin, 1979) from the exercise of public functions and political power. These discussions are still going on today and are centred on powerful female political figures such as Hilary Clinton, Benazir Bhutto, Sonia Ghandi, and others contending for top positions in the political sphere.

However, equally strong is the gender research on the productive and necessary forms of civil disobedience that ranges from the already quoted Woolf who defended feminists as 'the society of outsiders' with their own social system (Woolf, 1978 [1936; 1938]) to the seminal work of Rich on the necessity of being 'disloyal to civilization' (Rich, 1979b; 1985a). Another important thinker here is Audre Lorde, who in the model of Martin Luther King and Ghandi defends non-violence as the highest way of fighting structural injustices (Lorde, 1984). This critical distance from nationalism and cultural determinism is of the greatest relevance today, given that we are caught in a global state of clashing civilizations (Huntington, 1996). Far too many women in today's world have enlisted to the cause of defending their own culture against pre-sumed, real or imaginary enemies, mostly Islamic or non-Western ones. Ethnicity and race trace civilization fault-lines in the world and make it difficult to uphold any critical distance, let alone civil disobedience. The tragic case of the Italian Fallaci (2002) comes to mind, as do many other leading European feminists, from Badinter in France (2003) to Dresselhuys in the Netherlands. These women used to be feminists but have turned hyper-nationalistic and conservative, taking it upon themselves to defend their own civilization, come what may.

The inter-connection between gender analysis and ethnicity, race, and immigration issues has generated a large body of scholarship. In the 1960s and 1970s, radical feminists in the United States started addressing this issue (Millett, 1973; Davis, 1981), by running an analogy between sexism and racism. The terms of this debate shifted in the 1980s, when ethnic and racialized differences became more central to gender research (Hull, *et al.*, 1982). Women of colour develop a critical approach to the white bias of feminist theory (Mohanty, 1988) and feminist orientalism is criticized (Spivak, 1987). A more transnational approach to gender issues is emerging (Mohanty, *et al.*, 1991; Grewal and Kaplan, 1994), while strong theoretical claims are made about Black and racialized feminist perspectives (Anzaldúa, 1987; Minh-Ha, 1989; Hill Collins, 1990; hooks, 1990).

In a European perspective, the early analyses of intrinsic racist structures in Western societies (Essed, 1991) have expanded into a full-fledged critique of white domination (Gilroy, 1987; Ware, 1992). The long history of European nationalism comes under scrutiny (Yuval-Davis and Anthias, 1989) while the fast-moving EU project provides a new frame of reference for the analysis of social and political subjects (Brah, 1993; Griffin and Braidotti, 2002).

Another line of enquiry is a socio-political interrogation of the access of migrants, refugees, and alien subjects to citizenship and participation in active social and cultural life. As said, the key point here concerns the extent to which non-citizens, or alien and foreign 'others', can contribute to social cohesion and the well-being of a society. I have strongly defended the relevance of hybrid identities in terms of a complex and multi-layered or 'nomadic' subjectivity and complex allegiances (Braidotti, 1994; 2006). This flexible approach to citizenship allows for multiple modes of participation, also known as alternative ecologies of belonging, as opposed to nationalism and cultural determinism.

A recent visit I paid to the city of Gheel – in Dympna's footsteps – not only confirmed these insights, but also added a new dimension to my understanding of the Dympna phenomenon.[1] The canonization process was finally and reluctantly undertaken by the Catholic church in the thirteenth century, after almost seven hundred years of popular worship of the holy woman had transformed Gheel into a pilgrimage site. Because of the huge number of foreign pilgrims that poured into the town, Gheel had to provide extra facilities and accommodation. Lots of these foreigners were sick, especially mentally ill people, and many of them were placed in foster families for the duration of their stay for the cure in Gheel. This is how the system of foster care of the mentally ill was started and Gheel earned its title as 'Merciful Town': a haven of tolerance and compassion.

The spirit of *caritas* that prompted the care system was violently disrupted by the French occupation of 1797, when the psychiatric hospital was established and the mentally ill were interned. Economic considerations, including the closing down of the mental asylum in Brussels, led to a concentration of patients in Gheel. This resulted in the formation of the 'colony' of the mentally ill which combined scientific methods with family care. A law in 1850 officialized this system, which survives today.

However, there is a perverse twist to this otherwise edifying tale. The Gasthuis Museum in Gheel devotes one of its display rooms to Dympna and shows a sixteenth-century wooden sculpture of the saint being decapitated. The father – an Irish king – is depicted wearing a turban, sporting a flowing beard, and his sword is an unmistakable Arabic scimitar. The same transformation of the Irish father into a Muslim occurs in the gorgeous stained-glass windows of the Dympna church. This has to be one of the few Catholic churches devoted to the issue of sexual violence and incest. The father, however, has become ethnically marked as other, and hence distanced from our sense of collective responsibility and memory. There was no other way for early modern Christianity to visually represent a hostile, homicidal rapist then through the image of the Muslim enemy. *Plus ça change. . .*

3 Political theory and the role of emotions

The case study of Dympna highlights the part played by emotions, passion, pathos, and affectivity in the constitution of social and political subjectivity. Several important distinctions need to be made here, the first one being that between identity-based private emotions and public or collectively shared forms of affective subjectivity. The public-private distinction has played a major part in structuring gender roles and fixing them into social relations. They have defined and confined the position of women inside the private sphere, within the home and family, leaving the government of the common-wealth, the *res publica*, to males of the same ethnicity and culture. Foreign men, immigrants, and refugees are marginalized through other mechanisms of exclusion.

This constitutive distinction between the public and the private naturally leaves many grey areas where power relations are exercised, such as domestic violence, rape by incest, and many other abuses which often are ignored by the law. It also qualifies certain modes of emotional behaviour. For instance, emotions are tolerated and even encouraged in the private sphere, but need to be controlled in public. Objectivity in the form of emotional detachment is the public composure that Western culture approves of and actively enforces. The art of government or institutional politics is defined according to this standard. Explosive displays of emotions, rage, wrath, and anger are condemned and instead rational debate, objective exchange of arguments, and consensus-seeking negotiations are preferred. Historically, women – like children, foreigners, non-nationals, and migrants – are deemed unfit for the exercise of political rationality. A great deal of the feminist struggle for the empowerment of women and minorities, therefore, has taken the form of a strong defence of women's ability to exercise the use of reason in all of its ramifications, including political agency (Lloyd, 1985).

Another feminist strategy has been the re-appraisal of grass-roots transformative political activism in opposition to institutional representative parliamentary politics. This militant approach has been the message of radical feminism, which opposes joyful acts of insurrection and selective civil disobedience to the dead seriousness of organized politics. However, throughout its long history, feminist activism has not been spared the criticism of Left wing revolutionary movements (Keohane, *et al.*, 1988). The dialogue between feminism and Marxism, on what exactly constitutes a revolutionary movement, has been of the highest historical significance, as is testified by the very early texts of Marxist-inspired radical feminist politics (Firestone, 1971; Mitchell, 1971; Rowbotham, 1972; de Beauvoir, 1990 [1949]). While the conceptual difference between the two regards the fact that feminism insisted on politicizing the private sphere, following the slogan 'the personal is the political', another crucial difference was caused precisely by the part that positive emotions were allowed to play. As the anarchist feminist Emma Goldman put it wittily: 'if I can't dance I don't want to be part of your revolution!' (Drinnon and Drinnon, 1975). Feminism stresses an embodied and embedded approach to political subjectivity and avoids both abstract perspectives and universalistic generalizations. I shall return to this in the section on epistemology below.

The second methodological remark about the emotions concerns the necessity to distinguish between an empowering or positive use of the emotions and a negative use. The earlier mentioned public rituals of mourning are an example of a productive display of emotions. However, there are other examples that can be considered as less positive, such as rage or excessive anger, up to the murderous violence of Dympna's father. How to disengage political subjectivity from the more destructive elements of intense passions or emotions is the challenge that feminist ethics addresses (see point 1 above).

4 Women, madness, and psychoanalysis

The notion that women are mentally unstable and prone to mental disorders is deeply engrained in a patriarchal society that protects the interests and desires of men and is blind to the reality of sexual and other differences. Feminist literary critics pointed out the extent to which nineteenth-century and early twentieth-century literature is rife with examples of female lunatics. This prompted the popular image of 'the madwoman in the attic' (Gilbert and Gubar, 1979). The second feminist wave was vocal in denouncing the social construction of female insanity as the effect of structural social oppression and sustained discrimination (Chessler, 1972; Millett, 1973). A younger generation of artists and writers, who were affected by feminism, addressed explicitly the theme of mental pathology, depression, self-destruction, and even suicide (Plath, 1965; Arbus, 1972; Millett, 1976).

The bulk of feminist critics concentrated their attacks on the medical institutions of psychiatry and mental health. In a classical text called *For Her Own Good*, Ehrenreich and English (1979) analyze the part played by clinical psychiatry in literally driving women crazy. Foucault's work on the parallel histories of madness and scientific rationality (1965) confirms and supports feminist scholarship. This is where feminist critics develop an interesting but also controversial relationship to the movement of thought that is most openly critical of clinical psychiatry, that is to say, psychoanalysis.

In the third millennium, surrounded as we are by a popular culture that trivializes Freud's explorations of the unconscious through television series such as *The Sopranos* and films such as *Analyze This*, it may be difficult to remember just how radical and woman-friendly Freud's intervention in clinical practice was at the turn of the last century. Psychoanalysis effectuates a fundamental denaturalization of both madness and human sexuality, by introducing a subtler understanding of the cause of neurotic behaviour – constituted by the standard result of successful socialization processes. Femininity and masculinity are the pillars of one's social identity (Freud, 1933b), but femininity bears the brunt of cultural norms and values. Literally, culture is negotiated on the bodies of women. As a result, psychoanalysis argues that all sexed and gendered identities, but the female in particular, are fraught with tensions and contradictions. Freud introduces an ethics of respect for the complexity of mental life and defends the notion that the subject is split by his/her unconscious structures. This means that an individual does not coincide with his/her rational consciousness, but rather is driven by unconscious drives and desires. Psychoanalysis singles out desire as the fundamental human passion and emotion and develops special techniques to decode and interpret it.

Marxists and radical feminists of the second wave took objection to some of Freud's more traditional statements on penis-envy and castration. Simone de Beauvoir (1990 [1949]) famously dismissed psychoanalytic discourse as being too sexist. The debate shifted in the 1980s, as the works of Jacques Lacan were translated into English (Mitchell and Rose, 1984), updating Freud's psychoanalytic legacy and making it relevant to the twentieth century (Coward and Ellis, 1977; Turkle, 1978). In her agenda-setting intervention, Juliet Mitchell (1974) argues for a strong alliance between feminism and psychoanalysis, in that both support transgressive desires and trans-formative practices. The generation of 1980s 'difference-minded' feminists (Eisenstein and Jardine, 1984) focuses on the issue of women's desire, on its embodied nature (Gallop, 1984; Grosz, 1989), and on its vulnerability (Brennan, 1989). The French school known as *écriture feminine* argues for radical sexual difference and the specificity of women's desire (Cixous, 1980; Kristeva, 1980; Irigaray, 1985). Object-relation psychoanalysis, as mentioned above, grounds its theory in social and political analysis of gender relations (Benjamin, 1990). By the end of the twentieth century, the long debate between feminism and psychoanalysis has become so intense and rich, as to fill a thick critical dictionary (Wright, 1992).

Because of the changing historical and social contexts, and in spite of the trivialization of psychoanalysis that I already commented on, psychoanalytic theory remains of the greatest relevance for our times. Mental distress, depression, stress, and pathological behaviour have not at all disappeared; it is just the symptoms that shifted. What sex-driven hysteria was in the nineteenth century, today is an epidemic of anorexia, bulimia, and eating disorders mediated by visual culture (Orbach, 1986, 1987). Neo-liberal societies have reverted to a callous and instrumental relationship to madness and mental instability. The use of officially prescribed psycho-pharmaceutical drugs such as Prozac and Ritalin has become standard medical practice, turning millions of women into official addicts. Instead of dismissing them in this way, they should be offered the therapies and frames of reference of psychoanalysis, now more than ever.

5   Epistemology, or feminist knowledge claims

Gender research is a way of producing alternative knowledge, both by bringing in a different agenda and by challenging the rules of knowledge production. The most basic feminist epistemological strategy consists in a double move. First, visibility and recognition is granted to the women of ideas whose contribution is usually neglected (Spender, 1983). Second, the accepted standards of scientific rationality are challenged (Harding and Hintikka, 1983; Lloyd, 1985), as well as mainstream scientific culture and the official administration of knowledge. This takes many forms: claims to specific women's ways of knowing (Irigaray, 1985; Hill Collins, 1990; Code, 1991) are matched by forceful defences of feminist theory's relevance for mainstream philosophy (Benhabib and Cornell, 1987; Braidotti, 1991; Nussbaum, 1999) and also epistemology (Fox-Keller, 1983; Harding, 1986;). From the mid-1980s, feminism intersects with postmodernism (Nicholson, 1990) and debates are focused on the politics of epistem-ological practice, in other words, on power and knowledge (Foucault, 1977; Haraway, 1988).

To continue the discussion about the emotions as a case in point, feminist theory argues that the emotional or affective elements can create structures of knowledge, political action, and subjectivity. This is because lived experience and the empirical evidence of women's and other marginals' lives are re-appraised, not only as evidence of a state of injustice or exclusion (negative moment), but also as untapped sources of knowledge claims by the excluded others (positive moment). As is argued by Harding

(1987), the claim about the epistemological value of the view from below or the margins is crucial to the main school of feminist epistemology, namely standpoint theory. The point of stressing the positive and empowering value of the views from the margins is twofold: first it deconstructs the vision of groups that are socially marginal as mere victims. By stressing the constructive contribution that the marginal subjects make to society, standpoint feminist theory also redresses the structural injustice of so much unpaid labour and unrecognized work. Women of colour had denounced this in early feminist classics such as *This Bridge Called My Back* (Moraga and Anzaldúa, 1981).

A crucial element of feminist knowledge claims is the positive role it attributes to creativity, the emotions, and especially the imagination. This faith in the creative power of critical thought forms an overt contrast to the standards of scientific reason, which banks on objectivity, rationality, and protocols of logical thinking. Another related opposition is that which is between myth making and the imaginative thinking that goes with figuration, in opposition to rationality as sterile objectivity. What counts as objectivity becomes the bone of contention in feminist theories of knowledge since the 1980s. A related aspect of this feminist style of knowledge production is an unusual degree of interest in alternative cosmologies and worldviews, as an alternative to teleological thinking in the theological tradition (Bryld and Lykke, 2000). Joan Kelly (1979) refers to this aspect of gender research in terms of the double-edge vision of feminist theory, which combines critique and creation with equal ease. De Lauretis (1990) picks up this point in defining feminist theory as ex-centric, that is, off-centre in relation to mainstream scientific thought; she also expands feminist theory in a Foucauldian direction (de Lauretis, 1986a).

The methodological implications of this approach are rich and important and concern the practice of interdisciplinarity. To make sense of the interdisciplinary character of gender research, it is important to keep in mind my opening remarks about the method of the politics of locations in relation to the use of figurations. A scholar's primary location is her/his discipline. Disciplines are also the organizing units of scientific research: they structure academic life in that they design the shape of university departments and examination boards, scholarly journals, and peer-review committees. It is consequently important for gender researchers to develop a genealogical perspective on their own discipline by studying its historical developments and epistemological assumptions, so as to be able to understand their own location.

The same issue of belonging and of civil disobedience applies to a feminist scholar's relationship to her/his discipline, as they do to women's access to citizenship. Flexible approaches should be encouraged, ranging from nomadic transitions to flows of exile, bitter divorces, and lingering attraction. Gender research entertains a dynamic, ongoing, and hence unresolved relationship to mainstream academic disciplines. Feminist scholars have to be undutiful daughters.

The situation looks different, however, if a scholar has from the start been trained in new, inter-disciplinary areas of study. Probably the most relevant of these, at least in the humanities, is the field of cultural studies. This field stems from classical feminist literary theory (Miller, 1985; Showalter, 1986) and has evolved into a wide-ranging tool for the analysis of cultural practice, combining sociological methods (Franklin, *et al.*, 1991) with cutting-edge post-structuralist theory (de Lauretis, 1986b). More recently, cultural studies has developed stronger ties to feminist science studies (Franklin, *et al.*, 2000).

The location in disciplines is different for gender scholars who emerge from such an interdisciplinary background. In these cases, doing gender is likely to provide a sharper navigational tool and may act as a zoom lens that focuses the researcher more precisely onto her/his research project. In this respect, interdisciplinary gender research provides its own foundation and mutates into a trans-disciplinary practice that relies on feminist epistemologies for its own justification. A question about style is formulated in this process, not as a rhetorical device, but rather as a rigorous inter-rogation of the practice of locations, the specific modes of expression that are suitable for them, and the forms of accountability they require. Integrating form and content, while avoiding jargon, are key elements in experimenting with an adequate feminist epistemological style.

Conclusion

The rich and thought-inspiring analysis of an archetypical warrior such as Dympna brings into clear focus what I consider the key features of feminist theory and gender analysis. The first one is the commitment to strike a productive balance between the necessary and often painful recognition of a negative situation – pain, violence, margin-ality, exclusion, and injustice – on the one hand, and the joyful creation of empowering alternatives on the other. Being a philosopher by training, I translate this into the balance between negativity and affirmation, with a strong preference for the latter.

The quest for affirmative empowerment requires the transcendence of the negative, that is to say the rejection of revengeful violence and the interruption of the chain of repetition of negative experiences and emotions. This is the transformative edge of the feminist knowledge project, of its politics, and its ethical passions. Although it is grounded in the historical position of women, lunatics, marginal, natives, refugees, immigrants, and excluded others, it has a much broader appeal and reach. I have argued that the transformation of the negative into life-affirming alternatives, which not only empower the marginal but also change the structures of the social order, is the key to the politics of Human Rights in the third millennium. As such, it is instrumental to the creation of sustainable futures (Braidotti, 2006).

The second and last but not least feature is the simple fact that Dympna is *my* figuration. The personal autobiographical aspect is very important to the theoretical analysis I am offering here. That statuette, after all, does stand on my writing desk and fulfils an important purpose in the general economy of my writing. In some ways it structures my writing environment by playing a productive function in my imaginary, much as it structures the lines of arguments in this essay. Dympna is associated with events in my private life – a relationship and a personal loss, as I stated at the start of this chapter – thus, she is emotionally very laden and dear to me. The choice of this figuration expresses my preference for the imagination, for the power of thinking in images and figurations, which allow for personal feelings but also produce rigorous knowledge because and not in spite of the affective elements. Dympna also symbolizes the technique I cherish – of thinking back through the women in history and the women in our lives (Woolf, 1978 [1936; 1938]; Walker, 1984). I am not sure I believe that Dympna actually watches over me, but she does intrigue me. The day I was honoured with the royal award of a knighthood I had to think back to Dympna. Specifically, I thought of the way her hand rests on that down-turned sword, with a touch of nonchalance, the suggestion of fatigue, but also the unmistakable message that *this* woman may be hurt, but she is not alone, nor is she desperate, although she is desperately seeking justice.

Notes

1   With thanks to Jef Bal, historian and Gheel city guide.

Questions for further research

1   Simone de Beauvoir and Kate Millet can be seen to represent equality feminism. Explain what thinking equality involves by means of at least two examples from contemporary (popular) culture and society.

2   Patricia Hill Collins and Luce Irigaray can be seen to represent difference feminism. Explain what thinking difference involves by means of at least two examples from contemporary (popular) culture and society.

3   What scholarly and intellectual criteria can be deployed in demonstrating and evaluating the relevance of research by previous generation feminists? Illustrate your answer with examples from this book.

4   Use the approach of thinking equality as a method for analyzing a myth, text, or cultural representation relevant in your particular study programme. Refer as best as you can to the chapters in this book and include a copy of the image or material you are analyzing in your paper.

5   Thinking difference can be used to argue for the need for creating alternative myth formations and alternative representations. Try and do this and illustrate your argument with examples retrieved from the net.

6   A contemporary social or cultural phenomenon can be understood in light of the psycho-analytical approach – think of artefacts such as films or social problems such as eating disorders. Try and achieve such an understanding in making use of Chapters 11 and 12 and Part II of this book.

Bibliography

Aaron, M. (ed.) (2004) *New Queer Cinema. A Critical Reader.* Edinburgh: Edinburgh University Press.

Adler, R. (1998) *Engendering Judaism: An Inclusive Theology and Ethics.* Boston: Beacon Press.

Ahmed, S. (2003) 'Feminist futures' in M. Eagleton (ed.) *A Concise Companion to Feminist Theory.* Malden: Blackwell Publishers.

—— (2004) *The Cultural Politics of Emotion.* Edinburgh and New York: Edinburgh University Press/Routledge.

Alcott, L.M. (1989 [1868]) *Little Women.* New York: Viking Penguin.

Alexander, J. (2005) *Pedagogies of Crossing.* Durham: Duke University Press.

Alexander, J. and Mohanty, C.T. (eds) (1997) *Feminist Genealogies, Colonial Legacies, Democratic Futures.* New York: Routledge.

Ali, K. (2006) *Sexual Ethics and Islam: Feminist Reflections on Qur'an, Hadith and Jurisprudence.* Oxford: Oneworld Publications.

Althusser, L. (1984) 'Ideology and ideological state apparatuses (notes towards an investigation)' in *Essays on Ideology.* London and New York: Verso.

Amara, F. (2003) *Ni putes ni soumises: Postface inédite de láuteure.* Paris: Découverte.

Anbeek, T. (1988) 'Een nieuwe geschiedenis van de moderne literatuur', *Ons Erfdeel,* 31(1): 25–35.

Andermahr, S., Lovell, T. and Wolkowitz, C. (2000) *A Glossary of Feminist Theory.* London: Arnold.

Anderson, B. (1983) *Imagined Communities.* London and New York: Verso.

Anthias, F. and Yuval-Davis, N. (1992) *Racialized Boundaries: Race, Nation, Gender, Colour and Class and the Anti-racist Struggle.* London and New York: Routledge.

Anzaldúa, G. (1987) *Borderlands/La Frontera: The New Mestiza.* San Francisco: Aunt Lute Books.

—— (ed.) (1990) *Making Face, Making Soul, Haciendo Caras. Creative and Critical Perspectives by Women of Color.* San Francisco: Aunt Lute Books.

—— (1993) *Friends from the Other Side/Amigos del otro Lado.* San Francisco: Children's Book Press.

—— (1996) *Prietita and the Ghost Woman/Prietita y La Llorona.* San Francisco: Children's Book Press.

Anzaldúa, G. and Keating, A. (eds) (2002) *This Bridge we Call Home. Radical Visions for Trans-formations.* New York: Routledge.

Anzaldúa, G. and Moraga, C. (eds) (1981) *This Bridge called my Back: Writings by Radical Women of Color.* Massachusetts: Persephone Press.

Apostolus-Cappadona, D. (2006a) 'Revisiting the "Journey of the Scarlet Lily": Mary Magdalene in Western art and culture' in D. Burstein and A.J. de Keijzer (eds) *Secrets of Mary Magdalene.* New York: CDS Books.

—— (2006b) 'Mary Magdalene: First witness', *Sacred History Magazine,* 2(3): 30–33.

Arbus, D. (1972) *Diane Arbus: An Aperture Monograph.* New York: Aperture.

Arditti, R., Duelli Klein, R. and Minden, S. (1984) *Test-tube Women: What Future for Motherhood?* London and Boston: Pandora Press.

Armstrong, N. (1987) *Desire and Domestic Fiction. A Political History of the Novel.* New York: Oxford University Press.

Arrington, C.W. (1991) 'Madonna in bloom: Circe at loom', *Time,* 137: 56–58.

Asad, T. (2003) *Formations of the Secular: Christianity, Islam, Modernity.* Stanford: Stanford University Press.

Åsberg, C. and Johnson, E. (2009) 'Viagra Selfhood: Pharmaceutical advertising and the visual formation of Swedish masculinity', *Health Care Analysis,* 17(1).

Atkinson, T.G. (1974) *Amazon Odyssey.* New York: Links Books.

Austen, J. (1856) *Northanger Abbey.* London: Penguin Classics.

Badinter, E. (2003) *Fausse route.* Paris: Odille Jacob.

Baert, B. (2002) *Maria Magdalena. Zondares van de middeleeuwen tot vandaag. Tentoonstellings-catalogus.* Gent: Museum voor de Schone Kunsten, Cahier 4.

—— (2008) 'The gaze in the garden: body and embodiment in *Noli me tangere.* With an emphasis on the 15th-century Low Countries' in A-S. Lehmann and H. Roodenburg (eds) *Body and Embodiment in Netherlandish Art 1400–1750* (Netherlandish Yearbook of Art History 58), Zwolle.

Baert, B., *et al.* (eds) (2006) *Noli me tangere,* Leuven: Peeters.

Bair, D. (1996 [1990]) *Simone de Beauvoir: Biografie.* Amsterdam: Diogenes.

Bakhtin, M. (1982) *The Dialogic Imagination. Four Essays.* Austin: University of Texas Press.

Bal, M. (1986) *Femmes Imaginaires.* Utrecht/Paris: Hes/Nizet.

Balsamo, A. (1997) *Technologies of the Gendered Body: Reading Cyborg Women.* Durham: Duke University Press.

—— (2000) 'Reading cyborgs writing feminism' in G. Kirkup, *et al.* (eds) *The Gendered Cyborg. A Reader.* London and New York: Routledge and Open University Press.

Barend-Van Haeften, M. and Paasman, B. (2003) *De Kaap: Goede Hoop halverwege Indië. Bloemlezing van kaapteksten uit de compagniestijd.* Hilversum: Verloren.

Barlas, A. (2002) *'Believing women' in Islam: Unreading Patriarchal Interpretations of the Qur'an.* Austin: University of Texas Press.

Barrie, J. (1995) *Peter Pan and Other Plays.* Oxford: Oxford University Press.

Barrow, J. (1806) *Nouveau voyage dans la partie meridionale de l'Afrique.* Paris: Dentu.

Barthes, R. (1981) *Camera Lucida.* New York: Hill & Wang.

Baudry, J.L. (1992 [1974]) 'Ideological effects of the basic cinematographic apparatus' in G. Mast, M. Cohen and L. Braudy (eds) *Film Theory and Criticism. Introductory Readings.* Oxford: Oxford University Press.

Bauer, J. (1997) 'Conclusion. The mixed blessings of women's fundamentalism. Democratic impulses in a patriarchal world' in J. Brink and J. Mencher (eds) *Mixed Blessings. Gender and Religious Fundamentalism Cross Culturally.* New York: Routledge.

Beard, M. (1933) *America through Women's Eyes.* New York: Macmillan.

Beauvoir, S. de (1988 [1949]) *The Second Sex.* Trans. H.M. Parshley. London: Picador.

—— (1990 [1949]) *De tweede sekse: Feiten, mythen en geleefde werkelijkheid.* Utrecht: Bijleveld.

Beccaria, M. (2005) *Candice Breitz.* Milan: Skira Editore.

Becher, T. (1989) *Academic Tribes and Territories.* Buckingham: Oxford University Press.

Bel, J. (1993) *Nederlandse literatuur in het fin de siècle.* Amsterdam: Amsterdam University Press.

Benhabib, S. and Cornell, D. (eds) (1987) *Feminism as Critique: On the Politics of Gender.* Minneapolis: University of Minnesota Press.

Benjamin, J. (1990) *The Bonds of Love: Psychoanalysis, Feminism, and the Problem of Domination*. London and New York: Routledge.

Berger, J. (1972) *Ways of Seeing*. London: BBC and Penguin.

Bergstrom, J. and Doane, M.A. (eds) (1989) 'Camera obscura. A journal of feminism and film theory', Special Issue, *The Spectatrix*, 20–21.

Bhabha. H. (1994) 'Of mimicry and man. The ambivalence of colonial discourse' in *The Location of Culture*. London and New York: Routledge.

Birke, L. (2000) *Feminism and the Biological Body*. Edinburgh: Edinburgh University Press.

Blainville, H. de (1816) 'Sur une femme de la race hottentote' in *Bulletin des sciences par la société philomatique de Paris*. pp. 183–190.

Blixen, K. (2002) *Seven Gothic Tales*. London: Penguin Books.

Blom, I., *et al.* (eds) (2000) *Gendering Nations. Nationalisms and Gender Order in the Long Nineteenth Century*. Oxford and New York: Berg.

Boer, E.A. de (2005) *The Gospel of Mary: Beyond a Gnostic and Biblical Mary Magdalene*. London and New York: Continuum.

Boomen, M. van den (1993) 'Hackers aller landen . . . !' *De Groene Amsterdammer*, August 1993.

Bordo, S. (1993) *Unbearable Weight. Feminism, Western Culture and the Body*. Berkeley: University of California Press.

Bosch, M. (1994) *Het geslacht van de wetenschap*. Amsterdam: Sua.

Bosma, H. and Pisters, P. (2000) *Madonna: De vele gezichten van een popster*. Amsterdam: Prometheus.

Boston Women's Health Book Collective (2005 [1971]) *Our Bodies, Ourselves*. New York: Simon & Schuster, Touchstone.

Botman, M., Jouwe, N. and Wekker, G. (2001) *Caleidoscopische Visies, de zwarte, migranten- en vluchtelingenvrouwen beweging in Nederland*. Amsterdam: KIT Publishers.

Boven, E. van (1992) *Een hoofdstuk apart: 'Vrouwenroman' in de literaire kritiek 1898–1930*. Amsterdam: Sara/Van Gennep.

—— (2000) 'De eeuwige verbinding van schrijfsters, massa's en middelmaat', *De Gids* (September 2000): 688–696.

Bracke, S. (2004) *Women Resisting Secularisation in an Age of Globalization. Four Case-Studies in a European Context*, Ph.D thesis. Utrecht: Utrecht University.

Brah, A. (1993) 'Re-framing Europe: Engendered racisms, ethnicities and nationalism in contemporary Western Europe', *Feminist Review,* 45: 9–27.

Braidotti, R. (1991) *Patterns of Dissonance: A Study of Women in Contemporary Philosophy*. Cambridge: Polity Press.

—— (1994) *Nomadic Subjects: Embodiment and Sexual Difference in Contemporary Feminist Theory*. New York: Columbia University Press.

—— (1996) 'Cyberfeminism with a difference'. (Available at www.let.uu.nl/womens_studies/rosi/cyberfem.htm, accessed 19 May 2007.)

—— (2002) *Metamorphoses: Towards a Materialist Theory of Becoming*. Cambridge: Polity Press.

—— (2006) *Transpositions: On Nomadic Ethics*. Cambridge: Polity Press.

Brennan, T. (ed.) (1989) *Between Feminism and Psychoanalysis*. London and New York: Routledge.

Brett, P., Thomas, G. and Wood, E. (eds) (1994) *Queering the Pitch: The New Gay and Lesbian Musicology*. New York and London: Routledge.

Bronfen, E. (1998*) The Knotted Subject: Hysteria and its Discontents*. Princeton: Princeton University Press.

Bronfen, E. (ed.) (2002) *Cindy Sherman: Photographic Works 1975–1995*. New York: Schirmer/Mosel.

Brooks, P. (1976) *The Melodramatic Imagination: Balzac, Henry James, Melodrama, and the Mode of Excess*. New Haven and London: Yale University Press.

Broude, N. and Garrard, M.D. (eds) (2005) *Reclaiming Female Agency. Feminist Art After Postmodernism*. Berkeley, Los Angeles and London: University of California Press.

Brouns, M. (1988) *Veertien jaar vrouwenstudies in Nederland: een overzicht*. Zoetermeer: Ministerie van Onderwijs en Wetenschappen.

Brouwers, J. (1985) *Hélène Swarth. Haar huwelijk met Frits Lapidoth 1894–1910*. Amsterdam: De Arbeiderspers.

—— (1986) 'Hélène *Swarth* 1859–1941' in A. Korteweg and M. Salverda (eds) *'t Is vol van schatten hier . . .* (2 dl.). Amsterdam: Joost Nijsen.

—— (1987) *De schemerlamp van Hélène Swarth. Hoe beroemd zij was en in de schemer verdween*. Amsterdam: Joost Nijsen.

Brown, D. (2003) *The Da Vinci Code*. New York: Doubleday.

Brownmiller, S. (1976) *Against our Will: Men, Women and Rape*. Harmondsworth, Middlesex: Penguin Books.

Bryld, M. and Lykke, N. (2000) *Cosmodolphins. Feminist Cultural Studies of Technology, Animals and the Sacred*. London and New York: Zed Books.

Buffon, G.L. le Clerc de (1837) *Oeuvres completes de Buffon*. Paris: Pourrat.

Buikema, R. (1995) *De loden Venus: biografieën van vijf beroemde vrouwen door hun dochters*. Kampen: Kok Agora.

Buikema, R. and Smelik, A. (1993) *Vrouwenstudies in de cultuurwetenschappen*. Muiderberg: Coutinho.

—— (1995) *Women's Studies and Culture. A Feminist Introduction*. London: Zed Books.

Burstein, D. and Keijzer, A. J. de (eds) (2006) *Secrets of Mary Magdalene*. New York: CDS Books.

Busken Huet, C. (z.j.) 'Nieuwe Nederlandse letteren', *Litterarische fantasien en kritieken*.

Butler, J. (1990) *Gender Trouble: Feminism and the Subversion of Identity*. New York and London: Routledge.

—— (1992) 'Contingent foundations: feminism and the question of "postmodernism"' in J. Butler and J.W. Scott (eds) *Feminists Theorize the Political*. New York and London: Routledge.

—— (1993) *Bodies that Matter. On the Discursive Limits of Sex*. New York and London: Routledge.

—— (2000) *Antigone's Claim. Kinship between Life and Death*. New York: Columbia University Press.

Butler, J. and Scott, J.W. (eds) (1992) *Feminists Theorize the Political*. New York and London: Routledge.

Caine, B. and Sluga, G. (2000) *Gendering European History*. London and New York: Berg.

Carson, F. and Pajaczkowska, C. (2001) *Feminist Visual Culture*. London: Routledge.

Cassell, J. and Jenkins, H. (eds) (1998) *From Barbie to Mortal Kombat. Gender and Computer Games*. Cambridge: MIT Press.

Chadwick, W. (1990) *Women, Art and Society*. London: Thames and Hudson.

Chessler, P. (1972) *Women and Madness*. New York: Double Day and Co.

Chodorow, N. (1978) *The Production of Mothering: Psychoanalysis and the Sociology of Gender*. Berkeley, CA: University of California Press.

Chopin, K. (1986) *The Awakening*. New York: Penguin.

Christ, C.P. (1987) *Laughter of Aphrodite: Reflections on a Journey to the Goddess*. San Francisco: Harper & Row.

Christian, B. (1990 [1987]) 'The race for theory' in K.V. Hansen and I.J. Philipson (eds) *Women, Class and the Feminist Imagination. A Socialist-Feminist Reader*. Philadelphia: Temple University Press.

Cixous, H. (1980) 'The laugh of the Medusa' in E. Marks and I. de Courtivron (eds) *New French Feminisms*. Amherst: University of Massachusetts Press.

Clague, J. (2005) 'Divine transgressions: the female Christ-form in art', *Critical Quarterly*, 47(3): 47–64.

Clover, C. (1992) *Men, Women, and Chain Saws. Gender in the Modern Horror Film*. London: British Film Institute Publishing.

Clynes, M.E. and Kline, N.S. (1995) 'Cyborgs and Space', reprinted from *Astronautics* [1960] in C. Hables Gray, H.J. Figueroa-Sarriera and S. Mentor (eds) *The Cyborg Handbook*. New York and London: Routledge.

Cockburn, C. (1998) *The Space between Us. Negotiating Gender and National Identities in Conflict*. London and New York: Zed Books.

Code, L. (1991) *What Does She Know?* Ithaka: Cornell University Press.

Colebrook, C. (2002) *Gilles Deleuze*. London: Routledge.

Collet, I. (2005) 'Vrouwen en ICT, in tijd en ruimte'. (Available at www.ada-online.org/nlada/article.php3?id_article=261, accessed 7 August 2008.)

Combahee River Collective (1986 [1977]) *The Combahee River Collective Statement*. New York: Kitchen Table, Womcn of Color Press.

Cooper, J., Hall, J. and Huff, C. (1990) 'Situational stress as a consequence of sex-sterotyped software', *Personality and Social Psychology Bulletin*, 16: 419–429.

Copier, M. (2007) *Beyond the Magic Circle: A Network Perspective on Role-play in Online Games*, Ph.D thesis. Utrecht: Faculty of Humanities, Utrecht University.

Corea, G., *et al.* (1985) *Man-made Woman: How New Reproductive Technologies affect Women*. Bloomington: Indiana University Press.

Coupland, D. (1995) *Microserfs*. London: Flamingo/HarperCollins.

Coward, R. and Ellis, J. (1977) *Language and Materialism: Developments in Semiology and the Theory of the Subject*. London and Boston: Routledge and Kegan Paul.

Creed, B. (2005) *Phallic Panic. Film, Horror and the Primal Uncanny*. Melbourne: Melbourne University Publishing.

Crenshaw, K. (1989) *Demarginalizing the Intersection of Race and Sex: A Black Feminist Critique of Antidiscrimination Doctrine, Feminist Theory and Antiracist Politics*. Chicago: University of Chicago Legal Forum.

Crimp, D. (1980) 'The photographic activity of postmodernism', *October*, 15: 98–99.

Cruz, A. (1997) *Cindy Sherman: Retrospective*. New York: Thames & Hudson.

Culley, L. (1993) 'Gender equity and computer in secondary schools: Issues and strategies for teachers' in J. Beynon and H. Mackay (eds) *Computers into Classrooms: More Question than Answers*. London: Falmer Press.

Cuvier, G. (1817) 'Extrait d'observations faites sur le cadavre d'une femme connue à Paris et à Londres sous le nom de Vénus Hottentotte', *Mémoires de Muséum d'histoire naturelle*, 3: 259–274.

Dalsimer, K. (1986) *Female Adolescence: Psychoanalytical Reflections on Literature*. New Haven and London: Yale University Press.

Daly, M. (1973) *Beyond God the Father: Toward a Philosophy of Women's Liberation*. Boston: Beacon Press.

—— (1978) *Gyn/Ecology: The Metaethics of Radical Feminism*. Boston: Beacon Press.

Davis, A. (1981) *Women, Race and Class*. New York: Random House.

Davis, K. (1995) *Reshaping the Female Body. The Dilemma of Cosmetic Surgery*. New York: Routledge.

—— (1997) 'Embody-ing theory: Beyond modernist and postmodernist readings of the body', in K. Davis (ed.) *Embodied Practices*. London: Sage.

—— (2002) 'Feminist body/politics as world traveller: translating our bodies ourselves', *European Journal of Women's Studies*, 9(3): 223–247.

Davis, T.C. (2005) '"Do you believe in fairies?" The hiss of dramatic license', *Theatre Journal*, 57: 57–81.

Davison, P. (1998) 'Museums and the reshaping of memory' in S. Nutall and C. Coetzee (eds) *Negotiating the Past: The Making of Memory in South Africa*. Oxford: Oxford University Press.

Deleuze, G. and Guattari, F. (1977) *Anti-Oedipus. Capitalism and Schizophrenia*. Minneapolis: University of Minnesota Press.

—— (1988) *A Thousand Plateaus. Capitalism and Schizophrenia*. London: Athlone Press.

Dery, M. (1993) 'Culture jamming: Hacking, slashing and sniping in the empire of signs', Open Magazine Pamphlet Series. (Available at www.markdery.com/archives/books/culture_jamming/#000005#more, accessed 23 October 2008.)

Devi, P. and Cuny, M.T. (1996) *Moi, Phoolan Devi, la reine des bandits*. Paris: Fixot.

Devi, P., Cuny, M.T. and Rambali, P. (2006) *The Bandit Queen of India: An Indian Woman's Amazing Journey from Peasant to International Legend*. Lyon: Lyon Press.

Deyssel, L. van (1979a) 'Aantekeningen en paralipomena' in H.G.M. Prick (ed.) *De scheldkritieken*.

—— (1979b) 'Rouwviolen' in H.G.M. Prick (ed.) *De scheldkritieken*.

Deyssel, L. van, Eeden, F. van and Verwey, A. (1889) 'Boekbeoordelingen', *De Nieuwe Gids 4*.

Djebar, A. (1992 [1980]) *Women of Algiers in Their Apartments*. Charlottesville: University of Virginia Press.

Doane, M.A. (1987) *The Desire to Desire: The Woman's Film of the 1940s*. Bloomington: Indiana University Press.

Doty, A. (1993) *Making Things Perfectly Queer: Interpreting Mass Culture*. Minneapolis: The University of Minnesota Press.

Dresen, G. (1998) 'Van Madonna tot Madonna, of: het ideaal van de onbevlekte vrouw' in Eadem, *Is dit mijn lichaam? Visioenen van het volmaakte lichaam in katholieke moraal en mystiek*. Nijmegen: Valkhof Pers.

Drinnon, R. and Drinnon, A.M. (eds) (1975) *Nowhere at Home: Letters from Exile of Emma Goldman and Alexander Berkman*. New York: Shocken Books.

DuBois, W.E.B. (1995) *On Sociology and the Black Community*. Chicago: University of Chicago Press.

Duinkerken, A. van (1965) 'Het noodlot van Hélène Swarth', *Dietsche Warande and Belfort*, 110(4): 266–279.

Duncan, C. (1973) 'Virility and domination in early 20th century Vanguard painting', *Artforum* (December 1973): 30–39.

Dworkin, A. (1976) *Our Blood: Prophecies and Discourses on Sexual Politics*. London: The Women's Press.

Dyer, R. (1997) *White*. London: Routledge.

—— (2003) *Now You See It. Studies on Lesbian and Gay Film*. London: Routledge.

Eagleton, M. (ed.) (2003) *A Concise Companion to Feminist Theory*. Oxford: Blackwell Publishing.

Eeten, P. van (1961) 'Kloos en zijn sonnetten aan Hélène Swarth', *De Nieuwe Taalgids*, 54: 289–295.

Ehrenreich, B. and English, D. (1979) *For her own Good: 150 Years of the Experts' Advice to Women*. London: Pluto Press.

Eisenstein, H. and Jardine, A.A. (eds) (1984) *The Future of Difference*. Boston: K.G. Hall.

Ellmann, M. (1979 [1968]) *Thinking about Women*. London: Virago.

Ensler, E. (2003) *The Vagina Monologues*. New York: Villard.

Erffa, H. von and Staley, A. (1986) *The Paintings of Benjamin West*. New Haven and London: Yale University Press.

Essed, P. (1991) *Understanding Everyday Racism: An Interdisciplinary Theory*. London: Sage.

Fallaci, O. (2002) *The Rage and the Pride*. New York: Rizolli International.

Fanon, F. (1965) 'Unveiling Algeria' in *A Dying Colonialism*. New York: Grove Press.

Farranda, A. (2006) *Il volo della farfalla*. New York: Rizolli International.

Fausto-Sterling, A. (1992) *Myths of Gender: Biological Theories about Women and Men*. New York: Basic Books.

—— (1995) 'Gender, race and nation: The comparative anatomy of "Hottentot" women in Europe, 1815–1817' in J. Terry and J. Urla (eds) *Deviant Bodies. Critical Perspectives on Difference in Science and Popular Culture*. Bloomington and Indianapolis: Indiana University Press.

Fernandes, L. (1999) 'Reading "India's bandit queen". A trans/national feminist perspective on the discrepancies of representation', *Signs: Journal of Women in Culture and Society*, 25(1): 123–152.

Ferris, L. (ed.) (1993) *Crossing the Stage. Controversies on Cross-dressing*. London and New York: Routledge.

Ferrus, D. (2003) 'A tribute to Saartjie Baartman' in S. Barry, M. Ndlovu and D. Khan (eds) *Ink@boilingpoint. A Selection of 21st Century Black Women's Writing from the Southern Tip of Africa*. Cape Town: 70.

Firestone, D. (1993) 'While Barbie talks tough, GI Joe goes shopping', *New York Times*, 31 December. (Available at http://query.nytimes.com/gst/fullpage.html?res=9F0CE6D9143E F932A05751C1A965958260&sec=&spon=&pagewanted=all, accessed 12 September 2008.)

Firestone, S. (1971) *The Dialectic of Sex: The Case for the Feminist Revolution*. London: Bantam Books.

Fisher, A. and Ramsay, H. (2000) 'Of art and blasphemy', *Ethical Theory and Moral Practice*, 3(2): 137–167.

Flaxman, G. (2000) *The Brain is the Screen. Deleuze and the Philosophy of Cinema*. Minnesota: University of Minnesota Press.

Foster, H. (1996) *The Return of the Real: The Avant-garde at the End of the Century*. Cambridge: MIT Press.

Foster, S.L. (1998) 'Choreographies of gender', *Signs: Journal of Women in Culture and Society*, 24(1): 1–33.

Foucault, M. (1965) *Madness and Civilization: A History of Insanity in the Age of Reason*. New York: Random House.

—— (1977 [1975]) *Discipline and Punish: The Birth of the Prison*. New York: Pantheon Books.

—— (1980) *Power/Knowledge: Selected Interviews and Other Writings 1972–1977*. C. Gordon (ed.). New York: Pantheon Books.

—— (1988) 'Technologies of the self' in L.H. Martin, P.H. Hutton and H. Goodman (eds) *Technologies of the Self: A Seminar with Michel Foucault*. Amherst: The University of Massachusetts Press.

—— (1990) *The History of Sexuality: An Introduction*. New York: Vintage Books.

—— (2006) *De woorden en de dingen. Een archeologie van de menswetenschappen*. Amsterdam: Boom.

Fouz-Hernández, S. and Jarman-Ivens, F. (eds) (2004) *Madonna's Drowned Worlds: New Approaches to her Cultural Transformations, 1983–2003*. Aldershot: Ashgate.

Fox-Keller, E. (1983) *A Feeling for the Organism: The Life and the Work of Barbara McClintock*. San Francisco: W.H. Freeman.

—— (1992) *Secrets of Life, Secrets of Death: Essays on Language, Gender and Science.* London and New York: Routledge.

Franklin, S., Lury, C. and Stacey, J. (1991) (eds) *Off-centre: Feminism and Cultural Studies.* London: HarperCollins Academic.

—— (2004) *Global Nature, Global Culture.* London: Sage.

Fraser, M. and Greco, M. (eds) (2005) *The Body: A Reader.* London: Routledge.

Freedman, B. (1991) *Staging the Gaze. Postmodernism, Psychoanalysis and Shakespearean Comedy.* Ithaka: Cornell University Press.

Freud, S. (1900) 'The interpretation of dreams' in J. Strachey, *et al.* (eds) *The Standard Edition of the Complete Psychological Works of Sigmund Freud, 4–5.* London: The Hogarth Press.

—— (1905) 'Three essays on the theory of sexuality' in *The Standard Edition of the Complete Psychological Works of Sigmund Freud* 7. London: The Hogarth Press.

—— (1933a [1931]) 'Female sexuality' in *New Introductory Lectures to Psychoanalysis: Standard Edition, 21.* London: The Hogarth Press.

—— (1933b [1932]) 'Femininity and civilization and its discontents' in *New Introductory Lectures to Psychoanalysis: The Standard Edition, 21.* London: The Hogarth Press.

—— (1961a [1925]) 'Some psychical consequences of the anatomical distinction between the sexes' in *The Standard Edition of the Complete Psychological Works of Sigmund Freud, 19.* London: The Hogarth Press.

—— (1961b [1927]) 'Fetishism' in *The Standard Edition of the Complete Psychological Works of Sigmund Freud, 21.* London: The Hogarth Press.

Friesen, I.L. (2001) *The Female Crucifix: Images of St Wilgefortis since the Middle Ages.* Waterloo, ON: Wilfrid Laurier University Press.

Fullbrook, E. and Fullbrook, K. (2008) *Sex and Philosophy: Rethinking de Beauvoir and Sartre.* London and New York: Continuum.

Gaines, J. (1988) 'White privilege and looking relations: Race and gender in feminist film theory', *Screen,* 29(4): 12–27.

Galienne, E. Le (1983) 'Acting Hamlet' in K. Malpede (ed.) *Women in Theatre: Compassion and Hope.* New York: Limelight.

Gallop, J. (1984) *The Daughter's Seduction: Feminism and Psychoanalysis.* Ithaca: Cornell University Press.

Garber, M. (1992) 'Fear of flying, or why is Peter Pan a woman?' in *Vested Interests: Cross-dressing and Cultural Anxiety.* New York and London: Routledge.

Gever, M. and Breyson, J. (eds) (1993) *Queer Looks, Perspectives on Lesbian and Gay Film and Video.* New York and London: Routledge.

Gilbert, S. and Gubar, S. (1979) *The Madwoman in the Attic: The Woman Writer and the Nineteenth Century Literary Imagination.* New Haven: Yale University Press.

Gilligan, C. (1988) *In a Different Voice: Psychological Theory and Women's Development.* Cambridge and Massachusetts: Harvard University Press.

Gilman, S. (1985) 'Black bodies, white bodies: Towards an iconography of female sexuality in late nineteenth-century art, medicine and literature' in H.L. Gates, Jr. (ed.) *'Race', Writing, and Difference.* Chicago: University of Chicago Press.

Gilroy, P. (1987) *There ain't no Black in the Union Jack: The Cultural Politics of Race and Nation.* London: Hutchinson.

Glazer, S. (2004) 'Lost in translation', *The New York Times,* 22 August. (Available at http://query.nytimes.com/gst/fullpage.html?res=9402EED6163FF931A1575BC0A9629C8B63&pagewanted=all, accessed 26 October 2007.)

Gleeson-White, S. (2003) *Strange Bodies: Gender and Identity in the Novels of Carson McCullers.* Tuscaloosa: The University of Alabama Press.

Goldenberg, N. (1979) *Changing of the Gods: Feminism and the End of Traditional Religions.* Boston: Beacon Press.

Goldin, C. (2006) 'The quiet revolution that transformed women's employment, education, and family', *AEA Papers and Proceedings,* 96(2): May. Boston. (Available at www.economics. harvard.edu/faculty/goldin/files/GoldinEly.pdf, accessed 7 August 2008.)

Gordon, L. (1976) *Woman's Body, Woman's Right. A Social History of Birth Control in America.* New York: Penguin Books.

Gray, S. (1979) *Hottentot Venus and other Poems.* Cape Town: David Philip.

Grayson, D.R. (ed.) (1995) 'Black women spectatorship and visual culture' in special issue of *Camera Obscura: Feminism, Culture and Media Studies,* 36, September 1995.

Greenfield, P.M. and Cocking, R. (eds) (1996) *Interacting with Video.* New York: Ablex Publishing.

Grever, M. (1994) *Strijd tegen de stilte. Johanna Naber (1859–1941) en de vrouwenstem in geschiedenis.* Hilversum: Verloren.

—— (2007) 'Plurality, narrative and the historical canon' in M. Grever and S. Stuurman, *Beyond the Canon. History for the Twenty-first Century.* Basingstoke/New York: Palgrave/Macmillan.

Grewal, I. and Kaplan, C. (1994) *Scattered Hegemonies: Postmodernity and Transnational Feminist Practices.* Minneapolis: University of Minnesota Press.

Griffin, G. and Braidotti, R. (eds) (2002) *Thinking Differently: A Reader in European Women's Studies.* London: Zed Books.

Griffin, G., Green, T. and Medhurst, P. (2005) *The relationship between professionalization in academe and Interdiciplinarity: A comparative study of eight European countries.* (Available at www.hull.ac.uk/researchintegration/Comparative%20Report%20-%20Professionalization %20and%20Interdisciplinarity.pdf

Grigat, N. (1995) *Madonnabilder: Dekonstruktive Ästhetik in den Videobildern Madonnas.* Frankfurt am Main: Lang.

Grosz, E. (1989) *Sexual Subversions: Three French Feminists.* Sydney: Allen & Unwin.

Guilbert, G.C. (2002) *Madonna as Postmodern Myth: How one Star's Self-construction Rewrites Sex, Gender, Hollywood, and the American Dream.* Jefferson: McFarland & Co.

Hacker, B.C. (1981) 'Women and military institutions in early modern Europe: A reconnaissance', *Signs: Journal of Women in Culture and Society,* 6(4): 643–671.

Häger, A. (1997) 'The interpretation of religious symbols in popular music', *Temenos,* 33: 49–62.

Hall, J.N. van (1910 [1894]) *Dichters van dezen tijd.* Amsterdam: Van Kampen.

Hall, S. (1997) *Representation. Cultural Representations and Signifying Practices.* London: Sage.

Hammonds, E.M. (2000) 'New technologies of race' in G. Kirkup, *et al.* (eds) *The Gendered Cyborg. A Reader.* London and New York: Routledge and Open University Press.

Haraway, D. (1985) 'A manifesto for cyborgs: Science, technology, and socialist feminism in the 1980s', *Socialist Review,* 80: 65–107.

—— (1989) *Primate Visions: Gender, Race and Nature in the World of Modern Science.* New York and London: Routledge.

—— (1991a) 'A cyborg manifesto: Science, technology, and socialist feminism in the late twentieth century' in *Simians, Cyborgs, and Women: The Reinvention of Nature.* London: Free Association Books.

—— (1991b [1988]) 'Situated knowledges. The science question in feminism and the privilege of partial perspective' in *Simians, Cyborgs, and Women. The Reinvention of Nature.* London: Free Association Books.

—— (1992) 'The promises of monsters: A regenerative politics for inappropriate/d others' in L. Grossberg, C. Nelson and P. Treichler (eds) *Cultural Studies.* New York and London: Routledge.

—— (1997) *Modest_witness@second_millennium. FemaleMan©_meets_oncoMouse™ Feminism and Technoscience*. New York and London: Routledge.

—— (2000) *How Like a Leaf. Donna J. Haraway,* interview with Thyrza Nichols Goodeve. New York and London: Routledge.

—— (2000/2003/2004) interview in two parts by N. Lykke, R. Markussen and F. Olesen, 'Cyborgs, coyotes, and dogs: A kinship of feminist figurations' and 'There are always more things going on than you thought!', *Kvinder, Køn og Forskning,* 2000 (4): 52–61; in D. Idhe and E. Selinger (eds) *Chasing Technoscience. Matrix for Materiality,* 2003. Indiana: Indiana University Press; in *The Haraway Reader,* 2004. New York and London: Routledge.

—— (2003) *The Companion Species Manifesto. Dogs, People, and Significant Otherness.* Chicago: Prickly Paradigm Press.

—— (2004) *The Haraway Reader.* New York and London: Routledge.

—— (2008) *When Species Meet.* Minneapolis: University of Minnesota Press.

Haraway, D. and Schneider, J. (2005) 'Conversations with Donna Haraway' in J. Schneider, *Donna Haraway: Live Theory.* London and New York: Continuum.

Harding, S. (1986) *The Science Question in Feminism.* Ithaka and London: Cornell University Press and Open University Press.

—— (1987) *Feminism and Methodology: Social Science Issues.* Ithaka and London: Cornell University Press and Open University Press.

—— (1991) *Whose Science, Whose Knowledge? Thinking from Women's Lives.* Ithaca and New York: Cornell University Press.

—— (1993) *The 'Racial' Economy of Science. Toward a Democratic Future.* Bloomington: Indiana University Press.

—— (1998) *Is Science Multicultural? Postcolonialisms, Feminisms and Epistemologies.* Bloomington: Indiana University Press.

—— (ed.) (2003) *The Feminist Standpoint Theory Reader, Intellectual and Political Controversies.* New York and London: Routledge.

Harding, S. and Hintikka, M.B. (eds) (1983) *Discovering Reality: Feminist Perspectives on Epistemology, Metaphysics, Methodology and Philosophy of Science.* Dordrecht: Reidel.

Hartsock, N. (1987 [1983]) 'The feminist standpoint. Developing the ground for a specifically feminist historical materialism' in S. Harding (ed.) *Feminism and Methodology: Social Science Issues.* Bloomington: Indiana University Press.

—— (1998) *The Feminist Standpoint Revisited and Other Essays.* Boulder, CO: Westview Press.

Hayles, N.K. (2005) *My mother was a Computer.* Chicago, London: Chicago University Press.

Heartley, E. (2004) *Postmodern Heretics: The Catholic Imagination in Contemporary Art.* New York: Midmarch Arts Press.

Hegel, G.W.F. (1977) *Phenomenology of Spirit.* Oxford: Clarendon Press.

Hemmings, C. (2005a) 'Telling feminist stories', *Feminist Theory,* 6(2): 115–139.

—— (2005b) 'Invoking affect. Cultural theory and the ontological turn', *Cultural Studies,* 19(5): 548–567.

Henry, A. (2004) *Not my Mother's Sister: Generational Conflict and Third-wave Feminism.* Bloomington: Indiana University Press.

Hill Collins, P. (1986) 'Learning from the outsider within: The sociological significance of black feminist thought', *Social Problems,* 33(6): 14–32.

—— (1990) *Black Feminist Thought: Knowledge, Consciousness and the Politics of Empowerment.* Boston and London: Unwin Hyman.

—— (1997) 'Comment on Hekman's truth and method: Feminist standpoint theory revisited: Where's the power?' *Signs: Journal of Women in Culture and Society,* 22(2): 375–381.

Hobsbawm, E. and Ranger, T. (eds) (1983) *The Invention of Tradition*. Cambridge: Cambridge University Press.

Holm, U.M. and Liinason, M. (2005) 'Disciplinary boundaries between the social sciences and humanities: Comparative report on interdisciplinarity'. (Available at www.hull.ac.uk/research integration/Comparative%20Report%20-%20Interdisciplinarity.pdf, accessed 24 October 2008.)

Holmes, R. (2007) *The Hottentot Venus. The Life and Death of Saartjie Baartman: Born 1789 – Buried 2002*. London: Bloomsbury.

hooks, b. (1984) *Feminist Theory from Margin to Center*. Boston: South End Press.

—— (1990 [1981]) *Ain't I a Woman: Black Women and Feminism*. Boston: South End Press.

—— (1990) *Yearning: Race, Gender and Cultural Politics*. Toronto: Between the Lines.

—— (1992) *Black Looks: Race and Representation*. Boston: South End Press.

Hoving, I. (1995) *The Castration of Livingstone and Other Stories: Reading African and Caribbean Migrant Women's Writing,* Ph.D thesis. Amsterdam, University of Amsterdam.

Hubbard, R. (1990) *The Politics of Women's Biology*. New Brunswick and London: Rutgers University Press.

Hull, T.G., Bell-Scott, P. and Smith, B. (eds) (1982) *But Some of Us are Brave: Black Women's Studies*. New York: The Feminist Press.

Huntington, S. (1996) *The Clash of Civilizations and the Remaking of World Order*. New York: Simon & Schuster.

Ibsen, H. (1992) *A Doll's House; The Wild Duck; The Lady from the Sea*. London: Dent.

Ikas, K. (1999) 'Interview with Gloria Anzaldúa' in G. Anzaldúa *Borderlands/La Frontera*: *The New Mestiza*. San Francisco: Aunt Lute Books.

Irigaray, L. (1974) *Speculum de l'autre femme*. Paris: Les Éditions de Minuit.

—— (1984) *Ethique de la différence sexuelle*. Paris: Les Éditions de Minuit.

—— (1985) *This Sex which is not One*. Ithaca: Cornell University Press.

—— (1987) 'Femmes Divines' in Sexes et Parentés. Paris: Les Éditions de Minuit, pp. 67–85.

Israel, J. (2006) *Enlightenment Contested. Philosophy, Modernity, and the Emancipation of Man 1670–1752*. Oxford: Oxford University Press.

Jacobs, C. (1996) 'Dusting Antigone', *MLN,* 111(5): 890–917.

Jaggar, A. (1983) *Feminist Politics and Human Nature*. Totowa, NJ: Rowman & Allanheld.

James, H. (1986) *Daisy Miller*. New York: Penguin.

Jansen, K.L. (1999) *The Making of the Magdalen. Preaching and Popular Devotion in the later Middle Ages*. Princeton: Princeton University Press.

Jenkins, H. (2001) 'From Barbie to Mortal Kombat: Further reflections', paper presented at the conference, *Playing by the Rules: The Cultural Policy Challenges of Video Games*. Chicago, 26–27 October. (Available at http://culturalpolicy.uchicago.edu/conf2001/papers/jenkins.html, accessed 11 September 2008.)

—— (2006) *Convergence Culture: Where Old and New Media Collide*. New York: New York University Press.

Jenkins, H. and Cassell, J. (2008) 'From Quake Girls to Desperate Housewives: A decade of gender and computer games' in Y.B. Kafai, C. Heeter, J. Denner and J.Y. Sun (eds) *Beyond Barbie® and Mortal Kombat: New Perspectives on Gender and Gaming*. Cambridge, MA: MIT Press.

Jones, A. (1996) *Sexual Politics: Judy Chicago's 'Dinner Party' in Feminist Art History*. Ewing: University of California Press.

Jones, A. (ed.) (2003) *The Feminism and Visual Culture Reader*. London: Routledge.

Jones, C. (2001) 'Lara Croft: Fantasy games mistress' in *BBC News Online*, 6 July. (Available at http://news.bbc.co.uk/hi/english/uk/newsid 1425000/1425762.stm, accessed 22 August 2007.)

Jordanova, L. (1989) *Sexual Visions: Images of Gender in Science and Medicine between the Eighteenth and the Twentieth Centuries.* Hemel Hempstead: Harvester Wheatsheaf.

Kaegi, W. (1947–1982) *Jacob Burckhardt: Eine Biographie*, 8 dl. Basel and Stuttgart: Schwabe.

Kafai, Y.B. (1996) 'Gender differences in children's construction of video games' in P.M. Greenfield and R. Cocking (eds) *Interacting with Video*. New York: Ablex Publishing.

Kaplan, C. (1994) 'The politics of location as transnational feminist critical practice' in I. Grewal and C Kaplan (eds) *Scattered Hegemonies: Postmodernity and Transnational Feminist Practices*. Minneapolis, University of Minnesota Press, pp. 137–152.

Kaplan, E.A. (1983) *Women and Film. Both Sides of the Camera*. New York and London: Methuen.

Kaufmann, D. (1986) 'Simone de Beauvoir: Questions of difference and generation' in *Yale French Studies,* 72, Simone de Beauvoir: Witness to a century: pp. 121–131.

Kear, A. and Steinberg, D.L. (eds) (1999) *Mourning Diana: Nation, Culture and the Performance of Grief.* London and New York: Routledge.

Keating, A. (ed.) (2000) *Interviews/Entrevistas*. New York: Routledge.

Kelan, E.K. (2007) 'Tools and toys: Communicating gendered positions towards technology', *Information, Communication and Society*, 10(3): 358–383.

Kelly, J. (1979) 'The double-edged vision of feminist theory', *Feminist Studies*, 5(1): 216–227.

—— (1984) *Women, History and Theory: The Essays of Joan Kelly*. Chicago: University of Chicago Press.

Kennedy, B. (2000) *Deleuze and Cinema. The Aesthetics of Sensation*. Edinburgh: Edinburgh University Press.

Kennedy, H.W. (2002) 'Lara Croft: Feminist icon or cyberbimbo? On the limits of textual analysis', *The International Journal of Computer Game Research,* 2(2): 1–12.

Keohane, N.O., Rosaldo, M.Z. and Gelpi, B.C. (eds) (1988) *Feminist Theory. A Critique of Ideology.* Chicago: University of Chicago Press.

King, K.L. (2003) *The Gospel of Mary of Magdalene: Jesus and the First Woman Apostle*. Santa Rosa, CA: Polebridge Press.

Klaver, M. (2008) 'Gamers zijn leiders van de toekomst', *NRC Handelsblad,* June 4.

Klinge, I. (1997) 'Female bodies and brittle bones. Medical interventions in osteoporosis' in K. Davis (ed.) *Embodied Practices. Feminist Perspectives on the Body*. London: Sage.

Kloos, W. (1887) 'Literaire kronieken XI', *De nieuwe gids,* 2(II): 462–465.

—— (1898) 'Hélène Swarth' in *Veertien jaar literatuurgeschiedenis 1880–1893*. Amsterdam: Van Looy.

Komrij, G. (1998) 'De pop,' aflevering van de rubriek 'Trou moet blijcken', *NRC Handelsblad*, 12 November.

Kool-Smit, J. (1967) 'Het onbehagen bij de vrouw', *De gids,* 130(9/10): 267–281, trans. Iris van der Tuin.

Kralt, P. (1986) 'De vrouwen, de vriend en de verborgen God. Willem Kloos, zomer 1884–winter 1885', *Maatstaf,* 34(1): 19–35.

Kramer, P. (1998) 'Post-classical Hollywood' in J. Hill and P. Gibson (eds) *The Oxford Guide to Film Studies*. Oxford: Oxford University Press.

Krauss, R. (1993) 'Cindy Sherman's gravity: A critical fable', *Artforum,* 9(1): 63–64.

Kristeva, J. (1981 [1980]) *Desire in Language: A Semiotic Approach to Literature and Art.* New York and Oxford: Columbia University Press.

—— (1990) 'The adolescent novel' in J. Fletcher and A. Benjamin (eds) *Abjection, Melancholia, and Love: The Work of Julia Kristeva*. London and New York: Routledge.

Krueger, B. (1983) *We won't Play Nature against your Culture*. London: ICA.

Kuhn, A. (1994 [1982]) *Women's Pictures. Feminism and Cinema*. London: Routledge and Kegan Paul.
—— (1999) 'Classic Hollywood cinema' in P. Cook and M. Bernink (eds) *The Cinema Book*. London: British Film Institute.
Kuhn, T. (1962) *The Structure of Scientific Revolutions*. Chicago: University of Chicago Press.
Kunstschrift (2005) 6, themanummer Maria Magdalena.
Kunzru, H. (1997) 'You are cyborg. For Donna Haraway, we are already assimilated', *Wired*, February 1997.
Kutscher, R.E. (1993) 'Historical trends, 1950–1992, and current uncertainties: The American work force, 1992–2005', *Monthly Labor Review*. (Available at http://findarticles.com/p/articles/mi_m1153/is_n11_v116/ai_14746067, accessed 6 August 2008.)
Lacan, J. (1977) *Écrits*. New York: Norton.
Laclau, E. and Mouffe, C. (1985) *Hegemony and Socialist Strategy. Towards a Radical Democratic Politics*. London: Verso.
Lacqueur, T. (1990) *Making Sex: Body and Gender from the Greeks to Freud*. Cambridge and London: Harvard University Press.
Latour, B. (1993) *We Have Never Been Modern*. Cambridge: Harvard University Press.
—— (2002) 'What is iconoclash? Or is there a world beyond the image wars?' in B. Latour and P. Weibel (eds) *Iconoclash: Beyond the Image Wars in Science, Religion and Art*. Karlsruhe: Center for Art and Media.
Lauretis, T. de (1984) *Alice Doesn't. Feminism, Semiotics, Cinema*. Bloomington: Indiana University Press.
—— (1986a) *Technologies of Gender: Essays on Theory, Film and Fiction*. Bloomington: Indiana University Press.
—— (1986b) *Feminist Studies/Critical Studies*. Bloomington: Indiana University Press.
—— (1987) 'The technology of gender' in *Technologies of Gender: Essays on Theory, Film, and Fiction*. Bloomington and Indianapolis: Indiana University Press.
—— (1990) 'Ex-centric subjects: Feminist theory and historical consciousness', *Feminist Studies*, 16(1): 115–150.
—— (1991) 'Queer theory: Lesbian and gay studies', *Differences*, 3(2): iii–xviii.
—— (1993) 'Feminist genealogies: A personal itinerary', *Women's Studies International Forum*, 16(4): 393–403.
—— (1994) *The Practice of Love. Lesbian Sexuality and Perverse Desire*. Bloomington: Indiana University Press.
Lawton, D. (1993) *Blasphemy*. New York: Harvester Wheatsheaf.
Leibovitz, A. (2006) *A Photographer's Life (1990–2005)*. New York: Random House.
Leloup, J.-Y. (2002) *The Gospel of Mary Magdalene*. Rochester: Inner Traditions.
Lerner, G. (ed.) (1977) *The Female Experience: An American Documentary*. Bloomington and Indianapolis: Indiana University Press.
Levy, A. (2006) *Female Chauvinist Pigs. Women and the Rise of Raunch Culture*. London: Simon & Schuster Pocket Books.
Lévy, B.H. (1979) *Le testament de Dieu*. Paris: Bernhard Grasset.
Levy, L.W. (1993) *Blasphemy: Verbal Offense against the Sacred from Moses to Salman Rushdie*. New York: Alfred A. Knopf.
Levy, S. (1984) *Hackers: Heroes of the Computer Revolution*. New York: Bantam Doubleday.
Liebaers, H. (ed.) (1964) *Hélène Swarths Zuid-Nederlandse jaren*. Gent: Ludion.
Lloyd, G. (1985) *The Man of Reason*: *'Male' and 'Female' in Western Philosophy*. London: Methuen.

Loftus, G. and Loftus, E. (1983) *Mind at Play: The Psychology of Video Games.* New York: Basic Books.

Loomba, A. (1993) 'Dead women tell no tales', *History Workshop Journal,* 36: 209–227.

Lord, M.G. (1994) *Forever Barbie: The Unauthorized Biography of a Real Doll.* New York: Walker & Co.

Lorde, A. (1984) *Sister Outsider: Essays and Speeches.* Trumansburg, NY: The Crossing Press.

Luijt, M. (2003) 'Automatisering blijft een mannenbolwerk: ondanks initiatieven neemt percentage vrouwen in ICT niet toe', *NRC Handelsblad,* 31 December.

Lykke, N. (1996) 'Introduction' in N. Lykke and R. Braidotti, *Between Monsters, Goddesses and Cyborgs. Feminist Confrontations with Science, Medicine and Cyberspace.* London and New Jersey: Zed Books.

—— (2000) 'Between monsters, goddesses and cyborgs: Feminist confrontations with science' in G. Kirkup, *et al.* (eds) *The Gendered Cyborg. A Reader.* London and New York: Routledge and Open University Press.

—— (2002) 'Feminist cultural studies of technoscience and other cyborg studies. A cartography' in *The Making of European Women's Studies IV:* Utrecht: Athena/Utrecht University.

—— (2004a) 'Between particularism, universalism and transversalism: Reflections on the politics of location of European feminist research and education', *Nora: Nordic Journal of Women's Studies,* 12(2): 72–83.

—— (2004b) 'Women's/Gender/Feminist Studies, a post-disciplinary discipline' in R. Braidotti, E. Just and M. Mensink (eds) *The Making of European Women's Studies V.* Utrecht: Athena/Utrecht University.

McCall, L. (2005) 'The complexity of intersectionality', *Signs: Journal of Women in Culture and Society,* 30(3): 1771–1800

McClintock, A. (1994) 'The return of female fetishism and the fiction of the phallus', *New Formations,* 19: 1–21.

—— (1995) *Imperial Leather: Race, Gender, and Sexuality in the Colonial Context.* London and New York: Routledge.

—— (1997) 'No longer in a future heaven: Gender, race, and nationalism' in A. McClintock, A. Mufti and E. Shohat (eds) *Dangerous Liaisons: Gender, Nation, and Postcolonial Perspectives.* Minneapolis: University of Minnesota Press.

McCullers, C. (1962) [1946] *The Member of the Wedding.* London: Penguin.

McDonald, H. (2001) *Erotic Ambiguities. The Female Nude in Art.* London and New York: Routledge.

MacDonald, L. (ed.) (2001) 'Florence Nightingale. An introduction to her life and family' in *Collected Works of Florence Nightingale, Vol. 1.* Waterloo, ON: Wilfrid Laurier University Press.

—— (ed.) (2004) 'Florence Nightingale on public health care' in *Collected Works of Florence Nightingale, Vol. 6.* Waterloo, ON: Wilfrid Laurier University Press.

MacDonald, L. and G. Vallée (eds) (2006) 'Florence Nightingale on health in India' in *Collected Works of Florence Nightingale, Vol. 9.* Waterloo, ON: Wilfrid Laurier University Press.

MacKinnon, C. (1982) 'Feminism, Marxism, method, and the state: An agenda for theory', *Signs: Journal of Women in Culture and Society,* 7(3): 515–544.

McNeil, M. (2000) 'Techno-triumphalism, techno-tourism, American dreams and feminism' in S. Ahmed, *et al.* (eds) *Transformations: Thinking through Feminism.* London: Routledge.

Mahmood, S. (2005) *Politics of Piety. The Islamic Revival and the Feminist Subject.* Princeton: Princeton University Press.

Mak, G. (1997) *Mannelijke vrouwen. Over grenzen van sekse in de negentiende eeuw.* Amsterdam and Meppel: Boom.

—— (2007) 'Gender in and beyond the canon' in S. Stuurman and M. Grever *Beyond the Canon.* Basingstoke/New York: Palgrave/Macmillan.

Marks, L. (2000) *The Skin of the Film. Intercultural Cinema, Embodiment and the Senses.* Durham: Duke University Press.

Martin, E. (1987) *The Woman in the Body: A Cultural Analysis of Reproduction.* Boston: Beacon Press.

—— (1991) 'The egg and the sperm: How science has constructed a romance based on stereotypical male-female roles', *Signs: Journal of Women in Culture and Society,* 16(3): 485–501.

Marx, K. (1994) 'The Eighteenth Brumaire of Louis Bonaparte (1851–1852)' in P. Williams and L. Chrisman (eds) *Colonial Discourse and Postcolonial Theory: A Reader.* New York: Harverster/Wheatsheaf.

Mbeki, T. (2002) 'Speech at the Funeral of Saartje Bartmann', 9 August. (Available at www.anc.org.za/ancdocs/history/mbeki/2002/tm0809.html, accessed 24 October 2008.)

Mda, Z. (2000) *The Heart of Redness.* Cape Town: Oxford University Press.

—— (2002) *Het rode hart,* vertaald door R. Dorsman, Breda and Den Haag: De Geus/Novib.

Meijer, I.C. (1996) *Het persoonlijke wordt politiek: Feministische bewustwording in Nederland 1965–1980.* Amsterdam: Het Spinhuis.

Meijer, M. (1988) *De lust tot lezen. Nederlandse dichteressen en het literaire systeem.* Amsterdam: Van Gennep/Sara.

—— (1993) 'Literaire apartheid: kritiek en sekse 1898–1930', *De Nieuwe Taalgids,* 86(2): 120–126.

—— (1997) 'Inleiding', *Nederlandse letterkunde,* themanummer Vrouwen en de canon, 2(3): 199–207.

—— (ed.) (1998) *The Defiant Muse. Dutch and Flemish Feminist Poems from the Middle Ages to the Present.* New York: The Feminist Press.

—— (2006) 'The return of melodrama. After the great divide: The Dutch case', in G.J. Dorleijn (ed.) *New Trends in Modern Dutch Literature.* Leuven: Peeters.

Merchant, C. (1980) *The Death of Nature: Women, Ecology and the Scientific Revolution.* San Francisco: Harper & Row.

Metz, C. (1982 [1977]) *Psychoanalysis and Cinema.* London: Macmillan.

Mikula, M. (2004) 'Lara Croft: Between a feminist icon and male fantasy', in R. Schubart and A. Gjelsik (eds) *Femme Fatalities. Representations of Strong Women in the Media.* Göteborg: Nordicom.

Miles, M.R. (1989) *Carnal Knowledge: Female Nakedness and Religious Meaning in the Christian West.* Boston: Beacon Press.

Miller, N. (1985) *The Poetics of Gender.* New York: Columbia University Press.

Millett, K. (1973) *Sexual Politics.* London: Virago Press.

—— (1976) *Flying.* New York: Paladin.

Minh-Ha, T. (1989) *Woman, Native, Other.* Bloomington: Indiana University Press.

Mitchell, J. (1971) *Women's Estate.* Harmondsworth: Penguin Books.

—— (1974) *Psychoanalysis and Feminism.* London: Allan Lane.

Mitchell, J. and Rose, J. (eds) (1984) *Feminine Sexuality: Jacques Lacan and the École Freudienne.* London: Macmillan.

Mohanty, C.T. (1988 [1984]) 'Under Western eyes: Feminist scholarship and colonial discourse', *Feminist Review,* 30: 60–86.

—— (1990) 'On race and voice: Challenges for liberal education in the 1990s', *Cultural Critique,* 14: 179–208.

Mohanty, C.T., Russo, A. and Torres, L. (eds) (1991) *Third World Women and the Politics of Feminism.* Bloomington: Indiana University Press.

Mol, A. (1989) '"Sekse" en "wetenschap": Een vergelijking met twee onbekenden' in L. Boon and G. de Vries (eds) *Wetenschapstheorie: De empirische wending.* Groningen: Wolters-Noordhoff.

Moore-Gilbert, B. (1997) *Postcolonial Theory. Contexts, Practices, Politics.* London: Verso.

Moraga, C. and Anzaldúa, G. (eds) (1981) *This Bridge called my Back: Writing by Radical Women of Color.* Watertown: Persephone.

Moran, J. (2002) *Interdisciplinarity (The New Critical Idiom).* London: Routledge.

Mori, A.M. (1978) *Il silenzio delle donne e il caso Moro.* Cosenza: Lerici.

Morton, S. (2003) 'The unhappy marriage of "third world" women's movements and Orientalism' in I. Boer (ed.) *After Orientalism. Critical Entanglement, Productive Looks.* Amsterdam: Rodopi.

Mosse, G.L. (1985) *Nationalism and Sexuality: Respectability and Abnormal Sexuality in Modern Europe.* New York: Fertig.

Mott, F.L. (1947) *Golden Multitudes: The Story of Best Sellers in the United States.* New York: Macmillan.

Moya, P. (1997) 'Postmodernism, "realism", and the politics of identity: Cherrie Moraga and Chicana feminism' in J. Alexander and C.T. Mohanty (eds) *Feminist Genealogies, Colonial Legacies, Democratic Futures.* New York: Routledge.

Mulinari, D. (2004) 'Out of Africa. Gender, medicine and postcolonial discourse' in *Medicinsk genusforskning – teori och begreppsutveckling* [Gender Research in Medicine – Theory and Definitions]. Vetenskapsrådets Rapportserie, Rapport (2), Uppsala.

Mulvey, L. (1975) 'Visual pleasure and narrative cinema' in *Visual and Other Pleasures.* London: Macmillan.

—— (1989) *Visual and Other Pleasures.* London: Macmillan.

—— (1996) *Fetishism and Curiosity.* London: British Film Institute.

Naber, J. (1909) *Wegbereidsters: Elizabeth Fry, Florence Nightingale, Josephine Butler, Priscilla Bright MacLaren.* Groningen: Römelingh.

NCWIT (2007) *NCWIT Scorecard 2007: A report on the status of women in information technology.* Boulder, CO: National Center for Women & Information Technology. (Available at www.ncwit.org/pdf/2007_Scorecard_Web.pdf, accessed 7 August 2008.)

Ndebele, N.S. (2003) *The Cry of Winnie Mandela.* Cape Town: David Philip.

Nead, L. (1993) *The Female Nude. Art, Obscenity and Sexuality.* London and New York: Routledge.

Nederveen Pieterse, J. (1992) *White on Black: Images of Blacks and Africa in Western Popular Culture.* New Haven: Yale University Press.

Newman, B. (2003) *God and the Goddesses: Vision, Poetry, and Belief in the Middle Ages.* Philadelphia: University of Pennsylvania Press.

NextGenderation Network (2004) 'Not in our names!' (Available at www.nextgenderation.net/projects/notinournames, accessed 24 October 2008.)

Nicholson, L. (ed.) (1990) *Feminism/Postmodernism.* London and New York: Routledge.

Nightingale, F. (1991 [1860]) *Cassandra and other Selections for Suggestions for Thought.* London: Pickering & Chatto.

Noble, D.F. (1992) *A World without Women: The Christian Clerical Culture of Western Science.* New York: Alfred A. Knopf.

Nochlin, L. (1971) 'Why have there been no great women artists?' *Art News,* 69(9): 22–39.

Nussbaum, M. (1999) *Cultivating Humanity: A Classical Defence of Reform in Liberal Education.* Cambridge, MA: Harvard University Press.

Ogletree, S. and Williams, S. (1990) 'Sex and sex-typing effects on computer attitudes and aptitude', *Sex roles*, 23, 703–712.

Okin, S.M. (1979) *Women in Western Political Thought*. Princeton: Princeton University Press.

Oldenziel, R. (1999) *Making technology masculine: Men, women and modern machines in America 1870–1945*. Chicago: Chicago University Press.

Orbach, S. (1986) *Hunger Strike: The Anorectic Struggle as a Metaphor for our Age*. New York: Avon Books.

—— (1987) *Fat is a Feminist Issue: The Anti-diet Guide to Permanent Weight Loss*. London: Hamlyn.

O'Sullivan, S. (2006) *Art Encounters Deleuze and Guattari. Thought Beyond Representation*. Basingstoke: Palgrave.

Oudshoorn, N. (1994) *Beyond the Natural Body: An Archeology of Sex Hormones*. London: Routledge.

Palmeri, C. (2007) 'Barbie goes from vinyl to virtual', *Business Week*, 7 May: 68.

Parker, R. and Pollock, G. (1981) *Old Mistresses. Women, Art and Ideology*. London: HarperCollins.

Pateman, C. (1988) *The Sexual Contract*. Cambridge: Polity Press.

Pearson, M. and Mullins, P.R. (1999) 'Domesticating Barbie: An archaeology of Barbie material culture and domestic ideology', *International Journal of Historical Archeology*, 3(4): 225–259.

Phelan, P (1993) *Unmarked. The Politics of Performance*. London and New York: Routledge.

Phoenix, A. and Pattynama, P. (eds) (2006) *European Journal of Women's Studies, Special Issue: Intersecionality,* 13(3).

Pilcher, J. and Whelehan, I. (2004) *50 Key Concepts in Gender Studies*. London: Sage.

Pizan, C. de (1984 [1405]) *Het boek van de stad der vrouwen*. Amsterdam: Sara.

Plant, S. (1997) *Zeroes and Ones: Digital Women and the New Technoculture*. New York: Doubleday.

Plaskow, J. (1992) *Terug naar de Sinaï: Het Jodendom vanuit feministisch perspectief*. Amersfoort: De Horstink.

Plate, S.B. (2006) *Blasphemy: Art That Offends*. London: Black Dog.

Plath, S. (1965) *Ariel and other Poems*. London: Faber & Faber.

Poelstra, J. (2000) 'De eerste vrouwelijke leden van de Maatschappij', *Nieuw Letterkundig Magazijn,* 18: 16–23.

Pollock, G. (ed.) (1996) *Generations and Geographies in the Visual Arts. Feminist Readings*. London: Routledge.

Pontecorvo, G. (1966) *The Battle of Algiers*. Algeria/Italy.

Ponzanesi, S. (2005) 'Beyond the black venus: Colonial sexual politics and contempory visual practices' in J. Andall and D. Duncan (eds) *Italian Colonialism. Legacies and Memories*. Oxford: Peter Lang.

Poovey, M. (1991) 'Introduction' in *Florence Nightingale, Cassandra and the Other Selections for Suggestions for Thought*. London: Scutari Press.

Postman, N. (1982) *The Disappearance of Childhood*. New York: Delacorte Press.

Prensky, M. (2001) 'Digital natives, digital immigrants', *On the Horizon*, 9(5). (Available at www.marcprensky.com/writing/Prensky%20-%20Digital%20Natives,%20Digital%20Immigrants%20-%20Part1.pdf, accessed 26 May 2008.)

Pryse, M. (2000) 'Trans/feminist methodology: Bridges to interdisciplinary thinking', *NWSA Journal,* 12(2): 105–118.

Puar, J.K. and Rai, A.S. (2002) 'Monster, terrorist, fag: The war on terrorism and the production of docile patriots', *Social Text,* 72(3): 117–148.

Puig de la Bellacasa, M. (2004) *Think we Must. Politiques féministes et construction des savoirs*, Ph.D thesis. Brussels: Université Libre de Bruxelles.

Quimby, K. (2003) 'Literary tomboys, little women, and the sexual-textual politics of narrative desire', *GLQ*, 10(1): 1–22.

Qureshi, S. (2004) 'Displaying Sara Bartman, the Hottentot Venus', *History of Science*, 10(2): 233–257.

Rand, E. (1995) *Barbie's Queer Accessories*. Durham: Duke University Press.

Raphael, M. (1996) *Theology and Embodiment: The Post-patriarchal Reconstruction of Female Sacrality*. Sheffield: Sheffield Academic Press.

Reitsma, A. (1985–1986) '"Ik heb niets dan de stem van mijn hart." Hélène Swarth (1859–1941)', *Bulletin*, 14: 59–63.

Rich, A. (1976) *Of Woman Born: Motherhood as Experience and Institution*. New York: W.W. Norton.

—— (1979a) *Uit vrouwen geboren: Moederschap als ervaring en instituut*. Amsterdam: Feministische Uitgeverij Sara.

—— (1979b) *On Lies, Secrets and Silence: Selected Prose 1966–1978*. New York: W.W. Norton.

—— (1980) 'Compulsory heterosexuality and lesbian existence' in A. Snitow, C. Sansell and S. Thompson, *Desire: The Politics of Sexuality*. London: Virago Press.

—— (1981) *Gedwongen heteroseksualiteit en lesbisch bestaan*. Amsterdam: Lust en gratie.

—— (1985a) *Blood, Bread and Poetry: Selected Prose 1979–1985*. London: The Women's Press.

—— (1985b) 'Een politiek van plaats/Aantekeningen' in *Bloed, Brood, and Poëzie. Essays 1971–1984*. Amsterdam: Feministische Uitgeverij Sara.

—— (1985c) 'Notes towards a politics of location' in *Blood, Bread and Poetry: Selected Prose 1979–1985*. London: Virago Press, 210–232.

Riley, D. (1988) *Am I that Name? Feminism and the Category of 'Women' in History*. Basingstoke: Macmillan Press.

Ringer, J.R. (1994) *Queer Words, Queer Images: Communication and the Construction of Homosexuality*. New York and London: New York University Press.

Rodgers, C. (1998) *Le deuxième sexe de Simone de Beauvoir: Un héritage admiré et contesté*. Paris: L'Harmattan.

Rodowick, D. (2001) *Reading the Figural; Or, Philosophy after the New Media*. Durham: Duke University Press.

Roof, J. (1997) 'Generational difficulties; or, the fear of a barren history' in D. Looser and E.A. Kaplan (eds) *Generations: Academic Feminists in Dialogue*. Minneapolis and London: University of Minnesota Press.

Rose, H. (1983) 'Hand, brain and heart: A feminist epistemology for the natural sciences', *Signs: Journal of Women in Culture and Society*, 9(1): 73–90.

Rose, J. (1993) *The Case of Peter Pan; or, The Impossibility of Children's Fiction*. Philadelphia: University of Pennsylvania Press.

Rose, S.O. (2007) 'Fit to fight but not to vote? Masculinity and citizenship in Britain, 1832–1918' in S. Dudink, K. Hagemann and A. Clark (eds) *Representing Masculinity: Male Citizenship in Modern Western Culture*. New York: Macmillan Press.

Rousseau, J. (1762) *Emile: On Education*. Charleston: BiblioBazaar.

Rowbotham, S. (1972) *Women: Resistance and Revolution*. London: Allan Lane.

Roy, A. (1994) 'The great Indian rape-trick. Parts I and II', *Sunday Magazine*, 22 August and 3 September, New Delhi.

Ruether, R. (1983) *Feminism and God-Talk: Toward a Feminist Theology*. Boston: Beacon Press.

Rushkoff, D. (1997) *Children of Chaos: Surviving the End of the World as We Know it.* London: Flamengo/HarperCollins.

Russ, J. (1984) *How to Suppress Women's Writing.* London: The Women's Press.

Said, E. (1978) *Orientalism.* London: Pantheon Books.

—— (1983) *The World, the Text and the Critic.* Cambridge, MA: Harvard University Press.

—— (2002) *Reflections on Exile: And other Literary and Cultural Essays.* Cambridge, MA: Harvard University Press.

Saldivar-Hull, S. (1999) 'Critical Introduction', in *Borderlands/La Frontera: The New Mestiza.* San Francisco: Aunt Lute Books.

Sandoval, C. (1991) 'US Third World feminism: The theory and method of oppositional consciousness in the postmodern world', *Genders,* 10: 1–24.

—— (2000) *Methodology of the Oppressed.* Minneapolis: University of Minnesota Press.

Schaberg, J. (2002) *The Resurrection of Mary Magdalene: Legends, Apocrypha, and the Christian Testament.* New York: Continuum.

Schäfer, M.T. (2008) *Bastard Culture! User Participation and the Extension of Cultural Industries,* Ph.D thesis. Utrecht: Faculty of Humanities Utrecht University.

Schenkeveld-van der Dussen, R., *et al.* (eds) (1997) *Met en zonder lauwerkrans. Schrijvende vrouwen uit de vroeg-moderne tijd 1550–1850 van Anna Bijns tot Elise van Calcar.* Amsterdam: Amsterdam University Press.

Schiebinger, L. (1993) *Nature's Body: Gender in the Making of Modern Science.* Boston: Beacon Press.

—— (2001) 'Collecting body parts: Georges Cuvier's Hottentot Venus' in H.E. Bödeker and L. Steinbrügge (eds) *Conceptualising Woman in Enlightenment Thought.* Berlin: Berlin Verlag, Arno Spitz GmbH.

Schlegel, A.W. (1996 [1799]) 'Die Gemählde: Gespräch' in L. Müller (ed.) *Verlag der Kunst.* Dresden: Verslag der Kunst.

Schwarzer, A. (1974) *Portret van Simone de Beauvoir.* Amsterdam: Cinemien.

Schwegman, M.J. (2001) 'Strijd om openbaarheid: Sekse, cultuur en politiek in Nederland' in D. Fokkema and F. Grijzenhout (eds) *Rekenschap 1650–2000.* Den Haag: Sdu Uitgevers.

Schwichtenberg, C. (ed.) (1993) *The Madonna Connection: Representational Politics, Subcultural Identities and Cultural Theory.* Boulder, CO: Westview Press.

Scott, J.W. (1986) 'Gender: A useful category of historical analysis', *American Historical Review,* 91(5): 1053–1075.

—— (1988) *Gender and the Politics of History.* New York: Columbia University Press.

—— (1989) 'French feminists and the rights of "man": Olympe de Gouge's declarations', *History Workshop: A Journal of Socialist Historians,* 28: 1–21.

—— (1992) 'Experience' in J. Butler and J.W. Scott (eds) *Feminists Theorize the Political.* New York and London: Routledge.

—— (1996) *Only Paradoxes to Offer: French Feminists and the Rights of Man.* Cambridge, MA: Harvard University Press.

Sedgwick, E.K. (1990) *The Epistemology of the Closet.* Berkeley, CA: University of California Press.

Sen, M. (1991) *India's Bandit Queen. The True Story of Phoolan Devi.* London: Pandora.

Shakespeare, W. (1990) *King Lear.* Cheltenham: Stanley Thornes.

Shiva, V. and Moser, I. (1995) *Biopolitics: A Feminist and Ecological Reader on Biotechnology.* London and New Jersey: Zed Books.

Showalter, E. (1972) 'Women writers and the double standard' in V. Gornick and B.K. Moran (eds) *Woman in Sexist Society.* New York: New American Library.

—— (1981) 'Florence Nightingale's feminist complaint: Women, religion, and "suggestions for thought"', *Signs*, 6(3): 395–412.

—— (ed.) (1986) *The New Feminist Criticism: Essays on Women, Literature and Theory*. London: Virago.

—— (1987) 'Miranda and Cassandra: The discourse of the feminist intellectual' in M. Meijer and J. Schaap (eds) *Historiography of Women's Cultural Traditions*. Dordrecht: Foris.

Silverman, K. (1983) *The Subject of Semiotics*. Oxford, Oxford University Press.

—— (1988) *The Acoustic Mirror. The Female Voice in Psychoanalysis and Cinema*. Bloomington and Indianapolis: Indiana University Press.

Simpson, M. (1993) *Male Impersonators. Men Performing Masculinity*. London: Cassell.

Smelik, A. (1998a) *And the Mirror Cracked: Feminist Cinema and Film Theory*. Houndmills: Palgrave.

—— (1998b) 'Gay and lesbian criticism' in J. Hill and P. Gibson (eds) *The Oxford Guide to Film Studies*. Oxford: Oxford University Press.

—— (2003) 'For Venus smiles not in a house of tears: Interethnic relations in European cinema', *European Journal of Cultural Studies* 6(1): 55–74.

—— (2007) 'Feminist film theory' in P. Cook and M. Bernink (eds) *The Cinema Book*, 3rd edn. London: British Film Institute Publishing.

Smelik, A., Buikema R. and Meijer, M. (1999) *Effectief Beeldvormen. Theorie, analyse en praktijkvan beeldvormingsprocessen*. Assen: Van Gorcum.

Smith, B.G. (1998) *The Gender of History. Men, Women and Historical Practices*. Cambridge: Harvard University Press.

Smith, D. (1987 [1974]) 'Women's perspective as a radical critique of sociology' in S. Harding (ed.) *Feminism and Methodology*. Bloomington and Indianapolis: Indiana University Press and Open University Press.

—— (1997) 'Comment on Hekman's "Truth and method: Feminist standpoint theory revisited"', *Signs: Journal of Women in Culture and Society,* 22(2): 392–398.

Smuckler, L. (2000 [1982]) 'Turning points' in K. Analouise (ed.) *Interviews/Entrevistas*. New York: Routledge.

Solanas, V. (1983) *Scum Manifesto*. London: The Matriarchy Study Group.

Solomon-Godeau, A. (1991) 'Suitable for framing: The critical recasting of Cindy Sherman', *Parkett,* 29: 112–115.

Sontag, S. (2001) *On Photography*. New York: Picador.

—— (2003) *Regarding the Pain of Others*. New York: Farrar, Straus & Giroux.

Sophocles (1994) *Antigone*. Trans. H. Lloyd-Jones, Cambridge: Harvard University Press.

Spender, D. (1983) *Women of Ideas and What Men have Done to Them*. London: The Women's Press.

Spigel, L. (1994) *Twist Barbie*. New York: Paper Tiger Television.

Spivak, G.C. (1985a) 'Can the subaltern speak? Speculation on widow-sacrifice', *Wedge,* Winter/Spring: 120–130.

—— (1985b) 'The Rani of Sirmur' in F. Barker (ed.) *Europe and its Others 1*. Essex: University of Essex.

—— (1987) *In Other Worlds. Essays in Cultural Politics*. New York: Basic Books.

—— (1988) 'Can the subaltern speak?' in C. Nelson and L. Grossberg (eds) *Marxism and the Interpretation of Culture*. Illinois; reprinted in P. Williams and L. Chrisman (eds) (1994) *Colonial Discourse and Postcolonial Theory: A Reader*. New York: Harvester Wheatsheaf.

—— (1993) *Outside in the Teaching Machine*. New York: Routledge.

—— (2004) 'Terror: Speech after 9-11', *Boundary,* 31(2): 81–111.

Stacey, J. (1993) 'Feminist theory: Capital F, Capital T' in V. Robinson and D. Richardson (eds) *Introducing Women's Studies: Feminist Theory and Practice*. Basingstoke: Macmillan.

—— (1994) *Star Gazing. Hollywood Cinema and Female Spectatorship*. London and New York: Routledge.

Stam, R. (2000) *Film Theory. An Introduction*. Oxford: Blackwell.

Stanley, L. and Wise, S. (1993 [1983]) *Breaking out Again, Feminist Ontology and Epistemology*. London: Routledge.

Steiner, G. (1984) *Antigones. How the Antigone Legend has Endured in Western Literature, Art, and Thought*. Oxford: Oxford University Press.

Stighelen, K. van der and Westen, M.G. (1999) *Elck zijn waerom: vrouwelijke kunstenaars uit België en Nederland, 1500–1950*. Gent: Ludion.

Stimpson, C.R. (1990) 'Reading for love: Canons, paracanons, and whistling Jo March', *New Literary History*, 21(4): 957–976.

Stoler, A.L. (1995) *Race and the Education of Desire: Foucault's History of Sexuality and the Colonial Order of Things*. Durham: Duke University Press.

Strachey, L. (1986 [1918]) 'Florence Nightingale' in *Eminent Victorians*. New York: Weidenfeld & Nicholson.

Streng, T. (1997) *Geschapen om te scheppen? Opvattingen over vrouwen en schrijverschap in Nederland 1815–1860*. Amsterdam: Amsterdam University Press.

Strohmeyer, S. (1997) *Barbie Unbound: A Parody of the Barbie Obsession*. Chicago: New Victoria Publishers.

Sturken, M. and Cartwright, L. (2001) *Practices of Looking. An Introduction to Visual Culture*. Oxford: Oxford University Press.

Stuurman, S. (2004) *François Poulain de la Barre and the Invention of Modern Equality*. Cambridge: Harvard University Press.

Sullivan, N. (2003) *A Critical Introduction to Queer Theory*. New York: New York University Press.

Sunrahmanyam, K. and Greenfield, P.M. (1998) 'Computer games for girls: What makes them play?' in J. Cassell and H. Jenkins (eds), *From Barbie to Mortal Kombat: Gender and Computer Games*. Cambridge, MA: MIT Press.

Svendsen, L. (2006) *Fashion: A Philosophy*. London: Reaktion.

Swarth, H. (z.j.[1952]) *Het zingende hart*. Keur uit haar gedichten bijeenverzameld en van een inleiding voorzien door J.C. Bloem. Amsterdam: Van Kampen.

—— (1973) *Een mist van tranen*. Verzameld en ingeleid door H. Roest. Hasselt: Heideland-Orbis.

Tasker, Y. (1993) *Spectacular Bodies: Gender, Genre and the Action Cinema*. London: Routledge.

Taylor, J. (2002) 'The decline of women in computer science from 1940–1982'. (Available at http://knol.google.com/k/jennifer-taylor/the-decline-of-women-in-computer/u67r-Ndua/5hwjo0#, accessed 7 August 2008.)

Thienen, J. van (2007) 'Madonna's kruis: De vrouwelijke verbeelding van Christus', *Lover*, 34(1): 8–10.

Thompson, C.J. and Haytko, D.L. (1997) 'Speaking of fashion: Consumers' uses of fashion discourses and the appropriation of countervailing cultural meanings', *The Journal of Consumer Research*, 24(1): 15–42.

Tijdens, K. (2006) *Een wereld van verschil: arbeidsparticipatie van vrouwen 1945–2005*. Rotterdam: Erasmus Universiteit.

Toffoletti, K. (2007) *Cyborgs and Barbie dolls: Feminism, Popular Culture and the Posthuman Body*. London: I.B. Tauris.

Tompkins, J.P. (1985a) 'Sentimental power: Uncle Tom's cabin and the politics of literary history' in E. Showalter (ed.) *The New Feminist Criticism*. New York: Pantheon, pp. 81–105.

—— (1985b) *Sensational Designs: The Cultural Work of American Fiction 1790–1860.* Oxford: Oxford University Press.

Trinh T.M.H. (1989) *Woman/Native/Other. Writing Postcoloniality and Feminism.* Bloomington: Indiana University Press.

Tronto, J. (1993) *Moral Boundaries: A Political Argument for an Ethic of Care.* London and New York: Routledge.

Tuin, I. van der (2009) 'Jumping generations: On second- and third-wave feminist epistemology', *Australian Feminist Studies*, 24(59): 17–31.

Turkle, S. (1978) *Psychoanalytic Politics: Freud's French Revolution.* New York: Basic Books.

—— (1984) *The Second Self: Computers and the Human Spirit.* New York: Simon & Schuster

—— (1995) *Life on the Screen: Identity in the Age of the Internet.* New York: Simon & Schuster.

—— (1996) 'Constructions and reconstructions of the self in virtual reality' in T. Druckrey (ed.) *Electronic Culture: Technology and Visual Representation.* New York: Aperture.

Turner, W.B. (2000) *A Genealogy of Queer Theory.* Philadelphia: Temple University Press.

Vaillant, F. Le (1790) *Voyage dans l'interieur de l'Afrique par le Cap Bonne Esperance, dans les annees 1780–85,* Paris: Dentu.

V-Day Foundation. (Available at www.vday.org, accessed 24 October 2008.)

Verstraete, G. (2002) 'Inleiding: Cultural studies of cultuur in conflict' in J. Baetens and G. Verstraete (eds) *Cultural Studies. Een Inleiding.* Nijmegen: Uitgeverij Vantilt.

Vintges, K. (1992) *Filosofie als passie: Het denken van Simone de Beauvoir.* Amsterdam: Prometheus.

Wadud, A. (1999) *Qur'an and Woman: Rereading the Sacred Text from a Woman's Perspective.* Oxford: Oxford University Press.

Wajcman, J. (2004) *TechnoFeminism.* Cornwall: Polity Press.

Walden, K. (2004) 'Run, Lara, run! The impact of computer games on cinema's action heroine' in R. Schubart and A. Gjelsik (eds) *Femme Fatalities. Representations of Strong Women in the Media.* Göteborg: Nordicom.

Walker, A. (1984) *In Search of our Mother's Garden: Womanist Prose.* London: The Women's Press.

Walker Bynum, C. (1987) *Holy Feast and Holy Fast: The Religious Significance of Food to Medieval Women.* Berkeley: University of California Press.

—— (1991) *Fragmentation and Redemption: Essays on Gender and the Human Body in Medieval Religion.* New York: Zone Books.

Ware, V. (1992) *Beyond the Pale: White Women, Racism and History.* London and New York: Pale.

Warner, M. (1995) *From the Beast to the Blonde: On Fairy Tales and their Tellers.* London: Vintage.

—— (2002) *Photography. A Cultural History.* London: Laurence King Publishing.

Wekker, G. and Lutz, H. (2001) 'Een Hoogvlakte met koude winden. De geschiedenis van het gender – en etniciteitsdenken in Nederland' in M. Botman, N. Jouwe and G. Wekker (eds) *Caleidoscopische Visies – de zwarte, migranten – en vluchtelingen vrouwenbeweging in Nederland.* Amsterdam: KIT Publishers.

Wells, L. (ed.) (2004) *Photography: A Critical Introduction.* London and New York: Routledge.

West, R. (1913) 'Mr Chesterton in hysterics', *The Clarion,* 14 November.

Wicomb, Z. (2001) *David's Story.* New York: The Feminist Press.

Widerberg , K. and Hirsch, S. (May 2005) 'Change in sisciplination: Two case studies. A comparative report of eight European countries'. (Available at www.hull.ac.uk/researchintegration/ Comparative%20Report%20-%20Change%20in%20Disciplinization.pdf, accessed 24 October 2008.)

Williams, P. and Chrisman, L. (eds) (1994) *Colonial Discourse and Post-Colonial Theory. A Reader.* New York: Colombia University Press.

Winkel, C. van (2006) *Het primaat van de zichtbaarheid.* Rotterdam: NAi Uitgevers.

Winterbach, I. (2004) 'De Gamtoosrivier over', *Armada*, 34: 19–27.

Wittig, M. (1992) *The Straight Mind and other Essays.* Boston: Beacon Press.

Wollstonecraft, M. (1982) *Vindication of the Rights of Woman.* Harmondsworth: Penguin Books.

WomenGamers.Com Discussion Forum (1999). (Available at http://forums.womengamers.com, accessed 22 August 2007.)

Woodhull, W. (1993) *Transfigurations of the Maghreb: Feminism, Decolonization, and Literatures.* Minneapolis: University of Minnesota Press.

—— (2003) 'Unveiling Algeria' in R. Lewis and S. Mills (eds) *Feminist Postcolonial Theory. A Reader.* Edinburgh: Edinburgh University Press.

Woolf, V. (1978 [1929, 1936, 1938]) *A Room of One's Own and Three Guineas.* Harmondsworth, Middlesex: Penguin Books.

Wright, E. (ed.) (1992) *Feminism and Psychoanalysis: A Critical Dictionary.* Oxford: Blackwell.

Yegenoglu, M. (2003) 'Veiled fantasies: Cultural and sexual difference in the discourse of Orientalism' in R. Lewis and S. Mills (eds) *Feminist Postcolonial Theory. A Reader.* Edinburgh: Edinburgh University Press.

Young, L. (1996) *Fear of the Dark: 'Race', Gender and Sexuality in the Cinema.* London: Routledge.

Yuval-Davis, N. (1997) *Gender and Nation.* London: Sage.

Yuval-Davis, N. and Anthias, F. (eds) (1989) *Woman, Nation, State.* London: Macmillan.

Index